FROM JOSEPH TO JOSHUA

BIBLICAL TRADITIONS
IN THE LIGHT OF ARCHAEOLOGY

FROM JOSEPH TO JOSHUA

BIBLICAL TRADITIONS
IN THE LIGHT OF ARCHAEOLOGY

BY

H. H. ROWLEY, F.B.A.

THE SCHWEICH LECTURES
OF THE BRITISH ACADEMY
1948

LONDON
PUBLISHED FOR THE BRITISH ACADEMY
BY GEOFFREY CUMBERLEGE, OXFORD UNIVERSITY PRESS
AMEN HOUSE, E.C. 4
1950

PRINTED IN GREAT BRITAIN
AT THE UNIVERSITY PRESS, OXFORD
BY CHARLES BATEY, PRINTER TO THE UNIVERSITY

DEDICATED TO THE
THEOLOGICAL FACULTY OF THE
UNIVERSITY OF UPPSALA
AS A TOKEN OF GRATITUDE
FOR THE HONORARY DEGREE OF
DOCTOR OF THEOLOGY
AND FOR THE GENEROUS
HOSPITALITY AND FELLOWSHIP
I ENJOYED IN THEIR MIDST

PREFACE

TO the Council of the British Academy for the high honour of their invitation to deliver the Schweich Lectures, and for the freedom allowed me in the choice of my subject, I express my gratitude. It was when I was working in China that I first became interested in this subject more than a quarter of a century ago, and a solution of the problems much along the lines of that here adopted was presented in my classes there. Indeed I prepared an article while still in China, and wrote a letter to Dr. S. A. Cook—whose *Notes on Old Testament History* I had recently read and found more stimulating than anything I knew in the field of Old Testament history—inviting his criticism before venturing to offer it to any journal. My courage failed me, however, as I had then never met Dr. Cook or had any contact with him, and my letter remained unposted and the article unsubmitted. Little did I know, as I came later to know, his generous willingness to help and encourage younger scholars and to place the rich stores of his learning and his acute critical judgement at their disposal. Some years later I gave the inaugural lecture to the Bangor branch of the Historical Association on this subject. Two years later again, I was invited to read a paper to the Manchester University Theological Society, and proposed to read the same lecture. Unfortunately I left the lecture on my table after writing to announce my subject, and that night my children—with an insight which some readers of the present lectures may commend—used most of it as scrap paper and afterwards consigned it to the flames. I was therefore forced to begin my work again, but this time I published it in the *Bulletin of the John Rylands Library* after reading it. This led to a number of subsequent studies which have been published in various journals, and to the request from more than one quarter that I would gather the material together in a more comprehensive treatment. Moreover, fresh material relevant to the issue was continually coming to light. How long my natural indolence and the pressure of other work would have continued to defer the more comprehensive study of the question I cannot say; but the invitation to deliver the Schweich Lectures offered the occasion, and I could no longer delay.

I am aware that I have read only a small part of the literature devoted to my subject, or to some of its details, and I therefore do not offer a Bibliography but only a list of works consulted. It may, however, serve some interested readers as an introduction to the study of the subject. They will perhaps find some of the works difficult of access, and especially some of the continental war-time publications which are no longer available, and which are not found in the great libraries in this country. For many of these I am indebted to authors who have sent me copies of their books, or offprints of their articles. Where that has been impossible I have in a number of cases received photostats of articles by the kindness of continental scholars, who have in some cases generously sent me such photostats of articles they had not themselves written. To acknowledge by name all the continental scholars to whom I am indebted in one or other of these ways, and all the British and American scholars who have helped me by gifts and loans, and the libraries on whose resources I have drawn, would yield a long catalogue of names which would weary the reader, and might seem to be a mere display of the riches of the friendship which I have enjoyed with a very wide circle of scholars. Probably at least a hundred names would have to be recorded. It seems therefore less invidious if I abstain from setting out the names of those to whom I am indebted, and ask all who have so generously helped me to accept my warmest thanks for their service.

It would have been easy to write a simpler book, building up the case for the view I adopt and saying little about its rivals or about the difficulties. I have preferred to risk bewildering the reader by the complexity of the issues and by introducing him to all the main contemporary views on the question. I hope I have omitted no material piece of evidence which favours any of the views I do not share, and that no reader will feel that any view has been unfairly presented. My debt to all who have studied any aspect of the problem will appear on every page, and not least to those whose views I do not share, but from whom I have again and again learned much. My debt to Professor W. F. Albright will be especially manifest; for though I have on a number of points differed from him, and sometimes find it hard to be sure that I have his latest pronouncement, I acknowledge with gratitude my immeasurable debt to him. His industry and erudition are phenomenal, and while he sometimes leaves me breathless in the effort to keep abreast of his readjustments of view, the wide range of his learning and his unequalled power to inspire his disciples fill me with admiration.

Part of the material of these lectures was used in Uppsala for two lectures which I delivered there in May 1948. Neither there nor in London could all the evidence be presented to my hearers, and the footnotes of the present book carry a good deal which had to be excluded. Even so, time did not permit of the delivery of the Schweich Lectures in full as they are here printed, and while they were before me in the present form they had to be curtailed in delivery.

I acknowledge with gratitude my debt to Professor A. R. Johnson, of Cardiff, who read through the proofs, and to the Rev. Bleddyn J. Roberts, of Bangor, who generously undertook the task of preparing the Indexes. To the Printers and Readers of the Oxford Press I am also indebted for the care with which they have printed the volume.

H. H. ROWLEY

MANCHESTER UNIVERSITY

February 1949

CONTENTS

ABBREVIATIONS

A.A.A.	= *Annals of Archaeology and Anthropology.*
A.A.S.O.R.	= *Annual of the American Schools of Oriental Research.*
A.f.O.	= *Archiv für Orientforschung.*
A.J.A.	= *American Journal of Archaeology.*
A.J.S.L.	= *American Journal of Semitic Languages and Literatures.*
A.J.Th.	= *American Journal of Theology.*
A.P.A.W.	= *Abhandlungen der preussischen Akademie der Wissenschaften.*
A.R.E.	= A. H. Breasted, *Ancient Records of Egypt.*
A.R.W.	= *Archiv für Religionswissenschaft.*
A.Th.R.	= *Anglican Theological Review.*
B.A.	= *The Biblical Archaeologist.*
B.A.S.O.R.	= *Bulletin of the American Schools of Oriental Research.*
B.D.B.	= F. Brown, S. R. Driver, and C. A. Briggs, *A Hebrew and English Lexicon of the Old Testament.*
B.E.H.J.	= *Bulletin des études historiques juives.*
Bi.Or.	= *Bibliotheca Orientalis.*
B.J.R.L.	= *Bulletin of the John Rylands Library.*
B.W.	= *The Biblical World.*
B.W.A.N.T.	= Beiträge zur Wissenschaft vom Alten und Neuen Testament.
B.Z.A.W.	= Beihefte zur *Zeitschrift für die alttestamentliche Wissenschaft.*
C.A.H.	= *The Cambridge Ancient History,* edited by J. B. Bury, S. A. Cook, F. E. Adcock, M. P. Charlesworth, and N. H. Baynes.
Camb.B.	= Cambridge Bible.
C.B.Q.	= *Catholic Biblical Quarterly.*
Cent.B.	= Century Bible.
C.Q.R.	= *Church Quarterly Review.*
C.R.A.I.B.L.	= *Comptes rendus de l'Académie des Inscriptions et Belles Lettres.*
D.B.	= *A Dictionary of the Bible,* edited by J. Hastings and J. A. Selbie.
D.T.T.	= *Dansk Teologisk Tidsskrift.*
E.B.	= *Encyclopaedia Biblica,* edited by T. K. Cheyne and J. S. Black.
E.B.	= Études Bibliques.
E.Brit.	= *Encyclopaedia Britannica.*
E.H.A.T.	= Exegetisches Handbuch zum Alten Testament, edited by J. Nikel and A. Schulz.
E.T.	= *The Expository Times.*
E.Tr.	= English translation.
EV.	= English versions.
F.u.F.	= *Forschungen und Fortschritte.*
H.A.T.	= Handbuch zum Alten Testament.
H.K.	= Handkommentar zum Alten Testament, edited by W. Nowack.
H.S.A.T.	= *Die Heilige Schrift des Alten Testaments,* 3rd ed., edited by E. Kautzsch; 4th ed., edited by A. Bertholet.
H.S.A.Tes.	= Die Heilige Schrift des Alten Testamentes, edited by F. Feldmann and H. Herkenne.
H.T.R.	= *Harvard Theological Review.*
H.U.C.A.	= *Hebrew Union College Annual.*
I.C.C.	= The International Critical Commentary, edited by S. R. Driver, A. Plummer, and C. A. Briggs.
J.A.O.S.	= *Journal of the American Oriental Society.*
J.As.	= *Journal asiatique.*
J.B.L.	= *Journal of Biblical Literature.*
J.E.A.	= *Journal of Egyptian Archaeology.*
J.E.O.L.	= *Jaarbericht Ex Oriente Lux.*

J.N.E.S.	= *Journal of Near Eastern Studies.*
J.P.O.S.	= *Journal of the Palestine Oriental Society.*
J.Q.R.	= *Jewish Quarterly Review.*
J.R.A.S.	= *Journal of the Royal Asiatic Society.*
J.S.O.R.	= *Journal of the Society for Oriental Research.*
J.T.S.	= *Journal of Theological Studies.*
J.T.V.I.	= *Journal of the Transactions of the Victoria Institute.*
K.A.T.	= Kommentar zum Alten Testament, edited by E. Sellin.
K.H.C.	= Kurzer Hand-Commentar zum Alten Testament, edited by K. Marti.
M.A.O.G.	= *Mitteilungen der altorientalischen Gesellschaft.*
M.D.O.G.	= *Mitteilungen der deutschen Orient-Gesellschaft zu Berlin.*
M.E.O.J.	= *Journal of the Manchester Egyptian and Oriental Society.*
M.G.W.J.	= *Monatsschrift für Geschichte und Wissenschaft des Judentums.*
M.J.U.P.	= *Museum Journal* of the University of Pennsylvania.
N.T.T.	= *Nieuw Theologisch Tijdschrift.*
O.L.Z.	= *Orientalistische Literaturzeitung.*
O.T.S.	= *Oudtestamentische Studiën.*
P.E.F.Q.S.	= *Quarterly Statement* of the Palestine Exploration Fund.
P.E.Q.	= *Palestine Exploration Quarterly.*
P.J.B.	= *Palästinajahrbuch des deutschen evangelischen Instituts für Altertumswissenschaft des Heiligen Landes zu Jerusalem.*
P.S.B.A.	= *Proceedings of the Society of Biblical Archaeology.*
R.Ass.	= *Revue d'assyriologie et d'archéologie orientale.*
R.B.	= *Revue biblique.*
R.E.S.	= *Revue des études sémitiques.*
R.E.S.-B.	= *Revue des études sémitiques et Babyloniaca.*
R.G.G.	= *Die Religion in Geschichte und Gegenwart,* edited by F. M. Schiele and L. Zscharnack (1st ed.), and by H. Gunkel and L. Zscharnack (2nd ed.).
R.H.P.R.	= *Revue d'histoire et de philosophie religieuses.*
R.H.R.	= *Revue de l'histoire des religions.*
R.S.	= *Revue sémitique.*
R.Th.Ph.	= *Revue de théologie et de philosophie.*
S.B.U.	= *Svenskt Bibliskt Uppslagsverk.*
S.E.Å.	= *Svensk Exegetisk Årsbok.*
TA	= Tell el Amarna text.
Th.R.	= *Theologische Rundschau.*
Th.W.B.	= *Theologisches Wörterbuch,* edited by G. Kittel.
T.L.Z.	= *Theologische Literaturzeitung.*
T.S.K.	= *Theologische Studien und Kritiken.*
W.C.	= Westminster Commentaries, edited by W. Lock and D. C. Simpson.
Z.A.	= *Zeitschrift für Assyriologie.*
Z.Ä.S.	= *Zeitschrift für ägyptische Sprache und Altertumskunde.*
Z.A.W.	= *Zeitschrift für die alttestamentliche Wissenschaft.*
Z.D.M.G.	= *Zeitschrift der deutschen morgenländischen Gesellschaft.*
Z.D.P.V.	= *Zeitschrift des deutschen Palästina Vereins.*

LECTURE I

THE EXTRA-BIBLICAL EVIDENCE

IT is now more than thirty years since an earlier Schweich Lecturer dealt with the range of problems to which the present lectures are devoted.[1] My own interest in those problems dates from my reading of the earlier lectures, which I found immensely stimulating, and it has continued ever since. My first duty is therefore to express my debt to Burney, and to say that even where my view varies from his I have learned much from him. Yet it will not be deemed superfluous, I trust, to return to this subject. For its whole discussion has been radically changed since Burney's day. In his discussion Palestinian archaeology scarcely figured, for the excavations which have dominated all recent treatment of the subject were not begun when he delivered his lectures. On the other hand, not a little of the more recent writing on the subject has ignored some of the aspects of the problem to which he drew attention. It is my hope that I may not lose sight of either side of the problem, though I cannot hope to reach a solution which will be accepted as final. That, however, is due to the nature of the problem. For it is safe to say that there will never be any general agreement on the chronological problems which lie at the base of our inquiry. As a recent writer says, 'the story of the Exodus has become, more than ever before, one of the most vexing historico-Biblical problems that confront us to-day'.[2]

That excellent scholar, Millar Burrows, from whom also I have learned much, in an unguarded moment permitted himself to suggest that chronology is of no moment.[3] That is a view I cannot share. Another American writer, with truer insight, says:

---

[1] C. F. Burney, *Israel's Settlement in Canaan*, Schweich Lectures for 1917.

[2] Cf. O'Callaghan, *Aram Naharaim*, 1948, p. 119 n.

[3] Cf. *B.A.S.O.R.*, No. 86, Apr. 1942, p. 36. Burrows also permitted himself to suggest that Moses was unaware of the date of the Exodus, when what was really at issue was not a date in terms of the Christian era, but in terms of the Pharaoh in whose reign the Exodus took place. Such a judgement, implying that Moses did not know whether he lived in the reign of Thothmes III or of Rameses II or of any other of the Pharaohs whose names have been brought into the discussion, ought only to be made after a convincing demonstration that the entire Old Testament story is an empty fabrication. It is because I do not think Burrows really intended such a judgement that I suppose that his statement was made in an unguarded moment, and that it does not reflect his serious opinion.

B

'Chronology is the backbone of history. Absolute chronology is the fixed central core around which the events of nations must be correctly grouped before they may assume their exact positions in history and before their mutual relationships may be properly understood.'[1] With this I wholly agree, and would add that nowhere is this of greater importance than in relation to the problems which are before us. For much more than chronology is really involved, since the view that we take of Israel's religious development is materially affected by the solution we adopt. At the same time, these fundamental chronological problems are of the utmost complexity, and new evidence is being continually brought forward to complicate them still more.

Various attempts have been made to synthesize the available evidence in consistent theories, and some ten years ago I reviewed several of these and offered my own synthesis.[2] Since then, in a series of papers, I have supplemented my study or considered objections to it,[3] though I have not been persuaded to make substantial changes in it. In the present lectures I desire to deal more comprehensively with the subject than has been possible in the separate studies, and to examine some recent discussions of the problems.

The material that must be taken into account is threefold. There are the Biblical traditions, surviving extra-Biblical texts, and the material provided by the excavation of ancient sites. In each case the question of interpretation arises. The Biblical traditions cannot be uncritically treated as regulative for the settling of the question, in view of our uncertainty as to their history before they reached their present form. The surviving extra-Biblical texts offer primary and contemporary evidence, but we must beware of supposing that the interpretation of their evidence, such as the equation of the Ḫabiru of the Amarna Letters with the Hebrews, is more than speculative and disputable. Again, excavation has provided factual evidence that must be accepted without question. Nevertheless, the interpretation of the evidence is a different matter. The same evidence is often very differently interpreted by different archaeologists, and even

[1] E. R. Thiele, in *J.N.E.S.* iii, 1944, p. 137.

[2] Cf. *Israel's Sojourn in Egypt*, 1938 (reprinted from *B.J.R.L.* xxii, 1938, pp. 243–90).

[3] Cf. *E.T.* l, 1938–9, pp. 503–8 (summarized in *Actes du XXe Congrès International des Orientalistes*, 1940, pp. 91–3); *E.T.* li, 1939–40, pp. 466–71; *P.E.Q.* 1940, pp. 90–4; ibid. 1941, pp. 152–7; ibid. 1942, pp. 41–53; *B.A.S.O.R.*, No. 85, Feb. 1942, pp. 27–31; ibid., No. 87, Oct. 1942, p. 40; *J.N.E.S.* iii, 1944, pp. 73–8.

the same archaeologist may vary from time to time the conclusions he draws from it.

At the beginning of the present century the view was common
that the Exodus took place towards the end of the thirteenth
century B.C.[1] In Hastings's *Dictionary of the Bible*, which is still
widely used half a century after its publication, it is stated that
Rameses II was the Pharaoh of the Oppression, and it is added
that 'this fact [*sic*!], long conjectured, has been definitely settled
by Naville's identification of Pithom, and discovery that it was
built by Rameses II'.[2] In the same article it is said that it was
generally accepted that the descent into Egypt was to be dated
in the Hyksos period.[2] The difficulties created by the mention
of the Ḥabiru in some of the Amarna texts, and by the mention
of 'Asaru in texts from the reigns of Seti I and Rameses II, where
the context indicates that they were already settled in Palestine,[3]
were got over by the view[4] that not all of the Israelite tribes were
in Egypt,[5] though there were not wanting those who disputed
the equation of Ḥabiru with Hebrews,[6] and of 'Asaru with Asher.[7]
Some evidence was found in the Biblical account to support the
view that there was an attack on Palestine from the south earlier
than the attack across the Jordan under Joshua, and while the
Bible represents this as an abortive attack, in that it was not
followed up, it was believed that this was due to a harmonistic
motive, and that really this was a separate movement in a

---

[1] This view was found in conservative as well as 'critical' works. Cf. Sayce,
The Early History of the Hebrews, 1897, pp. 158 ff.; Mangenot, in *Dictionnaire
de la Bible*, ed. by Vigouroux, iii, 1903, col. 998.

[2] Cf. Curtis, in his article on 'Chronology of the Old Testament', *D.B.* i,
1898, p. 398 b.

[3] Cf. Müller, *Asien und Europa*, 1893, pp. 236-9.

[4] McClellan (*Ecclesiastical Review*, lxxxviii, 1933, p. 91) calls this 'a ground-
less bit of subterfuge'.

[5] Gemoll (*Israeliten und Hyksos*, 1913, p. 65) went so far as to maintain that
only Caleb was in Egypt. More common has been the view that the Rachel
tribes were in Egypt, while the Leah and Concubine tribes were settled in
Canaan earlier. This was the view still taken by Böhl in 1930 (*Das Zeitalter
Abrahams*, pp. 46 f.; cf. *Kanaanäer und Hebräer*, 1911, p. 81). Niebuhr (in Hel-
molt's *The World's History*, E.Tr. iii, 1903, pp. 627 f.) thought that either the
Israelites were never in Egypt at all, or they must be identified with the
Hyksos.

[6] Cf. Hommel, in Hastings's *D.B.* i, p. 228 a; Dhorme, in *R.B.*, N.S. vi,
1909, pp. 68 f., 72, and many other scholars (see below).

[7] Cf. Eerdmans, *Alttestamentliche Studien*, ii, 1908, p. 56. See also Jack, *The
Date of the Exodus*, 1925, p. 230. On the other hand, Prášek (*E.T.* xi, 1899-
1900, p. 504) speaks of the unquestionable identity of the names found in the
Egyptian texts and the Biblical Asher.

different age. Several scholars placed this movement in the Amarna age,[1] and this was the view worked out by Burney in his Schweich Lectures.[2]

There is not a feature of this reconstruction which has not been challenged in recent years, so that while in many respects it seems to me to be sound, it is in great need of defence. In particular, the recent tendency on the part of those who have maintained a twofold entry into Palestine in different ages has been to reverse the order, and to reject the Biblical evidence on this point. Thus Albright[3] and Meek[4] placed the settlement of Judah later than the settlement of the central highlands. In an important study which has greatly influenced several American writers, Albright[5] maintained that the Joseph tribes, which he identified with the Ḥabiru, were in Palestine about 1400 B.C., while the Leah tribes, and especially the tribe of Judah, were led out of Egypt by Moses early in the reign of Rameses II, after a short period of oppression. Several elements of Albright's view have been subsequently modified, though I believe he still adheres to this broad picture. Somewhat similarly Meek identi- fied the attack on the central highlands with the activities of the

[1] Cf. Steuernagel, *Die Einwanderung der israelitischen Stämme in Kanaan*, 1901; Paton, *J.B.L.* xxxii, 1913, pp. 1–53 (cf. id., *B.W.* xlvi, 1915, pp. 82 ff., 173 ff.); Asmussen, *Memnon*, vii, 1915, pp. 185–207. Similarly Barton, *J.B.L.* xlviii, 1929, p. 144. Paton identified the Ḥabiru with the older Leah tribes Reuben, Simeon, Levi, and Judah, and a later wave with the younger Leah tribes Zebulun and Issachar, while the tribes that came out of Egypt at the Exodus he identified with the Rachel tribes only. Of the Concubine tribes he finds Gad and Asher, i.e. the Zilpah tribes, to be Canaanite tribes that amalgamated with the Leah tribes, while Dan and Naphtali, i.e. the Bilhah tribes, were Canaanite tribes that amalgamated with the Rachel tribes. The complete elimination of any Levite element from the group that came out of Egypt is the chief weakness of this view. Steuernagel more simply identified the Ḥabiru with the Leah tribes, and placed their occupation of the Negeb *circa* 1400 B.C., while the central highlands he held to have been occupied *circa* 1385 B.C. This would bring both movements into the Amarna age, and would make them almost synchronous.

[2] *Israel's Settlement in Canaan*, 1918.

[3] Cf. *B.A.S.O.R.*, No. 58, Apr. 1935, pp. 10–18. See also ibid., No. 74, Apr. 1939, pp. 11–23.

[4] Cf. *A.J.Th.* xxiv, 1920, pp. 209–16; *B.A.S.O.R.*, No. 61, Feb. 1936, pp. 17–19; and *Hebrew Origins*, 1936, chap. i.

[5] *B.A.S.O.R.*, No. 58, pp. 10–18. Albright's view is followed in the main by Burrows, *What Mean These Stones?* 1941, p. 79; Wright, *The Westminster Historical Atlas to the Bible*, 1945, pp. 39 f.; Finegan, *Light from the Ancient Past*, 1946, pp. 105–8; Earle, *The Asbury Seminarian*, i, 1946, pp. 96–104 (but more hesitatingly).

Ḥabiru in the Amarna age, but put the settlement of Judah in the south rather later in the thirteenth century than Albright did. In his view Joshua led the former attack and hence long antedated Moses.[1] More radically T. H. Robinson[2] has denied that the tribe of Judah was originally an Israelite tribe at all, and argued that it was a Canaanite element which was later accepted into the Israelite federation.[3]

[1] For a brief summary of these and other views and some criticisms of their positions see below, pp. 140 ff.

[2] Cf. *Amicitiae Corolla* (Rendel Harris Festschrift), 1933, pp. 265–73, and *History of Israel*, i, 1932, pp. 169 f.

[3] That the tribe of Judah contained considerable non-Israelite elements is clear from the Old Testament, and recognized by all scholars. Calibbite, Kenite, and Kenizzite elements are said to have accompanied them in their attack on Canaan, and major achievements are credited to Caleb and Othniel. Moreover, Gen. xxxviii would seem to indicate some intermarriage with the Canaanites, and hence some Canaanite blood in the tribe of Judah. Cf. Burney, *Israel's Settlement in Canaan*, p. 30; Waterman, *A.J.S.L.* lv, 1938, p. 31. Waterman holds that 'it appears to have been David who first brought these Edomite clans to a group-consciousness, and to have identified the group with a definite geographical area under the name Judah'. He therefore holds that this tribe was of Edomite, and not of Israelite, origin. Robinson's view is that Judah was a Canaanite tribe, established in the Hebron district, which became subject to pressure from the Kenites and Kenizzites, until, under Philistine pressure, the two groups combined against the new aggressors, and became fused into a single people. The Canaanite name of Judah was borne by them all, but Caleb became the hero of the whole group, and Judahite traditions were attached to his name. The continued pressure of the Philistines brought this new Judah group into association with the Israelites in the north, and then by a fiction Judah was recognized to be Israelite. He holds that the non-mention of Judah in the Song of Deborah is explained by this view. But, as he points out, Simeon and Levi are also unmentioned in the Song of Deborah, and the theory fails to account for their origin. If Simeon also belonged to the anti-Philistine bloc, it might have been expected to be included in the reinforced 'Judah'. It is scarcely probable that in the period of Saul and David Simeon would have been independently recognized alongside Judah, since Simeon seems to have been of slight independent account at that time. Moreover, Robinson holds that the Kenites and the Kenizzites were Yahweh-worshipping, and that this facilitated the fiction that they were Israelite when they were accepted into the federation of the northern tribes, who were also Yahweh-worshipping. But again, if Simeon stood outside this Yahweh-worship, it is not clear why the fiction extended to her; while if she was already within it, it must have been through Kenite and Kenizzite influence, and she might have been expected to have been already incorporated in 'Judah'. It is also to be noted that in the period of the Judges, before the days of Saul and David, we find a Levite from Mount Ephraim with connexions in Judah, who clearly did not regard Judah as non-Israelite in the same way as he did the Jebusites, and who regarded Benjamites equally with Judahites as associated peoples (Judges xix f.). It therefore

Of those who have held that the Israelite immigration into
Palestine was made by separate waves, and that only some of the
tribes came out of Egypt, none appear to me to have sufficiently
related the various movements together. If certain tribes went
into Egypt in the Hyksos period and came out again in the
thirteenth century B.C., after a sojourn in Egypt of anything in the
neighbourhood of the 430 years of Ex. xii. 40, it would be surprising for them to feel much unity with tribes which quite independently entered Palestine in the fourteenth century B.C. For
while there are remnants of a tradition of a twofold entry into
Palestine preserved in the Bible, there is little trace of a double
Exodus from Egypt,[1] and no reason to suppose that the Amarna

seems better to accept the Biblical tradition that in the admittedly mixed tribe
of Judah there were some genuinely Israelite elements, and to explain the non-
mention of the southern tribes in the Song of Deborah by the geographical
isolation of tribes that had entered the land from the south (see below,
pp. 102 f.). It will be seen in the third lecture that I share Robinson's view
that by the time the southern group came into full association with the northern group in the age of Saul and David they were Yahweh-worshipping, and
that they derived that worship from their Kenite element. I also share his
view of the part Philistine pressure played in that association. My only disagreement with him is that I find the original Judah that gave its name to the
mixed group to be Israelite, and find the Levite and Simeonite elements that
were with them to be also Israelite. Even though the latter were weak elements
in the time of Saul and David, if they were genuinely Israelite associates of
the tribe of Judah, with traditions interlocked with theirs from their first
entry into the land, their recognition would not be surprising. Noth (*P.J.B.*
xxx, 1934, p. 31 n.) rejects Robinson's view out of hand, saying simply 'Die
These Th. H. Robinsons . . . halte ich für unbegründet'.

[1] Albright (*J.B.L.* xxxvii, 1918, pp. 138 ff.; *B.A.S.O.R.*, No. 58, p. 15 n.)
holds that there were two Exodi, but confesses (*J.B.L.*, loc. cit.) that he knows
of no Biblical passage bearing on the first of them. Mercer (*A.Th.R.* v, 1922–3,
pp. 96–107) holds that there were several migrations from Egypt, spread over
a long period, and that Simeon entered Palestine before 1375 B.C. and Asher
before 1313 B.C. These tribes and also Gad, Dan, Zebulun, Naphtali, Issachar,
and perhaps Levi and Reuben, are held to have left Egypt before Judah and
the Joseph tribes, who left in the reign of Merneptah, but then separated
from one another at Kadesh. S. H. Hooke (*In the Beginning*, 1947, p. 83) suggests that 'the tradition contained in Genesis xii. 10–xiii. 1 may well represent
the earliest entry of Hebrews into Egypt', and adds 'It should also be noted
that cc. xx and xxvi are duplicates of the same story and reflect some elements
of the Exodus traditions, e.g. the favoured treatment of the Hebrews on their
first entry, the intervention of Jahveh, and the triumphant exodus with the
spoils of Egypt'. This, however, is rather to find a double tradition of the
Sojourn in Egypt and the Exodus, than a double Exodus. Toffteen (*The
Biblical Exodus*, 1909) argued for a double entry into Egypt and a double
Exodus, the first sojourn dating from 1877 to 1447 B.C., and the second dating
from *circa* 1340 to *circa* 1144 B.C. He claimed that only the first was known to

age wave of settlement came from Egypt. The histories of the two groups would thus have lain along separate ways for so long that this problem cannot be lightly swept aside or tacitly ignored. If the group that went into Egypt was descended from those who had left Mesopotamia some considerable time before they went into Egypt, and if they went into Egypt in the Hyksos period and spent forty years in the wilderness after the Exodus before they entered Palestine, then even if they were of the same ultimate stock as the Ḥabiru, their ways would have been separate for half a millennium before they came together in Palestine. Nor is the question of the common worship of Yahweh by both groups sufficiently dealt with.

Further, there is commonly a failure to give any clear explanation of the connexion of Levites with both waves of immigration. For Moses is said to have been born of Levite stock in Egypt, while there is much evidence in the Bible to connect Levites with the tribe of Judah.[1] This consideration is not valid against the view of Albright and Meek, who connect Moses with the tribe of Judah and not with the Joseph tribes. But this is offset by their dissociation of the Joseph tribes from those who came out of Egypt with Moses, despite the fact that deeply embedded in the tradition we find the Ark associated with Moses and with Joshua, while it was certainly intimately associated with Ephraim. Moreover, it was the Ephraimite document E which cherished the tradition that the divine name was first mediated to Israel through Moses. This would certainly be odd if Moses had nothing to do with Ephraim, and if his work lay with the tribe of Judah, which completely forgot this important aspect of it.[2]

J, E, and D, while only the second was known to P, and that surprisingly enough each Exodus was preceded by a similar oppression and produced leaders with similar names. This improbable thesis is not sustained by convincing arguments, and it has found no other adherents. Its author confesses his belief 'that the Hexateuchal stories of the Exodus are reliable even to the most minute details, except where the later compiler of the documents has misunderstood and changed his material, and where the copyists of later ages have miscopied the text or annotated it with their own explanations. The Bible, we are convinced, in dealing with the Exodus, is *absolutely* historical, in the best sense of the word, and trustworthy in its evidence, even to details, contrary to the usual modern hypothesis' (p. 279). It is hard to see how the writer can claim in the same breath that the evidence of the Bible is both garbled and completely trustworthy. Without making such extravagant claims for the absolute historical accuracy of the Biblical texts, I attach more real reliability to them than does Toffteen.

[1] Cf. S. A. Cook, *A.J.Th.* xiii, 1909, pp. 370–88, and *E.B.* ii, 1901, cols. 1665 f.   [2] See further below, pp. 143 ff.

By some recent writers this particular problem is eliminated by the view that Levi was never a secular tribe, and that the term always indicated a functional class of priests.¹ In support of this, evidence from the south Arabian inscriptions is adduced.² It is doubtful, however, if they are of sufficient antiquity to decide the issue.³ Moreover, the certainly ancient Blessing of Jacob pronounces on Simeon and Levi a common curse for some act of violence which they had committed.⁴ This is generally believed to be the act of treachery at Shechem, referred to in Gen. xxxiv. If this view is correct—and there seems little reason to doubt it—great antiquity must attach to the tradition of Gen. xxxiv, which tells of hostile activity in the Shechem district long before the age of Moses and Joshua. In actual fact Simeon and Levi did not share a common fate, and it is therefore certain that the prophecy that they would must go back to a time when it seemed likely that they might. This means that at that time Levi cannot well have been honourably scattered by reason of its priestly function, and that it had always been so scattered, but that it was then a secular tribe, comparable with Simeon.⁵ Hence it seems to me that the evidence of the history of the tribe

¹ Cf. Hölscher, in Pauly-Wissowa, *Realencyclopädie der klassischen Altertumswissenschaft*, xii, 1925, cols. 2155 ff. Hölscher says (ibid., col. 2161): 'Die Leviten, die wir geschichtlich kennen, sind von Anfang an nichts anderes als der Priesterstand, als dessen mythischer Ahnherr in der Sagengenealogie L., d.h. der 'Priester', gilt. Die Organisation solcher Berufsgenossenschaften war im hebräischen Altertum die eines fiktiven Blutsverbandes, eine Fiktion, die dadurch erleichtert wurde, dass der Beruf sich in den Familien zu vererben pflegte.' Cf. also Dhorme, *La Religion des Hébreux nomades*, 1937, pp. 226 f., and Haldar, *Associations of Cult Prophets among the Ancient Semites*, 1945, pp. 95 f. Mowinckel (*Norsk Geografisk Tidsskrift*, ix, 1942, pp. 22 f.) derives the name Levi from a root meaning 'to swing round' (*dreie, svinge rundt*), which he connects with the ecstatic dance. He thinks the Levites were originally the cultic officials of Kadesh, who were ousted from their office, and whose God was Yahweh (ibid., pp. 21 f.).

² In the Minaean inscriptions *lw'* and *lw't* are found, apparently meaning *priest* and *priestess*. The references are given in Pauly-Wissowa, loc. cit. Cf., too, Gray, *Sacrifice in the Old Testament*, 1925, pp. 242 ff.

³ Cf. S. A. Cook, *E.Brit.*, 11th ed., xvi, 1911, pp. 514 f., Gray, op. cit., p. 244. Meek (*Hebrew Origins*, 1936, p. 128) thinks that some of the Israelite Levites migrated southwards into Arabia, and became priests there, and thus explains the Minaean references.   ⁴ Gen. xlix. 5–7.

⁵ Cf. what I have written elsewhere, *J.B.L.* lviii, 1939, pp. 116 f. n.: 'If . . . Levites were from the first priests, and the term denoted a function, and not a community, it is hard to see how the dispersion that was involved in their honorable function could be recorded to their dishonor, or how it could be associated with the wholly different dispersion of Simeon, or why its cause should be traced to an act of treachery in which, *ex hypothesi*, the Levites

of Levi calls for integration into a consistent and satisfying view of the whole question.[1]

With all these questions Burney appears to have grappled seriously, and to have gone far towards their solution. He believed the Joseph tribes to have broken off from the others after the Ḥabiru invasion, and then to have gone down into Egypt,[2] to be later joined by Levite and Simeonite elements,[3] after the Shechem treachery. He then assumed a second breaking-off, however, when the Joseph tribes with some Levites separated from Judah and Simeon after the Exodus from Egypt.[4] This is represented as taking place at Kadesh-Barnea, when the main body of Levi moved northward with Simeon and Judah, while the Joseph tribes journeyed round Edom to attack from the east of Jordan. There is no trace in the Biblical tradition of the assumed migration of Simeon and Levi to Egypt after the installation in Goshen of an earlier wave of immigration into Egypt, and the assumption that Simeon and Levi joined the Joseph tribes in Egypt and then separated from them after the Exodus to rejoin Judah, from whom they had by now been separated for at least the duration of the Sojourn in Egypt, seems improbable. Nor is it clear how much remained of the achievements of the Ḥabiru on Burney's view. Since the tribe of Judah was somewhere in the neighbourhood of Kadesh-Barnea, with the victory at Hormah still before her, her conquest had scarcely begun, though *ex hypothesi* she had been continuously in the south of Palestine for a century and a half. Despite the measure of my agreement with Burney, therefore, I am not wholly satisfied with his reconstruction.

Between the two World Wars a marked change came over the discussion of the whole question, and the centre of gravity in all treatment of the whole complex of problems involved here

as a community could not have been concerned. If Levi were originally a secular tribe, it is possible to understand how the two groups followed unexpectedly different courses after their common disaster, but it is not easy to see how a common disaster could have been created to account for such wholly different courses, and quite impossible to suppose that any writer who knew that in fact Levi and Simeon were not on any comparable footing in his day should have created an oracle that pronounced a common doom upon them.' Cf. Burney, *Israel's Settlement in Canaan*, pp. 44 f.; Gray, *Sacrifice in the Old Testament*, 1925, pp. 244 f.; Meek, *Hebrew Origins*, 1936, pp. 118 f., 128. [1] Cf. *J.N.E.S.* iii, 1944, pp. 73–8.

[2] Cf. *Israel's Settlement in Canaan*, p. 87. [3] Ibid., pp. 46 f.

[4] Ibid., p. 48. Cf. also Burney's earlier presentation of his view, *J.T.S.* ix, 1907–8, pp. 321 ff., esp. p. 340.

moved into the field of present-day excavations of Biblical sites.[1]
This led to a radical change of view on the date of the Exodus
in some circles, and particularly in Great Britain.

Already, on the ground of previously known evidence, J. W.
Jack had argued for the fifteenth-century date of the Exodus,[2]
and this view received a powerful impetus from the excavations
at Jericho conducted by Garstang. When that scholar announced
that the date of the fall of Jericho was before 1400 B.C.[3] this
seemed to confirm the chronology of 1 Kgs. vi. 1,[4] and to place

---

[1] Kennett (*Old Testament Essays*, 1928, pp. 21 ff.) offers a reconstruction of
the history which almost entirely ignores the archaeological evidence. He
finds a series of waves of Israelite immigration, but does not sufficiently relate
them to one another, or explain how or when all the tribes became Yahweh-
worshipping.

[2] *The Date of the Exodus*, 1925. To this view Peet had inclined (*Egypt and
the Old Testament*, 1922, p. 121), as also had Desnoyers (*Histoire du peuple
hébreu*, i, 1922, pp. 407 ff.), and it had been held by Hommel (*E.T.* x, 1898–9,
pp. 210–12), Miketta (*Der Pharao des Auszuges*, 1903), Orr (*Expositor*, 5th
series, v, 1897, pp. 161–77; *The Problem of the Old Testament*, 7th imp., 1909,
pp. 422 ff.), and other older scholars. Some of those who adopted this view
held that Hatshepshut, the sister and wife of Thothmes III, was the Pharaoh's
daughter who rescued Moses from the Nile. So Orr, *Expositor*, 5th series, v,
1897, pp. 174 f.; Jack, op. cit., pp. 251 ff. Some older writers who assigned the
Exodus to the Ramesside dynasty placed it in the fourteenth century B.C.,
using a chronology for the Egyptian rulers that is now known to be wrong.
Thus Prášek (*E.T.* xi, 1899–1900, pp. 503 ff.) placed the Exodus under Seti II,
whose reign was said to have extended from 1273 to 1271 B.C., and Mahler
(*J.R.A.S.* 1901, pp. 33–67) placed it in the thirteenth year of Rameses II,
which he equated with the year 1335 B.C. Mahler claimed that his dates were
established astronomically (cf. *Handbuch der jüdischen Chronologie*, 1916) and that
they could be determined with great precision. The promise to Abraham he
fixed at 8 Oct. 1764 B.C. by an eclipse which enabled the patriarch to see the
stars in the daytime (Gen. xv. 5), and the date of the Exodus at 27 Mar.
1335 B.C. by an eclipse on Thursday, 13 Mar. 1335 B.C., which he identified
with the darkness of Nisan 1 in Ex. x (pp. 231 ff.). Mahler's astronomical
and mathematical skill cannot make up for the complete *non sequitur* of his
argument. Nor does he relate the story to the background of history.

[3] Cf. *Joshua–Judges*, 1931, p. 146.

[4] This verse locates the Exodus 480 years before the founding of the
Temple in the fourth year of Solomon's reign. The date of Solomon's acces-
sion is put by modern scholars variously from 976 B.C. to 952 B.C. Thus T. H.
Robinson (*History of Israel*, i, 1932, p. 463) assigns it to 976 B.C.; Hall (*The
Ancient History of the Near East*, 7th ed., 1927, facing p. 516) to *circa* 975 B.C.;
Cook (*C.A.H.* iii, 1925, p. 356) to *circa* 974 B.C.; Smith (*Old Testament History*,
1911, p. 499) to 973 B.C.; Kleber (*Biblica*, ii, 1921, p. 172), Kittel (*Geschichte
des Volkes Israel*, ii, 5th ed., 1922, p. 271), and Ricciotti (*Storia d'Israele*, i, 2nd
ed., 1934, p. 341; French Tr., 1939, p. 352) to 972 B.C.; Coucke (*Supplément
au Dictionnaire de la Bible*, i, 1928, col. 1247), Jirku (*Geschichte des Volkes Israel*,

the Exodus securely in the middle of the fifteenth century B.C. Many writers accepted this date,[1] and some hailed the signal vindication of the accuracy of the Bible, as though the only text

1931, p. 146), Jean (*Initiation biblique*, 1939, table to p. 436), and Lusseau-Collomb (*Histoire du peuple d'Israël*, 6th ed., 1945, p. 867) to 971 B.C.; H. W. Robinson (*History of Israel*, 1938, Appendix III) to *circa* 970 B.C.; Jack (*The Date of the Exodus*, 1925, pp. 201 f.) to 969 B.C.; Lewy (*Chronologie der Könige von Israel und Juda*, 1927, p. 27) to 960 B.C.; Olmstead (*History of Syria and Palestine*, 1931, p. 338) and Mowinckel (*Chronologie der israelitischen und jüdischen Könige*, 1932, p. 271) to 955 B.C.; von Gall (*Beiträge zur alttestamentlichen Wissenschaft* (Budde Festschrift), 1920, pp. 52–60) to 952 B.C.

[1] Cf. Dussaud, in *Syria*, xi, 1930, pp. 298, 390–2 (see also ibid. iv, 1923, pp. 76 f.); T. H. Robinson, *History of Israel*, i, 1932, p. 80 (see also *Theology*, xxv, 1932, pp. 267–74, and *E.T.* xlvii, 1935–6, pp. 53–5); Yahuda, *The Accuracy of the Bible*, 1934, pp. 116–28; Phythian-Adams, *The Call of Israel*, 1934, p. 52 n.; Dennefeld, *Histoire d'Israël*, 1935, pp. 64–70; Caiger, *Bible and Spade*, 1936, pp. 68–71, 191 f.; Kalt, *Biblisches Reallexikon*, 2nd ed., 1938, col. 972; de Koning, *Studiën over de El-Amarnabrieven*, 1940, p. 92; Lusseau-Collomb, *Histoire du peuple d'Israël*, 6th ed., 1945, pp. 599–611; Bendixon, *Israels Historia*, i, 1948, p. 84. T. H. Robinson (*E.T.*, loc. cit., p. 54) goes so far as to say: 'With very few exceptions serious Old Testament scholars have abandoned the nineteenth dynasty date.' Amongst the scholars who have not abandoned the nineteenth-dynasty date are: Dhorme (*Supplément au Dictionnaire de la Bible*, i, 1928, col. 224); Gunkel (*R.G.G.*, 2nd ed., iv, 1930, col. 234); Hempel (*Althebräische Literatur*, 1930, pp. 8 f.); Jirku (*Geschichte des Volkes Israel*, 1931, pp. 67 ff.); Vincent (*R.B.* xli, 1932, pp. 264 ff.; xliv, 1935, pp. 583 ff.); Barton (*Archaeology and the Bible*, 6th ed., 1933, pp. 41 f.); Schmidtke (*Die Einwanderung Israels in Kanaan*, 1933, p. 66); Petrie (*Palestine and Israel*, 1934, pp. 55 ff.); Heinisch (*Das Buch Exodus*, 1934, pp. 16 ff.); Albright (*B.A.S.O.R.*, No. 58, Apr. 1935, pp. 10 ff., and often); Sellin (*Geschichte des israelitisch-jüdischen Volkes*, i, 1935, p. 57); Duncan (*New Light on Hebrew Origins*, 1936, pp. 148, 180 ff.; with this contrast his earlier view, *Digging up Biblical History*, ii, 1931, pp. v f.); Wardle (*History and Religion of Israel*, 1936, p. 33, and *Record and Revelation*, 1938, p. 114); Meek (*Hebrew Origins*, 1936, pp. 33 f.); Lavergne (*Chronologie Biblique*, 1937, p. 48); H. W. Robinson (*History of Israel*, 1938, pp. 30 ff.); Schofield (*The Historical Background of the Bible*, 1938, pp. 79 ff.); de Vaux (*Z.A.W.*, N.F. xv, 1938, pp. 225 ff., and *Supplément au Dictionnaire de la Bible*, iv, 1947–8, cols. 736 f.); Jean (in *Initiation biblique*, 1939, pp. 430 f.); Beer (*Exodus*, 1939, pp. 16, 79); Mould (*Essentials of Bible History*, 1939, pp. 91 f.); Noth (*Die Welt des Alten Testaments*, 1940, p. 173); Burrows (*What Mean these Stones?* 1941, p. 79); Gordon (*The Living Past*, 1941, pp. 36 f.); Daniel-Rops (*Histoire sainte*, 1943, p. 105); Wright (*The Westminster Historical Atlas*, 1945, pp. 39 f.); Finegan (*Light from the Ancient Past*, 1946, pp. 105 ff.). A few scholars who do not definitely commit themselves to the nineteenth-dynasty date appear to incline to it: Lods (*Israël*, 1930, pp. 203 ff.; E.Tr., 1932, pp. 181 ff.; cf. *Mélanges Franz Cumont*, 1936, pp. 847 ff.); Mallon (*Supplément au Dictionnaire de la Bible*, ii, 1934, cols. 1340 ff.); Ricciotti (*Storia d'Israele*, i, 2nd ed., 1934, pp. 225 ff.; French Tr., 1939, pp. 230 ff.); James (*Personalities of the Old Testament*, 1939, p. 6); Alleman and Flack (*Old Testament Commentary*, 1948, pp. 208 f.).

that mattered was 1 Kgs. vi. 1.[1] It was sometimes claimed that all that really pointed to Rameses II as the oppressing Pharaoh was Ex. i. 11, which gives the names of the cities the Israelites were set to build as Pithom and Raamses, and that its evidence could hardly be determinative.[2]

In reality the problem is extremely complex, and any attempt to reduce it to simplicity is inadequate. Certainly the issue cannot be decided on the date of the fall of Jericho, even if that were established beyond all question. For many other sites have been excavated, and the evidence they provide must also be taken into account. Moreover, as has been said, archaeological evidence is but one of the types of evidence to be considered. Beside it the Biblical traditions, and surviving non-Biblical texts from several sources, fall to be considered. Nor does it need to be added that the Biblical traditions include far more than such a chronological note as 1 Kgs. vi. 1, and such an antiquarian note as Ex. i. 11. Here it will be convenient first to review the evidence from excavated Palestinian sites, since these have received so much attention in recent discussion, and then to pass to other extra-Biblical evidence, before considering the Biblical evidence and attempting a synthesis.

The date of the fall of Jericho is not yet finally settled.[3] Garstang at one time stated that 'the fourteenth century had not begun at the time the walls fell'.[4] Later he modified this somewhat, and in a joint statement he issued with Rowe he declared that 'we may logically conclude that the fall of Jericho took place between 1400 B.C. and the accession of Akhenaton. No

---

[1] Cf. Lucas, *P.E.Q.* 1941, pp. 110 ff. Vincent, with more discrimination, observes (*R.B.* xlviii, 1939, p. 582 n.): 'Quant à la Bible, après qu'on a vainement répété l'indication chronologique, incidente et précaire, que le Temple salomonien fut fondé 480 ans après la sortie d'Égypte (1 Rois vi, 1), personne encore, que je sache, n'y a découvert quelque indice concret d'une aussi lointaine prise de possession du pays de Canaan par les Israélites.'

[2] Cf. T. H. Robinson: 'The whole theory of a nineteenth dynasty date for the Exodus rests on two names in that verse' (*History of Israel*, i, p. 79). Even more emphatically, in *T.L.Z.* lvii, 1932, col. 77, he says: 'Die Erwähnung der beiden Städte in Ex. i, 11 ist den meisten Forschern entscheidend erschienen und man hat sich nicht vergegenwärtigt, dass die ganze Theorie einzig und allein an der Ursprünglichkeit dieser beiden Namen hängt.'

[3] Cf. Hennequin, *Supplément au Dictionnaire de la Bible*, iii, 1936, col. 413: 'Il ne saurait être question de faire état des "résultats" acquis à Jéricho pour déterminer la date de l'entrée des Israélites en Canaan. *Adhuc sub judice lis est.*'

[4] Cf. *Joshua–Judges*, p. 146 n. Cf. also *P.E.F.Q.S.* 1930, p. 132, where the date was given 'in round figures, about 1400 B.C.'

other conclusion will satisfy the archaeological evidence as a whole.'[1] Albright was at first inclined to agree with Garstang in the earlier date just mentioned,[2] but later modified this to a date somewhere in the fourteenth century, probably in the second or third quarter,[3] or to a date between *circa* 1375 and *circa* 1300 B.C.[4] He has been followed by Burrows[5] and Wright,[6] though the latter had earlier concluded a brief survey of the question by saying: 'Absolutely all that we can now say with any certainty is that the city fell to the Hebrews some time between cir. 1475 and 1300 B.C.'[7] According to a recent American writer,[8] however, Albright has now considerably modified his view, and concedes the possibility that the fall of Jericho may be brought down a century to a date early in the thirteenth century B.C. As this was in a private letter, and Albright has not yet published any statement of this view or of the grounds on which it rests, it should perhaps be regarded as a tentative modification, rather than one to which he is definitely committed.[9] It is of interest in that it would bring Albright much nearer to the view of Vincent,

[1] Cf. *P.E.F.Q.S.* 1936, p. 170; *A.A.A.* xxiii, 1936, pp. 75 f.

[2] Cf. Garstang, *Joshua–Judges*, p. 146 n.

[3] Cf. *Haverford Symposium*, 1938, p. 21. Also *B.A.S.O.R.*, No. 58, Apr. 1935, p. 13, where it is dated between 1360 and 1320 B.C. In the meantime Albright had announced his acceptance of Vincent's date for the capture of Jericho, in the thirteenth century B.C. (cf. *B.A.S.O.R.*, No. 56, Dec. 1934, p. 10, and *Archaeology of Palestine and the Bible*, 1932, p. 101).

[4] Cf. *B.A.S.O.R.*, No. 74, Apr. 1939, p. 20; also No. 57, Feb. 1935, p. 30, where it is assigned to the second half of the fourteenth century B.C. Cf. *A.J.A.* xxxix, 1935, p. 140 b, where he says: 'For a number of reasons the writer is unable to accept a date at the beginning of the fourteenth century, but the evidence certainly is against a date later than the end of this century.' Albright states roundly (*B.A.S.O.R.*, No. 74, p. 23): 'The views of Professor Garstang, Sir Charles Marston, and others are devoid of concrete archaeological foundation.' On the other hand Vincent (*R.B.* xlviii, 1939, p. 580) dismisses Albright almost equally roundly, saying: 'M. Albright n'a produit aucun solide argument technique pour limiter à ±1320 l'évolution céramique de Jéricho.'

[5] Cf. *What Mean these Stones?* 1941, p. 79.

[6] Cf. *The Westminster Historical Atlas to the Bible*, p. 40 a.

[7] Cf. *B.A.S.O.R.*, No. 86, Apr. 1942, p. 34. See also Finegan, *Light from the Ancient Past*, 1946, p. 136.

[8] J. Bright, in *Interpretation*, i, 1947, p. 84.

[9] While the present work has been in the press, Albright has published *The Archaeology of Palestine*, 1949, in which he says (pp. 108 f.): 'At present the evidence points to a date . . . in the latter part of the fourteenth century or the early thirteenth for the fall of Jericho; it must, however, be frankly confessed that our evidence against a date somewhat later in the thirteenth century . . . is mainly negative.'

who in a series of articles[1] has expressed his disagreement with
Garstang, and adhered to a date between 1250 and 1200 B.C.
for the fall of Jericho[2]—a date to which Wright had declared
that the final blow had been given.[3]

With Vincent Schaeffer is in substantial agreement. He brings
Garstang's date for the fall of City C down to 1365 B.C. when
he finds evidence of an earthquake that brought widespread
destruction throughout Syria and Palestine and beyond, and
holds that City D, which followed, was destroyed by fire towards
the end of the thirteenth century B.C.[4]

The excavations of Garstang proved that part of the wall of
Jericho collapsed, and that the city was utterly burned.[5] This
agrees so well with the Biblical account of the fall of Jericho that
there would seem to be every probability that it is this fall which
is in question. Petrie maintains that there is evidence of a second
and later burnt layer, and while he agrees substantially with
Garstang in the dating of the earlier destruction, claims that the
final destruction did not take place until two centuries later.[6]
Garstang, however, finds the evidence to show that such settlements as continued after the destruction *circa* 1400 B.C. were
unimportant, and were unprotected by a wall.[7] For the dating

---

[1] Cf. *R.B.* xxxix, 1930, pp. 403–33; *P.E.F.Q.S.* 1931, pp. 104 f.; *R.B.* xli,
1932, pp. 264–76; ibid. xliv, 1935, pp. 583–605. Cf. also *Mélanges E. Podechard*, 1945, p. 273. Similarly de Vaux, *Z.A.W.*, N.F. xv, 1938, p. 237, where
it is stated that Jericho continued to be occupied until towards 1250–
1225 B.C., after which all occupation ceased for some centuries. Cf. also
Pidoux, *R.Th.Ph.*, N.S. xxvii, 1939, pp. 48–61.

[2] Cf. *R.B.* xlviii, 1939, p. 580, where Vincent more narrowly indicates the
date of the fall of Jericho as 'towards 1230 B.C.' Pidoux (*R.Th.Ph.*, N.S. xxvii,
1939, p. 60) concludes for a date towards 1200 B.C.

[3] Cf. *B.A.S.O.R.*, No. 86, Apr. 1942, p. 33.

[4] Cf. *Stratigraphie comparée et chronologie de l'Asie occidentale*, 1948, pp. 129 ff.,
esp. 135 f., 149; also pp. 560 f.

[5] Cf. Garstang, *P.E.F.Q.S.* 1931, pp. 105 ff.; ibid., pp. 186 ff.; ibid.
1932, pp. 149 ff.; *A.A.A.* xix, 1932, pp. 3 ff., 35 ff., xx, 1933, pp. 3 ff., xxi,
1934, pp. 99 ff., xxii, 1935, pp. 143 ff., xxiii, 1936, pp. 67 ff.; *P.E.F.Q.S.* 1935,
pp. 61 ff.   [6] Cf. *Palestine and Israel*, 1934, p. 55.

[7] Cf. *P.E.F.Q.S.* 1932, pp. 152 f.; *Joshua–Judges*, pp. 146 f. Lods (*R.E.S.*
1936, p. lx) says: 'Le point de divergence principal entre M. Garstang et le
P. Vincent paraît être celui-ci: le savant anglais a relevé, sur le tell et dans la
nécropole voisine, des débris provenant du dernier âge du bronze (Br. III),
donc d'une époque voisine de 1200, mais en si minime quantité qu'il les
attribue à quelque petit poste militaire que les pharaons auraient installé
temporairement au milieu des ruines de la ville, détruite vers 1400. Le P.
Vincent, au contraire, y reconnaît les restes de la puissante cité cananéenne
que Josué doit avoir conquise et anéantie. L'interprétation des constatations

of the collapse he relies in part, as all archaeologists to-day do, on the evidence of the broken pottery.[1] For the precision of his dating, however, he relies on scarabs bearing the names of Egyptian kings, found in some graves which he excavated. In a cemetery containing many hundreds of graves[2] a large number were opened.[3] In some of these were found the scarabs, three of which bore the name of Amenhotep III, and of these three two were found in a single tomb.[4] As no scarabs of later Pharaohs were found, and as Amenhotep's reign fell *circa* 1400 B.C., the date of the fall of Jericho was held to be established.[5]

That it is not really so simple as it sounds is sufficiently shown by the eminence of some of the archaeologists who are not convinced, such as Vincent, de Vaux, and Albright. Amongst the ceramic finds were some imitations of Mycenaean vases. Both Albright and Vincent independently found these to be evidence against Garstang's dating. Vincent held that their character pointed to a date *circa* 1250 B.C.[6] while Albright noted that the importation of Mycenaean ware into Egypt was only slight before the middle of the fourteenth century B.C., and it was therefore very improbable that it would have been both imported into Palestine and copied there at an earlier date.[7] So far as the scarabs of Amenhotep III are concerned, Albright observes that scarabs of this Pharaoh continued to be used for long after his death, and notes that four of them were found at Tell ed-Duweir

archéologiques, on le voit, est ici particulièrement délicate.' More recently Garstang has advanced the view that the remains of this later occupation date from the time of Eglon (*A.J.S.L.* lviii, 1941, pp. 371 f.).

[1] Dussaud (*Syria*, xi, 1930, p. 391 b) says: 'La céramique de Jéricho correspond à la céramique du deuxième niveau de Ras Shamra, c'est-à-dire qu'elle ne peut pas descendre plus bas que 1400 avant J.-C.'

[2] Cf. *A.A.A.* xix, 1932, p. 19, where 300 to 400 are mentioned.

[3] Cf. *P.E.F.Q.S.* 1932, p. 150, where twenty-five are said to have been opened.

[4] Cf. *A.A.A.* xix, 1932, p. 36, xx, 1933, pp. 21 f.

[5] Cf. Garstang, *P.E.F.Q.S.* 1935, p. 68: 'Five seasons devoted to the examination and excavation of this site have convinced me that no other conclusion can satisfy the abundant circumstantial evidence bearing upon this date.' Cf. *A.J.S.L.* lviii, 1941, p. 370: 'Our excavations, logically interpreted, point to the fall of the city in the reign of Amenhotep III, possibly late in his reign (which is well represented), but before that of his successor Akhenaton, of whose period there is no trace.' Similarly *The Story of Jericho*, 1940, pp. 121 f. De Koning (*Studiën over El Amarnabrieven*, 1940, p. 114) dates the fall of Jericho *circa* 1380 B.C. [6] Cf. *R.B.* xliv, 1935, pp. 598 f.

[7] Cf. *B.A.S.O.R.*, No. 58, Apr. 1935, p. 12. See also *A.A.S.O.R.* xvii, 1938, p. 79. Cf. also Pidoux, *R.Th.Ph.*, N.S. xxvii, 1939, p. 56; Wright, *B.A.* iii, 1940, p. 35.

in remains that are dated in the thirteenth century B.C.[1] Moreover, scarabs of the Pharaohs who reigned during the century
and a half after Amenhotep III are uncommon, and particularly so in Palestinian finds.[2] Further, it is to be noted that Fairman thinks the name Jericho may stand in an Egyptian text
from the time of Rameses II.[3] If this were a certain reference it
would be of the highest importance.

As I am not an archaeologist, I am not qualified to express an
opinion on these questions. To choose the date that best fits my
own general view and to pin my faith to the archaeologist who
proposes it would merely reflect on the objectivity of my own
scholarship. When there is a stable agreement amongst the
archaeologists, I am prepared to accept it, and to recognize that
our view must somehow accommodate its evidence. It is clearly
out of the question at the moment to make any one archaeologist's dating of this event the determining factor of our whole
view of the Exodus and Settlement.[4] Nor, indeed, if there were
agreement here, could we make this date regulative for our whole
view. We should still have to consider all the other evidence and
strive to piece it together in an integrated and consistent whole.
Albright has long held that the archaeological evidence quite
clearly proves that the main weight of Israel's conquest of Palestine fell in the thirteenth century B.C,[5] and his view that Jericho

---

[1] Cf. ibid., pp. 13 f. Albright dated these remains in the latter half of the
reign of Rameses II, while Starkey at first dated them in the first half of that
reign (cf. *P.E.F.Q.S.* 1934, p. 174), but later appears to have associated himself with Albright's dating (*P.E.Q.* 1937, p. 239). It should be noted that
Vincent draws attention (*R.B.* xlviii, 1939, p. 580 n.) to the fact that 'un
beau scarabée d'Aménophis III a été découvert dans l'édifice de l'acropole
que les explorateurs dataient de l'époque perse et qui paraît représenter une
écurie royale de l'ère israélite' to point his warning against using isolated
scarabs for the dating of ruins.

[2] Cf. *B.A.S.O.R.*, No. 58, p. 12. See also Wright, *B.A.* iii, 1940, p. 34, who
observes: 'Every Palestinian and Egyptian archaeologist knows that scarabs
are not good evidence, since they were handed down as keepsakes and charms,
and were widely imitated some centuries later;' and Pidoux, *R.Th.Ph.*, N.S.
xxvii, 1939, p. 57: 'La seule chose, en effet, que puisse nous fournir la présence d'un scarabée, c'est un *terminus a quo*. Il permet d'établir que le con-
texte archéologique dans lequel il se trouve n'est pas antérieur au souverain
dont il porte le nom, mais il peut, sans difficulté, lui être postérieur de
plusieurs siècles.'   [3] Cf. *J.E.A.* xxv, 1939, pp. 141 f.

[4] Cf. Contenau, *Manuel d'Archéologie orientale*, iv, 1947, pp. 1752 f.: 'En
présence des arguments de poids exposés en faveur des deux solutions (M.
Garstang conclut à 1400, le P. Vincent à 1250–1200), on ne peut trouver là un
critérium pour fixer la date de l'Exode plus haut qu'on ne le fait généralement.'

[5] Albright goes so far as to declare that the fifteenth-century dating of the

fell in the previous century therefore compelled him to separate this event from the activities of the group of Israelites whom
Moses led out of Egypt. Wright, who followed him in this, supposed that the attack on Jericho might have been made not from
across the Jordan but from the neighbourhood of Shechem by
the immigrants of the earlier wave who were operating in that
district.[1] While I must confess that I am not happy about this
solution, since the Biblical tradition so strongly associates the
fall of Jericho with the passage of the Jordan and with the leadership of Joshua, it could not be ruled out merely on this ground.
If, however, Albright's new date or Vincent's date should ultimately gain general favour, the integration of Biblical and non-
Biblical material at this point would be easier. I would emphasize,
however, my complete suspense of judgement on the question of
the date of the fall of Jericho.

The evidence from other sites does not appear to be so keenly
disputed. The fall of Lachish is dated archaeologically towards
the end of the thirteenth century B.C.[2] and by the Bible shortly
after the fall of Jericho.[3] Albright,[4] who is followed by Wright,[5]
fixes the date with great precision. He says: 'In 1937 the discovery in the remains of the latest Canaanite Lachish of a
hieratic inscription dated to the year 1231 B.C. (or possibly
somewhat later, but in no case earlier) proved that the fall of
this town into Israelite hands took place in or after that year.'[6]
Vincent is less precise than Albright, but assigns the fall of

Exodus is scarcely worth considering. He says (in Alleman and Flack, *Old
Testament Commentary*, 1948, p. 141): 'Some scholars wish to date the Exodus
much higher, even in the 15th cent. B.C., but the high chronology offers
such insoluble historical difficulties that it scarcely seems worth considering
at all.' [1] Cf. *The Westminster Historical Atlas*, p. 40 a.

[2] Cf. Tufnell–Inge–Harding, *Lachish II: The Fosse Temple*, 1940, pp. 22 f.;
Burrows, *What Mean these Stones?* p. 76; Schaeffer, *Stratigraphie comparée et
chronologie de l'Asie occidentale*, 1948, p. 188. Starkey at first dated the fall not
later than 1260 B.C. (cf. *P.E.F.Q.S.* 1934, p. 174), but later modified this to a
date 'towards the close of the XIXth dynasty' (ibid. 1937, p. 239; cf. Tufnell–
Inge–Harding, op. cit., p. 22). [3] Cf. Josh. x. 31 f.

[4] Cf. *B.A.S.O.R.*, No. 68, Dec. 1937, p. 24, and No. 74, Apr. 1939, p. 21.
In the former passage Albright says: 'The earliest possible date for the fall
of Canaanite Lachish into the hands of the Israelites is 1231 B.C. . . . This new
evidence is, therefore, of decisive value for the question of the date of the
main phase of the Israelite Conquest.' In *A.J.A.* xxxix, 1935, pp. 139 f.,
Albright had been inclined to a rather earlier date.

[5] Cf. *B.A.* i, 1938, p. 26; *J.N.E.S.* v, 1946, p. 111. See also Finegan, op.
cit., p. 139.

[6] Cf. *From the Stone Age to Christianity*, 2nd ed., 1946, p. 194. Similarly,
Noth (*P.J.B.* xxxiv, 1938, p. 16), who gives as the *terminus a quo* 1230 B.C.

C

Lachish to a date after 1250 B.C.[1] The conjecture of Jack,[2] that the burning of Lachish took place *circa* 1400 B.C., has for its basis the already-mentioned presence of scarabs of Amenhotep III amongst the Lachish finds, and the lack of scarabs of the succeeding Pharaohs until the reigns of Ay, Horemheb, and Rameses II. That this is insufficient to sustain his conclusion has been said above, and the argument is turned the other way round by Vincent.[3] In the case of Lachish there are additional grounds to control the date, and the general consensus of archaeological opinion is impressive. Since, then, the ceramic finds of Jericho reflect a similar development to that of Lachish, and since an identical situation exists in the matter of the scarabs of Amenhotep III but not of the succeeding Pharaohs, the evidence of Lachish is significant for the dating of the fall of Jericho.[4]

The date of the fall of Debir, with which Tell beit Mirsim has been identified by Albright,[5] is assigned either generally to the thirteenth century B.C.[6] or to approximately the same time as the fall of Lachish.[7] Here again in the C stratum a scarab of Amenhotep III was found, and also a scarab of Ramesside type, which Albright says 'can hardly be dated before the middle of the thirteenth century'.[8] These are of importance as showing that this phase of the city's life cannot have begun earlier than 1400 B.C. and cannot have closed until later than the middle

[1] Cf. *R.B.* xlviii, 1939, p. 419 n.   [2] Cf. *E.T.* xlviii, 1936–7, p. 551.
[3] Cf. Vincent, *R.B.* xlviii, 1939, p. 580.
[4] Cf. Vincent, ibid., where after referring to 'l'évolution céramique de Jéricho' and 'l'évolution identique de Douweir' he says: 'Cette similitude finale de la poterie dans les deux sites ne saurait être mise en échec par les arguments négatifs tant rebattus: absence d'importations mycéniennes et absence de scarabées égyptiens plus tardifs qu'Aménophis III dans la nécropole et la ville à Jéricho.'
[5] On the identification cf. Albright, *The Archaeology of Palestine and the Bible*, 1932, pp. 63 ff.; id., *A.A.S.O.R.* xvii, 1938, pp. 5 f. n.; Wright, *J.N.E.S.* v, 1946, p. 110 n. On the equation Kirjath-sepher = Debir, cf. Noth, *J.P.O.S.* xv, 1935, pp. 44 ff.
[6] Cf. Burrows, *What Mean these Stones?* p. 77.
[7] Cf. Albright, *A.A.S.O.R.* xvii, 1938, pp. 78 f.; Wright, loc. cit., p. 111; Finegan, op. cit., p. 140. Albright has devoted a whole chapter of his *Archaeology of Palestine and the Bible* (chap. ii) to the excavations at Tell beit Mirsim, and in addition to brief reports in *B.A.S.O.R.* (No. 23, Oct. 1926, pp. 2–14; No. 31, Oct. 1928, pp. 1–11; No. 38, Apr. 1930, pp. 9 f.; No. 39, Oct. 1930, pp. 1–10; No. 47, Oct. 1932, pp. 3–17) and *J.P.O.S.* (xi, 1931, pp. 105–29) has published extensive accounts of the excavations in *A.A.S.O.R.* (*The Excavation of Tell Beit Mirsim*, I = *A.A.S.O.R.* xii, 1932; I A = ibid. xiii, 1933; II = ibid. xvii, 1938; III = ibid. xxi–xxii, 1943).
[8] Cf. ibid. xvii, 1938, p. 71.

of the thirteenth century B.C. Albright notes the absence of Mycenaean pottery in the earlier part of this stratum.[1]

In the case of Bethel, Albright suggested as the date of its fall 'the first half of the thirteenth century',[2] or even a slightly earlier date,[3] but more recently he has assigned it simply to 'some time in the thirteenth century B.C.',[4] and in this form it is accepted by Burrows,[5] while Wright places it 'during the middle of the thirteenth century'.[6]

The problem of Ai is more complex. That city is said by the archaeologists to have been destroyed long before the earliest date suggested for the Israelite incursion, and to have lain in ruins from *circa* 2000 to *circa* 1200 B.C.[7] The story of its capture by Joshua[8] is therefore dismissed by some writers as fictitious,[9] or as the transfer to Joshua of the ancient story of its destruction long before his day,[10] or even as the reflection back to Joshua's day of events of much more recent occurrence.[11] Some writers have preferred to follow a harmonizing path, and have suggested that there has been confusion between Ai and the neighbouring Bethel,[12] which was perhaps built to take the place of the anciently

---

[1] Ibid., p. 79. Cf. *J.P.O.S.* xi, 1931, p. 31.

[2] Cf. *B.A.S.O.R.*, No. 57, Feb. 1935, p. 30. So Bentzen, *D.T.T.* iv, 1941, p. 19.

[3] Cf. *B.A.S.O.R.*, No. 58, Apr. 1935, p. 13.

[4] Cf. *From the Stone Age to Christianity*, 2nd ed., p. 212; *B.A.S.O.R.*, No. 74, Apr. 1939, p. 17. Already ibid., No. 56, Dec. 1934, p. 11, Albright had contented himself with these broader limits. Cf. also Hennequin, in *Supplément au Dictionnaire de la Bible*, iii, 1936, col. 376. Petrie (*Palestine and Israel*, 1934, p. 57) refers to 'the break after 1200 B.C. due to Israelite conquest'.

[5] Op. cit., p. 76.   [6] Cf. loc. cit., p. 113.

[7] Cf. J. Marquet-Krause, *Syria*, xvi, 1935, pp. 325–45; Vincent, *R.B.* xlvi, 1937, pp. 231–66; *B.A.S.O.R.*, No. 56, Dec. 1934, pp. 2–15.

[8] Josh. viii. 28.

[9] Cf. Dussaud, *Syria*, xvi, 1935, p. 351; Phythian-Adams, *P.E.F.Q.S.* 1936, pp. 141–9; Alt, in *Werden und Wesen des Alten Testaments*, 1936, pp. 20 ff.; Lods, *Mélanges Franz Cumont*, ii, 1936, pp. 847–57; Thomsen, *A.f.O.*, xi, 1936–7, p. 95. In *R.H.R.* cxv, 1937, pp. 125–51, Dussaud argues that the original name of Ai was Beth-Hadad.

[10] Cf. Albright, *B.A.S.O.R.*, No. 74, Apr. 1939, p. 17. See also Noth, *P.J.B.* xxxi, 1935, pp. 7–29, xxxiv, 1938, p. 14 n., and *Das Buch Josua*, 1938, pp. 23 ff.

[11] Cf. Möhlenbrink, *Z.A.W.*, N.F. xv, 1938, p. 261.

[12] Cf. Albright, *B.A.S.O.R.*, No. 56, Dec. 1934, p. 11; Jack, in *Companion to the Bible*, 1939, p. 178; Burrows, op. cit., p. 76; Wright, *The Westminster Historical Atlas*, p. 40; id. *B.A.* iii, 1940, p. 36; Finegan, op. cit., p. 137. This solution seems to me to be the most probable. The Book of Joshua gives no account of the capture of Bethel, though in Josh. vii. 17 the men of Bethel are said to have joined the men of Ai in their fight with Israel. The word ובית־אל is unrepresented in the LXX, however, and is treated as a gloss, out of har-

destroyed ruin, or that the natural strength of the position of Ai may have made it a temporary stronghold in the time of Joshua.[1] A further suggestion is that the identification of Et Tell with Ai is not secure.[2] New light may yet be shed by further excavations on this site, but meanwhile, since the case of Ai is an equal embarrassment to every view of the Exodus, and cannot be integrated at present into any synthesis of Biblical and non-Biblical material, it must be left out of account.[3]

The explorations of Nelson Glueck in the south and in Transjordan have established that there was no settled population

mony with its context, by Burney (*Book of Judges*, 2nd ed., 1920, p. 21), Noth (*Das Buch Josua*, 1938, p. 24) and others. In Jg. i. 22 ff. the capture of Bethel is singled out as the first exploit of the house of Joseph, and the only one worthy of note. Budde's conjecture (*Die Bücher Richter und Samuel*, 1890, pp. 57 f., 86) that the text originally preceded the account of the capture of Bethel by an account of the capture of Ai is improbable in view of the archaeological evidence of the wide gap that separated the fall of Ai from the fall of Bethel, and it is much more probable that the neighbouring ruined site attracted to itself the story of the Israelite capture of Bethel. Since the Book of Joshua only records the capture of Ai and Jg. i only that of Bethel, neither narrative provides evidence of a double capture in this neighbourhood. It should be added that Josh. xii. 16 mentions the king of Bethel amongst those who were smitten by Joshua. Dussaud holds that the non-mention of Ai in the account of Jg. i implicitly confirms the archaeological findings, since if the site had been occupied, the invaders would have been forced to reduce it before they could take Bethel (cf. *R.H.R.* cxv, 1937, p. 132).

[1] Cf. Vincent, *R.B.*, xlvi, 1937, pp. 258 ff. So also Pidoux, *R.Th.Ph.*, N.S. xxvii, 1939, p. 59, and Chaine, *Le Livre de la Genèse*, 1948, p. 184 n.

[2] Cf. Kenyon, *The Bible and Archaeology*, 1940, p. 190. Similarly Simons, *J.E.O.L.* vi, 1939, p. 156, and more fully ix, 1944, pp. 157–62. Bea (*Biblica*, xxiv, 1943, p. 258 n.) observes: 'Dell' identificazione di *Hai* con *et-Tell*, poco distante da Bethel verso E, non vi può essere dubbio ragionevole.' Cf. Van Selms, *J.E.O.L.* iv, 1936, p. 208, and Auvray, in *Supplément au Dictionnaire de la Bible*, iv (fasc. xxii, 1948), col. 1138: 'Jamais, peut-être, un site palestinien n'a mérité, comme cet énorme tas de pierres écroulées depuis des siècles, le titre de Ha-'Aï, "la Ruine". Nom propre ou simple qualificatif, le terme frappe ici par sa justesse. Dès lors, n'est-il pas téméraire de rejeter une identification généralement acceptée pour appliquer le nom de "Ruine" à un site qui ne cessa jamais d'être habité?'

[3] Fernández (*Commentarius in librum Josue*, 1938, p. 118) observes somewhat tartly: 'Verum, si paucis abhinc annis adeo fidenter asserebatur nullum esse dubium quin urbs Hai c. annum 1500, diruta esset, idque potissimum ex operibus fictilibus ibi inventis, nemo mirabitur plures viros non illico assentiri iisdem archaeologis, qui nunc aeque fidenter affirmant c. annum 1500 nullam exstitisse urbem Hai, quippe quae iam anno 2000 certo certius destructa esset. Hanc autem diffidentiam confirmat, nedum minuit, diversitas opinionum quae longo annorum decursu ferebantur, immo feruntur adhuc de tempore moenium urbis Jericho.'

there before the thirteenth century B.C.[1] It is therefore hard to
see how any historical value can be attached to the Biblical
traditions of these districts if the entry into Palestine was associated with an attack on Jericho at the beginning of the fourteenth
century B.C. Glueck observes: 'Had the Exodus through southern
Transjordan taken place before the thirteenth century B.C., the
Israelites would have found neither Edomites nor Moabites
who could have given or withheld permission to traverse their

[1] Cf. *B.A.S.O.R.*, No. 55, Sept. 1934, pp. 3–21, No. 86, Apr. 1942, pp. 14–
24, and *The Other Side of the Jordan*, 1940 (also *B.A.S.O.R.*, No. 90, Apr. 1943,
pp. 2–23). Glueck's positions are criticized by Phythian-Adams, *P.E.F.Q.S.*
1934, pp. 181–8, but they have convinced many scholars. Cf. Albright,
B.A.S.O.R., No. 58, Apr. 1935, p. 15; Bergman, *J.P.O.S.* xvi, 1936, p. 251;
de Vaux, *Z.A.W.*, N.F. xv, 1938, p. 236; Gordon, *The Living Past*, 1941,
pp. 36 f.; Kirk, *P.E.Q.* 1944, pp. 186 ff.; Wright, *The Westminster Historical
Atlas*, p. 40 a; Finegan, op. cit., pp. 131 f.; Ginsberg, *Legend of King Keret*,
1946, p. 7. Grdseloff (*B.E.H.J.*, No. i, 1946, pp. 69–99) argues that Egyptian
sources entirely corroborate Glueck's findings, and concludes that the Exodus
of the Israelites 'n'a pu donc se produire avant 1314, date de l'établissement
définitif des Édomites en Séïr' (p. 99). De Vaux (*R.B.* xlv, 1937, p. 450)
observes that Edom and Seir are unmentioned in Egyptian texts before
Rameses II, and Grdseloff (loc. cit., p. 86) observes that the first occurrence
of the name Edom so far known from Egyptian sources comes from the reign
of Merneptah. There is a reference to the land of Seir in the Amarna letters,
however (Knudtzon, *Die El-Amarna Tafeln*, 288: 26 (i, 1908, pp. 870 f.; cf. ii,
1915, p. 1340)). It has been thought that Edom is mentioned in the Keret
text from Ras Shamra (so Virolleaud, *La Légende de Keret*, 1936, pp. 19, 79 f.;
Schaeffer, *The Cuneiform Texts of Ras Shamra-Ugarit*, 1939, pp. 73 ff.; Dussaud,
Les Découvertes de Ras Shamra et l'Ancien Testament, 2nd ed., 1941, pp. 68 f.,
163 ff.; Barton, *Mémorial Lagrange*, 1940, pp. 29 f.; cf. Lods, *R.H.P.R.* xvi,
1936, pp. 104 ff.). This was associated with the Negebite hypothesis, which
is now generally rejected. Pedersen, while not subscribing to that hypothesis,
and taking a very different view of the text, yet allowed the reference to
Edom, but thought it was mentioned as a distant land (cf. *Berytus*, vi, 1941,
pp. 90 ff.). Others, however, while maintaining a geographical reference,
have located it elsewhere. Thus Weill (*J.As.* ccxxix, 1937, pp. 20 ff.) and de
Vaux (*R.B.* xlvi, 1937, pp. 362 ff., 536 ff.; cf. Bea, *Biblica*, xix, 1938, pp.
437 ff.; de Langhe, *Les Textes de Ras Shamra-Ugarit et leurs apports à l'histoire des
origines israélites*, 1939, pp. 53 ff., and *Les Textes de Ras Shamra-Ugarit et leurs
rapports avec le milieu biblique de l'Ancien Testament*, ii, 1945, pp. 499 ff.) proposed a location in Galilee, Eissfeldt one between Lebanon and Anti-
Lebanon (*Z.D.M.G.* xciv, 1940, pp. 59 ff.; cf. Baumgartner, *Th.R.* xiii, 1941,
pp. 18 f.), and Ginsberg one in southern Phoenicia (cf. *The Legend of King
Keret*, 1946, pp. 7 f.). Albright believed the text was not of an historical but of
a mythological character (cf. *B.A.S.O.R.*, No. 63, Oct. 1936, pp. 23 ff., No. 70,
Apr. 1938, pp. 22 f.; cf. Mowinckel, *Norsk Teologisk Tidsskrift*, xlii, 1941,
pp. 142 ff., xliii, 1942, pp. 24 ff.), and Engnell that it was cultic, and that
'*udm* was a cultic term and not a geographical name (cf. *Studies in Divine
Kingship*, 1943, pp. 163 ff., and *Horae Soederblomianae*, i, fasc. 1, 1944, pp. 1 ff.).

territories.'[1] To the suggestion that a nomad population might have been there it is replied that the Biblical tradition is not of passage through a district inhabited by nomads, but through a district which already had towns.[2]

Moreover, it has been frequently noted that according to the Biblical account the Exodus and Settlement in Canaan fell within the Iron Age,[3] whereas the fourteenth century B.C. fell within the Late Bronze Age. Schofield observes that 'a fairly accurate date for the introduction of iron through Asia Minor into Egypt is given by the discovery at Boghaz Keui of the cuneiform copy of a letter from Rameses II to Hattushil, the Hittite king in the first half of the thirteenth century, asking him to supply him with smelted iron'.[4] Too much weight must not be put on this consideration, however, in view of the fact that iron is already mentioned in the Amarna letters of the fourteenth century B.C.[5] and of the further fact that a wrought-iron hatchet, which is assigned to the fifteenth or fourteenth century B.C., was found at Ras Shamra.[6]

Nor can we attach much importance to the references to the Philistines in the Biblical account of the wandering.[7] The date of

On the character of the text cf. de Langhe, in *Miscellanea Historica Alberti de Meyer*, 1946, pp. 92 ff. So far as the text known as II Keret is concerned, Virolleaud recognizes that its scene is not in the Negeb, but in the north (*Mélanges Syriens* (Dussaud Festschrift), ii, 1939, pp. 755 ff.), though he still adheres to the Negebite view of I Keret (ibid., p. 755). It is clearly impossible to build anything on this reference until there is a greater agreement as to the nature of the text in which it stands, and it is, in any case, highly improbable that it has anything to do with the land of Edom. Albright observes that the entire Negebite hypothesis 'is now virtually extinct in serious scholarly circles' (cf. *Archaeology and the Religion of Israel*, 2nd ed., 1946, p. 60). It is accepted by Barton, however (*Mémorial Lagrange*, 1940, pp. 29 ff.).

[1] Cf. *B.A.S.O.R.*, No. 55, Sept. 1934, p. 16. See also *The Other Side of the Jordan*, 1940, pp. 146 f. Kirk (*P.E.Q.* 1944, p. 188) says that this evidence would appear to make it impossible for the Exodus to have taken place before the twelfth century B.C. It is unnecessary to come down into the twelfth century, however, and so late a date would run into other difficulties.

[2] Cf. Wright, *The Westminster Historical Atlas*, p. 40 a.

[3] Cf. Cook, *P.E.F.Q.S.* 1932, p. 92; Petrie, *Palestine and Israel*, 1934, p. 56; Duncan, *New Light on Hebrew Origins*, 1936, p. 79; Schofield, *The Historical Background of the Bible*, 1938, p. 79.   [4] Ibid.

[5] Cf. TA 22 I : 38; 22 II : 1, 3, 16; 25 II : 22 (?), 28 (Knudtzon, *Die El-Amarna Tafeln*, i, 19, pp. 158, 162, 200).

[6] Cf. Schaeffer, *Ugaritica*, 1939, pp. 107 ff. Albright (*The Archaeology of Palestine*, 1949, p. 110) observes that 'it was not until the fourteenth century B.C. that iron began to be used rather extensively for weapons'.

[7] Ex. xiii. 17, xxiii. 31.

the Philistines' entry into the land was early in the twelfth century
B.C.[1] and more than one writer has drawn attention to this as
an objection to the theory of a fifteenth-century Exodus.[2] These
references are to the land and sea of the Philistines, rather than
to the people, and are as easily intelligible as a reference to
Julius Caesar's crossing the English Channel would be to British
readers to-day. They are in any case less harsh anachronisms
than the references to the Philistines in the accounts of Abraham
and Isaac.[3]

More weighty than such considerations are the archaeological
evidences of a break in the cultural development of Palestine
at the end of the thirteenth century B.C., and of the fall of
Canaanite cities in that age, with the disputed exception of
Jericho. Albright says: 'The date of the Israelite conquest
of Palestine still remains obscure, though the available evidence
proves that the main wave of destruction fell in the thirteenth
century and that the reoccupation of the more important towns
must be dated between 1250 and 1150 B.C.'[4] This evidence is so
strong that a scholar like T. H. Robinson, who follows Garstang
in the dating of the fall of Jericho and assigns its conquest to
Joshua, is compelled to deny that leader any part in the battle
for Bethel,[5] while Albright and the American scholars who follow
him place Joshua at the end of the thirteenth century B.C., and
therefore dissociate him entirely from the campaign for Jericho.

Turning now to the evidence that comes from outside Palestine, and viewing it in relation to some items of the Biblical data,
we may note that the fifteenth-century date for the Exodus

[1] The date is usually given as 1192 B.C. Albright, however, places it
slightly later, in 1188 B.C. (cf. B.A.S.O.R., No. 58, pp. 17 f.), following the
researches of Borchardt (Z.Ä.S. lxx, 1934, pp. 97 ff.); but for a criticism of
Borchardt's chronological views on an earlier period, cf. Edgerton, A.J.S.L.
liii, 1936–7, pp. 188–97. On the question of possible advance settlements of
Philistines earlier than the main wave, cf. Garstang, Joshua–Judges, 1931,
pp. 285–7, and Garofalo, Biblica, xviii, 1937, pp. 9 ff.
[2] Cf. Petrie, Palestine and Israel, p. 56; Duncan, New Light on Hebrew Origins,
p. 189; Schofield, The Historical Background of the Bible, p. 79.
[3] Gen. xxi. 32, 34; xxvi. 1, 8, 14 f., 18. Grintz (Tarbiz, xvii, 1945–6,
pp. 32–42; xix, 1947–8, p. 64) has maintained that these references are not
anachronisms, but that there were two waves of Philistine immigration.
[4] Cf. Haverford Symposium, p. 23.
[5] Cf. Companion to the Bible, ed. by Manson, 1939, p. 221: 'Archaeologists
date the fall of Jericho with confidence near the beginning of the fourteenth
century, and though the date of the destruction of Bethel is put at some century and a half later, this may easily be explained on the ground of the slow
advance of the central body through the land.'

would make Thothmes III the Pharaoh of the Oppression. No
known building operations of this Pharaoh took place in the
Nile Delta region, and he is not known to have had a royal
residence in that district.[1] It is of the essence of the Biblical tradition of the Exodus that the building operations on which the
Israelites were engaged were close to the palace, so that at the
time of the birth of Moses Pharaoh's daughter might find herself in the vicinity of the Israelites when she went out for a walk,[2]
and at the time when Moses led them out they were still in the
neighbourhood of the court.[3] On the other hand, when the
Israelites went into Egypt, they were assigned a district far from
the court, where the Egyptians would run no risk of contact
with the disliked shepherds.[4] This raises a serious difficulty
against the commonly accepted Hyksos date[5] for the descent

[1] Cf. Mallon, *Supplément au Dictionnaire de la Bible*, ii, 1934, col. 1340:
'L'activité monumentale de ces pharaons s'exerça principalement en haute
Égypte et l'on en a retrouvé peu de traces dans le Delta. Au contraire, avec
Ramsès II, nous avons une splendide résidence à Pi-Ramessé, qui était comme
la seconde capitale de l'empire.'   [2] Ex. ii. 1–10.

[3] Cf. Ex. xii. 23, 31 ff.

[4] Gen. xlvi. 34. In Gen. xlv. 10 Goshen is described as 'near' to the court
of Pharaoh, but there it is in comparison with Palestine. That it was actually
at some distance from the court is clear from the fact that Judah goes on in
advance to Joseph, who comes by chariot to Goshen (xlvi. 28 f.).

[5] It is commonly said that the Hyksos kings would be naturally well disposed towards Semitic immigrants in view of their own Semitic, or Asiatic,
stock. The precise ethnic composition of the Hyksos is hard to determine.
Gelb (*Hurrians and Subarians*, 1944, p. 68) observes: 'In spite of an immense
literature devoted to the Hyksos problem, we do not yet know who the
Hyksos really were' (cf. Galling, *Z.D.P.V.* lxii, 1939, pp. 106 ff.). That they
contained a Semitic element is indicated by some of the proper names known
to us, but there are other names which are not Semitic, and which are thought
to indicate a Hittite or Hurrian element (cf. Speiser, *A.A.S.O.R.* xiii, 1933,
pp. 47 f., 51; Meek, *Hebrew Origins*, 1936, p. 5; in addition to the works noted
below). But Albright (*J.P.O.S.* xv, 1935, pp. 228 f.; cf. Dussaud, *Les Découvertes de Ras Shamra et l'Ancien Testament*, 2nd ed., 1941, p. 114) says that the
most recent efforts to show that the non-Semitic Hyksos names are Hurrian
cannot be said to be successful, and that none of the equations proposed by
Gustavs (*Z.Ä.S.* lxiv, 1929, pp. 55 f.) and others (cf. Ginsberg and Maisler,
J.P.O.S. xiv, 1934, pp. 243 ff., esp. p. 265) is at all convincing, while Dussaud (*Syria*, xxi, 1940, p. 344) criticizes Engberg for not recognizing the
Canaanites in the Hyksos. That the Hyksos were of mixed race, and that they
contained some Semites seems, however, certain, and it may be agreed that
they would be likely to treat Semites in Egypt with kindness. But this is not
to establish the thesis that the Descent of Jacob into Egypt took place in the
Hyksos period in the absence of any other evidence, Biblical or other, and
in the teeth of evidence provided by the Biblical traditions, when tested by
the archaeological evidence. Albright has frequently associated the Descent

into Egypt.[1] For the Hyksos monarchs had their capital at Avaris, which has been identified with the Delta residence of Rameses II by recent writers. A descent in the Hyksos period and Exodus in the thirteenth century B.C. would therefore mean that the proximity of the Hebrews to the court would be the same in both ages, and this is in disagreement with the Biblical tradition.[2] On the other hand, a descent in the Hyksos period and an Exodus in the fifteenth century B.C. would mean proximity to the court at the time of the descent, but an impossible distance from the court at the time of the Exodus, to the complete reversal of the Biblical tradition. It would be quite impossible to suggest any suitable location for the Israelites in the Delta region that

into Egypt with the Hyksos Conquest (cf. *J.P.O.S.* i, 1921, pp. 65 f.; *J.S.O.R.* x, 1926, p. 268; *B.A.S.O.R.*, No. 58, Apr. 1935, p. 15; *J.P.O.S.* xv, 1935, p. 227; *From the Stone Age to Christianity*, 2nd ed., 1946, p. 150; cf. Galling, *Z.D.P.V.* lxii, 1939, p. 107, where Albright's view is rejected), and has assumed that the Israelites formed a part of the conquering host, but this is not supported by the Biblical tradition or by probability. Dussaud (*R.H.R.* cix, 1934, p. 123; cf. Weill's criticism, *J.As.* ccxxix, 1937, pp. 52 f.) also holds that the Hyksos took groups of Israelites into Egypt with them, and similarly de Vaux (*R.B.* lv, 1948, p. 336) thinks the entry of the Hebrews was connected with the entry of the Hyksos. Somewhat incomprehensibly, however, Dussaud finds Ex. i. 8 to carry us to a later dynasty (cf. loc. cit., p. 127: 'Cela'—i.e. the Exodus—'se passe sous un pharaon qui n'avait pas connu Joseph (Ex. i. 8), autrement dit sous un roi de race égyptienne et non plus hyksos'), while identifying the Pharaoh of the Oppression mentioned in Ex. i. 11 with a Hyksos ruler (cf. p. 126: 'Les grands travaux des rois hyksos, notamment à Tanis, obligeaient à lever des corvées parmi eux. Le souvenir en est conservé Exode, i. 11 et 14, et surtout Exode, v'). On the whole complex Hyksos problem cf. Gunn and Gardiner, *J.E.A.* v, 1918, pp. 36 ff.; Wolf, *Z.D.M.G.* lxxxiii, 1929, pp. 67 ff.; Jirku, *J.P.O.S.* xii, 1932, pp. 51 ff.; Dussaud, *R.H.R.* cix, 1934, pp. 113 ff.; von Bissing, *A.f.O.* xi, 1936–7, pp. 325 ff.; Engberg, *The Hyksos Reconsidered*, 1939 (on which cf. Dussaud, *Syria*, xxi, 1940, pp. 343 f., and von Bissing, *A.f.O.* xiv, 1941, pp. 84 ff.); Galling, *Z.D.P.V.* lxii, 1939, pp. 89 ff.; Stock, *Studien zur Geschichte und Archäologie der 13. bis 17. Dynastie Ägyptens*, 1942 (cf. Galling's review, in *Deutsche Literaturzeitung*, lxvi–lxviii, Heft 1/2, Oct.–Nov. 1947, cols. 13 ff.); Bea, *Biblica*, xxiv, 1943, pp. 249 ff. Galling (*Biblisches Reallexikon*, 1937, col. 461) suggested that Akkadian was the official language of the Hyksos; but cf. now *Z.D.P.V.* lxii, 1939, pp. 114 f.

[1] Cf. Wright, *B.A.S.O.R.*, No. 86, Apr. 1942, pp. 34 f., and my reply, ibid., No. 87, Oct. 1942, p. 40. The Hyksos period was formerly believed to run from *circa* 1800 B.C. (so *C.A.H.* i, 2nd ed., 1924, p. 664), but more recently scholars date it from 1730 B.C. (cf. Sethe, *Z.Ä.S.* lxv, 1930, pp. 85 ff.; Engberg, *The Hyksos Reconsidered*, 1939, pp. 1, 9), while Albright puts it slightly later at 1720 B.C. (cf. *J.P.O.S.* xv, 1935, pp. 225 f.).

[2] Montet (*Le Drame d'Avaris*, 1940, p. 147) wrongly states that at the entry and departure the Egyptian court is quite close to the strangers. The Biblical data clearly suggest a different relative location.

would be at once appropriately distant from Avaris and yet in
the neighbourhood of Thothmes III's capital.[1] Moreover, the
Biblical statement that the susceptibilities of the Egyptians were
studied in assigning a district to the Israelites[2] does not suggest
the Hyksos. The depth of the hatred they inspired in the Egyptians does not naturally accord with such an attitude of studied
consideration. Hooke adds the further consideration that in the
period of the Hyksos it would be no honour to give Joseph the
daughter of the priest of On to wife,[3] since the Hyksos promoted
the worship of Set and despised the sun-god Ra, whose chief
temple was at On, or Heliopolis.[4]

The question of the location of Avaris, however, which seemed
settled a few years ago, has been reopened, and if it is differentiated from the Ramesside residence it would be possible on
geographical grounds to maintain a descent in the Hyksos period
and an Exodus in the thirteenth century B.C., since a Hebrew
residence near the palace of Rameses II might then be sufficiently far from the palace of the Hyksos, save that the palace

[1] Jack (*The Date of the Exodus*, pp. 242 ff.) draws attention to the extensive
building operations of Thothmes III in all parts of Egypt, including Heliopolis in the Delta region, and claims that 'there is a probability, almost
amounting to certainty, that the old capital'—i.e. of the Hyksos—'was not
abandoned by the Pharaohs of the XVIIIth Dynasty' (pp. 249 f.). As he
says Thothmes had another capital in the Delta, or on the borders of it, probably at or near Memphis (p. 250), in addition to his chief capital at Thebes,
a plethora of capitals is alleged. This rather throws a cloud round the subject
than offers any clear or consistent view. Neither Heliopolis nor Memphis
will satisfy the Biblical conditions, since a Pharaoh who pursued the Israelites
from either of these places in chariots, as soon as he learned that they had
fled, would have easily overtaken them long before they could have reached
the place where they crossed the sea. Nor could the Goshen in which the
Israelites dwelt be anywhere near either place, if the Biblical data are in any
way reliable. For Joseph is said to have come in a chariot from the court to
meet his father in Goshen (Gen. xlvi. 29). In the period of the Hyksos, when
the Eisodus is held to have taken place (pp. 219 f.), the court at Avaris was
much nearer to Palestine than a Goshen which is located near Heliopolis or
Memphis. Further, the assumed maintenance of the Hyksos capital of Avaris
in the days of Thothmes III is not evidence, either of residence or of building
activity there, and the excavator of Avaris found none (see below).

[2] Gen. xlvi. 34. Albright would seem to attach little value to the Israelite
traditions as to their occupation; for he says the Hebrew settlement in Goshen
must have been a military foundation, designed to protect the Asiatic frontier
of Egypt (*J.A.O.S.* xlviii, 1928, p. 184). I see no reason for this assumption,
however.   [3] Gen. xli. 45.

[4] Cf. *In the Beginning*, 1947, p. 117. Yahuda also opposes the view that the
descent is to be assigned to the Hyksos period (cf. *The Accuracy of the Bible*,
1934, pp. 45 ff.).

of Rameses would have to be located nearer to Palestine than that of the Hyksos to fit the Biblical conditions.[1]

About thirty years ago Gardiner maintained that Pi-Ramesse, the Delta capital of Rameses II, was to be identified with Pelusium, and so to be differentiated from Tanis or Zoan,[2] and this view was followed by Mallon[3] and others.[4] Then Montet[5] so brilliantly argued that Avaris, Tanis, and Pi-Ramesse were three names for the same place that Gardiner retracted his own view and announced his conversion.[6] More recently Weill has[7] challenged this and argued for the separateness of Avaris and Tanis,[8] while refraining from offering any secure identification of Avaris.[9] Montet has replied to his arguments,[10] and still maintains his view,[11] to which Albright continues to adhere,[12] as also do some other scholars.[13] In the most recent survey of the question

---

[1] If Joseph drove from the Hyksos capital in a chariot to meet Jacob at a spot in the immediate vicinity of what became the capital of Rameses II (Gen. xlvi. 29), the latter must have been nearer the Palestinian border.

[2] Cf. *J.E.A.* v, 1918, pp. 127 ff., 179 ff., 242 ff.; also ibid. 1916, pp. 99 ff., and *Recueil d'Études égyptologiques dédiées à la mémoire de J. F. Champollion*, 1922, pp. 203 ff. See also Gunn and Gardiner, *J.E.A.* v, 1918, p. 38. Lepsius had earlier argued that Avaris was to be located in the neighbourhood of Pelusium (*Königsbuch der alten Ägypter*, 1858, p. 45 n.).

[3] Cf. *Les Hébreux en Égypte*, 1921, pp. 106–19.

[4] Cf. Peet, *Egypt and the Old Testament*, 1922, pp. 83–91; Breasted, in *C.A.H.* ii, 1924, p. 152; Power, *Biblica*, x, 1929, pp. 103 f.; Lods, *Israël*, 1930, p. 198 (E.Tr., 1932, p. 174); Beer, *Exodus*, 1939, p. 16.

[5] Cf. *R.B.* xxxix, 1930, pp. 1–28. Alt had already (*Die Landnahme der Israeliten in Palästina*, 1925, p. 6 n.) declared both the identification of Avaris with Pelusium and that with Kantara (see below) 'durchaus unsicher'.

[6] Cf. *J.E.A.* xix, 1933, pp. 122–8. In *Ancient Egyptian Onomastica*, ii, 1947, pp. 171*–5*, Gardiner is less sure of this identification, though he still thinks the balance of evidence is in its favour.

[7] Cf. *J.E.A.* xxi, 1935, pp. 10–25.

[8] Brugsch had distinguished between Avaris and Tanis, identifying Pi-Ramesse with the latter. Cf. *Z.Ä.S.* x, 1872, pp. 16–20.

[9] Weill had earlier suggested somewhat hesitantly that Avaris might be located at Heliopolis. Cf. *J.As.*, 10th series, xvi, 1910, p. 544; xvii, 1911, p. 11 n. (= *La Fin du moyen empire égyptien*, 1918, pp. 132, 173 n.).

[10] Cf. *Syria*, xvii, 1936, pp. 200 ff.   [11] Cf. *Le Drame d'Avaris*, 1941.

[12] Cf. *From the Stone Age to Christianity*, 2nd ed., pp. 169, 194; *B.A.S.O.R.*, No. 109, Feb. 1948, p. 15.

[13] Cf. Dhorme, *La Religion des Hébreux nomades*, 1937, p. 138; Junker, *Z.Ä.S.* lxxv, 1939, pp. 83 f.; Celada, *Sefarad*, i, 1941, pp. 415–35; Wright, *B.A.S.O.R.*, No. 86, Apr. 1942, p. 34; Bea, *Biblica*, xxiv, 1943, p. 249; Finegan, op. cit., pp. 84, 103 f. Dussaud (*Syria*, xxi, 1940, p. 344) complains that Engberg (*The Hyksos Reconsidered*, 1939) has not given sufficient attention to the identification of Tanis–Avaris–Pi-Ramesse.

Couroyer would loose Pi-Ramesse from Tanis, but instead of locating it at Pelusium tends to favour Qantir, while yet recognizing that any identification is uncertain.[1] This location at Qantir was earlier proposed by Hamza,[2] adopted by Hayes,[3] and favoured by Lucas.[4] Yet another proposed location was at Kantara,[5] but Gardiner replied to this some years ago,[6] and Wright regards it as improbable.[7] Equally improbable is Petrie's identification of Raamses with Tell el Retabeh,[8] and Avaris with Tell el Yehudiyyeh.[9] While it is clear that this question cannot be regarded as closed, the identification of the Hyksos capital, Avaris, with Pi-Ramesse, the Delta residence of Rameses II, and of both with Tanis, which figures in the Old Testament as Zoan, seems most probable, and this would mean that if Rameses II were the oppressor, the descent into Egypt could not have taken place under the Hyksos rulers. It should be added that even though the geographical argument were disposed of, there would still remain other difficulties against the Hyksos date for the descent into Egypt. The difficulty about the Biblical tradition as to Joseph's wife has been noted. Other difficulties will emerge as we proceed.

It is frequently noted that a fifteenth-century date for the Exodus would make surprising a lack of mention of Egyptian activities in Palestine between the Exodus and the early

---

[1] Cf. *R.B.* liii, 1946, pp. 75–98.

[2] Cf. *Annales du Service des Antiquités de l'Égypte*, xxx, 1930, pp. 31 ff., esp. 64 ff.

[3] Cf. *Glazed Tiles from a Palace of Ramesses II at Ḳantir*, 1937, p. 8. See also *J.E.A.* xxiv, 1938, p. 216, where Wainwright seems to favour this view. Gardiner, in his latest discussion of the subject (*Ancient Egyptian Onomastica*, ii, 1947, pp. 171* ff.), despite some strictures on Hayes, does not close the door against this identification.

[4] Cf. *The Route of the Exodus*, 1938, pp. 25 f., 28. It is to be observed, however, that Lucas notes (p. 27) that there is no evidence that this city existed before the reign of Seti I, and he is compelled to rely on the possibility that some may yet be found, in order to maintain his preference for the early date for the Exodus. So far as evidence at present goes, this identification would be definitely in favour of the later date.

[5] Cf. Naville, *J.E.A.* x, 1924, pp. 18–39; Clédat, in *Recueil d'Études égypto-logiques dédiées à la mémoire de J. F. Champollion*, 1922, pp. 185–201.

[6] Cf. *J.E.A.* x, 1924, pp. 87–96.

[7] Cf. *B.A.S.O.R.*, No. 86, Apr. 1942, p. 34: 'There is an outside chance . . . that the site may have been Qantir.' Also cf. *The Westminster Historical Atlas*, p. 37 b.

[8] Cf. *Hyksos and Israelite Cities*, 1906, pp. 28 ff. On this identification cf. Gardiner, *J.E.A.* v, 1918, pp. 266 f. Wiener (*Ancient Egypt*, 1923, pp. 75 ff.) still adheres to Petrie's view.   [9] Cf. *Hyksos and Israelite Cities*, pp. 9 f.

monarchy, and in particular the lack of any reference to the campaigns of Seti I and Rameses II.[1] The suggestion that Rameses may have been satisfied to secure the coast road without interfering with the Israelite districts[2] does not seem probable. In a later age Pharaoh Necho had more military wisdom than to leave Judah uncontrolled, and it is not to be supposed that Rameses II had so little as to leave even the central highlands uncontrolled. Even more unlikely is Jack's suggestion that the Pharaohs were afraid to intervene in Palestine. He says:[3] 'Egypt knew well that the Ḥabiru-SA-GAZ were not to be meddled with.' Since the Palestinian princes in their letters to the Pharaoh suggested that a handful of Egyptian troops would be sufficient to deal with them in the Amarna age,[4] and since we have evidence of a probable encounter between Seti I and 'Aperu in the neighbourhood of Beth-shan,[5] and of an encounter between Merneptah and Israel towards the end of the thirteenth century B.C.,[6] if Ḥabiru, 'Aperu, and Hebrews are equated[7] and the Exodus is placed earlier than the Merneptah stele, we have ample evidence to set against Jack's unsupported conjecture. Where so feeble a Pharaoh as Merneptah could meddle, it is idle to suppose that Rameses II was afraid to exert himself. Garstang has boldly suggested that the references to Egyptian activity are veiled, and that the successive periods of peace recorded in the book of Judges are the periods of effective Egyptian control.[8] He supposes that for religious reasons the Israelites suppressed all mention of this, since they wished their God to have the undivided credit.[9] It is doubtful, however, if the Israelites would recognize

[1] There is force in the remark of Henderson (*C.Q.R.* xcvii, 1923–4, p. 115): 'It is not merely that the Book of Judges does not mention the passage of Egyptian armies . . . but nowhere in the whole history from start to finish is there a word to suggest Egyptian suzerainty at the time of the occupation.'

[2] Cf. Jack, *The Date of the Exodus*, pp. 78 f.

[3] Cf. ibid., p. 79. Cf. also pp. 76, 78.   [4] See below.

[5] Cf. Rowe, *The Topography and History of Beth-shan*, 1930, pp. 29 f., and Grdseloff, *B.E.H.J.*, No. i, 1946, p. 77 n.

[6] In the Merneptah stele. See below, p. 30.

[7] On this question cf. below. Jack accepted the equation.

[8] Cf. *Joshua-Judges*, pp. 258 ff.

[9] It is a little surprising to find that a scholar whose defence of 1 Kgs. vi. 1 has been so hailed as vindicating the accuracy of the Bible should be so completely sceptical about the book of Judges. For if it is taken seriously, his theory means that the achievements of the Judges were hollow, and the total impression of the book of Judges completely unhistorical. Other alien power is acknowledged and resented. If the Egyptian power was known to have been beneficent, such absence of mention would be a complete falsification of

Egyptian rule to be beneficent, especially since Egypt was the symbol of oppression to her, and it is much more probable that such periods would have been reckoned with the foreign oppressions.

On the other hand, if the Exodus took place in the thirteenth century B.C., the absence of mention of Egyptian activity would be less surprising. There would still be the Merneptah stele to account for. In its text, as is well known, there is found the earliest non-Biblical mention of the name Israel, and amongst a series of claims which the Pharaoh makes, he states that 'Israel is desolate, her seed is not'.[1] It is frequently pointed out that Israel has here the determinative of a people, as distinct from the geographical terms of the rest of the text,[2] but it is likely that she is a people already within the borders of Palestine. The chastisement which the Pharaoh claims to have meted out ranged from the districts inhabited by Hittites to the far south of Palestine. It is therefore unlikely that Merneptah is here distorting his unsuccessful pursuit of Israel at the time of their leaving history, while the ascription to the Judges of a deliverance that was in fact achieved by the Egyptians would not be consistent with the accuracy or reliability of the Bible. There is, indeed, no theory which can maintain the complete reliability of every Biblical statement. It is possible conveniently to ignore every Biblical statement which cannot be integrated into a theory, or to ignore extra-Biblical evidence that is intractable. But every honest investigator is compelled to acknowledge, as Garstang here does, that some Biblical statements will not fit into his theory.

[1] Breasted renders the concluding strophe of the inscription as follows (*Ancient Records of Egypt*, iii, 1906, pp. 263 f.):

'The kings are overthrown, saying: "Salâm!"
Not one holds up his head among the Nine Bows.
Wasted is Tehenu,
Kheta is pacified,
Plundered is Pekanan with every evil,
Carried off is Askalon,
Seized upon is Gezer,
Yenoam is made as a thing not existing,
Israel is desolated, his seed is not;
Palestine has become a widow for Egypt:
All lands are united, they are pacified:
Everyone that is turbulent is bound by King Merneptah, given life like Re, every day.'

[2] So, e.g., Sayce, *The Early History of the Hebrews*, 1897, p. 159; Brown, *J.E.A.* iv, 1917, p. 18; Griffiths, *The Exodus in the Light of Archaeology*, 1923, p. 49; Barton, *Archaeology and the Bible*, 6th ed., 1933, p. 375. Jack (*E.T.* xxxvi, 1924–5, p. 41) thinks the lack of the determinative should not be pressed too much, since Israel could not be said to be settled for one or two centuries after their entry into Canaan.

Egypt.[1] Yet if Merneptah was the Pharaoh of the Exodus, then the Israelite traditions carry ample memory of their relations with him, and the non-mention of his activity as recorded on the stele is not seriously surprising. For there is no pretence to record every detail of history in the book of Judges, and there can be no doubt that the event recorded on the stele was of trivial significance for Israel's history compared with the event of the Exodus. It is, however, necessary to find some place in any view that is ultimately adopted for a body of Israelites in Palestine early in the reign of Merneptah.

The evidence of Ex. i. 11 is not so negligible as is sometimes supposed. It is claimed that the names may be secondary,[2] or that the names that were later familiar were anachronistically substituted for the ones the cities bore at the time of the Oppression.[3] In this there would be nothing surprising. Whatever view is taken of the date of the Exodus, there can be no doubt that the descent into Egypt preceded the reign of Rameses I,[4] and

[1] Montet (*Le Drame d'Avaris*, p. 149) believes that it is the Exodus that is referred to in Merneptah's stele, and so Brown (*J.E.A.* iv, 1917, p. 19). The view of Griffiths (op. cit., pp. 49 ff.) is even more improbable. He connects the events recorded on the stele with Num. xiv. 40 ff., Dt. i. 41 ff., and thinks Merneptah was claiming a victory which was won by tribes under the suzerainty of the Pharaoh. The stele mentions so many other places that it is improbable that all represent local victories and more probable that Merneptah carried out some sort of raid on Palestine, on which the Egyptian hold was vanishing. Naville (*J.E.A.* ii, 1915, pp. 195 ff.) argues that the stele does not record any expedition of Merneptah into Syria at all, but merely states that the Palestinian peoples were powerless to disturb his peace. This interpretation seems to have gained no following.

[2] Cf. Miketta, *Der Pharao des Auszuges*, 1903, pp. 39 ff.; Hall, *The Ancient History of the Near East*, 7th ed., 1927, p. 405; T. H. Robinson, *History of Israel*, i, 1932, p. 73; Kalt, *Biblisches Reallexikon*, 2nd ed., 1937, col. 344. Cf. Orr, *Expositor*, 5th series, v, 1897, p. 167 n.

[3] Cf. Jack, *The Date of the Exodus*, 1925, pp. 24 f.; Yahuda, op. cit., pp. 126 f.; McClellan, *Ecclesiastical Review*, lxxxviii, 1933, p. 90; Dussaud, *R.H.R.* cix, 1934, p. 127. T. H. Robinson takes the opposite way, and suggests that they were inserted by a writer 'dessen archäologischen Kenntnisse besser waren als seine historischen' (*T.L.Z.* lvii, 1932, col. 77).

[4] Eerdmans (*Alttestamentliche Studien*, ii, 1908, pp. 67–76, reaffirmed in *The Religion of Israel*, 1947, pp. 13 f.), advanced the view that the Descent into Egypt is to be dated 1210 B.C. On this view see below, p. 135 n. Toffteen (*The Historic Exodus*, 1909, p. 223) places his second Descent after the accession of Rameses II precisely on the ground of this name, but it is difficult to take this view seriously. Since Toffteen accepts the numbers of Ex. xii. 37 (though suggesting the rendering 'six hundred clans') for the first Exodus, the second Descent could only have been of a handful of the people if the numbers of Gen. xlvi. 27 are to be relied on—and Toffteen maintains that the details

that the Biblical reference to the settlement of Jacob and his family 'in the land of Rameses' at the time of their entry is an anachronism.[1] A similar anachronism here would be readily intelligible. The Delta capital of Rameses II was not a new site, hitherto unoccupied,[2] especially if it is to be identified with Avaris,[3] and it is sometimes suggested that the Israelite forced labour may have been employed during its pre-Ramesside history.[4] All of this ignores a number of considerations. It is strange that the Biblical tradition has preserved the name which suggests Rameses, who is known to have occupied and rebuilt a Delta site, and has used the name as the name of a town[5] only in connexion with this incident, if the name was not given to the site until after they had left Egypt. Further, if the name were an anachronism, we should expect the contemporary name at the time of the composition of the narrative to be employed. But Albright notes that Tanis was called Pi-Ramesse for about 200 years only,[6] and this makes it improbable that the tradition

of all the accounts are reliable. He is compelled to identify Eli with Eleazar the son of Aaron (p. 205) and to date the beginning of the judgeship of Samson in the year of the second entry into Palestine (p. 234). It seems much easier to find an anachronism in the use of the name Rameses in Gen. xlvii. 11 than to reshuffle all the history of Israel in order to avoid it. Again C. A. Simpson (*Revelation and Response in the Old Testament*, 1947, pp. 23 ff.; cf. *The Early Traditions of Israel*, 1948, pp. 425, 427) has advanced the view that the sojourn in Egypt occupied but a very few years at some time later than the thirteenth century B.C., and that Moses never was in Egypt and had nothing to do with leading the Israelites out, while the Israelite escape was not from Pharaoh, but from the headman of some obscure village. As no serious reasons are offered for preferring these speculations to the Biblical traditions, they can hardly claim to be discussed.   [1] Gen. xlvii. 11.

[2] Already Rashi (ad loc.) commented that Pithom and Raamses were not originally suitable for store-cities, but were strengthened and fortified for this purpose, but this conjecture was probably based on Gen. xlvii. 11.

[3] On the identification of the second city, Pithom, cf. Albright, *From the Stone Age to Christianity*, p. 194, and *B.A.S.O.R.*, No. 109, Feb. 1948, p. 15. Naville's identification (*The Store City of Pithom and the Route of the Exodus*, 1885) is now abandoned. Cf., however, Wiener, *Ancient Egypt*, 1928, pp. 75–7, where Naville's identification is defended and declared to be 'in a stronger position than ever'.

[4] Cf. Lods, *Israël*, 1930, p. 211 (E.Tr., 1932, p. 186); Dennefeld, *Histoire d'Israël*, 1935, pp. 68 f.

[5] The 'land of Rameses' is found in Gen. xlvii. 11 as the location of Israel in Egypt. This, as noted above, is certainly an anachronism, probably carrying back to the time of the entry into Egypt the name the locality had at the time of the coming out. It is not there used of a town, though it probably extends to the neighbourhood of a town the later name of the town.

[6] Cf. *From the Stone Age to Christianity*, p. 194. Montet (*Le Drame d'Avaris*,

could arise if it were spurious.[1] Further, since the Bible elsewhere refers to Tanis as Zoan,[2] and locates the miracles associated with the Exodus in 'the fields of Zoan',[3] we should rather have expected that name to be employed here unless Raamses was preserved in the tradition as the accurate reflection of the contemporary name. Nor should it be forgotten that the suggestion that the names may be interpolated or anachronistic in Ex. i. 11 still requires to be supported by evidence that there was royal building activity and residence in the cities referred to in the earlier age in which the story is located. To dismiss the names because they are inconvenient is not to invoke a serious textual argument.[4] Yet no other reason for their dismissal is advanced. Nor does such dismissal carry with it the slightest proof that Thothmes III was the Pharaoh of the Oppression, and that he set the Israelites to build cities for him in the Delta region. Of that evidence is required, and none is offered.

On the other hand, we cannot ignore the evidence that has been brought forward from Egyptian and Ugaritic sources to show that some of the Israelite tribes were already in Palestine before the days of Rameses II. It has already been noted that the Egyptian references to 'Asaru[5] have long been felt to provide a difficulty for those who adopt a thirteenth-century date for the Exodus, since they show that in the reign of Seti I, as well as in that of Rameses II, the tribe of Asher was already settled in its portion.[6] The equation of the names was more readily allowed,

---

p. 188) notes that the Wen-Amon text already refers to the city as Tanis. Cf. also Montet, *Tanis*, 1942, p. 227.

[1] Henderson (*C.Q.R.* xcvii, 1923–4, p. 111) says: 'The names Pithom and Ramses are nothing to go by, for they only give a clue to the date of the documents in which they occur, not of the events which they describe.' If this were sound, the documents would have to be dated before 1100 B.C., when the name Pi-Ramesse had already passed out of use. It is improbable that Ex. i. 11 was extracted from a document so old as that, but if it were it would claim not less but more respect.

[2] Cf. Num. xiii. 22.   [3] Cf. Ps. lxxviii. 12, 43.

[4] Caiger (*Bible and Spade*, 1936, p. 66) says the names are suspect on textual grounds, but none are specified.

[5] Cf. *C.A.H.* ii, pp. 319, 326 f.; T. H. Robinson, *History of Israel*, i, 1932, pp. 75 f. n.

[6] Cf. Burney, *Israel's Settlement in Canaan*, p. 82; T. H. Robinson, loc. cit., p. 76 n. Dussaud, however, rejects the view that this Israelite tribe is referred to in the inscriptions of Seti I and Rameses II. Cf. *Syria*, xix, 1938, p. 177 b, and *Les Découvertes de Ras Shamra et l'Ancien Testament*, 2nd ed., 1941, p. 163 n. See also de Langhe, *Les Textes de Ras Shamra-Ugarit et . . . le milieu biblique de l'Ancien Testament*, ii, 1945, pp. 472 ff. and cf. *supra*, p. 3, n. 7. It seems

D

however, by the advocates of the thirteenth-century date of the
Exodus than by some advocates of the fifteenth-century date,
and the embarrassment was turned by the view that only part
of the Israelite tribes went into Egypt. Jack was very dubious
about the equation,[1] and preferred not to build on it. More
recently, however, there has been added evidence from Ras
Shamra, where alleged references to Asher and also to Zebulun[2]
are found at a date considerably earlier than the thirteenth-
century date of the Exodus would allow, if these tribes came
out of Egypt with Moses. Here again the references are less
secure than could be wished, and less secure than some who have
appealed to them have claimed. De Vaux,[3] no less than Virolleaud,[4] has accepted the references, and finds them to indicate

probable that we should find here evidence that the tribe of Asher had
entered Canaan before the reign of Seti I, and since in the Amarna letters we
learn that Zurata, of Acco, which lay within the borders of what became the
territory of Asher, was fighting the SA-GAZ (TA 290a: 22 ff.; cf. Mercer, *The
Tell El-Amarna Tablets*, ii, 1939, pp. 724 f. and Thureau-Dangin, *R. Ass.* xix,
1922, p. 99) it seems likely that the settlement of Asher took place in the Amarna
age. Cf., however, Gardiner, *Ancient Egyptian Onomastica*, i, 1947, pp. 191*-3*.

[1] Cf. *The Date of the Exodus*, p. 230. On p. 233 Jack expresses doubts as to
whether the tribe of Asher was acknowledged to be an Israelite tribe until
some time after the Exodus.

[2] Cf. Virolleaud, *La Légende de Keret*, 1936, pp. 38, 44 (I: 94 f., 182 f.) for
Asher, and p. 34 (I: 17) for Zebulun. See also id., *R.E.S.* 1934, No. i, pp. vi,
xi. Cf. also Dussaud, *Les Découvertes de Ras Shamra et l'Ancien Testament*, 2nd ed.,
1941, p. 163, where it is held that Zebulun and Asher were at this time in the
south, in accordance with Dussaud's Negebite theory of these texts. It should
be added that Sethe (*A.P.A.W.* 1926, No. 5, p. 47) thinks there is a possibility that Zebulun stands on one of the *Ächtungstexte* (e. 6), which he ascribes
to the period of the XIth Dynasty. If this reading and dating are correct
(Dussaud agrees with the dating; cf. *Syria*, vii, 1927, pp. 216 f.; and Albright
says the identification is either certain or practically so; cf. *Vocalization of the
Egyptian Syllabic Orthography*, 1934, p. 7), this Zebulun is either not to be
equated with the Biblical Zebulun, or the Biblical traditions on any dating
of the Exodus are completely unreliable, and Zebulun existed as a tribe long
before the earliest possible dating.

[3] Cf. *R.B.* xlvi, 1937, pp. 446, 542. So, too, Weill, *J.As.* ccxxix, 1937,
pp. 16, 18; Barton, *Mémorial Lagrange*, 1940, p. 30. It would appear, however,
from *R.B.* lv, 1948, pp. 326 f. that de Vaux no longer accepts these references.
Humbert (*R.E.S.-B.* 1941, pp. 61 ff.) finds a reference to Asher in Εἰσίριος,
which figures in one of the sources cited by Philo of Byblos. He also accepts
the references to Asher which have been alleged to stand in the inscriptions
of Seti I and Rameses II, and in the Keret text from Ras Shamra, and holds
that Asher was originally the name of a divinity, which was transformed into
the name of an eponymous hero of a Canaanite canton, which in turn gave
its name to the Israelite tribe. With this view cf. Virolleaud, loc. cit., p. 18.

[4] Loc. cit., pp. 16, 18.

that the tribes of Asher and Zebulun were already settled in their districts in the fifteenth century B.C. On the other hand, Albright[1] and several other scholars[2] deny any reference to these tribes in the passages concerned. The better of the argument seems here to lie with Albright, though to concede a reference to these two tribes in the Ras Shamra texts could only strengthen the evidence of the texts of Seti I and Rameses II, rather than provide a new embarrassment for the view of the thirteenth-century Exodus. Despite the improbability of the Ras Shamra references, therefore, we may reasonably allow the likelihood that at least Asher was in Palestine at the end of the fourteenth century B.C., on the strength of the Egyptian texts.

Much more problematical are the alleged references to Jacob and Joseph in the place-names Jacob-el and Joseph-el, inscribed in the temple at Karnak in the time of Thothmes III and ascribed to *circa* 1479 B.C.,[3] and to Jacob in the names of some of the Hyksos leaders, Jacob-el and Jacob-baal.[4] So far as the latter are concerned they can have no connexion with the Biblical

[1] Cf. *B.A.S.O.R.*, No. 63, Oct. 1936, pp. 27 n., 29 n.; ibid., No. 71, Oct. 1938, pp. 38 f. Albright takes *zblnm* = *patricians*, and '*tr* = *march*.

[2] Cf. Goetze, *J.A.O.S.* lviii, 1938, p. 277 n.; de Langhe, *Les Textes de Ras Shamra-Ugarit et leurs rapports avec le milieu biblique de l'Ancien Testament*, ii, 1945, pp. 472 ff., 477 ff., and earlier *Les Textes de Ras Shamra-Ugarit et leurs apports à l'histoire des origines israélites*, 1939, pp. 76 ff., 79 ff.; Gordon, *Ugaritic Grammar*, 1940, pp. 34, 36; Pedersen, *Berytus*, vi, 1941, p. 68; Engnell, *Studies in Divine Kingship in the Ancient Near East*, 1943, pp. 150, 157 f. All of these share Albright's view. Cf. Lettinga, *J.E.O.L.* ix, 1944, p. 120. Ginsberg, *The Legend of King Keret*, 1946, pp. 14, 34, takes *zblnm* to mean *sickness*, and pp. 16, 18 '*tr* to mean *after*. Cf. also Herdner, *Syria*, xxv, 1946–8, p. 137 b: 'Il est certain aussi qu'on ne trouve à Ras Shamra aucune mention des tribus israélites de Dan, d'Ašer, de Zabulon et d'Issachar.'

[3] Cf. Mariette, *Les Listes géographiques des pylônes de Karnak*, 1875, pp. 36, 40; Petrie, *History of Egypt*, ii, 1896, pp. 323 ff.; Jirku, *Die ägyptischen Listen palästinensischer und syrischer Ortsnamen*, 1937, pp. 14 f. The two names are Nos. 78 and 102 in the list. It should be noted that Mariette thought No. 78 was שפיר = Σαφείρ of St. Jerome, and described No. 102 simply as 'ville inconnue'. On these names cf. Meyer, *Z.A.W.* vi, 1886, pp. 2 ff., and *Die Israeliten und ihre Nachbarstämme*, 1906, pp. 281 f.; Maspero, in *J.T.V.I.* xxii, 1888–9, pp. 60 f., 83 f.; Müller, *Asien und Europa*, 1893, pp. 162 ff.; Gressmann, *Z.A.W.* xxx, 1910, pp. 6 ff. It should be noted that the former name is found again in a list of the time of Rameses II (cf. Jirku, op. cit., p. 38, No. 9), and the latter in a short later list (ibid., p. 50, No. 3).

[4] Cf. Hall, *The Ancient History of the Near East*, 7th ed., 1927, p. 217. Also Stock, *Studien zur Geschichte und Archäologie der 13. bis 17. Dynastie Ägyptens*, 1942, p. 67. Albright (*From the Stone Age to Christianity*, 2nd ed., 1946, p. 184) prefers to read *Ya'kob-har* = *May the Mountain-god protect*, for the first of these names. Cf. id., *J.B.L.* xxxvii, 1918, p. 137 n.

patriarch. For even if the Israelites went into Egypt in the period of the Hyksos—and it has already been seen that such a view encounters serious difficulties—it is improbable that one whose presence was regarded as offensive to the court[1] would become the namesake of the Hyksos leaders.[2] The mere fact that the name Jacob is met more than once is no evidence of any association between the holders,[3] in the absence of any other evidence. Moreover, the name is said to occur in Babylonia in the age of Ḥammurabi,[4] and it stands three times in texts from Chagar Bazar.[5]

So far as the place-names, Jacob-el and Joseph-el, are concerned, the latter is but doubtfully so read, the sibilant in the Egyptian text not being the normal equivalent of the Hebrew sibilant;[6] and even if both were fully demonstrated, they could

[1] Gen. xlvi, 28–34.

[2] Cf. Jack, op. cit., p. 231: 'It is possible that these chieftains may have been called after the patriarch, whose name may have been in high favour at the Egyptian court.'

[3] Scheil (R.Ass. xii, 1916, pp. 5 ff.) published a cylinder from the period of Agade containing the name Išre-il, with which Scheil compared Israel. Yet there can be no reason to connect its owner with the Biblical Israel.

[4] Cf. S. R. Driver, in Hastings's D.B. ii, 1899, p. 526 b; Cheyne, E.B. ii, 1901, col. 2306; Dictionnaire de la Bible, ed. by Vigouroux, iii, 1903, col. 1074.

[5] In the form Ia-aḫ-qu-ub-él. Cf. Gadd, Iraq, vii, 1940, p. 38 a. For an account of the excavations at Chagar Bazar, cf. Mallowan, Iraq, iv, 1937, pp. 91–154, ix, 1947, pp. 1–257; Gadd, ibid. iv, 1937, pp. 178–85, vii, 1940, pp. 22–66.

[6] Cf. Burney, Israel's Settlement in Canaan, pp. 89 f.; Gressmann, in ΕΥΧΑΡΙΣΤΗΡΙΟΝ (Gunkel Festschrift), i, 1923, p. 4; Jack, op. cit., p. 231. On the other hand, cf. Müller, O.L.Z. ii, 1899, cols. 396 ff., where the possibility of the equation is defended; also Heyes, Bibel und Ägypten, i, 1904, pp. 104 f. Jirku (op. cit., p. 14) fails to make the equation and Dussaud comments: 'On est surpris que l'auteur se refuse au rapprochement de Išpir avec Yoseph-El. Encore voudrait-on savoir pourquoi' (Syria, xviii, 1937, p. 395 a). Dussaud would find the same name in one of the Ächtungstexte edited by Sethe (A.P.A.W. 1926, No. 5, pp. 54 f., 58, e 31, f. 21), where Sethe reads the name 'Ijsỉpj, but does not identify it. Dussaud (Syria, viii, 1927, p. 231) thinks it may be the same as Yšpir = ישפאל. Similarly, in Posener's collection of these texts, attributed to the end of the XIIth Dynasty (cf. Mélanges Syriens (Dussaud Festschrift), i, 1939, p. 314; also Couroyer, Vivre et Penser, i (= R.B. l), 1941, p. 260; Noth, Z.D.P.V. lxv, 1942, p. 13; de Vaux, R.B. liii, 1946, p. 341), the name 'Isỉpỉ occurs (Princes et pays d'Asie et de Nubie, 1940, p. 71, E 12), and this Dussaud (Syria, xxi, 1940, p. 172) would connect with 'Ijsỉpj. If this is correct, and the Sethe collection is rightly dated in the period of the XIth Dynasty (cf. Alt. Z.D.P.V. lxiv, 1941, p. 24; Noth, ibid. lxv, 1942, p. 13), then it would be established that the name Joseph-el goes back to a much earlier period than the one to which the Biblical Joseph is assigned on any possible

not prove that the Israelites Jacob and Joseph gave them their names.[1] Further, even if this could be proved, it would still not be proved that they were in Palestine at this time, but only that at some unknown time in the near or remote past they had been there. And even this would be as serious an embarrassment to the fifteenth-century date for the Exodus as for the thirteenth-century date. For the Joseph tribes would still be in Egypt in 1479 B.C., and a Joseph who had been carried into Egypt as a youth would scarcely have left his name to be enshrined in a place-name in Palestine during the period of the Sojourn in Egypt.

When we turn to the Amarna letters we find once more that they give rise to problems on which there is still no agreement. Those letters, as is well known, were found at Tell el Amarna, which is the modern name for the site of the new capital to which the Pharaoh Ikhnaton transferred the seat of government from Thebes. They formed part of the state archives that lay forgotten in the sand from the time when the government was transferred back to Thebes until they were unearthed, and amongst them are many letters from the Palestinian city-states

dating, and the name would be irrelevant for the chronology of Israel's settlement in Canaan. Dussaud identifies this place with Yasif, known to-day as Tell or Kafr Yasif in the Plain of Acre (*Syria*, viii, 1927, p. 231), while Vincent (*Vivre et Penser*, ii (= *R.B.* li), 1942, p. 195) thinks 'Isîpi has the value of a divine name. Albright (*J.P.O.S.* viii, 1928, p. 249) identifies it with Arabic Yasâf, and says 'it has no connection either with Yôséf, Yasîf, or Yasuf'. It is further to be noted that it is thought that the name Simeon also stands in one of Posener's texts (E 55; cf. Posener, op. cit., p. 91, *Syria*, xviii, 1937, p. 191, and *Chronique d'Égypte*, No. 27, Jan. 1939, p. 44; Vincent, loc. cit., pp. 200 f.), though Alt (*Z.D.P.V.* lxiv, 1941, p. 35) differently identifies the name (cf. also Albright, *B.A.S.O.R.*, No. 81, Feb. 1941, p. 19 n., No. 83, Oct. 1941, p. 34; Maisler, *B.E.H.J.*, No. 1, 1946, pp. 60 f.). Dussaud suggests that this was an old Canaanite tribe, which was settled in southern Palestine as early as the XIIth Dynasty. If it had been continuously settled there from that period, the tradition of Gen. xxxiv could hardly have arisen, and it seems to me probable that Simeon migrated northwards and reached Shechem, but was afterwards forced to fall back again on the south. All of these identifications are somewhat hazardous, however, and we cannot build solidly on them. At the most they can only be said to be possible.

[1] Albright (*A.A.S.O.R.* vi, 1926, p. 19 n.) says: 'The name Ya'qobel is the same as that of the Patriarch Jacob, but was certainly common in the second millennium, and probably has no connexion with him.' Weill, on the other hand, by assuming a connexion reaches 'aisément' the conclusion that the patriarchs were mythical persons who figured in Canaanite traditions before the Israelites entered the land, and who were taken over by Israel after the Conquest (*R.H.R.* lxxxvii, 1923, pp. 69 ff., lxxxviii, 1923, pp. 1 ff.).

concerning affairs in that land. It is known with certainty that they date from the first half of the fourteenth century B.C., and most of them come from the reign of Ikhnaton and his predecessor, Amenhotep III. One of the letters was written from Ras Shamra,[1] and in others there are references to that city,[2] but the letters which are of importance to us tell of conditions farther south, in Palestine. Of the religious and administrative conditions in Egypt I shall say something later. Here I must confine myself to the Palestinian conditions as they are reflected in these documents.

There is clearly much trouble in the land, and people who are called in most of the letters by the ideogram SA-GAZ, but in the letters of Abdi-ḫiba[3] the king of Jerusalem, Ḫabiru,[4] are seeking to get control of the country. The little city-states appeal for help to the Pharaoh and bandy against one another charges and

---

[1] TA 45 (cf. Knudtzon, *Die El-Amarna Tafeln*, ii, 1915, p. 1098).

[2] Cf. Knudtzon, op. cit. ii, p. 1016 f.; Dussaud, *Les Découvertes de Ras Shamra et l'Ancien Testament*, 2nd ed., 1941, p. 16 n.

[3] I retain the common form of this name, which is compounded of an ideogram meaning *servant* and the name of the Hittite goddess, Ḫiba or Ḫepa. Cf. Knudtzon, op. cit. ii, pp. 1332 f. In view of the fact that the divine name is Hittite, Burney is doubtful if the ideogram should be read as the Semitic *abdi*, and prefers to retain the ideogram ARAD-Ḫiba (*Israel's Settlement in Canaan*, pp. 66 f. n.; similarly, Speiser, *A.A.S.O.R.* xiii, 1933, p. 52), holding that the first element is of unknown pronunciation, while Dhorme (*J.P.O.S.* iv, 1924, p. 165) prefers the form Arta-Ḫepa. Gustavs, however (*O.L.Z.* xiv, 1911, cols. 341 ff.), argues for the reading Puti-Ḫepa, and this is followed by Meek (*Hebrew Origins*, 1936, p. 18 n.). This gives to the ideogram a Ḫurrian interpretation, since the divine name is now regarded as Ḫurrian. Weill retains the form Abd-Ḫepa, and says that it is 'un théophore sémitique pur comportant un nom de dieu non sémitique', and says that this divine name, which is found over a wide area, belongs to the pre-Indo-European stock of this area (cf. *R.H.R.* cxv, 1937, p. 180). Cf. also Thureau-Dangin in *Mémorial Lagrange*, 1940, pp. 27 f.

[4] This form seems to be preferable to the form Ḫabiri which is frequently used, since in the only two cases in the Amarna letters where the word is found in the nominative it has this form. Cf. Knudtzon, op. cit. i, 1908, p. 45 n. Burney contests Dhorme's statement (*R.B.*, N.S. vi, 1909, p. 72) that the word is a participle, since we never find it written Ḫa-a-bi-ru = Ḫâbiru (op. cit., p. 69). Böhl (*Kanaanäer und Hebräer*, 1911, pp. 88 f.) appears to regard it as participial, and so Lewy, *Z.A.*, N.F. ii, 1925, p. 26 n., *O.L.Z.* xxx, 1927, p. 745 n., and *H.U.C.A.* xiv, 1939, pp. 587 ff., where the word is spelt Ḫābiru. Despite the fact that a single example of the name with the additional *a* has now been found (cf. *P.E.Q.* 1946, p. 81 n.), it is unlikely that it is a participle. Cf. Opitz, *Z.A.*, N.F. iii, 1927, p. 99. Langdon (*E.T.* xxxi, 1919–20, p. 327) says the reading ḫa-ab-bi-ri, which was given by some older writers, is now known to be erroneous.

counter-charges of disloyalty to their overlord and of giving
assistance to the enemy. That the Habiru and the sa-gaz are
associated peoples is quite certain,[1] though it is improbable that
the ideogram sa-gaz was intended always to be read as Habiru.[2]

For those who hold the fifteenth-century date for the Exodus,
nothing is simpler than to equate the Habiru with the Hebrews,
and to connect the Biblical story of the Conquest with the conditions reflected in these letters. Before the excavations of Garstang
at Jericho had provided a new sheet-anchor for the advocates
of that view, these letters provided the anchor on which they
relied. It was principally on these that Jack rested his case. Nor
can it be denied that the Biblical chronology of 1 Kgs. vi. 1
and of the wanderings seemed to fit most excellently. An Exodus
in the middle of the fifteenth century, followed by forty years of
wandering in the wilderness, would bring the entry into Palestine at the turn of the century and would make the period of
Joshua and of the Conquest fall in the first part of the fourteenth
century b.c., which is precisely the period covered by these
letters. For the short reign of Ikhnaton commenced about 1375
b.c.,[3] so that we have reflected in these letters the conditions of

[1] This was proved by Winckler, who showed that in Hittite texts from
Boghaz-Keui the expressions 'gods of the Habiru' and 'gods of the sa-gaz'
were used interchangeably (cf. *M.D.O.G.*, No. 35, Dec. 1907, p. 25 n.). See
also Böhl, *Kanaanäer und Hebräer*, 1911, pp. 87 ff.; Dhorme, *R.B.* xxxiii, 1924,
pp. 12–16 and *Supplément au Dictionnaire de la Bible*, i, 1928, col. 220 (where
Dhorme says: 'Il est incontestable que les sa-gaz et les Habiri sont une
seule et même chose'). Meek (*Hebrew Origins*, 1936, pp. 7 ff.) lists the occurrences of the two terms where they appear to be the same.

[2] Cf. Burney, *Israel's Settlement in Canaan*, pp. 70 ff.; Hallock, in Mercer's
The Tell El-Amarna Tablets, 1939, ii, pp. 844 f. That sa-gaz is sometimes to
be equated with Habiru would appear from the fact that in Abdi-Hiba's
letters his enemies are referred to as Habiru, whereas in another letter (TA
290 a: 20 f.; cf. Mercer, *The Tell El-Amarna Tablets*, ii, 1939, pp. 724 f., and
Thureau-Dangin, *R.Ass.*, xix, 1922, p. 99) they are called sa-gaz. Cf. Jirku,
O.L.Z. xxiv, 1921, col. 247, where it is argued that sa-gaz is sometimes to be
read Habiru, since in parallel passages in Akkadian texts from Boghaz-Keui
we have [ilâni]Habiri, [ilâni]sa-gaz and [ilâni]-ša [amêlu]sa-gaz. Dhorme goes
so far as to say (*J.P.O.S.* iv, 1924, p. 165): 'L'écriture sa-gaz n'est qu'une
écriture idéographique pour représenter le nom qu'on lisait Habiru.' It
seems best, however, to say with Meek (*Hebrew Origins*, 1936, p. 9): 'In some
of these documents sa-gaz seems to interchange with *ha-bi-ru*, but it does not
necessarily follow that sa-gaz in every instance is to be interpreted as *habiru*,
because the only definitely attested equivalent of the ideogram is *habbatu*.'

[3] So Breasted, *History of Egypt*, 1906, p. 354. Baikie (*History of Egypt*, ii,
1929, p. 387) gives the date of Ikhnaton's accession as 1376 b.c., Albright
(*B.A.S.O.R.*, No. 77, Feb. 1940, p. 29) as 1377 b.c., Dhorme (*Supplément au*

the first four decades, roughly, of this century, and particularly of the latter half of that period.

The difficulties arise as soon as we look more closely into the question. Some of those who took the view that these letters come from the period of Joshua, following the Exodus from Egypt, supposed that we have here the Canaanite view of the incursion of the Israelites.[1] Such a view cannot really be maintained. Here Garstang agrees, saying: 'No historical connection can be traced between the Habiru revolution and the original invasion of Canaan by the Israelites under Joshua. The two movements were essentially distinct.'[2]

Dictionnaire de la Bible, i, 1928, col. 207) as 1379 B.C., while Steindorff and Seele (*When Egypt ruled the East*, 1942, p. 275) assign to him the years 1387–1366 B.C.

[1] So Hall, *The Ancient History of the Near East*, 7th ed., p. 409; Caiger, *Bible and Spade*, 1936, pp. 102 f. ('The Tell el Amarna tablets are believed to paint from the Canaanite side the same picture which the historian of Joshua–Judges paints from the Hebrew side'); Meek, *Hebrew Origins*, 1936, p. 20 ('This contemporaneous account of the settlement of the Habiru in Palestine so exactly parallels the Old Testament account of the Israelite conquest of Jericho and the invasion of the highlands of Ephraim under Joshua that the two manifestly must have reference to the same episode'). See also de Koning, *Studiën over de El-Amarnabrieven*, 1940, pp. 311 ff., and cf. Alt's comment (*A.f.O.* xiv, 1941–4, p. 351 b): 'Dass er mehrere Ereignisse, die sich nach der Darstellung des Buches Josua bei der Einwanderung des Volkes Israel nach Palästina abgespielt haben sollen, wie z. B. die Zerstörung von Jericho, den Zug nach Sichem und die Eroberungen in Judäa, in den Amarna-Briefen direkt erwähnt und damit bestätigt findet, scheint seiner Rekonstruktion ja auch eine Sicherheit zu geben, die jedes ernstliche Schwanken verbietet.' Paton (*B.W.*, N.S. xlvi, 1915, p. 86) says: 'It is possible, therefore, that the Amarna letters contain the Canaanite version of Israel's conquest.' Here, however, it is not the conquest of those who came out of Egypt under Moses that is thought of, but of an earlier and independent wave, and it will be seen below that I am in substantial agreement with Paton, though I think he fails to relate his two movements to one another.

[2] Cf. *Joshua–Judges*, p. 255. So Dhorme (*La Religion des Hébreux nomades*, 1937, p. 80): 'L'histoire de ces Habiri . . . n'a rien de commun avec celle des Hébreux'; Cook (*C.A.H.* ii, 1924, pp. 256 f.): 'The events in the Amarna Letters cannot be identified with Joshua's invasion from the south without entirely stultifying the Biblical narrative. The Habiru, who are mentioned only in Abdi-Khiba's letters from Jerusalem, are evidently the SA.GAZ, who are found also in the north with Abd-Ashirta, and can scarcely be the Israelites under Joshua'; Baikie (*History of Egypt*, ii, p. 308): 'If the Hebrews are the Habiru, and the letters of the loyal Egyptian residents are to be accepted as presenting a true picture of the events of the time, then it is impossible to regard the Biblical account of the Conquest of Canaan as anything more than a romance, and a romance which can scarcely be even said to be based upon fact. There are not any two facts in the two stories which

THE EXTRA-BIBLICAL EVIDENCE

In the first place, it is clear that in the Amarna age we have small groups of people acting simultaneously in different parts of the country, and not the united army that the book of Joshua brings before us. Some of the letters plead for a garrison of fifty to be sent for their protection.[1] This would scarcely suffice for defence against a force of more than half a million men of military age,[2] and by whatever specious devices the Biblical numbers are reduced to what might seem more manageable proportions[3] they could not be brought down to anything against which a force of fifty would appear adequate.

Even if the Biblical numbers are dismissed as wholly unreal,[4] and it is recognized that the company that came out of Egypt was only a small one,[5] it is still impossible to relate the Biblical picture of a united group acting under a single leader with the pattern of the Amarna correspondence. Moreover, wherever the

agree with one another.' Hommel, in a work written to defend the Bible against the Higher Criticism, says (*Ancient Hebrew Tradition*, 1897, pp. 232 f.): 'Their inroads [i.e. of the Ḥabiru] into Palestine have nothing whatever to do with the Israelite invasion of Canaan. Had the two been identical, the sensational fact would lie before us that 'Abdi-Khiba of Jerusalem had given us really the record of such an event as the conquest of the region west of the Jordan, but the existence of any such record would be a severe blow to the credibility of the Old Testament tradition.'

[1] Cf. TA 238 : 11, 295: Rev. 6 (Knudtzon, *Die El-Amarna Tafeln*, i, pp. 782 f., 888 f.). The king of Tyre asks for so few as ten infantrymen, TA 148 : 14, or sometimes twenty, TA 149 : 18, 151 : 15 (Knudtzon, op. cit., pp. 612 f., 616 f., 622 f.).   [2] Ex. xii. 37.

[3] Cf. McNeile, *The Book of Exodus*, 2nd ed., 1917, p. 75.

[4] Cf. Driver, *The Book of Exodus*, 1911, pp. 100 f. To the considerations there noted it may be added that a disciplined army of half a million men could not have been got away from their camp and across the sea in the time between the sighting of the Egyptians and their arrival on the scene, even if they had not had the impediment of women and children, and if they had abandoned all their baggage.

[5] Cf. Lucas, *P.E.Q.* 1943-4, pp. 164 ff., where it is stated that if the original seventy Israelites had increased at the average rate of increase shown in Egypt during the period 1907-37 throughout a Sojourn in Egypt of 430 years, they would have become 10,363 at the end. The case is somewhat overstated, however, since Gen. xlvi. 26 f. excludes Jacob's sons' wives from the original seventy, and a modern rate of increase is scarcely a fair criterion. On the other hand, it is improbable that the Sojourn in Egypt was so long as 430 years. But even granting that duration and making due allowance for the addition of wives to the total and a higher rate of increase, it is impossible to reach anything like the total of something in the neighbourhood of 2 million that Ex. xii. 37 requires. For devices to reduce the Biblical numbers to more probable limits, cf. Heinisch, *Das Buch Exodus*, 1934, pp. 104 f., and Petrie, *Egypt and Israel*, 1911, pp. 40 ff.

names of persons can be checked, they disagree in the Biblical and in the Amarna records.[1] Currency has been given to the statement that Joshua and Benjamin are referred to in the Amarna letters,[2] but there is no ground whatever for this. Philologically the Yashuia of the Amarna correspondence and Joshua are not to be equated,[3] and still less are Benenima and Benjamin.[4] Moreover, the Amarna letters convey appeals to the Egyptian court for help in suppressing the Ḫabiru or SA-GAZ, and it is quite improbable that one of the Canaanite chiefs would refer the chancellery to Benjamin and Joshua for confirmation of his statements.[5] Yet it is solely as witnesses to the reliability of Mutbaʿlu's word that Benenima and Yashuia are invoked.[6]

Further, the activity of Joshua was especially associated with the central districts, and his own tribe of Ephraim was settled in that area. It is true that we are also told of his conquests in the north and in the south. At the account of the latter we shall have to look later, but it may here be noted that the Bible itself offers good reason to doubt the northern victory ascribed to him. In Jg. iv the account of a victory over Jabin, king of Hazor, achieved by the two tribes of Zebulun and Naphtali, is combined with the story of the victory over Sisera, of Harosheth,

[1] Cf. Burney, *Israel's Settlement in Canaan*, p. 92 n.; Lods, *Israël*, 1930, pp. 207 f. (E. Tr., 1932, p. 183). Jack tries to turn this by some forced argument that Abdi-Ḫiba might be equated with Adonizedek, but it is improbable that he even convinced himself (op. cit., pp. 158 ff.).

[2] Cf. Olmstead, *History of Palestine and Syria*, 1931, pp. 188, 198; Caiger, *Bible and Spade*, 1936, p. 103; Barton, *E.T.* xlvii, 1935–6, p. 380 (cf. T. H. Robinson's reply, ibid., and further discussion by Barton and Robinson, ibid., pp. 476 f.); Simpson, *Revelation and Response in the Old Testament*, 1947, p. 105. Schofield (*The Historical Background of the Bible*, 1938, p. 78) says the name of Joshua has been discovered in one of the letters, though he does not identify him with the Israelite leader. Similarly, Meek (*Hebrew Origins*, 1936, p. 21; cf. *B.A.S.O.R.*, No. 61, Feb. 1936, p. 17) thinks the names are to be equated, but says there is no ground for identifying the persons.

[3] Cf. Albright, *B.A.S.O.R.*, No. 89, Feb. 1943, p. 12 n.

[4] Albright (ibid., p. 11) reads Ben-elima = 'Son of the Gods', and says the *li* value of NI is common in these letters, adding that 'Olmstead's identification of the name "Benjamin" was phonetically very difficult, and has now been disproved by the discovery that the name already belonged to a tribe or groups of tribes, Banû-yamîna . . . in the Middle Euphrates region in the eighteenth century B.C. (Mari documents).'

[5] It is improbable that Rommel's dispatches to Hitler ran: 'If you do not believe me, ask Montgomery'; and as improbable that the Palestinian princes in writing to their overlord referred him to the chiefs of the Ḫabiru.

[6] Cf. TA 256: 15, 18 (Knudtzon, op. cit., i, pp. 816 f.).

achieved by a much wider combination of tribes.[1] In Josh. xi
the great victory in the north is said to have been over Jabin,
the king of Hazor. As that victory is stated to have been sealed
by the death of Jabin and the entire population of the city, and
by the complete destruction of the city,[2] there is no room for
another powerful Jabin to have been ruling in the same city in
a comparatively short time, and it is quite certain that we have
two variant traditions of a single victory. That a victory actually
won by a united people under Joshua was later ascribed to
Zebulun and Naphtali is far less probable than that a local victory of these tribes has been magnified into the exploit of the
whole people under Joshua. Such a name tends to attract to
itself traditions[3] rather than to dissipate them.

The actual historical exploits of Joshua were therefore mainly,
if not entirely, confined to the central districts, whereas the only
place in that area where Ḫabiru activity is recorded in the
Amarna letters is Shechem.[4] In the book of Joshua we are given
no account of the conquest of Shechem, though the tribes are
said to have assembled there when the conquest was complete.[5]
That we cannot suppose that an unrecorded victory of Joshua's
had given the invaders Shechem is clear from the fact that that
city was still Canaanite in the period after Joshua.[6]

The evidence of the Amarna letters would seem rather to connect the Shechem incident with things that are recorded in the
Bible as having happened before the going down into Egypt, and
not after the Exodus. Abdi-ḫiba of Jerusalem refers in one of his
letters to Labaya and the land of Shechem having given all to
the Ḫabiru.[7] There is another letter, which comes from Labaya
himself, which refers to the conquest by enemy activity of a city
whose name does not stand in the surviving text.[8] In view of

[1] Cf. Burney, *The Book of Judges*, 1920, pp. 78 ff. Also Moore, *Judges*, 2nd
ed., 1898, pp. 107 ff.   [2] Josh. xi. 10 f.
[3] Cf. McFadyen, *E.T.* xxxvi, 1924–5, pp. 103 ff.
[4] Cf. TA 289:23 (Knudtzon, op. cit. i, pp. 874 f.).
[5] Josh. xxiv, 1. Möhlenbrink (*Z.A.W.*, N.F. xv, 1938, pp. 250 ff.) thinks
this localizing of the Covenant in Shechem is secondary. He finds evidence
of an older Gilgal-amphictyony which was later replaced by a Shiloh-
amphictyony of twelve tribes, to which he attaches more historical value
than the Shechem Covenant, which could hardly have antedated the Abimelech incident.   [6] Cf. Jg. ix.
[7] Cf. TA 289:22 ff. (Knudtzon, loc. cit.). Dhorme, however, takes 'the
land of Shechem' as the object rather than the subject and renders 'Labaya
has given even the land of Shechem to the Ḫabiru' (*J.P.O.S.* iv, 1924,
p. 163).
[8] Cf. TA 252:9 ff. (Knudtzon, op. cit. i, pp. 806 f.). Mercer (*The Tell*

Labaya's association with Shechem in the other text, it is not improbable that it was Shechem. This incident is reminiscent of the story recorded in Gen. xxxiv, where, however, Shechem is treated as a person living in an unnamed city instead of as the name of a city.[1] But that story is represented as belonging to the age of Jacob, and not to the age of Joshua.

The Amarna letters offer evidence of trouble in the south and in the north. We learn of the following places in the south that were affected: Gezer and Askelon,[2] Lachish,[3] Gath, and Keilah and possibly Rabbah.[4] In the north there is evidence of groups of SA-GAZ operating with Abdi-Ashirta.[5] The general picture is thus of trouble in the south and north, but with the centre affected only by the action at Shechem; whereas the general picture of the Biblical account of Joshua is of a movement that began in the centre and spread north and south from there.[6] If the Shechem story is rightly connected with Gen. xxxiv, then it would not seem to have led to any lasting control of the district, for Jacob complains that the treachery is likely to react unfavourably on the fortunes of the whole kindred of the traitors,[7] and in

El-Amarna Tablets, ii, 1939, p. 657) renders: 'The city was conquered by treachery. As with one who had made peace, and as one who had taken an oath, was the chief with me. Hence the city was conquered.' This rendering is of doubtful authority, however. Knudtzon's rendering is: 'Durch Feindschaft ist die Stadt erobert worden. Ist die Treue unversehrt oder ist die Treue zerstört worden? I Grosser ist bei mir; erobert ist die Stadt.'

[1] Gen. xxxiii. 18 f. connects Shechem with the city of Shechem, however, and it is probable that in Gen. xxxiv Shechem is a personification of the city. Similarly, Hamor may be a personification of a neighbouring city.

[2] Cf. TA 287:14 (Knudtzon, op. cit. i, pp. 86 f.).

[3] Cf. TA 287:15, 288:42 (Knudtzon, ibid., pp. 864 f., 870 f.).

[4] Cf. TA 290:9 ff. (Knudtzon, ibid., pp. 876 f.). On the identification of Gimti with Gath cf. Knudtzon, op. cit. ii, 1915, p. 1311.

[5] Abdi-Ashirta figures in a large number of the letters. Amongst the places in whose neighbourhood the SA-GAZ are mentioned as active are Beirut (TA 118:28 ff., cf. Knudtzon, op. cit., pp. 514 ff.), Gebal (TA 87:21 ff.; cf. ibid., pp. 602 f.), Ashtaroth and Boṣrah (TA 197:10 ff.; cf. ibid., pp. 726 f.), Acco (TA 290a:21 ff.; cf. Mercer, *The Tell El-Amarna Tablets*, ii, 1939, pp. 724 f.). It will be seen that some of these places lie outside the range of Joshua's activities as recorded in the Bible. Cf. de Koning, *Studiën over de El-Amarnabrieven*, 1940, pp. 129 ff., 295 ff.

[6] It is to be noted that while Albright places the settlement of the Joseph tribes in the Amarna age, he does not identify the campaigns of Joshua with the events of that age, but holds that Joshua's work fell at the end of the thirteenth century B.C., and lay first in the neighbourhood of Gibeon, and then in Judah, and finally in Galilee. Cf. *B.A.S.O.R.*, No. 58, Apr. 1935, pp. 10–18. Speiser (*A.A.S.O.R.* xiii, 1933, pp. 52 f.) says the Amarna Ḥabiru and the Josephite Ḥabiru were centuries apart.   [7] Gen. xxxiv. 30.

Gen. xlix we find the two tribes cursed and promised dispersion.[1] Moreover, it is certain that Simeon and Levi did not retain any hold on Shechem,[2] and we are therefore not surprised to find that in the time of Abimelech it was still a Canaanite city[3]—as we should be if Joshua had conquered it and made it the headquarters of an Israelite amphictyony.

We must not, however, ignore Josh. x. That chapter relates how Joshua, after the defeat of the confederation of kings at Aijalon, attacked the cities of Judah one by one and smote them with the edge of the sword, and wiped out their entire populations. Wright has recently argued for the historical worth of this account,[4] and for its integration with the different picture presented by Jg. i, but since he does not locate the events of either chapter in the Amarna age, his view does not fall to be considered at this point. Here it is relevant only to note that if Joshua is located in the Amarna age, then the statements of the second part of this chapter cannot be reconciled with the Amarna letters. For Josh. x says that Joshua wiped out the entire population of Lachish, Gezer, and indeed of the entire south of the land. But the Amarna letters tell only of assistance given to the Ḥabiru by Lachish and Gezer, and it has already been said that the archaeological evidence is against any destruction of these places in the Amarna age.

There remains the vexed question of the philological equation of the word Ḥabiru with the name Hebrews.[5] There have always been scholars who have doubted the equation,[6] though most

---

[1] Gen. xlix. 7. On Gen. xlix. 5–7 cf. Burney, *Israel's Settlement in Canaan*, pp. 38 ff.

[2] Burney (ibid., pp. 43, 86) holds that Gen. xlviii. 22 is evidence that Shechem was once held by non-Ephraimite Israelites.   [3] Jg. ix.

[4] Cf. *J.N.E.S.* v, 1946, pp. 105–14.

[5] Cf. Ryle, *The Book of Genesis*, 1921, pp. 460 ff.; Hallock, in Mercer, *The Tell El-Amarna Tablets*, ii, 1939, pp. 838 ff.

[6] Cf. Sayce, *P.S.B.A.* x, 1887–8, p. 496, xi, 1888–9, p. 347, *E.T.* xi, 1899–1900, p. 377; Hommel, in Hastings's *D.B.* i, 1898, p. 228 a, and *Ancient Hebrew Tradition*, 1897, p. 234; Halévy, *R.S.* xii, 1904, pp. 246 ff.; Eerdmans, *Alttestamentliche Studien*, ii, 1908, pp. 61 ff.; Dhorme, *R.B.*, N.S. vi, 1909, pp. 68 f., 72, xxxiii, 1924, pp. 12 ff., *J.P.O.S.* iv, 1924, pp. 162 ff., *Supplément au Dictionnaire de la Bible*, i, 1928, col. 220, *R.B.* xxxix, 1930, pp. 171 ff., *La Religion des Hébreux nomades*, 1937, pp. 79 ff.; Kraeling, *Aram and Israel*, 1918, p. 34, *B.A.S.O.R.*, No. 77, Feb. 1940, p. 32; Friedrich, *Aus dem hethitischen Schrifttum*, i, 1925, p. 18 n.; von Baudissin, *Kyrios als Gottesname*, iii, 1929, pp. 172 f.; Ricciotti, *Storia d'Israele*, i, 2nd ed., 1934, pp. 56, 180 f. (French Tr. i, 1939, pp. 59, 182). Several scholars have held that the Ḥabiru were Kassites rather than Hebrews. So Reisner (*J.B.L.* xvi, 1897, p. 143),

have allowed that it is possible,¹ even if they have not claimed
that it is certain. Like so many others of our problems, this one
is much more complex to-day than it once appeared. For the
Ḥabiru of the Amarna letters no longer stand alone.² The word
is found in Babylonian sources,³ in Nuzu texts,⁴ and also in at
least one Ras Shamra text.⁵ Moreover, it cannot be discussed
without reference to the 'Aperu, who figure in Egyptian
texts.⁶

There is a reference to the 'Aperu in a list dealing with the
reign of Thothmes III, who is the Pharaoh of the Oppression on
the fifteenth-century view of the date of the Exodus,⁷ but the

and Halévy (R.S. xii, 1904, pp. 246 ff.). Cf. Scheil (R.Ass. xii, 1915, pp.
114 ff.), who says the Ḥabiru were Elamite, Kassite, or Lower Mesopotamian people; Gustavs (T.L.Z. l, 1925, cols. 604 f.), who notes the character
of the only names of the Ḥabiru known to us; and Gemoll, Israeliten und
Hyksos, 1913, p. 27.
    ¹ Cf. Alt, in R.G.G., 2nd ed., ii, 1928, cols. 1668 f., where it is held that
the equation is possible, but uncertain. While most scholars have gone beyond
this, and have accepted the equation as probable, or highly probable, some
have gone so far as to say that the equation is complete. Thus Burney (The
Book of Judges, 1920, p. lxxiv) says: 'The philological equivalence of (amêlûtu)
Ḥa-bi-ru with עברי . . . is perfect.' Similarly Schofield (The Historical Background of the Bible, 1938, p. 71) says: 'In central and southern Palestine
the anti-Egyptian element revealed in the Amarna tablets is spoken of as the
Sa-Gaz—a word that means plunderer, but the king of Jerusalem calls the
attackers in his district the Habiru—which exactly corresponds to the word
Hebrew.' This is certainly going too far. Weill (R.E.S. 1937, p. 154) says:
'L'équation Ḥabiri = Hébreux . . . est acceptée aujourd'hui . . . par la
presque unanimité des travailleurs.' It will be seen below that this is not quite
true to-day.
    ² Meek (Hebrew Origins, 1936, pp. 7 ff.) lists all the occurrences of Ḥabiru
and SA-GAZ, where they appear to be the same, so far as they were known at
that time.
    ³ Jirku (Die Wanderungen der Hebräer, 1924, pp. 14 ff.) lists references to all
the occurrences of the word known at that time in Babylonian, Hittite, and
Amarna sources. Cf., too, Scheil, R.Ass. xii, 1915, pp. 114 f.
    ⁴ Cf. Chiera, A.J.S.L. xlix, 1932–3, pp. 115 ff.
    ⁵ Cf. Virolleaud, C.R.A.I.B.L. 1939, p. 329 f. See also A.f.O. xiii, 1938,
p. 88; Kraeling, B.A.S.O.R., No. 77, Feb. 1940, p. 32; and Jack, P.E.Q. 1940,
pp. 95 ff.
    ⁶ Cf. Heyes, Bibel und Ägypten, i, 1904, pp. 146–58; Eerdmans, Alttesta-
mentliche Studien, ii, 1908, pp. 52 ff.; Wilson, A.J.S.L. xlix, 1932–3, pp. 275 ff.
The occurrences of the term then known are recorded in Jirku, op. cit.,
pp. 23 ff., and also in A.A.S.O.R. xiii, 1933, p. 38, and Meek, Hebrew Origins,
1936, p. 11. Cf. also S. R. Driver, The Book of Exodus, 1911, pp. xli f.
    ⁷ This stands in Papyrus Harris 500, which contains what Jirku (op. cit.,
p. 24) calls a 'historical romance, dealing with the capture of the Palestinian
town of Jaffa by Thothmes III'.

text itself is assigned to the reign of Seti I, or later.[1] But the earliest reference to the 'Aperu as being in Egypt comes from the time of Amenhotep II.[2] There are further references to them in texts from the times of Seti I,[3] Rameses II,[4] Rameses III, and Rameses IV.[5] They are found not alone in Egypt, but also in the neighbourhood of Beth-shan, where they are probably mentioned as engaged in fighting.[6]

Some of those who have identified the Ḥabiru with the Hebrews have resisted any equation of Ḥabiru and 'Aperu.[7]

[1] Cf. Gunn, *apud* Speiser, *A.A.S.O.R.* xiii, 1933, p. 38 n.; cf. Wilson, *A.J.S.L.* xlix, pp. 277 f., and Gardiner, *Ancient Egyptian Onomastica*, i, 1947, p. 184* n.

[2] This text has been published more recently than the works mentioned on p. 46, n. 6. Cf. Badawi, *Annales du Service*, xliii, 1943, pp. 21 ff. This text contains the mention of 3,600 'Aperu prisoners of war. Cf. also Grdseloff, *B.E.H.J.* i, 1946, p. 75, and Gardiner, loc. cit.   [3] Cf. Gunn, loc. cit.

[4] It has been frequently stated that the 'Aperu are referred to on an inscription of Rameses II found at Beth-shan as engaged on the building of Pi-Ramesse. So, for example, Schofield, *The Historical Background of the Bible*, 1938, facing p. 110. Cf. Fisher, *M.J.U.P.* xiv, 1923, p. 234; Cook, *P.E.F.Q.S.* 1924, p. 199; Hall, ibid. 1925, p. 117; Vincent, *R.B.* xxxiii, 1924, p. 429 n.; Jack, *The Date of the Exodus*, 1925, p. 22. This statement is quite unwarranted. Cf. Mallon, *Biblica*, vii, 1926, p. 112. The inscription mentions Pi-Ramesse, but does not say who built it. Cf. Rowe, *M.J.U.P.* xx, 1929, pp. 88–98, esp. p. 95, and *The Topography and History of Beth-shan*, 1930, p. 34; Caiger, *B.A.* ix, 1946, pp. 64 ff.

[5] Cf. Gunn, *apud* Speiser, loc. cit.; Wilson, *A.J.S.L.* xlix, p. 276.

[6] Cf. Rowe, *The Topography and History of Beth-shan*, 1930, pp. 29 f. Rowe observes that 'an invasion by tribes from the east side of the Jordan is distinctly referred to in the text of the other Seti stele from Beth-shan', and by analogy with this he thinks the text which mentions the 'Aperu is doubtless to be reconstructed to indicate that they invaded Canaan. On the other hand, Albright (*A.A.S.O.R.* vi, 1926, p. 36 n.) says it is impossible to tell certainly whether they are the allies or the enemies of Egypt, but the former appears the more natural, and Mallon (*Biblica*, vii, 1926, p. 109) says that they appear to be the allies of the Egyptians. Albright (loc. cit.) connects the 'Aperu with the Midianite tribe of 'Epher. Zoller (*M.G.W.J.* lxxii, 1928, p. 241) thinks it improbable that they should be identified with the Israelites. On the other hand, Grdseloff is persuaded that they are to be identified with the Hebrews and that they were in revolt against Egypt. Cf. *B.E.H.J.*, No. i, 1946, p. 77 n. See also *Chronique d'Égypte*, No. 39–40, Jan. and July 1945, pp. 116 f.

[7] So, for example, Miketta, who states that the 'Aperu have nothing in common with the Hebrews of the Bible (*Der Pharao des Auszuges*, 1903, p. 55). Cf. Breasted, *A.R.E.* iv, 1906, p. 150 n.: 'These are the people supposed by Chabas to have been Hebrews, a theory long since exploded'; Luckenbill, *A.J.Th.* xxii, 1918, p. 36: 'At the present time the majority of scholars are inclined to reject the first identification'—i.e. 'Aperu = Hebrews—'while they accept the second'—i.e. Ḥabiru = Hebrews; Böhl, *Kanaanäer und Hebräer*, 1911, p. 83: 'Sprachlich unwahrscheinlich, sachlich verlockend,

Since the latter are not referred to as being in Egypt until after
the Exodus had already taken place on the fifteenth-century dating of that event, the denial of this equation left that dating
unembarrassed. Yet the philological possibility of the equation
was maintained by many scholars,[1] and the fact that the 'Aperu
figure as labourers working on state buildings under the *corvée*,[2]
precisely as the Hebrews figure in the narratives of the Oppression, led others to maintain the equation, but to argue that not
all the Hebrews came out of Egypt.[3] Since the 'Aperu are referred
to so late as the time of Rameses IV, a little before the middle of
the twelfth century B.C., when 800 of them are mentioned as
engaged on some enterprise, some of those who adopt the 'late
date' view of the Exodus, placing it in the thirteenth century
B.C., share this view. Alternatively, these later 'Aperu might be
regarded as prisoners of war, who were set to task-work as
slaves,[4] though neither Rameses III nor Rameses IV seems to have
been militarily active in Palestine to make prisoners.[5] Possibly

chronologisch unmöglich ist die Gleichsetzung der '*pr*-Leute mit den Hebräern
aufzugeben.'
    [1] Cf. Heyes, *Bibel und Ägypten*, i, 1904, pp. 147 ff.; Skinner, *Genesis*, 1910,
pp. 218 f. n.; Albright, *Z.A.W.*, N.F. vi, 1929, pp. 12 f., and *Archaeology and
the Religion of Israel*, 2nd ed., 1946, p. 200; Wilson, *A.J.S.L.* xlix, 1932–3,
p. 280; Noth, *Festschrift Otto Procksch*, 1934, pp. 99 f.; Speiser, *A.A.S.O.R.* xiii,
1933, p. 38. Cf., too, Meek, *Hebrew Origins*, 1936, p. 10: 'The Egyptian word
'*apiru* is the exact equivalent of the cuneiform *ḫabiru* and the Hebrew '*ibri*';
Gardiner, *Ancient Hebrew Onomastica*, i, 1947, p. 184* n. On the other hand,
Gunn (*apud* Speiser, *A.A.S.O.R.* xii, p. 39 n.) says: 'No case is known in
which the Egyptians wrote a foreign ḥ or ḫ by ', so that of the two words (or
forms) '*br* (Hebrew) and *Ḫabīru* it can have been only the former that was
reproduced as '*pr*.'
    [2] Cf. Burney, *Israel's Settlement in Canaan*, p. 62: 'Other allusions . . . pic-
ture the 'Apuriu in Egypt, performing (like the Hebrews of Exod. i. 11 ff.)
heavy manual labour in connexion with the building operations of the
Pharaohs, especially the quarrying and transportation of stone.' Cf. Wilson,
A.J.S.L. xlix, p. 276.
    [3] Cf. Driver, *The Book of Exodus*, 1911, p. xlii; Burney, ibid.; Speiser,
A.A.S.O.R. xiii, p. 53.
    [4] Hall so accounts for 'Aperu in all cases. Cf. *P.E.F.Q.S.* 1925, p. 118.
Chiera (*A.J.S.L.* xlix, 1932–3, pp. 115 ff.) and Wilson (ibid., pp. 275 ff.) both
thought the original meaning of the word was *captive*. But Speiser (loc. cit.,
p. 36) says that while this might satisfy the Nuzu evidence, it will not fit the
Babylonian.
    [5] That Rameses III retained some hold on the coast road and the Vale
of Esdraelon is indicated by the evidences of Egyptian control in Beth-shan
in his reign, and by the statue of him found in that city. Cf. Rowe, *The
Topography and History of Beth-shan*, 1930, p. 38, and *The Four Canaanite
Temples of Beth-shan*, i, 1940, pp. 22 ff. His control is scarcely likely to have been

Merneptah may have taken some captives home from the raid which is commemorated on his stele, and their children have continued to serve as slaves of the State, though this is not very probable.

In view of the latest evidence from Ras Shamra, however, the philological equation of Ḫabiru and ʿAperu has taken a new turn. For here we find that a town which is referred to in an Accadian Ras Shamra text as ^{âlu}Ḫal-bi-^{amêlûti}SAG-GAZ appears in an alphabetic text as Ḫlb-ʿprm.[1] This makes it certain that the ʿprm are the same as the Ḫabiru, and since ʿprm and ʿAperu provide no obstacles to their equation, it seems more highly probable than ever that ʿAperu = ʿprm = Ḫabiru.[2] But doubt is now cast on the reading Ḫabiru, and it has been claimed that the Ras Shamra text has finally closed the door against the equation of Ḫabiru and Hebrews.[3] For the word that is usually read as Ḫabiru could equally be read as Ḫapiru, and indeed some had already claimed that it should be so read.[4] If now it is agreed that it should be so read, the difficulty of the equation between Ḫapiru and Hebrews is certainly increased.[5] For the r is left as

effective after the settlement of the Philistines, however. That the incoming Israelites were not able to get possession of Beth-shan is stated in Jg. i. 27.

[1] Cf. Kraeling, B.A.S.O.R., No. 77, Feb. 1940, p. 32, and Jack, P.E.Q. 1940, p. 97. The texts were published by Virolleaud in Syria, xxi, 1940, pp. 125 (II. 7), 132 (VIII. 1), 134 (X. 12). Cf. ibid., p. 143. See also Virolleaud, R.E.S.-B. 1940, pp. 74–6; de Vaux, R.B. lv, 1948, pp. 339 f. Goetze (B.A.S.O.R., No. 79, Oct. 1940, pp. 32–4) argues that the reference is to the quarter of the city of Ḫalbi where the Ḫabiru lived.

[2] Kraeling (B.A.S.O.R., No. 77, p. 32) observes that the new evidence makes this equation 'all the more certain'. Cf. O'Callaghan, Aram Naharaim, 1948, p. 32; Cazelles, Études sur le Code de l'Alliance, 1946, p. 45.

[3] Cf. Virolleaud (C.R.A.I.B.L. 1939, p. 329): 'Les nouveaux documents permettent . . . d'établir que les Khabiri . . . n'ont rien de commun avec les Hébreux. Il faut lire, en effet, Khapiri . . . et ce simple fait met fin à une controverse qui divisait les érudits depuis un demi-siècle.' Kraeling also (B.A.S.O.R., No. 77, p. 32) claims that the issue is settled, though he finishes on a more doubtful note by saying that 'the equation with the Hebrews is rendered still more difficult', and more recently (A.J.S.L. lviii, 1941, pp. 237 ff.) he prefers to transcribe by Ḫa-BI-ru, where BI stand for both bi and pi.

[4] Cf. Albright, The Archaeology of Palestine and the Bible, 1932, p. 206: 'Since the cuneiform orthography Kha-BI-ru may just as well be read Khapiru, and Canaanite ʿain is regularly transcribed kh in the Amarna tablets, it is difficult to avoid the conclusion that the true form of the name is ʿApiru.' Cf. id., Vocalization of Egyptian Syllabic Orthography, 1934, p. 42 (VII B 4); Speiser, A.A.S.O.R. xiii, p. 39; Meek, Hebrew Origins, 1936, p. 11.

[5] It is thus no longer possible to speak with the confidence of Barton, who

the only letter in common between the two words. Against that, however, it should be set that the equation of the Accadian *ḫ* and the Hebrew ע, which had earlier been challenged by those who doubted the equation, is now proved to be sound by the Ras Shamra 'prm[1] while the interchange of the labial provides no real difficulty.[2] Further, it should be noted that some years ago Virolleaud had found the form 'brm in a Ras Shamra fragment,[3] which he had connected with Ḥabiru, and it is therefore possible that forms with both *b* and *p* were found at Ugarit.[4] This, however, must remain doubtful in view of the fragmentary character of the text in which the *b* form is found.

Some of those who had earlier denied the equation of Ḥabiru and Hebrews favoured the view that Ḥabiru was a word of Canaanite origin,[5] and that it was connected with the root חבר and perhaps with the name Hebron, and that it means *con-*

said (*Semitic and Hamitic Origins*, 1934, p. 86): 'There can be little doubt that it'—i.e. the name Ḥabiru—'is the real original of the name "Hebrews."'

[1] Cf. Knudtzon, *Die El-Amarna Tafeln*, i, 1908, p. 48; Burney, *The Book of Judges*, 1920, p. lxxiv; Schmidtke, *Die Einwanderung Israels in Kanaan*, 1933, p. 43; and many other writers.

[2] Cf. what I have written in *P.E.Q.* 1940, pp. 92 f.: 'An early tendency to substitute *b* for *p* in some words is amply attested, e.g. Acc. *parzillu* = Heb. and Phoenician ברזל; Acc. *dišpu* = Heb. דבש (with metathesis); Acc. *napištu*, Heb. נפש = נבש in the Aramaic of Zenjirli (Hadad, 17, 21, 22 (Cooke, *North Semitic Inscriptions*, No. 61, p. 160). So also in the Phoenician inscription of Kilamu from the same locality, line 13 (Lidzbarski, *Ephemeris*, iii, 1909–15, p. 223) and Soudschin (Bb 21, 23 (Ronzevalle, *Mélanges de l'Université St-Joseph*, xv, 1931, pp. 237 ff.))). In the Ras Shamra tablets we find some instance of this substitution of *b* for *p*, e.g., *bšn* = serpent (I D, 223; II D, vi. 14 (Virolleaud, *La Légende phénicienne de Danel*, 1936, pp. 182, 208); V AB, D 38 (Virolleaud, *La Déesse 'Anat*, 1938, p. 50)) = Heb. פתן (cf. Ar. بثن); *nbt* = honey (I K 72, 165 (Virolleaud, *La Légende de Keret*, 1936, pp. 38, 44; cf. p. 69)) = Heb. נפת (cf. also *ḫpš* (I K 91), which Virolleaud (op. cit., p. 74) would connect with *ḫubši* of the Amarna letters, of doubtful meaning (cf. Knudtzon, op. cit., ii, p. 1165)).' Cf. also Jack, ibid., pp. 99 f.; Albright, *B.A.S.O.R.*, No. 77, p. 33; Kraeling, *A.J.S.L.* lviii, 1941, p. 239; and my comment in *P.E.Q.* 1942, pp. 42 f.

[3] Cf. *Syria*, xv, 1934, p. 317 n.; and *La Légende de Keret*, p. 74 n. Cf. also Jack, *The Ras Shamra Tablets*, 1935, p. 35. Kraeling, however (*A.J.S.L.* lviii, 1941, p. 238), disputes Virolleaud's interpretation, and renders 'passers-by'.

[4] In *R.E.S.-B.* 1940, pp. 75 f., Virolleaud suggests that 'brm = Hebrews and 'prm = 'Aperu. This seems very doubtful.

[5] Albright (*J.B.L.* xliii, 1924, p. 391 n.) notes that Ḥabiru is once marked in the Amarna tablets as a Canaanite word in TA 290:24. Cazelles (*Études sur le Code de l'Alliance*, 1946, p. 45 b) suggests that the Israelites borrowed the name from the Egyptians, but because they pronounced *p* as *f* in this position (i.e. after a vowel), they substituted *b* for it. De Vaux (*R.B.* lv, 1948, p. 342 n.) rightly pronounces this theory ingenious but insecure.

federates or *allies*.[1] The Ras Shamra text with the form ʿprm rules this view out, while it still leaves it possible that ʿAperu = ʿprm = Ḥapiru or Ḥabiru = עברים. It must be emphasized, however, that these equations can in no sense be said to be proved.

[1] Cf. Sayce, *P.S.B.A.* xi, 1888–9, p. 347, and *E.T.* xi, 1899–1900, p. 377, xxxiii, 1921–2, pp. 43 f.; Kraeling, *Aram and Israel*, 1918, p. 34; Dhorme, *R.B.* xxxiii, 1924, pp. 12 ff., *J.P.O.S.* iv, 1924, pp. 166 f., *Supplément au Dictionnaire de la Bible*, i, 1928, p. 220, and *La Religion des Hébreux nomades*, 1937, pp. 80 ff.; von Baudissin, *Kyrios als Gottesname*, iv, 1929, p. 203; Ricciotti, *Storia d'Israele*, i, pp. 56, 180 (French Tr. i, pp. 59, 182). Speiser had already (*A.A.S.O.R.* xiii, p. 39) observed that this view was ruled out. Reisner (*J.B.L.* xvi, 1897, p. 143) said this view had been universally rejected because the determinative for country occurs after the word. Similarly Jack, *P.E.Q.* 1940, p. 105. In view of the Nuzu evidence Dhorme modified his view, and suggested that the original meaning was *captive* (cf. *R.H.R.* cxviii, 1938, pp. 184 ff.; *Actes du XXᵉ Congrès international des Orientalistes*, 1940, pp. 123 f.), while Albright (*Archaeology of Palestine and the Bible*, p. 206) agreed with Landsberger (*Kleinasiatische Forschungen*, i, 1929, pp. 321 ff.) in holding that Ḥabiru = *condottiere*. De Vaux (*R.B.* lv, 1948, pp. 341 n., 343) suggests that it means *man of the steppe land*. Kraeling (*A.J.S.L.* lviii, pp. 248 ff.) suggested that the word is formed from the preposition עֵבֶר, and that it means ʿone from the other side of the river' (cf. Speiser, loc. cit., p. 41; Jack, *P.E.Q.* 1940, pp. 105 f.), while others have connected it with the root from which this preposition is formed, and have found its original meaning to be *nomad* (so Albright, *J.A.O.S.* xlviii, 1928, p. 184; Meek, *Hebrew Origins*, 1936, p. 9; Guillaume, *P.E.Q.* 1946, p. 82; cf. Speiser, loc. cit., p. 41, Jack, loc. cit.). Lewy (*H.U.C.A.* xiv, 1939, pp. 587 ff.) derived it from the same root, but held that it meant a foreigner with the status of a servant (cf. *J.B.L.* lix, 1940, p. 302, where Albright observes that the latest evidence from Ras Shamra rules out any derivation from this root). Not a few writers have claimed that it was an appellative and not a gentilic (so, for example, Luckenbill, *A.J.Th.* xxii, 1918, pp. 36 f. and *A.J.S.L.* xxxvi, 1919–20, pp. 244 f.), while Sidney Smith (*Isaiah, Chapters xl–lv*, 1944, p. 137) regards it as a gentilic, and so Jack (loc. cit., pp. 103 ff.). Guillaume (*P.E.Q.* 1946, p. 83) holds that it is both an appellative and a gentilic. He brings together the words Ḥabiru, Hebrews, and Arabs, and argues that the last is a late formation with metathesis. Albright (*J.B.L.* xliii, 1924, pp. 389 f.) had earlier made a similar suggestion. In *A.A.S.O.R.* vi, 1926, p. 36 n., and *B.A.S.O.R.*, No. 77, Feb. 1940, p. 33, Albright suggested a connexion with Epher (Gen. xxv. 4), and a similar suggestion was made apparently independently by Mallon (*Biblica*, vii, 1926, p. 109 n.) and Zoller (*M.G.W.J.* lxxii, 1928, p. 241), and adopted by Meek (*Hebrew Origins*, 1936, p. 11), while Eerdmans (*Alttestamentliche Studien*, i, 1908, pp. 64 f.) argued that Ḥabiru = Ḥa-wi-ru, which he connected with Egyptian Ḥaru, which was a name for part of Palestine, and Sidney Smith (*The Early History of Assyria*, 1928, pp. 192 ff.) suggested that Ḥabiru meant people from the district of Ḥabir (perhaps a place in the desert west of Babylonia, cf. Ḥafiru mentioned in a late Aramaic document). Jirku (*Z.A.W.*, N.F. v, 1928, p. 211) says the question whether Ḥabiru is appellative or not ʿein Streit um des Kaisers Bart ist', and adds ʿJedes Nomen propr. war einmal ein Appellativum'. Similarly Gustavs, *T.L.Z.* l, 1925, col. 603.

They are philologically possible, but no more can be said.[1] I am happy to find that de Vaux, for whose sober judgement I have a very great respect, now confesses himself less sure of this equation than he was.[2] If the equation is maintained, it must be on the basis of non-philological evidence, and to that we must next turn.[3]

In the Nuzu texts the word Ḥabiru appears to be a social, rather than an ethnic, term,[4] and it is claimed that this was its fundamental meaning.[5] It stood for a class of slaves.[6] This meaning well fits the Egyptian references to the ʿAperu[7] and it is argued that in the Amarna letters we have to do, not with an external invasion of tribes pressing into the land, but with social revolution.[8] This seems to me to be a precarious hypothesis. The reference to the gods of the Ḥabiru[9] in Hittite texts suggests that

[1] Cf. what I wrote in *P.E.Q.* 1940, p. 93: 'It is to be observed that while the equation Ḥapiru = עברים is still possible, it remains as uncertain as it has always been.'

[2] Cf. *R.B.* liv, 1947, p. 286. Earlier he had said (*Z.A.W.*, N.F. xv, 1938, p. 233): 'L'équivalence entre Hébreux, Ḥabiru et ʿApiru, à laquelle d'ailleurs la philologie ne fait pas d'objection sérieuse, peut être considérée comme solide.'

[3] Albright (*J.B.L.* xliii, 1924, p. 392) observes: 'The picture of the Ḥabiru which we draw from our inscriptional sources is very like that we draw from our analysis of the Old Testament traditions concerning the Hebrews.' Cf. de Vaux, *R.B.* lv, 1948, pp. 340 ff.

[4] Cf. Speiser, *A.A.S.O.R.* xiii, 1933, p. 35: 'The Ḥabiru of Arrapḫa have only one thing in common: they do not enjoy full civic rights.' See also Chiera, *A.J.S.L.* xlix, 1932–3, pp. 115–24; Lewy, *H.U.C.A.* xiv, 1939, pp. 587–623, xv, 1940, pp. 47–58.

[5] Speiser (loc. cit., p. 37) holds that though originally an appellative it developed an ethnic meaning. So also Meek, *Hebrew Origins*, 1936, p. 12. Cf. O'Callaghan, *Aram Naharaim*, 1948, p. 32.

[6] Lewy (*H.U.C.A.* xiv, 1939, pp. 687 ff.) holds that they were not slaves but servants, and he brings them into relation with the Hebrews of Ex. xxi. 2 ff., Dt. xv. 12 ff. (cf. *H.U.C.A.* xv, 1940, pp. 47 ff.). Jack, however, is not convinced (*P.E.Q.* 1940, pp. 113 f.). It is frequently emphasized that these Ḥabiru slaves were voluntary slaves (so Speiser, loc. cit., p. 35). That they were also foreigners is also clear (cf. Speiser, loc. cit.; Lewy, *H.U.C.A.* xiv, 1939, pp. 603 ff.).

[7] Chiera (*A.J.S.L.* xlix, 1932–3, pp. 115 ff.) and Wilson (ibid., pp. 275 ff.) both think that in Nuzu and in Egyptian texts a contemptuous note came into the word.

[8] Cf. Kraeling, *A.J.S.L.* lviii, 1941, p. 240. This is not a recent view, but one that has been held for half a century. Cf. Reisner, *J.B.L.* xvi, 1897, p. 145: 'The part the Ḥabiru play in Canaan is that of foreign mercenaries, and not that of an invading horde or of a confederacy of tribes.'

[9] Cf. Albright, *J.B.L.* xliii, 1924, p. 391 n.; Jack, *P.E.Q.* 1940, p. 107; Rowley, ibid., 1942, pp. 44 f. In Hittite texts there are references to the gods

we are dealing with ethnic tribes, rather than with a social class, since it is unlikely that social classes had their own deities. Moreover, it is easy to see how an ethnic term could develop a non-ethnic usage, and become equivalent to slave, in a community where large numbers of people of this tribal group were reduced to slavery.[1] We know that in later times the originally ethnic

of the SA-GAZ and to the gods of the Ḥabiru. It has been argued that the latter should be read 'the gods Ḥabiru', though Gustavs (*Z.A.W.*, N.F. iii, 1926, p. 31 n.) observes that ilâni Ḥabir*u* is nowhere found. An Assyrian text, however (cf. Schroeder, *Keilschrifttexte aus Assur verschiedenen Inhalts*, 1920, 42 II:9, Pl. 37; cf. p. xiv), refers to 'the god Ḥabiru' in the singular. Cf. Jirku, *O.L.Z.* xxiv, 1921, pp. 246 f.; id., *Z.A.W.*, N.F. iii, 1926, pp. 237 ff.; Gustavs, *Z.A.W.* xl, 1922, pp. 313 f., N.F. iii, 1926, pp. 25 ff., and *A.f.O.* xiv, 1941–4, p. 202; Landsberger, *Kleinasiatische Forschungen*, i, 1929, pp. 326 f. Cf. also Gustavs, *Z.A.W.*, N.F. xvii, 1940–1, pp. 158 f., where evidence for the god Ḥabiru is adduced from Kirkuk. Kraeling (*A.J.S.L.* lviii, 1941, p. 253 n.) is doubtful if the god Ḥabiru derived his name from the Ḥabiru people, and argues that the fact that the Ḥabiru were a social class makes it difficult to believe that they could lend their name to a divinity. It is equally difficult to believe that a social class—so widely spread as the Ḥabiru are now known to have been—had special gods. It is certainly much easier to believe that an ethnic group had its own deities, and even shared its name with a deity, but that its name fell on bad days where many of its members sank in the social scale.

[1] Cf. Wilson, *A.J.S.L.* xlix, 1932–3, pp. 275–80. Speiser thinks a non-ethnic term could develop an ethnic meaning (loc. cit., p. 37), but this view is criticized by Jack (*P.E.Q.* 1940, pp. 113 ff.) and by Kraeling (*A.J.S.L.* lviii, 1941, pp. 243 f.), though from quite different angles. Cf. *P.E.Q.* 1942, p. 51, where I have said: 'Speiser's view that a non-ethnic term tended to develop an ethnic use is very improbable, since there is nothing to suggest that in a later age any ethnic unity was felt, in association with this term, between Ḥabiru of the various districts where they are known to have been found.' If Hebrews and Ḥabiru are associated together we have an intelligible development. The Hebrews came from Babylonia to Palestine via northern Mesopotamia, yet in neither stage of their migration did all their kin accompany them. It is not, therefore, surprising that we find Ḥabiru in Babylonia and in northern Mesopotamia as well as in Palestine. (Cf. *R.Ass.* xii, 1915, pp. 114 f., where Scheil publishes evidence of the presence of Ḥabiru in Babylonia in the time of Rim Sin.) The Hebrews retained for a time their links with their kindred in the north, and Isaac and Jacob both sought wives from among them, as they would hardly have been expected to do if the only real link between them was social status. In the north, however, where we know that Ḥabiru acquired a social significance, the ethnic consciousness faded and the term fell out of use. The Hebrews of Palestine, therefore, who retained their ethnic consciousness, though transferred to the name Israel, lost their contacts with their kindred, and no longer felt any ethnic unity with the northern peoples of their own day, though they remembered that their fathers had come from those regions. The contrary theory offers no explanation (*a*) of the gods of the Ḥabiru, or (*b*) of the Hebrew traditions that at the

term Chaldaean was used for a soothsayer, and in a similar way Ḥabiru or 'Aperu could be used with a nuance of contempt, and be applied loosely to non-members of the ethnic group from which the social class derived its name.[1]

Parzen draws attention to the derogatory nuance that attaches to the word 'Hebrew' in the Old Testament,[2] and others have noted the same thing.[3] As Kraeling says: 'It is a fact that the term is chosen (when chosen at all) in situations where the Israelite is not a free citizen in a free community or on a free soil.'[4] Kraeling himself thinks it is an attractive possibility that the term 'Hebrews' came into vogue amongst the Israelites at some time in the early monarchy 'as a result of Israelite self-orientation in the world in which it had become a power'.[5] This seems doubly improbable. In the first place, the term disappears almost completely from the Old Testament with the establishment of the monarchy,[6] and there is no evidence that it was ever associated with Israelite nationalism.[7] Indeed, the Old Testa-

---

beginning of the development there was a sense of ethnic links between the districts in which Ḥabiru are known to have been found, viz. Babylonia, northern Mesopotamia, and Palestine. Moreover, if it is supposed that an originally non-ethnic term developed an ethnic meaning in Palestine only, we are still faced with the difficulty of the gods of the Ḥabiru, and in addition are left without explanation of the fact that the Biblical traditions of its ethnic use relate to early and not to late times.

[1] Cf. Scheil (*R.Ass.* xii, 1915, p. 114): 'On les appela bientôt les Ḥabiri, du nom d'un de leurs principaux groupes. Entre temps, le mode et le milieu de leur recrutement avaient pu changer, mais leur rôle primordial de défendre ces contrées contre l'ingérence égyptienne, au profit de l'influence babylonienne, persista avec le nom de Ḥabiri, jusque sous la dynastie Kassite, aux temps de la dix-huitième dynastie égyptienne.' It is doubtful how far we should give them a pro-Babylonian role.

[2] Cf. *A.J.S.L.* xlix, 1932–3, pp. 254 ff.

[3] Cf. Lewy, *O.L.Z.* xxx, 1927, pp. 828 ff.; Noth, *Festschrift Otto Procksch*, 1934, p. 110; Meek, *Hebrew Origins*, 1936, pp. 6 ff.; von Rad, in Kittel's *Th.W.B.* iii, 1938, pp. 357–9.

[4] Cf. *A.J.S.L.* lviii, 1941, p. 245.   [5] Ibid., p. 246.

[6] It stands in 1 Sam. xiii. 3, where, however, ישמעו העברים = 'Let the Hebrews hear', sounds somewhat strange on the lips of Saul. LXX has ἠθετήκασιν οἱ δοῦλοι = 'the slaves have rebelled' = פשעו העבדים (ἀθετέω frequently renders פשע and its synonyms). Since these would appear to be the words of the Philistines, they should perhaps be transferred to follow פלשתים, though there is no need to follow the LXX in reading העבדים. Cf. Kittel, *Biblia Hebraica*, 3rd ed., 1933, ad loc. König (*Z.A.W.*, N.F. v, 1928, pp. 204 ff.) reviews the passages in the Old Testament where the Hebrews are referred to.

[7] Cf. Alt, *Die Ursprünge des israelitischen Rechts*, 1934, p. 21 n., where it is said that on Israelite lips with this word 'ein Ton der Selbstdemütigung oder

ment itself indicates that Hebrews, a gentilic formed from the eponymous ancestor Eber,[1] covered a much wider group of peoples.[2] And in the second place, it is improbable that a term which is generally employed in a pejorative sense was actually the symbol of self-esteem. Its use in the Old Testament is, as Kraeling observes,[3] 'spotty' in its distribution. In the time of Jacob, before the Descent into Egypt, we find references to the Hebrews being in Palestine, and we find a Hebrew messenger being sent from Hebron to Shechem in the age when treachery at Shechem was being perpetrated.[4] Those who went down into Egypt are called Hebrews, and they are still called Hebrews in the days of the Oppression. But when they came out of Egypt and entered Palestine they ceased to have this name, though it reappears in the period of the establishment of the monarchy, when they were crushed by the Philistines. We find it on the lips of the Philistines, where it is used contemptuously,[5] but never does it stand as a term of national pride. In the pejorative use, both in the Old Testament and elsewhere, therefore, we have a non-philological ground of association of the terms 'Aperu and Ḥabiru with the Hebrews.[6]

That Ḥabiru is of much wider application than to cover the Israelites is abundantly clear from the non-Biblical sources already referred to. But that is in full accord with the evidence of the Old Testament in respect to Hebrews, as has been noted. The dictum of Böhl, that 'all Israelites were Hebrews, but not all Hebrews were Israelites',[7] is often quoted. It is criticized by

im anderen Fall der Verachtung, aber niemals ein nationales Hochgefühl mitschwingt'. Rapaport (*P.E.Q.* 1941, pp. 161 f.) denies this.

[1] Gen. x. 25. [2] Cf. Guillaume, *P.E.Q.* 1946, pp. 64 ff.
[3] Cf. *A.J.S.L.* lviii, 1941, p. 241. [4] Gen. xxxvii. 13. Cf. Gen. xxxiv.
[5] 1 Sam. iv. 9.
[6] Hempel (*Althebräische Literatur*, 1930, p. 8) says of the Ḥabiru: 'Ich sehe in ihnen Stammverwandte der später einbrechenden Israeliten, auf deren Konto die Eroberung von Jericho und ha-'Ai zu setzen ist und die allmählich, wie schon die Aufnahme der Traditionen über ihre Taten unter die israelitische Sagenüberlieferung zeigt, in dem israelitischen Volke aufgegangen sind, nach 1. Sam. 14, 21 nicht vor dem 11. Jahrhundert.' The incursion of the Israelite tribes he places at 1230–1220 B.C., thus distinguishing between the Hebrews and the Israelites.
[7] Cf. *Kanaanäer und Hebräer*, 1911, p. 67. Hallock (*apud* Mercer, *The Tell El-Amarna Tablets*, ii, 1939, pp. 883 f.) endorses this view, and also maintains that SA-GAZ is a wider term than Ḥabiru = Hebrews. Albright (*J.A.O.S.* xlviii, 1928, p. 184) observes: 'SA-GAZ were naturally of every race, but predominantly Ḥabiru, a fact which naturally accounts for the secondary equivalence SA-GAZ = Ḥabiru'.

Jirku,[1] and it is perhaps better to hold that the areas of meaning
of the two terms overlapped than to claim that one was wholly
included in the other.[2] We should also recognize that if the terms
'Aperu, 'prm, Ḥabiru, and עברים are allowed to be philologically
equatable, we must not equate their areas of meaning in the different communities where they were used.[3] Again, the terms
more probably overlapped in their use. Yet, in view of what has
been said above, in so far as the equation of Ḥabiru and Hebrews
is maintained, it tells against the fifteenth-century date of the
Exodus, rather than in its favour, since in the Biblical sources
the term Hebrews is not used of the invading Israelites under
Moses and Joshua, whereas it is used of those who went down
into Egypt when they were in Palestine prior to the Descent. In
so far as this doubtful equation carries any weight, therefore, it
does not favour the identification of Joshua's attack with the
events recorded in the Amarna letters.

[1] Cf. *Die Wanderungen der Hebräer*, 1924, pp. 31 f.
[2] Cf. Guillaume, *P.E.Q.* 1946, p. 68, and Jirku, op. cit., p. 32.
[3] Cf. what I have written in *P.E.Q.* 1942, p. 53: 'So long as the philological equation of Ḥabiru or Ḥapiru with 'Aperu and Hebrews remains
possible but uncertain, it seems wiser to refrain from offering an etymology
for 'ibrim, since any suggestion must assume either the admittedly doubtful
equation or the equally doubtful lack of equation. And for the view that
Ḥabiru and Hebrews are terms that overlap, and that the Amarna letters
are relevant to the history of the Hebrews, it seems wiser to continue to rely
on non-philological grounds. . . . They do not yield any "proof", but I think
they yield stronger probability than anything that can be alleged against
them.'

THE BIBLICAL TRADITIONS

I N the previous lecture we examined the extra-Biblical evidence
relevant to the consideration of the period of Israel's Sojourn
in Egypt and the Conquest and Settlement of the land of Canaan.
We now turn to examine some elements of the Biblical traditions, at which we must look in the light of the archaeological
evidence. And here we find that within the Bible we have a
chronological framework, as well as traditions which are fitted
into the framework. 1 Kgs. vi. 1 places the Exodus 480 years
before the founding of the Temple, or *circa* 1447 B.C. Exod. xii.
40 places the Descent into Egypt 430 years before the Exodus, or
circa 1877 B.C. This would bring the Descent into Egypt long
before the Hyksos period, while for Abram's migration from
Ḥarran to Palestine we should be carried back a further 215
years to *circa* 2092 B.C. For in Gen. xii. 4 we read that Abram
was seventy-five years old when he left Ḥarran, and in Gen. xxi. 5
that he was one hundred years old when Isaac was born. Since
Gen. xxv. 26 states that Isaac was sixty years old when Jacob
was born, and Gen. xlvii. 9 puts the age of Jacob at 130 when he
went into Egypt, we have a total of 215 years from the migration
of Abram to the Descent into Egypt.

Here we find ourselves immediately in the midst of a highly
complex problem once more. For the date of Abraham reliance
has commonly been put on Gen. xiv. 1, and the identification of
Amraphel, king of Shinar, with Ḥammurabi, king of Babylon.
But modern research and discovery have made Ḥammurabi
career about among the centuries in a most disturbing fashion,
and there can be no security for the Biblical chronology by link-
ing Abraham to Ḥammurabi. A quarter of a century ago the
Cambridge Ancient History assigned Ḥammurabi to 2123–2081 B.C.[1]

---

[1] Cf. *C.A.H.* i, 2nd ed., 1924, p. 154. So, also, King, *History of Babylon*, 1919,
pp. 106–11. Albright (*R.Ass.* xviii, 1921, p. 94) considered this date practically certain, and emphasized its agreement with Nabonidus's statement
which placed Ḥammurabi 700 years before Burnaburiash (ibid., p. 86). See
also Langdon and Fotheringham, *The Venus Tablets of Ammizaduga*, 1928,
pp. 66 f., where Ḥammurabi's reign was assigned to 2067–2025 B.C. For a
criticism of the arguments here presented cf. Neugebauer, *O.L.Z.* xxxii, 1929,
cols. 913–21 (see also ibid. xlii, 1939, cols. 407–11), and for support for the
positions of Langdon and Fotheringham, cf. Sidersky, in *Dissertationes in
honorem E. Mahler*, 1937, pp. 253 ff., and Shortt, *The Journal of the British
Astronomical Association*, lvii, 1947, p. 208. Thureau-Dangin (*R.Ass.* xxiv, 1927,

This date seemed to agree very closely with the Biblical chronology, which would put Abraham's migration from Ḥarran some
eleven years before the death of Ḥammurabi. Recently found
evidence from Mari, however, has brought about a re-dating of
Ḥammurabi, and while there is much divergence of opinion as to
his date, there is agreement that he must be brought much lower
down in time.[1] In 1937 Thureau-Dangin published evidence
that Shamshi-Adad I of Assyria was contemporary with the early
part of Ḥammurabi's reign,[2] on the basis of which Albright
argued that the accession of Ḥammurabi must be dated *circa*
1870 B.C.[3] In 1940, however, on the basis of further evidence
found at Mari and discussed by Sidney Smith,[4] Albright brought
this date down a further seventy years, and dated Ḥammurabi
1800–1760 B.C.,[5] while in the same year Sidney Smith published
an important monograph in which he argued that the Babylonian king should be dated 1792–1750 B.C.[6] In the same year
Ungnad quite independently and along other lines reached the
conclusion that his reign covered the years 1791–1749 B.C.,[7] while
Sidersky, again apparently independently, assigned it to the
years 1848/7–1803/2 B.C.[8] Two years later further material was

pp. 181 ff.) argued for the date 2003–1961 B.C., while Pirot (*Supplément au
Dictionnaire de la Bible*, i, 1928, cols. 7–14) decided in favour of the date
1947–1905 B.C.

[1] For a brief review of the discussion cf. Contenau, *Manuel d'Archéologie
orientale*, iv, 1947, pp. 1804 ff.

[2] Cf. *R.Ass.* xxxiv, 1937, pp. 135–9. See also Jean, ibid. xxxv, 1938,
pp. 107 ff.

[3] Cf. *B.A.S.O.R.*, No. 69, Feb. 1938, pp. 18 f. Parrot (*Syria*, xix, 1938,
p. 184) held that this date was too low.

[4] Cf. *Antiquaries Journal*, xix, 1939, pp. 45 ff.

[5] Cf. *B.A.S.O.R.*, No. 77, Feb. 1940, pp. 25 f. Meanwhile Thureau-
Dangin had briefly discussed the date of Ḥammurabi but without reaching
any definite conclusion, save that Albright's earlier date for Ḥammurabi's
accession was too high (cf. *R.Ass.* xxxvi, 1939, pp. 24–8).

[6] Cf. *Alalakh and Chronology*, 1940. This date was followed by Noth,
Z.D.P.V. lxv, 1942, p. 15. Cf. also Kern, *J.E.O.L.* x, 1945–8, pp. 481–90.
Engnell (cf. *S.B.U.* i, 1948, col. 777) gives Ḥammurabi's date as 1800–1750 B.C.

[7] Cf. *Die Venustafeln und das neunte Jahr Samsuilunas*, 1940, p. 17. Cf. Ungnad,
Orientalia, xiii, 1944, pp. 83 ff. In *A.f.O.* xiii, 1940, pp. 145 f. Ungnad dated
Ḥammurabi 1801–1759 B.C. Hrozný (*Histoire de l'Asie Antérieure*, 1947, pp. 121,
125) follows Ungnad in assigning Ḥammurabi to the years 1791–1749 B.C.

[8] Cf. *R.Ass.* xxxvii, 1940, pp. 45–54. Thureau-Dangin (*Mémoires de
l'Académie des Inscriptions et Belles Lettres*, xliii, 2ᵉ partie, 1942, p. 258) observes:
'La position que Sidney Smith et Ungnad sont amenés à donner au début de
la dynastie cassite relativement à la première dynastie babylonienne se heurte
à des invraisemblances historiques qui suffisent, je crois, à faire écarter la solu-

published by Poebel in the form of the Khorsabad King List,[1] and this led Albright to bring the date of Ḥammurabi down still lower to 1728–1686 B.C.[2] This date has been rejected by Smith, who adheres to his own dates,[3] and who is followed by Mallowan, who finds that Albright's date creates many difficulties in connexion with Cretan evidence,[4] while Rowton,[5] de Vaux,[6] and O'Callaghan[7] follow Albright; Rowton concluding his study of Mesopotamian chronology by saying: 'Should it be established that our present interpretation of the KKL[8] is the right one, it will have to be considered that Albright's date for Ḥammurabi is almost certainly correct.'[9] Along entirely different lines and again quite independently, using the materials preserved by Berossus, Cornelius reached the same conclusion in the same year as Albright.[10] More recently Böhl has expressed some hesita-

tion qu'ils proposent. Tel n'est pas le cas en ce qui concerne la solution Sidersky. Il serait sûrement exagéré d'en déduire qu'elle est historiquement probable, mais elle est "possible".' For a brief account of the discussions of the question published in 1940, cf. Dussaud, *Syria*, xxi, 1940, pp. 238, 357 f. Cf. also Vernet, *Sefarad*, viii, 1948, pp. 428–34.

[1] Cf. *J.N.E.S.* i, 1942, pp. 247 ff., 460 ff.; ii, 1943, pp. 56 ff. Poebel dated Shamshi-Adad I 1726–1694 B.C. (pp. 285 ff.). Cf. also Cavaignac, *R.Ass.* xl, 1945–6, pp. 17 ff. Weill (*Chronique d'Égypte*, No. 41, Jan. 1946, p. 42) refers to this list as 'd'autant plus célèbre qu'elle reste mystérieuse', and prefers to leave it out of account until fuller information about it and study of its contents are available.

[2] *B.A.S.O.R.*, No. 88, Dec. 1942, pp. 28–31. Already Neugebauer (*J.A.O.S.* lxi, 1941, p. 59) had said: 'If historical evidence places Hammurabi around 1800, then the Venus observations require for his reign either the years 1792–1750 or an interval 56 (or even 64) years earlier or later.' Schaeffer (*Ugaritica*, 1939, p. 18 n.) on the basis of Ras Shamra evidence had suggested an eighteenth- or seventeenth-century date, and more recently has decided for a date between 1800 and 1700 B.C. (*Syria*, xxv, 1946–8, p. 187).

[3] Cf. *A.J.A.* xlix, 1945, pp. 18–23. Cf. Albright, *B.A.S.O.R.*, No. 99, Oct. 1945, p. 10 n., and *Bi.Or.* v, 1948, p. 126, where some reply is given.

[4] Cf. *Iraq*, ix, 1947, p. 4 n. Cf. also p. 86 n.: 'A reduction of the date of Khammurabi's accession to 1728 B.C. is therefore in my opinion hardly compatible with the stratigraphic evidence.'

[5] Cf. *Iraq*, viii, 1946, pp. 94–110.

[6] Cf. *R.B.* liii, 1945, p. 335.   [7] Cf. *Aram Naharaim*, 1948, pp. 6–11.

[8] i.e. the Khorsabad King List.

[9] Cf. *Iraq*, loc. cit., p. 110. In *Bi.Or.* v, 1948, p. 126, Albright states that Schaumberger, in an unpublished paper, supports the date 1728 B.C. for the accession of Ḥammurabi, but with an alternative date 1736 B.C. Cavaignac (*R.Ass.* xl, 1945–6, p. 22) places the beginning of Ḥammurabi's reign in 1720 B.C., with 1728 as a possible alternative.

[10] Cf. *Klio*, xxxv, 1942, p. 7. Weidner (*A.f.O.* xiv, 1941–4, p. 367) says: 'so würde der Ansatz von Cornelius für Ḥammurapi: 1728–1686 v. Chr. recht gut passen.' In *F.u.F.* xx, 1944, p. 75, Cornelius gives Ḥammurabi's date as

tion about the precision of this result, while agreeing substantially with it, and contents himself with saying that the greater part of Ḥammurabi's reign of forty-two years is to be placed after the year 1700 B.C.[1] Finally, van den Waerden in an important article[2] has shown that the mathematical probability that Cornelius and Albright are right is very far greater than that Ungnad and Smith are right.

The evidence on which Albright's view rests[3] consists of: (1) the year formula of the eighth year of Ammiṣaduqa, tenth king of the First Dynasty of Babylon—of which Ḥammurabi was the sixth king—in terms of the risings and settings of the planet Venus; (2) Mari evidence that Ḥammurabi was contemporary with Shamshi-Adad I;[4] (3) the approximate fixation of the date of Shamshi-Adad I by the Khorsabad King List; (4) a Mari reference to a Byblian prince named Yantin-ḥamu who appears to figure in the form Entin in an Egyptian inscription which must come from the period 1740–1720 B.C.;[5] (5) evidence of Mesopotamian pottery which would date levels in which cunei-form tablets of the time of Shamshi-Adad I were found about three centuries earlier than levels which can be dated by Nuzu evidence in the fifteenth century B.C.[6]

1729–1687 B.C. Weill, however, in *Chronique d'Égypte*, No. 41, Jan. 1946, p. 42, speaks of Cornelius's 'méthode de datation hasardeuse, certes! tendancieuse, croit-on sentir, dans le sens d'une sorte de vertige de rajeunissement des dates'.

[1] Cf. *King Ḥammurabi of Babylon in the Setting of his Time*, 1946, p. 12. See also *Bi.Or.* i, 1944, pp. 55 ff., 76 ff., 101 ff. Van der Meer (*J.E.O.L.* ix, 1944, pp. 143 f.) took a position between those of Smith and Albright, dating Ḥammurabi 1778–1736 B.C. but more recently has proposed (*The Ancient Chronology of Western Asia and Egypt*, 1947, p. 22) a later but less precise date, $1712+x$ to $1670+x$, where x (cf. p. 13) cannot be more than twenty years, and may be but a few years (cf. *Orientalia Neerlandica*, 1948, pp. 38 ff.). Kramer (*A.J.A.* lii, 1948, p. 163 n.) says: 'On the data available at present it seems difficult to decide between the conflicting views, and the date 1750 for the beginning of Ḥammurabi's reign is merely a makeshift compromise which may prove to be some four decades off one way or the other.'

[2] Cf. *J.E.O.L.* x, 1945–8, pp. 414–24.

[3] An excellent and clear, but brief, summary of the evidence is given by O'Callaghan, op. cit., pp. 6–11. Cf. also de Vaux, *R.B.* liii, 1946, pp. 328–36.

[4] Gelb (*Hurrians and Subarians*, 1944, pp. vi f.) has reserves about this equation, and says that intensive study of the Mari texts leads him to think that Ḥammurabi's reign synchronized with the period of disorganization under Shamshi-Adad's successor.

[5] Cf. *B.A.S.O.R.*, No. 99, Oct. 1945, pp. 9–18. Cf. earlier *B.A.S.O.R.*, No. 77, Feb. 1940, pp. 27 f., and Noth, *Z.D.P.V.* lxv, 1942, pp. 30 f. n.

[6] Cf. Rowton, loc. cit.; de Vaux, loc. cit.; O'Callaghan, loc. cit.; also Mallowan, *apud* Thureau-Dangin, *R.Ass.* xxxvi, 1939, pp. 26 f.

Almost every one of these pieces of evidence involves highly technical questions, on which there is some difference of opinion. Yet it is significant that the margin of difference between Smith's date and Albright's is less than three-quarters of a century, and in either case Ḥammurabi of Babylon cannot be placed anywhere near the date at which the Biblical chronology places Abraham.[1] Moreover, it now transpires that there were no less than three Ḥammurabis[2] at that time, so that if Amraphel is to be identified with any of them, Abraham must have belonged to the eighteenth or seventeenth century B.C.[3] If the Biblical chronology would put the Descent into Egypt long before the Hyksos period, the identification of Amraphel with Ḥammurabi would now seem to put it after the Hyksos period.

That identification has never been unchallenged, however, and O'Callaghan observes that 'the number of those who identify Amraphel of Gen. 14:1 with the great Ḥammurabi of Babylon grows steadily smaller'.[4] More than twenty years ago Albright

[1] It should, however, be added that Parrot is doubtful of the new chronology, and thinks it involves serious difficulties. Cf. *Archéologie mésopotamienne*, 1946, p. 12.

[2] These were Ḥammurabi of Babylon, Ḥammurabi of Aleppo, and Ḥammurabi of Kurda. For the last of these cf. Jean, *R.Ass.* xxxv, 1938, pp. 107 ff. See also *Actes du XXᵉ Congrès international des Orientalistes*, 1940, pp. 116 f., where a fourth Ḥammurabi is mentioned.

[3] Cf. Böhl, *King Ḥammurabi of Babylon in the Setting of his Time*, 1946, p. 17: 'If, therefore, there is, notwithstanding all difficulties, question of a certain Ḥammurabi, it is at any rate the Ḥammurabi of Aleppo.' Already in *A.J.S.L.* liii, 1936–7, pp. 253 ff., Gelb had suggested the region of Aleppo as a more likely home for Amraphel than Babylon, while Albright in *A.J.S.L.* xl, 1923–4, pp. 125 ff., had suggested that it was in northern Mesopotamia. Cf. Jean, *Bi.Or.* v, 1948, p. 128. Böhl prefers, however, to think of Amûr-pî-el as a possible corruption of Amût-pî-el, king of Qaṭna on the Orontes (loc. cit., pp. 17 f.). O'Callaghan (*Aram Naharaim*, 1948, p. 31 n.) thinks this suggestion attractive but hazardous; while Dougherty inclines to accept it (*Scripture*, iii, 1948, p. 99). Jean thinks the identification of Amraphel with Amûr-pî-el probable enough, but finds it difficult to think of Amût-pî-el of Qaṭna, since the shift from *r* to *t* is doubtful (cf. *Bi.Or.* v, 1948, p. 128).

[4] Cf. op. cit., p. 31. Cf. Hooke, *In the Beginning*, 1947, p. 72: 'the now generally rejected identification of Hammurabi with Amraphel'. Similarly de Vaux (*Z.A.W.*, n.f. xv, 1938, p. 231) regards this identification as 'trop fragile', while Speiser (*A.A.S.O.R.* xiii, 1933, p. 45 n.) says the equation of the names is philologically impossible. While not ruling out the equation of the names, Böhl (op. cit., p. 18) says 'Ḥammurabi of Babylon is out of the question here and has nothing to do with Genesis xiv.' Nyberg, on the other hand (*A.R.W.* xxxv, 1938, p. 357), finds no difficulty in the identification of Amraphel and Ḥammurabi. Thirty years earlier Dhorme had said (*R.B.*,

maintained that 'Amraphel and Ḥammurabi are entirely distinct persons',[1] and observed that 'we may, as sober historians,
breathe a sigh of relief at the passing of this mirage'.[2] It is,
indeed, probable, as de Vaux observes,[3] that the identification
of Amraphel and Ḥammurabi has only enjoyed such favour
because it made it possible to place Abraham in the setting of
world history.

On quite other grounds, however, a seventeenth-century date
for Abraham has long been maintained.[4] Thirty years ago Kraeling maintained this date,[5] and it was adopted by Jirku[6] and
Albright.[7] It was also followed by Böhl,[8] who had earlier adopted
an even later date,[9] in the thirteenth century B.C. Böhl based
himself, not on the doubtful Amraphel, but on Tidal, king of Goim,
who had always been a problem to earlier identifiers. Here
he proposed the identification with Tudḫalia, king of the Hittites. At first Böhl suggested Tudḫalia II, but then instead proposed Tudḫalia I, who belonged to the seventeenth century B.C.
Dhorme opposed this view, and argued for a date for Abraham
in the latter part of the twentieth century B.C.[10] Albright moved

N.S. v, 1908, p. 208): 'Il nous semble donc hors de conteste que le nom
d'Amraphel roi de Šinʿâr est bien dû à une déformation de Hammourabi et
que, par conséquent, l'auteur du chapitre xiv de la Genèse a pu utiliser un
original cunéiforme.' Deimel also accepted the identification (*Biblica*, viii,
1927, pp. 350 ff.).

[1] Cf. *J.P.O.S.* vi, 1926, p. 179. See also *J.S.O.R.* x, 1926, p. 232.
[2] Cf. *J.P.O.S.* i, 1921, p. 71.
[3] Cf. *R.B.* lv, 1948, p. 331.
[4] Schmidtke (*Die Einwanderung Israels in Kanaan*, 1933, pp. 50 f.) assigns
Abraham to *circa* 1400 B.C.   [5] Cf. *Aram and Israel*, 1918, p. 32.
[6] Cf. *Z.A.W.* xxxix, 1921, pp. 152–6, 313 f., and *Geschichte des Volkes Israel*,
1931, pp. 61–5.
[7] Cf. *A.J.S.L.* xl, 1923–4, pp. 125–33; *B.A.S.O.R.*, No. 14, Apr. 1924, p. 7;
A.A.S.O.R. vi, 1926, pp. 62 f. In *J.P.O.S.* vi, 1927, p. 227, Albright gave the
date as 1800–1600 B.C. Cf. Procksch, *Genesis*, 1924, p. 513.
[8] Cf. 'Tud'alia I, Zeitgenosse Abrahams, um 1650 v. Chr.', in *Z.A.W.*,
N.F. i, 1924, pp. 148–53; *Das Zeitalter Abrahams*, 1930. Cf. also Kroeze,
Genesis Veertien, 1937, pp. 3 ff.
[9] Cf. 'Die Könige von Genesis 14', in *Z.A.W.* xxxvi, 1916, pp. 65–73,
where he had assigned Abraham to the time of Tudḫalia II, *circa* 1250 B.C.
Schmidtke (*Die Einwanderung Israels in Kanaan*, 1933, pp. 50 f.) placed him in
the Amarna age.
[10] Cf. *R.B.* xl, 1931, pp. 506–14. Gruenthaner (*C.B.Q.* iv, 1942, pp. 360–63,
v, 1943, pp. 85–7) held that Chedorlaomer is to be identified with an unnamed king of the Elamites who overthrew the third dynasty of Ur, and who
is to be dated about 2100 B.C.; that Amraphel is not to be identified with
Ḥammurabi but with a puppet king of Babylonia under the suzerainty of
Chedorlaomer, of whose existence no evidence is offered; that Tidal may have

back some way towards this date, and on the basis of his own and others' explorations in the Dead Sea area thought of a date not earlier than the nineteenth century B.C.[1] Here Wright[2] and Burrows,[3] who so frequently follow Albright, went all the way to Dhorme's date, and assigned Abraham to the twentieth century B.C.—Burrows to the beginning of that century. Albright, however, has now returned to the seventeenth-century date, and again maintains that there seems to be 'historical warrant for dating the expedition described in Gen. xiv in the late seventeenth century B.C.'[4] and adds that 'if this view proves to be correct, the events described from oral sources in Gen. xii–l could be dated between 1700 and 1550 B.C.'[5] He bases himself now on the identification of Chedorlaomer—which had earlier been supposed to be equivalent to Kudur-Lagamar, an unrecorded name, but one which bore a likely form for an Elamite sovereign—with Kuter-Naḫḫunte,[6] the third predecessor of an Elamite contemporary of Ammiṣaduqa, who would therefore most likely fall towards the end of the seventeenth century B.C., 'when Hyksos power was declining'.[7] This last observation is especially to be noted, since we are not told what becomes of the view that the Descent into Egypt took place in the Hyksos period. This latter view is still advanced by Albright in the latest edition of his book

been the leader of a wandering horde; and that Arioch was a Ḥurrian sub-king of Larsa, of whose existence again no evidence is offered. This is so completely speculative and unrelated to evidence that it can scarcely be convincing.

[1] Cf. *The Archaeology of Palestine and the Bible*, 1932, p. 137. Similarly Meek (*Hebrew Origins*, 1936, p. 14) says the nineteenth century is the upper limit for Abraham. Cf. Bea (*Biblica*, xxiv, 1943, p. 248): 'Qualunque sia la data esatta di Ḥammurapi, l'insieme dei fattori storici e culturali rende assai probabile che Abramo non sia entrato in Palestina prima del secolo XIX.' Similarly de Vaux, *R.B.* lv, 1948, p. 336.

[2] Cf. *B.A.S.O.R.*, No. 71, Oct. 1938, p. 34.

[3] Cf. *What Mean these Stones?* p. 71—'about 2000 B.C.'

[4] Cf. *B.A.S.O.R.*, No. 88, Dec. 1942, p. 35. Cf. also *J.P.O.S.* i, 1921, pp. 68 ff.

[5] Cf. *B.A.S.O.R.*, No. 88, p. 36.

[6] Cf. ibid., pp. 33–6. Cf. also O'Callaghan, *Aram Naharaim*, 1948, p. 31; de Vaux, *R.B.* lv, 1948, p. 334. Böhl (*King Ḥammurabi of Babylon*, 1946, p. 18) thinks this identification is impossible on the ground that this king was junior by some decades to the others in Gen. xiv. 1. It should be added that Böhl (op. cit., p. 17) identifies Arioch with Arriwuk, the son of Zimrilim of Mari. Cf. *Bi.Or.* ii, 1945, p. 66. Zimrilim was defeated by Ḥammurabi of Babylon in the thirty-second year of his reign (cf. Thureau-Dangin, *Symbolae Paulo Koschaker dedicatae*, 1939, pp. 119 f.).

[7] Ibid., p. 36.

From the Stone Age to Christianity.[1] If Abraham flourished at the end of the seventeenth century B.C., it is hard to see how the Descent into Egypt can be placed a hundred years earlier.[2]

By earlier writers the narrative of Gen. xiv was treated as a late Midrash, devoid of historical worth.[3] It was felt to be improb-

---

[1] Cf. pp. 150, 184.

[2] Albright at one time suggested that the story of Abraham's going into Egypt and the Descent of Jacob are but duplicates of the same tradition. Cf. *J.B.L.* xxxvii, 1918, p. 137, where he suggested that Abraham may have commanded some Hebrew elements in the Hyksos army of invasion, while Jacob and Joseph were tribal deities of the people Abraham led. More recently he has abandoned this view, and stated that 'the figures of Abraham, Isaac, Jacob, and Joseph appear before us as real personalities' (*From the Stone Age to Christianity*, p. 183). Cf., too, *J.S.O.R.* x, 1926, p. 268: 'The writer formerly regarded Abram and Jacob as representing contemporary phases of Hebrew history.' He has continued to connect the Descent of Jacob into Egypt with the Hyksos movement (cf. *J.P.O.S.* i, 1921, pp. 65 f.; *J.S.O.R.* x, 1926, p. 268; *B.A.S.O.R.*, No. 58, p. 15; *J.P.O.S.* xv, 1935, p. 227; *From the Stone Age to Christianity*, 2nd ed., 1946, p. 150), but by adding three or four generations arrived at the date 'somewhere between 1900 and 1750 B.C.' for Abraham's migration (ibid., p. 150). As it was in 1942 that he had transferred Abraham to the end of the seventeenth century B.C. (see above) to the period when the Hyksos power was declining, we might have expected some clearer guidance on the inconsistency with which we are left. Does Albright now really place Abraham a century later than Jacob and Joseph, or does he abandon the equation of the Descent into Egypt with the Hyksos invasion? If he does the latter, does he renew his equation of Abraham's entry into Egypt with Jacob's—falling now at the end of the Hyksos period, however, and not at their entry—or does he bring Jacob down below the Hyksos period to an appropriate time after Abraham? Between these possibilities we are left very much in the dark. While the present work has been in the press, Albright has published his work on *The Archaeology of Palestine*, 1949, in which the answer to these questions is given in the abandonment once more of the late date for Abraham. He says (p. 83): 'In the writer's present opinion the Terachid movement from Ur to Harran and westward may have taken place in the twentieth and nineteenth centuries, and Jacob's migration to Egypt may have fallen somewhere in the eighteenth or more likely the seventeenth century, in connexion with the Hyksos movement.' This leaves the identification of the names in Gen. xiv. 1 in the air once more, and he now confesses (p. 237) that this is an enigma which only the future can solve. So far as I know he has nowhere formally repudiated his earlier article of 1942, but has merely abandoned it by implication here. It should be noted that some writers have held the view that the Hyksos secured control of Egypt by gradual penetration, rather than by conquest. So Mallon, *Les Hébreux en Égypte*, 1921, p.54; Engberg, *The Hyksos Reconsidered*, 1939, p. 32. Against this view cf. von Bissing, *A.f.O.* xiv, 1941–4, p. 85.

[3] This view has still been maintained by some writers. Cf. Meinhold, *1 Mose 14*, 1911; Richardson, *B.W.* xlv, 1915, pp. 160 ff; Gunkel, *Die Psalmen*, 1926, p. 485; Budde, *Z.A.W.*, N.F. xi, 1934, p. 43; Pfeiffer, *Introduc-*

able that four powerful kings would form a confederacy against a few small towns in the neighbourhood of the Dead Sea, and even more unlikely that the household of a single man should be able to put to flight such a powerful confederacy. The fact that the Elamite king headed the alliance inspired especial doubts. For while there is evidence that Elamite power once reached far to the west, it was felt to be improbable that Ḥammurabi would have followed at the heels of the Elamite king. S. A. Cook wrote: 'The leader of the kings is Chedorlaomer, whereas Ḥammurabi was no vassal of Elam, but its chief foe; and the story, which contains anachronisms and misunderstandings, and introduces old primitive inhabitants of the land, aims chiefly at describing the glory and piety of the great ancestor of Israel.'[1] This consideration is still felt by Böhl to be very weighty. He says: 'The difficulty is not in the name, which is genuinely Elamitic, but in the identification in connexion with the question how Elam could take action so far in the West.'[2] On the whole, however, there is a tendency to-day to regard this chapter as resting on an ancient tradition,[3] and it does seem to be significant that all four

tion to the Old Testament, 1941, p. 161; Simpson, The Early Traditions of Israel, 1948, p. 72. Cf. also La Bible du Centenaire, i, 1941 (actually published in 1916), p. 16: 'D'autres, plus nombreux, ne voient dans ce récit qu'un simple midrach, c'est à dire une histoire librement imaginée dans un but d'édification, comme le judaïsme postérieur à l'exil en vit éclore beaucoup.' This view was already rejected by Winckler, who wrote (in Schrader–Winckler–Zimmern, Die Keilinschriften und das Alte Testament, 3rd ed., 1903, p. 211 n.): 'Gen. 14 ist nach meiner Auffassung bereits Bestand der alten Überlieferung und nicht erst im Exil aus nachbabylonischen Quellen entstanden.'

[1] Cf. C.A.H. i, 2nd ed., 1924, p. 236. See also S. R. Driver, The Book of Genesis (W.C.), 1904, pp. 171–3; Skinner, Genesis (I.C.C.), 1910, pp. 271–6.

[2] Cf. King Ḥammurabi of Babylon, p. 18.

[3] Cf. Hooke, In the Beginning, 1947, p. 76: 'Thus it may be said that the old view that Genesis 14 is a late midrash is no longer tenable. It suggests a dependence upon written sources and presents a political situation which is not historically impossible. Hence we may legitimately use the story to gain some idea of the historical setting of Abraham's activities.' See also Kroeze, Genesis Veertien, 1937, pp. 117 ff. There is indeed a much greater respect for the historical worth of the patriarchal narratives in general than there used to be. Wellhausen (Prolegomena to the History of Israel, E.Tr., 1885, pp. 318 f.) held that we could know nothing of the age of the patriarchs, but that the stories merely reflected the age when they were written down, while others dissolved the patriarchs into personifications of tribes. Similarly Weill (R.E.S. 1937, pp. 145–206) found little historical substance in the traditions which are embodied in the stories of Genesis. A greater respect is apparent in the work of Hooke (op. cit., p. 62) no less than of Dhorme (R.B. xxxvii, 1928, pp. 367 ff., 481 ff.; xl, 1931, pp. 364 ff., 503 ff.) and de Vaux (R.B. liii, 1946, pp. 321 ff.). Dougherty (Scripture, iii, 1948, p. 98) judiciously observes: 'There can

F

names can now be identified with a large measure of probability with seventeenth-century monarchs. Böhl's identification of Amraphel with the prince of Aleppo or of Qatna and of Arioch with the prince of Mari, with Chedorlaomer left unidentified,[1] does not appear to be very convincing, since we are left with this unidentified prince heading a confederacy which included the Hittite monarch, Tudḫalia I. Clearly Chedorlaomer would have to be the monarch of a powerful state if the Hittite king acted under his leadership, and it is not clear where there is room for a sufficiently powerful state. It would seem to be much more likely that originally, in the form of the tradition which lies behind Gen. xiv, the initial statement was intended to indicate the period when the incident recorded took place, rather than the protagonists,[2] and that it was misunderstood to name the protagonists.[3] The northern overlord's name is perhaps lost, and has been replaced by the Elamite king's. For the dating of the event we should expect famous kings to be named, and the Elamite, Babylonian, and Hittite states would appear to be more likely than obscure states, while if Arioch is correctly identified by Böhl with the prince of Mari, it should be remembered that Abraham is said to have but recently migrated from Ḥarran, and the prince of Mari may have seemed a more important person in contemporary eyes than he does to us.

In so far as Gen. xiv is of use to us for dating Abraham, therefore—and I would not press it, in view of the uncertainties that still surround it[4]—it would seem to-day to point to the seventeenth century B.C. for the migration from Ḥarran, and therefore to be quite inconsistent with the Biblical chronology of the passages to which reference has been made.

It is frequently observed that ancient tradition scaled down the Biblical chronology by 215 years by the simple device of adding the words 'in the land of Canaan' in Ex. xii. 40. This reading is found in the Samaritan Pentateuch and in the LXX, and its

be no question that certain traits of the narrative indicate tribal history, but it is unlawful to draw from this the conclusion that the Patriarchs are nothing more than figures of tribes. In this ancient literary *genre*, personal and tribal history shade off into each other.'

[1] Cf. *King Ḥammurabi of Babylon*, pp. 17 f.   [2] Cf. Lk. iii. 1 f.

[3] The commentators call attention to the defective syntax of Gen. xiv. 1 f., whereby the subject of the verb in verse 2, 'they made war', is unexpressed. Originally it may have been other than the kings of verse 1, but the editor of the chapter clearly understood it to refer to them, as he shows later in the story. Cf. Kroeze, *Genesis Veertien*, 1937, pp. 20 ff.

[4] Cf. *B.J.R.L.* xxii, 1938, p. 285.

effect is to make the 430 years cover not alone the Sojourn in Egypt, but the entire period from Abraham's migration from Ḥarran to the Exodus. It was followed by Paul[1] and by Josephus[2] and is represented in Jewish tradition,[3] and has been adopted by

[1] Gal. iii. 17. [2] *Antiquities*, II. xv. 2 (ii. 318).

[3] I am indebted to Mr. P. R. Weis for the following references: (*a*) *Gen. Rabba* lxiii. 3 (ed. Theodor, i, 1912, p. 680): 'Jacob was called Israel; for it says: "Thy name shall be called no more Jacob, but Israel" (Gen. xxxii. 28). Isaac was called Israel; for it says: "And these are the names of the children of Israel which came into Egypt, Jacob ..." (Gen. xlvi. 8). Abraham was called Israel ... R. Nathan said: "This is a deep matter ... 'Now the sojourning of the children of Israel, which they sojourned in Egypt and in the land of Canaan and in the land of Goshen was four hundred and thirty years' (Ex. xii. 40)."' (Some editions wrongly cite the irrelevant Exod. i. 1 for the second text.)

(*b*) *Mekilta of R. Simeon*, ed. Hoffmann, 1905, p. 27: '"Now the sojourning of the children of Israel, which they sojourned in Egypt was four hundred and thirty years" (Ex. xii. 40). Were the children of Israel 430 years in Egypt? Were they not there for 210 years only? Why then does it say 430 years? They sojourned many sojournings: the sojourning of Abraham in the land of the Philistines (Gen. xx. 1); the sojourning of Isaac in the land of Canaan (Gen. xxv. 11); the sojourning of Jacob "in the land wherein his father was a stranger" (Gen. xxxvii. 1) You collect all these [sojournings] and they add up to four hundred years [*sic*, for "four hundred and thirty years"]'.

(*c*) *Mekilta of R. Ishmael*, I. xiv. 7 (ed. Lauterbach, i, 1933, p. 111); 'And the sojourning of the children of Israel, which they sojourned in Egypt and in the land of Canaan and in the land of Goshen was four hundred and thirty years.'

(*d*) *Tanḥuma*, שמות 22 (Choreb ed., p. 177): 'in Egypt and in the land of Goshen and in the land of Canaan four hundred and thirty years.'

(*e*) *Tanḥuma*, שמות 19 (ed. Buber, 1885, p. 11): 'in Egypt and the other lands'.

(*f*) *Sopherim*, i. 8: 'in Egypt and in the land of Canaan four hundred and thirty years'.

(*g*) *T. J. Meg.* 1, 11 (Krotoschin ed., 71 d): 'in the land of Egypt and in all the lands four hundred and thirty years.'

(*h*) *T. B. Meg.* 9 a: 'in Egypt and in other lands four hundred [*sic*] years.' (The Munich MS has 'four hundred and thirty years' (cf. Goldschmidt, *Der babylonische Talmud*, iii, 1899, p. 564). Mr. Weis thinks, however, that the number was deliberately changed to 400 to agree with Gen. xv. 13. But cf. *Mekilta of R. Simeon* above). It is to be observed that the Rabbis make the Sojourn in Egypt 210 years, rather than 215. This is because they reckon the 430 years from a point of time five years before Abraham's departure from Ḥarran (see below). They support this figure by gematria and by reference to the life of Job, who was supposed to have lived for 210 years, which synchronized with the sojourn. To Mr. Weis I am again indebted for the following references:

Seder 'Ōlām (Warsaw ed., 1877), chap. iii: 'Our father Abraham was told on the occasion of the covenant "between the pieces" (Gen. xv. 13): "Know of a surety that *thy seed* shall be a stranger in a land that is not theirs, and shall serve them; and they shall afflict him four hundred years." Who is meant by "thy seed"? Isaac. For it is written (Gen. xxi. 12): "For in Isaac

some harmonists,[1] but is more generally rejected. That the words were not original to the text is generally felt to be indicated by the fact that they stand in a different place in the Samaritan and Greek texts. Moreover, it is often pointed out that their addition would make the sojourning of the children of Israel include the period of Abraham and Isaac and Jacob, who could scarcely be reckoned as 'children of Israel'. This difficulty was felt by Jews who adopted the reading, and efforts were made to turn it.[2] Even if the reading were adopted, we should still be carried to *circa* 1877 B.C. for Abraham's migration, and if any reliance is placed on Gen. xiv. 1 this would still be too high.

Nor should we omit to notice Gen. xv. 13, which appears to give general support to Ex. xii. 40. Here it is said that in a revelation to Abraham God said: 'Know of a surety that thy seed shall be a stranger in a land that is not theirs, and shall serve them; and they shall afflict them four hundred years.' To this passage Stephen referred,[3] and Josephus sometimes uses it,[4] without any

shall thy seed be called." In the case of Isaac it says (Gen. xxv. 26): "And Isaac was sixty years old when she bare them." Our father Jacob said to Pharaoh (Gen. xlvii. 9): "The days of the years of my pilgrimage are an hundred and thirty years." This adds up to one hundred and ninety, and two hundred and ten remain. An allusion to this matter is to be found in the year of the life of Job, who was born at that time. For it is written (Job xlii. 16): "After this lived Job an hundred and forty years", and it says (Job xlii. 10): "The Lord gave Job twice as much as he had before. Hence Job was born when Israel descended to Egypt and died when they went forth from it. Or I might have said that Israel was in Egypt for four hundred years? But did not Kohath belong to those who went down to Egypt (with Jacob, Gen. xlvi. 11), and it is written (Ex. vi. 18): "And the years of the life of Kohath were an hundred and thirty-three years", and (Ex. vi. 20): "The years of the life of Amram were an hundred and thirty-seven years." The eighty years of Moses (Ex. vii. 7) (must be added). All this makes three hundred and fifty years (i.e. even if there was no overlap of these successive generations, it would be impossible to reach a total of four hundred). What then is meant by "and shall serve them; and they shall afflict them four hundred years"? It teaches that the total amount of time which "thy seed" will spend in a land which is not theirs will be four hundred years.' (The same statement is found with variations in several other works.) *Tanḥuma*, מקץ 8 (Choreb ed., p. 129): 'And he (Jacob) said: "Behold, I have heard that there is corn in Egypt: get you down (רדו) thither" (Gen. xlii. 2). What is the significance of the expression רדו? He foresaw that they would go down thither and serve the Egyptians for a period lasting as many years as the numerical value of the word רדו (i.e. two hundred and ten.' (This, too, is found elsewhere.)

[1] Cf. Whiston, note on *Antiquities*, ii. xv. 2; Birks, *The Exodus of Israel*, 1863, pp. 39 f.

[2] Cf. *Gen. Rabba*, lxiii. 3, cited above.　　　　　　　　　　[3] Acts vii. 6.

[4] *Antiquities*, ii. ix. 1 (ii. 204), and *Wars*, v. ix. 4 (v. 382).

apparent awareness of its inconsistency with the form in which he uses Ex. xii. 40. Here the Rabbis sought an explanation of the discrepancy of thirty years between Gen. xv. 13 and Ex. xii. 40, and found it in the different point from which the reckoning was made.[1] Here, however, it is to be noted that Gen. xv. 16 estimates the period of the Oppression in different terms. It says: 'In the fourth generation they shall come hither again.' Here, however, the precise significance of the word דוֹר cannot be fixed, and we should beware of being too much influenced by the associations of the English word 'generation'.[2] The verse could mean what we should mean by 'fourth generation', and it would then agree with other Biblical evidence at which we must look. But it would have to be assigned to a different hand from

[1] Again I am indebted to Mr. P. R. Weis for references: *Mekilta of R. Ishmael*, loc. cit.: 'One verse (Ex. xii. 40) says: "Now the sojourning of the children of Israel . . . in Egypt was four hundred and thirty years", and another verse (Gen. xv. 13) says: "And they shall afflict them four hundred years." How can these two verses be harmonized? . . . Thirty years before the birth of Isaac was the decree pronounced "between the pieces".' (This is also found elsewhere.)

Baraita of the Thirty-Two Rules, example for the final rule: ' "And he said unto him" (Gen. xv. 7). When was this section spoken? After the war with the kings (Gen. xiv). For it says: "And it came to pass at the end of the four hundred and thirty years" (Ex. xii. 41), and R. Jose said "You cannot find this calculation unless you reckon from the seventieth year of Abraham, when the decree was pronounced 'between the pieces'. Hence the decree 'between the pieces' was pronounced five years before Abraham's departure from Ḥarran (Gen. xii. 4), but was written later." ' Mr. Weis comments: 'The actual wanderings of the patriarchs began thirty years before the birth of Isaac, which justifies the number four hundred and thirty given in Ex. xii. 40. In Gen. xv. 13, however, no reference was made to these thirty years, as the person addressed there was Abraham who experienced these wanderings himself. Yet since Abraham left Ḥarran only twenty-five years before the birth of Isaac (Gen. xxi. 4), some Rabbis assumed that Abraham wandered to Canaan a first time five years earlier, and argued that the section of the covenant "between the pieces" (Gen. xv. 7–21) is misplaced. Others, however, preferred the simple explanation that the wanderings of Abraham began with his leaving Ur (Gen. xi. 31), which may have taken place five years before he left Ḥarran at the command of God (Gen. xii. 1). This view is quoted in the name of the Midrash by R. Elijah Wilna, in his annotations to Seder 'Ōlām (Warsaw ed., 1877, p. 4), but is not found in the printed Midrashim. Among the commentators it is Ibn Ezra who holds this view (*ad* Gen. xii. 1, xv. 7).'

[2] Cf. *B.D.B.*, s.v. Cf., too, what I wrote in *B.J.R.L.* xxii, 1938, p. 246 (= *Israel's Sojourn in Egypt*, p. 6): 'The word *dor* in Hebrew far more commonly means *cycle of time* than *cycle of birth*, and in view of the preceding "four hundred years" (xv. 13), it most probably means the large cycle of a century here.'

the one that wrote Gen. xv. 13. I am reluctant to press this, however, and think it is likely that each דור, or age, was here thought of as a century, and that the two neighbouring verses were not in disagreement. This does not mean that it was supposed that a 'generation', in our sense of the term, was a hundred years, for it was clearly regarded as most unusual that Isaac should be born when his father was a hundred years old. A more serious objection to Gen. xv. 13 than any supposed disagreement with Gen. xv. 16 is its disagreement with the recorded history. For the Oppression in Egypt is not represented in the Bible as lasting for anything like 400 years.[1] The period of Joseph is hardly to be reckoned as a time of oppression, and indeed we are told that it was in the reign of one Pharaoh that the Oppression was begun, and in the reign of his successor that it was terminated in the Exodus. The reign of the first oppressor is represented as a long one,[2] but certainly one that fell far short of 400 years.

It must be emphasized that the earlier claim that the Biblical chronology correctly placed Abraham in the twenty-first century B.C., when Hammurabi was believed to belong to that age, rested on the acceptance of the figures of Gen. xii. 4, xxi. 5, xxv. 26, and xlvii. 9 as correct, while completely ignoring many other similar figures which are given in the Old Testament. Why should it be supposed that we have accurate information about the ages of the patriarchs when their children were born and the length of their lives, but completely untrustworthy information about the period nearer to the Exodus? In particular it is hard to understand why those who maintain the Mosaic authorship of the Pentateuch should attach no importance to the statements it contains about the father and grandfather of Moses. According to Gen. xlvi. 11, Kohath was one of those who went down into Egypt, and according to Ex. vi. 18 he lived 133 years. His son was Amram the father of Moses, according to Ex. vi. 18, 20. We are not told the age of Kohath when he went into Egypt, but if we suppose that his grandson Moses was born eighty years after the Descent, when Kohath was upwards of eighty years of age, and if we allow to Moses the full eighty years he is said to

[1] Here again the difficulty was already noted by the Rabbis. Mr. Weis cites *Gen. Rabba* xliv. 18 (ed. Theodor, i. 1912, p. 440; in some editions this is numbered xliv. 21 and reads slightly differently): 'Thy seed shall be a sojourner in a land that is not theirs, and shall serve them; and they shall afflict them four hundred years' (Gen. xv. 13). Rabbi Judah says: 'The sojourning and the servitude and the affliction in a land that is not theirs will last four hundred years.' Cf. *Pesiqta Rabbati*, ed. Friedmann, 1880, p. 71 a.
[2] Ex. ii. 23.

have reached at the time of the Exodus,[1] we reach a total of only 160 years for the Sojourn in Egypt. Again, Jochebed, Moses' mother, is said to have been born to Levi after the Descent.[2] As Levi is said to have had three sons already at the time of the Descent,[3] if we allow a further forty years before the birth of Jochebed we exceed the limits of the probable. At the time of the birth of Moses Jochebed can scarcely have been more than forty years old, or Pharaoh's daughter would not have chosen her for nursing mother to her foundling. Hence, again, if we add the eighty years of Moses at the time of the Exodus, we reach a maximum of 160 years to satisfy with reasonable probability the Biblical traditions. I am not arguing that all these figures are reliable, but simply that there is as much reason to accept them as there is to accept the traditions about the age of the patriarchs. And that means that Ex. xii. 40 is in flat contradiction of other Biblical statements, as the Jewish Rabbis perceived. For if Kohath was in his first year at the time of the Descent, and his son Amram—the eldest of four brothers—was born in the year of his father's death, and Amram's son Moses was also born in the year of his father's death, Moses would still have reached his eightieth year in the 350th year after the Descent. Not even a theory of posthumous births could span the remaining eighty years to accord with Ex. xii. 40.

It has frequently been observed that the genealogies of the Pentateuch are in persistent disagreement with the 430 years of Ex. xii. 40. Five of Kohath's grandsons are said to have belonged to the generation of the Exodus: Mishael,[4] Elzaphan,[5] Korah,[6] Moses, and Aaron.[7] On their mother's side Moses and Aaron were grandsons of Levi[8] and through her Kohath was their uncle. Hezron, the grandson of Judah, is said to have been born before the Descent into Egypt.[9] Nahshon and Elisheba, who figure in the generation of the Exodus, are represented as his

---

[1] Ex. vii. 7.   [2] Num. xxvi. 59.   [3] Gen. xlvi. 11.

[4] Cf. Ex. vi. 16, 18, 22; Lev. x. 4. The genealogy is Jacob, Levi, Kohath, Uzziel, Mishael, of whom the first three were amongst those who went down into Egypt (cf. Gen. xlvi. 11).

[5] Cf. Ex. vi. 16, 18, 22; Lev. x. 4; Num. iii. 17, 19, 30. The genealogy is Jacob, Levi, Kohath, Uzziel, Elzaphan.

[6] Cf. Ex. vi. 16, 18, 21; Num. xvi. 1. The genealogy is Jacob, Levi, Kohath, Izhar, Korah.

[7] Cf. Ex. vi. 16, 18, 20; Num. xxvi. 57–59. The genealogy is Jacob, Levi, Kohath, Amram, Moses, and Aaron.

[8] Cf. Ex. vi. 20; Num. xxvi. 59. The genealogy is Jacob, Levi, Jochebed, Moses, and Aaron.   [9] Cf. Gen. xlvi. 12.

great-grandchildren.[1] Joseph's son Manasseh is said to have been born before the Descent into Egypt.[2] In the period of the Wandering in the Wilderness we meet the five daughters of Zelophehad, who are of the fifth generation from Manasseh,[3] while Machir, the son of Manasseh, is said to have been alive and vigorous not only in the time of Moses,[4] but in the time of the Conquest under Joshua.[5] In this last case, however, it is probable that we should see in Machir the personification of a clan.[6] Such a view would not serve for the others, however. Again, Zerah is said to have been amongst those who went down into Egypt.[7] His great-grandson Achan figures in the story more than forty years after the Exodus.[8] All of this is quite insufficient to cover a period of more than 400 years. Some measure of variation in the number of generations is inevitable, since all children are not born together in a family, and all parents are not of the same age when their first child is born. Moreover, three generations might be expected to be contemporary at the time of the Exodus, as they are said to have been at the time of the Descent into Egypt. But it is surely significant that the fourth generation from Jacob is normally the one which is said to have belonged to the generation of the Exodus, and the extreme case of Zelophehad's daughters carries us only to the seventh generation from Jacob, and this is quite insufficient to span the period.

The favourite resort of harmonists in all such cases is the assumption that some links may have been left out in these genealogies. It is undeniable that Hebrew often uses 'son' for 'grandson', and it is supposed that the edge of the argument from the genealogies can be simply turned by recalling that fact. But here such an assumption is irrelevant. We are told that Kohath was born before the Descent into Egypt,[9] and that Amram

---

[1] Cf. Ex. vi. 23; Num. i. 7; Ruth iv. 19 f. The genealogy is Jacob, Judah, Perez, Hezron, Ram, Amminadab, Nashhon and Elisheba.

[2] Cf. Gen. xlvi. 20.

[3] Cf. Num. xxvi. 33; xxvii. 1. The genealogy is Jacob, Joseph, Manasseh, Machir, Gilead, Hepher, Zelophehad, five daughters.

[4] Cf. Num. xxxii. 40.   [5] Cf. Josh. xvii. 1.

[6] Machir is said to have been a father before Joseph died (Gen. l. 23)— i.e. some seventy years after the Descent into Egypt. If he was still alive, therefore, after the death of Moses, he must, on the chronology of Ex. xii. 40, have been about 430 years of age. Even on the view which will be taken below, which greatly shortens the period from Joseph to Joshua, it would still not be possible to take the statements about Machir literally, unless he were about 100 years old in the time of Joshua.   [7] Cf. Gen. xlvi. 12.

[8] Cf. Josh. vii. 1. The genealogy is Jacob, Judah, Zerah, Zabdi, Carmi, Achan.   [9] Gen. xlvi. 11.

was his 'son'.[1] It cannot be supposed that 'son' here means 'grandson' or more distant descendant, for we are also told that Amram married his father's sister, Jochebed.[2] We can hardly resort to fantastically improbable suggestions that Amram married his grandfather's sister, or his great-grandfather's sister. Yet we should have to go far beyond this to cover the period required by Ex. xii. 40. For we are expressly told that Jochebed was the daughter of Levi, who was born to him after the migration to Egypt.[3] To suppose that this means that she was a long-range descendant of Levi's born centuries after his migration to Egypt is to reduce it to nonsense. The clear meaning of the passage is that whereas Levi took with him three sons when he went into Egypt, Jochebed was born to him later, and the genealogy of Moses and Aaron, which linked them with Levi through their mother by a single link, and through their father by two links, is clearly intended to be a firm one.

Again I would insist that I am not arguing that all these Biblical statements are reliable, but that we cannot assume that Ex. xii. 40 is reliable and ignore all that is in disagreement with it. And the persistent tradition of the genealogies is not confined to a single verse but widely scattered through the Old Testament. Moreover, to all these passages we may add those relating to Joseph. We are told that he was thirty when he was appointed to control Egypt,[4] and if we add to this the seven good years and part of the seven years of famine before the Descent into Egypt, he must have been about forty at that time. He is represented as reaching a total age of 110,[5] and therefore as dying some seventy years after the Descent. Two verses after his death is recorded we read of the rise of a new Pharaoh who knew not Joseph.[6] Were it not for Ex. xii. 40 no one would suppose that a leap of more than two centuries was made at this point, and Ex. i by itself would suggest a very much more modest interval.[7]

---

[1] Ex. vi. 18.   [2] Ex. vi. 20.   [3] Num. xxvi. 59.
[4] Gen. xli. 46.   [5] Gen. l. 22.
[6] Cf. Ex. i. 6: 'And Joseph died and all his brethren, and all that generation'; and Ex. i. 8: 'Now there arose a new king over Egypt, which knew not Joseph.'
[7] Cook (*The Old Testament: a Reinterpretation*, 1936, p. 59) notes that according to Gen. l. 23 and Num. xxxii. 40 Joseph lived to see the birth of the sons of the man to whom Moses gave Gilead, and that therefore Joseph and Moses overlapped. On the other hand, however, Moses is represented as having been born after the Oppression began, and the Pharaoh of the Oppression is said to have arisen after the death of Joseph.

It should be remembered that whereas it is easy for us, who work with a fixed era, to measure the period between one event and another, once we have them both expressed in terms of that era, the Biblical chronologers were working under very different conditions. They had no fixed era, and for large parts of the periods covered by Ex. xii. 40 and 1 Kgs. vi. 1 they did not even have a monarchy. Even with a monarchy, it is not easy to reckon long periods, when the length of each reign must be remembered and the total calculated; but where there is no monarchy generations are a more reliable guide to chronology than anything else. It is altogether improbable that the Hebrews in Egypt, whether pursuing their pastoral occupation or supplying slave labour for the Pharaoh, would be interested in chronology. It is probable that some people in this country remember that their grandfather fought in the Crimean War without remembering the date of that war, though everyone has had more opportunity of knowing that date than the Hebrews could have had of knowing the 'date' of events a century before their time.

To this it may be replied that there is some evidence of an era in Egypt, and Albright has frequently claimed that there is Biblical evidence that the Israelites knew and used it. Indeed he associates Ex. xii. 40 with that era. For that verse he has always had peculiar respect. For 1 Kgs. vi. 1, which to many writers is of peculiar sanctity, he has had none, while for the Biblical chronology of the patriarchial period prior to the Descent into Egypt his respect has varied from time to time.[1] But he has often argued that the Old Testament shows a knowledge of the Era of Tanis,[2] and has connected the entry of Israel into Egypt with the founding of Tanis by the Hyksos in 1720 B.C.[3] Here he has in

---

[1] Cf. *supra*, p. 64, n. 2.

[2] Cf., e.g., *J.P.O.S.* i, 1921, p. 64; *The Archaeology of Palestine and the Bible*, p. 143; *B.A.S.O.R.*, No. 58, Apr. 1935, p. 16; *From the Stone Age to Christianity*, p. 184. Griffiths (*The Exodus in the Light of Archaeology*, 1923, p. 66) supposes that the 430 years of Ex. xii. 40 is probably based on the Era of Tanis, but does not explain how.

[3] Cf. *J.P.O.S.* xv, 1935, pp. 225 f. Drioton and Vandier give the date as *circa* 1730 B.C. (cf. *Les Peuples de l'Orient méditerranéen*: II. *L'Égypte*, 1946, pp. 282 f.), following Sethe (*Z.Ä.S.* lxv, 1930, p. 88); and so Engberg (*The Hyksos Reconsidered*, 1939, p. 9). Albright earlier dated it *circa* 1675 B.C. (cf. *J.S.O.R.* x, 1926, p. 268; so also Winlock, *The Rise and Fall of the Middle Kingdom in Thebes*, 1947, pp. 97 f.). With the latter cf. Meyer, *Die Israeliten und ihre Nachbarstämme*, 1906, p. 447, where the date is given as 1670 B.C., and Gressmann, *Z.A.W.* xxx, 1910, p. 31, where it is given as 1650 B.C. Stock (*Studien zur Geschichte und Archäologie der 13. bis 17. Dynastie Ägyptens*, 1942, p. 70) puts the beginning of the Hyksos period 1720–1710 B.C., and the begin-

mind the Four Hundred Year Stele, once found by Mariette and lost and again found by Montet at Tanis,[1] recording the first founding of the city 400 years before the time of Rameses I. Albright finds peculiar significance in the fact that the 430 years of Ex. xii. 40, when added to his own dating of the Exodus *circa* 1290 B.C., would bring the Descent into Egypt *circa* 1720 B.C., or at the very time of the founding of Tanis.[2] Since, however, Albright now places Abraham at the end of the seventeenth century B.C., about a century after the founding of Tanis[3], there would seem to be no vestige of support for this hypothesis in Ex. xii. 40. For there is no adequate reason to prefer this theory to the content of the Biblical traditions by placing Jacob and Joseph before Abraham. Moreover, Albright has associated Jacob's entry into Egypt with the Hyksos invasion, and has held that Jacob was an ally of the invaders, or a leader of their hosts. Yet it is hard to find in the Biblical traditions anything at all in common with the story of the Hyksos invasion. For they tell of the entry of suppliants at an already established court, and not of a victorious entry of conquering hosts.

Into the discussion of this question, however, Num. xiii. 22 has been drawn. This verse states that Hebron was built seven years before Zoan, or Tanis, in Egypt. Albright links this verse with his view that the Era of Tanis was known to the Israelites, and finds it to mean that Hebron was first built seven years before the Hyksos establishment of Avaris, or Tanis, as their capital in 1720 B.C.[4] It would be a little surprising if this era were used for dating events both ways, like our B.C. and A.D., and we should either have to assume that the Era of Tanis was also known and used in pre-Israelite Hebron, or Kirjath-arba as it was then called,[5] or else assume that when the Israelites captured it—

ning of the 400 years of the Four Hundred Year Stele not earlier than 1690 B.C. It should be added that Weill would greatly foreshorten the Hyksos period. He says (*Chronique d'Égypte*, No. 41, Jan. 1946, p. 39): 'L'intervalle de la fin de la xiie dynastie au début de la xviiie est de l'ordre de 20 ans, 30 ans tout au plus.' On this view cf. Capart (ibid., pp. 44 f.) and Schaeffer (*Syria*, xxv, 1946–8, pp. 188 ff.).

[1] Cf. Engberg, op. cit., pp. 8 f.

[2] Cf. *B.A.S.O.R.*, No. 58, p. 16.

[3] For his more recent modification of this, while the present work was in the press, cf. *supra*, p. 64 n.

[4] Galling (*Z.D.P.V.* lxii, 1939, p. 106 n.) finds in this verse some evidence that the Hyksos were in Palestine before they entered Egypt. He says: 'Wenn in Num. 13, 22 Hebrons Gründung "sieben Jahre vor Tanis" angegeben wird, so ist das ein beachtlicher Hinweis darauf, dass die Hyksos aus Syrien über Palästina nach Ägypten eindrangen.'   [5] Cf. Jg. i. 10.

nearly 500 years later on Albright's view—some antiquarian
Israelite investigated the precise age of the city and converted it
into the Era of Tanis, which he was still using. There is no
evidence elsewhere in the Old Testament that the Israelites used
the Era of Tanis, and therefore no reason why an antiquarian
writer should use it here and here alone. Moreover, it is unlikely
that Caleb or his followers were interested in delving 500 years
into the past to determine the age of the cities they captured, and
there seems no special reason why the Era of Tanis should have
been remembered and used in Kirjath-arba alone. It seems to
me much more natural to understand the passage, with Winnett,[1] to mean that Caleb captured Hebron seven years before
the rebuilding of Avaris-Tanis by Israelite forced labour for
Rameses II.[2] We have already noted that in the Bible the toils
of the Israelites are elsewhere located in 'the fields of Zoan', so
that we know that this name was used anachronistically for the
city in the period when it was known in Egypt as Pi-Ramesse.
This verse would then, as Winnett notes,[3] carry some memory of
the fact that Hebron was captured by Caleb while the tribes that

[1] Cf. 'The Founding of Hebron', in *Bulletin of the Canadian Society of Biblical
Studies*, No. 3, June 1937, pp. 21–9. With Winnett's further views as elaborated
in this article I am not in agreement. He assigns Abraham to the Amarna
age, and ascribes the abortive attempt from the south (Num. xxi. 1–3) to the
group that came out of Egypt. He emphasizes Caleb's Edomite connexions,
and dissociates him from Judah. Since he holds that Judah entered Palestine
circa 1400 B.C., it would appear that he allows little achievement to that
tribe. If Hebron and Debir were held by Edomites, who by the time of the
Exodus are held to have reached the height of their power, and if the
Canaanites still possessed Arad in the south, Judah's position would be
unenviable. It would seem more probable that we should recognize that
Kenites and Calibbites and Kenizzites were non-Israelites, who were associated with Judah in her adventure and who ultimately became welded into
a unity with her; and that we should attribute to these associated tribes the
victory over Arad and a steadily increasing hold on the land that included
Caleb's capture of Hebron *circa* 1300 B.C. So far as the assignment of Abraham
to the Amarna age is concerned, this would mean, on Winnett's view, that
Abraham lived long subsequently to the Descent into Egypt. It would be
curious if people who could so nicely relate the date of the capture of Hebron
to the experiences of the Hebrews in Egypt were so entirely confused about
the date of Abraham.

[2] Montet (*Le Drame d'Avaris*, 1941, pp. 188, 212) would bring the reference
down later still. He thinks the meaning is that the city of Hebron was founded
seven years before Tanis was founded on the ruins of Avaris and Pi-Ramesse,
circa 1110 B.C. Like Winnett he thinks the verse refers to the Israelite building
of Hebron, not the pre-Israelite founding of Kirjath-arba, but he does not
allow any anachronism in the use of the name Tanis.

[3] Loc. cit., p. 24.

Moses led were still in bondage in Egypt. This view relates the building of both Zoan and Hebron to Israelite history, which would be more likely to command the interest of an Israelite writer than a precise date running back half a millennium before the Israelites came on the scene.[1] The verse then carries its item of evidence that the south of the country was occupied first by the Israelites.

Of any real Biblical evidence, either for a knowledge or use of the Era of Tanis, or for a Descent into Egypt in the Hyksos period, whether at the beginning of that period or later, there is none. The Biblical chronology of Ex. xii. 40 and 1 Kgs. vi. 1 does not accord with a Descent in the Hyksos period. If Gen. xiv gives any clue to the date of Abraham he must be placed towards the end of the Hyksos period, and Jacob correspondingly later. The only possible period for the Exodus that would accord with the Biblical tradition that the court resided in the neighbourhood of Goshen is the Ramesside period, and the probability that Avaris is to be identified with Pi-Ramesse means that, if the Descent was in the Hyksos period, the relation of the court to the Hebrew settlements would be the same in both ages, whereas the Biblical tradition is of a different geographical relation. If the Hyksos view is put forward in the form adopted by Albright, that the Israelites were part of the invading force, there is the added difficulty that the whole essence of the Biblical tradition of the Descent is quite other.[2]

When we turn to the 480 years of 1 Kgs. vi. 1 we find ourselves in equally involved questions, to which no simple answers can be given. It has been said that an Exodus in the middle of the fifteenth century B.C. is not easy to square with the Egyptian evidence, since the residence of the court in that age would not be suitable, while there is no evidence of building operations in the 'fields of Zoan' at that time. Here, however, it is the conflict with other Biblical evidence that calls for attention.

Once again we find that genealogical and other similar information preserved in the Old Testament does not accord with 1 Kgs. vi. 1. For we are told that Nahshon, who belonged to the period

[1] Engberg (*The Hyksos Reconsidered*, 1939, p. 49) observes: 'The oft-quoted statement that Hebron was built seven years before Zoan (Tanis-Avaris) has never been tested archaeologically.'

[2] In addition to these considerations there are those noted in the previous lecture, where it was pointed out that the Biblical tradition of tenderness towards Egyptian susceptibilities on the part of the rulers of Egypt does not suggest the Hyksos period, and the tradition that Joseph was given the daughter of the priest of Heliopolis to wife is fatal to it.

of the Exodus,[1] was separated from Solomon by six generations.[2] This is quite inadequate to cover a period of 480 years. Against this it is once more often remarked that genealogies are not always complete, and that some links may be left out. Here we can hardly resort to this, however. For there can be no doubt that the table is intended to be complete from Boaz to David and Solomon.[3] Between Nahshon and Boaz, therefore, a lacuna of more than 300 years would have to be presumed to be bridged by a single obscure name. But this is to reduce the genealogy to complete worthlessness.

Again, in Gen. xxxvi. 31 ff. we are given the list of kings who ruled over Edom before there reigned any king in Israel. Here the *terminus ad quem* is probably the institution of the monarchy in the time of Saul. The *terminus a quo* is harder to fix, but since we learn from Num. xx. 14 that there was already a king in Edom in the time of Moses, it cannot be later than his day, if any value is attached to this tradition. The first king is said to have been Bela the son of Beor,[4] whose name is so similar to that of Balaam the son of Beor[5] that not a few scholars have supposed that they were one and the same person.[6] This identification is not without difficulties, however, and cannot be pressed.[7] If it could be established it would mean that the list of kings given in Gen. xxxvi. 31 ff. spanned the period from Moses to Saul—a period of more than 400 years, on the chronology of 1 Kgs. vi. If the identification is rejected we are in no better case, but rather worse. For the list of kings would still not span a lesser period, but possibly a longer. For this period of more than 400 years we

---

[1] Cf. Num. i. 7. Moreover, Ex. vi. 23 states that his sister married Aaron.

[2] Cf. Ruth iv. 20–2. The genealogy is Nahshon, Salmon, Boaz, Obed, Jesse, David, Solomon.

[3] Cf. ibid. 17. It should be added that the genealogy in Ruth iv. 18–22 is commonly held to be quite separate from the preceding work. While I do not agree with some of the grounds on which this is argued, I agree that it is of independent origin and not part of the original book. Cf. *H.T.R.* xl, 1947, pp. 77 ff.   [4] Gen. xxxvi. 32.   [5] Num. xxii. 5.

[6] So Hommel, *Ancient Hebrew Tradition as illustrated by the Monuments*, 1897, pp. 153, 222 f. n.; Sayce, *The Early History of the Hebrews*, 1897, pp. 224, 229; Meyer, *Die Israeliten und ihre Nachbarstämme*, 1906, p. 376; Lods, *Israël*, 1930, p. 210 (E.Tr., 1932, p. 185).

[7] Balaam is said to have come from Pethor on the Euphrates, and he could scarcely be the Edomite king who had already opposed the Israelites by force of arms (Num. xx. 14–21). Cf. S. R. Driver, *The Book of Genesis*, 1904, p. 317. Albright (*J.B.L.* lxiii, 1944, p. 231) declares categorically that 'Balaam has nothing to do with Bela of Edom', whom he dates in the middle of the twelfth century and therefore later than Balaam.

are given a list of eight kings. An average of more than fifty years each for a succession of eight kings would be most remarkable, and it can scarcely be seriously maintained. An average of twenty-five years would seem more probable, and this would bring the period from the Exodus to the fourth year of Solomon to something in the neighbourhood of 260 years.[1]

Further, we learn that the migrating Danites, who moved northwards to Laish and occupied and renamed it, took with them Micah's image and Micah's priest, who was none other than the grandson of Moses.[2] Once more we find ourselves involved in complex problems of chronology when we try to determine the age of this migration.[3] For there is a reference to Dan in the Song of Deborah,[4] and we are compelled to ask what is the date of the events recorded in that song, and whether the migration of Dan preceded or followed those events. On neither question is there any general agreement.

Garstang assigns the victory over Sisera to *circa* 1200 B.C.,[5] and T. H. Robinson agrees with this since he believes that it preceded the entry of the Philistines into Palestine.[6] On the other hand, Albright dates the victory over Sisera *circa* 1125 B.C.,[7] while Wheeler Robinson comes down even lower to 1100 B.C.[8] Not all the arguments used are equally cogent. Thus Albright[9] appeals to the fact that in the Song of Deborah[10] Shamgar

---

[1] Cf. Grdseloff (*B.E.H.J.*, No. i, 1946, p. 71), who reckons an average of twenty-two years, and so reckons the chronology of the kings of Elam from *circa* 1200 B.C. Lods (*Israël*, 1930, p. 210; E.Tr., 1932, p. 185) allows a mean length of twenty-five to thirty years.

[2] Cf. Judges xvii f., and for the name of the priest Judges xviii. 30, where the Massoretic text adds a suspended Nun in the name of Moses, to convert it into Manasseh. There can be little doubt that the original reading was Moses. It is found in the Vulgate, and the Talmud declares it to be the true reading, which was changed for edification (cf. *T. B. Baba-bathra*, 109 b). Cf. Burney, *The Book of Judges*, 1920, pp. 434 f.

[3] Cf. my paper 'The Danite Migration to Laish', in *E.T.* li, 1939–40, pp. 466–71.   [4] Jg. v. 17.

[5] Cf. *Joshua–Judges*, 1931, p. 298. Similarly Hall, *The Ancient History of the Near East*, 7th ed., 1927, p. 413.

[6] Cf. *History of Israel*, i, 1932, p. 79. The entry of the Philistines is normally put at 1192 B.C., but Albright brings it down slightly to 1188 B.C. (cf. *B.A.S.O.R.*, No. 58, Apr. 1935, pp. 17 f.). Albright's date rests on the researches of Borchardt (*Z.Ä.S.* lxx, 1934, pp. 97–103).

[7] Cf. *B.A.S.O.R.*, No. 62, Apr. 1936, p. 29; No. 68, Dec. 1937, p. 25.

[8] Cf. *History of Israel: its Facts and Factors*, 1938, p. 42. So, too, O'Callaghan, *Aram Naharaim*, 1948, p. 121 n.

[9] Cf. *J.P.O.S.* i, 1921, pp. 55–62.

[10] Jg. v. 6.

ben-Anath[1] is said to have been a precursor of Sisera, while elsewhere[2] we are told that Shamgar ben-Anath slew 600 Philistines with an ox-goad. The latter passage reckons him amongst the Israelite Judges, but this is denied by some writers, including Garstang[3] and Sellin.[4] Graham and May think he was actually a Philistine,[5] while Albright says his name is Hittite[6] and Maisler that it is Ḥurrian.[7] Whether the Shamgar of the one passage is to be identified with the Shamgar of the other is not certain, though it may be agreed that when we meet this name in two passages so close together it is antecedently likely that the same person is referred to. Albright suggests that he first drove off the Philistines when they entered the land and sought to establish themselves in the coastal plain, and then afterwards became an oppressor of the Israelites, being succeeded by Sisera of Harosheth.[8] All of this is most problematical. If the Shamgar of these two passages is one and the same, then the Song of Deborah must record things that took place after the Philistine settlement, and the same conclusion would follow if the Shamgar of the Song of Deborah were himself a Philistine.

These doubtful considerations are reinforced by archaeological considerations which are stronger, though not as strong as might be wished. Albright argues that Megiddo itself was unoccupied at the time of the battle,[9] since Taanach is named rather than Megiddo,[10] despite the fact that whereas the latter was but half a mile from the river Kishon the former was nearly four miles away. Archaeologically one of the destructions of Megiddo is dated *circa* 1150 B.C., and since this is the only one of its destructions which could be considered in this connexion, and since it

---

[1] Albright holds that this name means Shamgar of Beth-Anath, in Galilee, and not Shamgar the son of Anath. Cf. *J.P.O.S.* i, 1921, p. 55 n. Cf. also Maisler, *P.E.F.Q.S.* 1934, p. 194.   [2] Jg. iii. 31.

[3] Cf. *Joshua–Judges*, 1931, pp. 287 f. Garstang holds that he is to be identified with a Syrian sailor of the time of Rameses II. Sir Charles Marston follows this view, and suggests that Shamgar's ship was named *The Ox Goad* (cf. *The Bible is True*, 1934, p. 248; *The Bible comes Alive*, 1937, p. 163).

[4] Cf. *Geschichte des israelitisch-jüdischen Volkes*, 2nd ed., i, 1935, pp. 102 f. Sellin supposes that Shamgar preceded Sisera in the city of Harosheth.

[5] Cf. *Culture and Conscience*, 1936, p. 150.

[6] Cf. *J.P.O.S.* i, 1921, p. 56.

[7] Cf. *P.E.F.Q.S.* 1934, pp. 193 f.

[8] Cf. *J.P.O.S.* i, 1921, pp. 55, 60 f. Cf. Haupt, in *Studien zur semitischen Philologie und Religionsgeschichte* (Wellhausen Festschrift), 1914, p. 199.

[9] Cf. *B.A.S.O.R.*, No. 62, Apr. 1936, pp. 27 ff.; No. 68, Dec. 1937, p. 25. But see Noth, *P.J.B.* xxxiv, 1938, p. 19 n.   [10] Jg. v. 19.

was followed by a period of abandonment,[1] Albright relies on this for his dating of the battle with Sisera *circa* 1125 B.C.[2]

My own feeling is that this allows insufficient time for the events that lay between the time of Deborah and the destruction of Shiloh in the middle of the following century.[3] I therefore incline to a somewhat earlier date, about the middle of the twelfth century for the victory over Sisera,[4] and think all probability lies on the side of its being later than the Philistine entry, though before the Philistines had begun to press inland.

As to whether this victory over Sisera was earlier than the Danite migration or later opinion is again divided. Many scholars hold that it was earlier,[5] while others of equal eminence hold that it was later.[6] The only clue we are given is in the reference to ships. For in the Song of Deborah we read: 'Why did Dan sojourn in ships?'[7] To find this consistent with the northern

[1] Cf. Loud, *Megiddo II*, 1948, Text, p. 5, where stratum vi B is held to cover the period 1150–1100 B.C., and pp. 33, 105, 114, where the remains of this stratum are described as very fragmentary. See also Noth, *P.J.B.* xxxiv, 1938, p. 17. Against this, cf. Simons, *O.T.S.* i, 1941–2, pp. 47 f.

[2] James (*Personalities of the Old Testament*, 1939, p. 58 n.) is not convinced that the battle was later than the fall of Megiddo, but is in general agreement with Albright as to the date.

[3] For the date of the destruction of Shiloh cf. Albright, *B.A.S.O.R.*, No. 35, Oct. 1929, p. 4; H. Kjaer, *J.P.O.S.* x, 1930, pp. 37–109; Mallon, *Biblica*, x, 1929, pp. 369–75; Hennequin, *Supplément au Dictionnaire de la Bible*, iii, 1936, col. 378.

[4] This was the view presented by Albright earlier, when he argued for the date *circa* 1150 B.C. Cf. *B.A.S.O.R.*, No. 58, Apr. 1935, p. 18. The same view was taken by Kittel (*Geschichte des Volkes Israel*, ii, 5th ed., 1922, p. 12), Graham and May (*Culture and Conscience*, 1936, p. 150), and James (*Personalities of the Old Testament*, 1939, p. 58), while Bergman (*J.P.O.S.* xvi, 1936, p. 248 n.) puts it *circa* 1140 B.C. Albright had previously maintained an even earlier date, *circa* 1175 B.C. (cf. *J.P.O.S.* i, 1921, p. 56; ii, 1922, p. 82 n.). Similarly Sellin (*Geschichte des israelitisch-jüdischen Volkes*, i, 2nd ed., 1935, p. 102) had declared himself in favour of a date in the first half of the twelfth century B.C.

[5] So Bertheau, *Das Buch der Richter und Rut*, 1845, p. 95; Wellhausen, *Prolegomena to the History of Israel*, 1885, p. 444; G. A. Smith, *The Historical Geography of the Holy Land*, 22nd ed., p. 220; Zapletal, *Das Buch der Richter*, 1923, p. 83; T. H. Robinson, *History of Israel*, i, 1932, p. 79; Albright, *B.A.S.O.R.*, No. 62, Apr. 1936, p. 27.

[6] So Budde, *Das Buch der Richter*, 1897, p. 46; Moore, *Judges*, 1898, p. 115; Meyer, *Die Israeliten und ihre Nachbarstämme*, 1906, p. 525; Haupt, in *Studien zur semitischen Philologie und Religionsgeschichte* (Wellhausen Festschrift), 1914, p. 204; Cooke, *Judges*, 1918, p. 63; Burney, *The Book of Judges*, 1920, p. 143; Garstang, *Joshua-Judges*, 1931, p. 247. Peake (*D.B.* i, 1898, p. 548 b) is undecided. [7] Jg. v. 17.

residence of Dan seems to me to involve an improbable straining of the meaning. Some have supposed that the ships were Phoenician ships, on which Danites were serving as sailors,[1] but it is hard to see how Danites under those conditions could be expected to desert and rally at Mount Tabor. Phoenician ships made long journeys, and the preparations of Deborah and Barak are not likely to have been long drawn out. Hence only such Danites as happened to be in port when the call came could be referred to on such a view, and they could only be a very small proportion of the tribe, the rest being unreferred to. Moore is dissatisfied with this view, and suggests that the meaning is that the tribe of Dan lived under the protection of the seafaring Phoenicians.[2] This is scarcely a natural interpretation of the words, and the story of the migration of Dan would suggest that they relied on their own resource. Garstang thinks the reference is to boats on Lake Huleh, in the neighbourhood of the northern Dan.[3] This seems unlikely,[4] and again could not be relevant to more than a handful of the tribe. The Biblical references to the northern Dan draw attention to its distance from Sidon,[5] and to the fertility of its soil.[6] Its principal occupation would therefore seem to have been agriculture, and it was so far inland that maritime connexions seem to be out of place.

On the other hand, the suitability of the words to the southern Dan is challenged. We are told that the Amorites would not suffer the Danites to descend to the coastal plain,[7] and we have little evidence that the tribe ever reached the coast. The border of the tribe is stated to have been very close to Joppa,[8] and it is possible that the tribe made some real bid to establish itself on the coast.[9] Robinson thinks that in pre-Philistine days Dan may have been a maritime tribe,[10] and Albright has advanced a similar

---

[1] Cf. Meyer, op. cit., p. 525; Haupt, loc. cit., p. 205; Cooke, op. cit., p. 63; Forster, in Alleman and Flack, *Old Testament Commentary*, 1948, p. 360. Zapletal, who holds the reference to be to the southern Danites, agrees with this view as to the meaning of the reference to ships (op. cit., p. 83). Cf. the rendering of Grether (*Das Deboralied*, 1941, p. 63): 'Warum weilte Dan auf fremden Schiffen?'   [2] Cf. *Judges*, p. 115.

[3] Cf. *Joshua–Judges*, p. 305. Presumably these would be fishing-boats and it would seem most natural to suppose that it is to such boats, whether on sea or on lake, that the words refer. Cf. Nöldeke, *E.B.* i, 1899, col. 993 n.

[4] There is no evidence that the tribe of Dan ever bordered on Lake Huleh.

[5] Jg. xviii. 7, 28.   [6] Jg. xviii. 9 f.   [7] Jg. i. 34.

[8] Josh. xix. 46.

[9] Cf. Nyberg (*S.B.U.* i, 1948, p. 342): 'I Deborasången, Dom. 5:17, synes Dan ännu bo kvar på sitt gamla område under fruktlösa försök att få fast fot vid kusten.'   [10] Cf. *History of Israel*, i, p. 128.

suggestion.[1] While this is very uncertain, and a maritime occupation for the southern Dan cannot be said to be established, it would seem to be more likely than for the northern Dan. It is possible, indeed, that the reference to ships is not original to the text, though there is no ancient evidence to throw doubt on the reading. Budde at one time[2] proposed to read נְאֹתָיו = *meadows*, for אֳנִיּוֹת = *ships*, but later abandoned this suggestion.[3] With some diffidence I have suggested the reading גֵּאָיוֹת = *valleys*,[4] and this would well fit the district occupied by the southern Dan. George Adam Smith describes that district as follows: 'The territory, which the book of Joshua assigns to Dan, lies down the two parallel valleys that lead through the Shephelah to the sea, Ajalon and Sorek, and the Song of Deborah seems to imply that they reached the coast.'[5] The real difficulty with the reference to ships is that it is hard to believe that maritime pursuits were ever the principal or characteristic occupation of the tribe of Dan in either of its locations. At the same time I do not suppose the emendation I have suggested can bring any added weight to the view that the southern Dan is referred to. An emendation that is born of a theory can never give any support to the theory, and it is rather on general grounds that I incline to the southern view, though without claiming that either it or the other view can be more than doubtful.[6]

Unfortunately, even if it were certain that the southern Dan were referred to, the verse could still not be held to prove that the victory over Sisera antedated the Danite migration to Laish. For there is no reason to believe that the whole tribe migrated.[7]

---

[1] Cf. *J.P.O.S.* ii, 1922, p. 82 n. See also ibid. i, 1921, p. 56.

[2] Cf. *Die Bücher Richter und Samuel*, 1890, p. 16 n. Cooke (*History and Song of Deborah*, 1892, p. 46) concluded that there must be some error in the text and pronounced Budde's suggestion ingenious.

[3] Cf. *Das Buch der Richter*, 1897, p. 46.

[4] Cf. *E.T.* li, 1939–40, p. 468.

[5] Cf. *The Historical Geography of the Holy Land*, 22nd ed., p. 220.

[6] The consideration that Asher is mentioned in the same verse as Dan (Jg. v. 17), and that Asher was the neighbour of the northern Dan should be mentioned, though it does not carry any weight. Jg. v. 16 f. mention four tribes that did not join in the fight against Sisera. These were Reuben, Gilead (i.e. Gad), Dan, and Asher, and actually Gilead is mentioned in the closest connexion with Dan. They were all peripheral tribes, lying at some distance from the enemy whose pressure brought about the battle. Two of them were west of the Jordan and two east. Their geographical proximity cannot be deduced from the fact that they are all named together for dishonour because of a common failure to share in the battle.

[7] Some have assumed that the whole tribe of Dan migrated. So T. H.

Samson may well have lived after the migration, and have belonged to the part of the tribe which did not go northwards.[1] The northern Dan appears never to have occupied more than a single town and its environs, while such part of the tribe as did not migrate became gradually absorbed in its neighbours. But such absorption did not take place immediately, and if Samson is placed after the migration it does not seem to have been effected by his day. It would therefore be possible to refer to the southern Dan even after the migration of a part of the tribe to Laish, and the reference in the Song of Deborah, even if it could be proved to refer to the southern Dan, would still not prove that the migration took place after the battle of Taanach.

Of more importance than the doubtful dating of this migration in terms of its relation to the victory of Deborah and Barak is the question of its relation to the Philistine immigration. It is commonly held that it was under the pressure of the Philistines that the Danites were dislodged,[2] though the Bible attributes it to Amorite resistance.[3] Even so, it might well be indirectly due

Robinson, *History of Israel*, i, p. 143. Others, with greater probability, have doubted it. So Kittel, *Geschichte des Volkes Israel*, ii, 5th ed., 1922, pp. 27 f.; Zapletal, *Das Buch der Richter*, 1923, p. 267; Fernández, *Biblica*, xv, 1934, p. 264.

[1] Cf. Fernández, ibid., pp. 263 f. Others have placed Samson before the migration. So Maspero, *The Struggle of the Nations*, E.Tr., 1925 ed., p. 704; Olmstead, *History of Palestine and Syria*, 1931, pp. 272 ff.; T. H. Robinson, *History of Israel*, i, 1932, p. 156. Olmstead places Samson before the migration, and the migration before the battle of Taanach. Since Samson must be placed after the Philistine entry, all these things are brought very close together.

[2] Cf. Maspero, op. cit., p. 704; Lods, *Israël*, 1930, p. 390 (E.Tr., 1932, p. 336); T. H. Robinson, op. cit., i, p. 157; Meek, *Hebrew Origins*, 1936, p. 90; Albright, *B.A.S.O.R.*, No. 62, Apr. 1936, p. 29. Schmidtke (*Die Einwanderung Israels in Kanaan*, 1933, p. 181) suggests that we should read 'Philistines' for 'Amorites' in Jg. i. 34.

[3] Jg. i. 34. Cf. Josh. xix. 47, where it is said that their border 'went out' from them. For M.T. ויצא גבול בני דן מהם, however, LXX there has καὶ οὐκ ἐξέθλιψαν οἱ υἱοὶ Δὰν τὸν Ἀμορραῖον τὸν θλίβοντα αὐτοὺς ἐν τῷ ὄρει· καὶ οὐκ εἴων αὐτοὺς οἱ Ἀμορραῖοι καταβῆναι εἰς τὴν κοιλάδα, καὶ ἔθλιψαν ἀπ' αὐτῶν τὸ ὅριον τῆς μερίδος αὐτῶν. This has suggested the reading וַיֵּצֶר for וַיֵּצֵא, giving the meaning 'was too strait for them'. So Ehrlich, *Randglossen*, ii, 1910, p. 55; S. R. Driver, in Kittel, *Biblia Hebraica*, 2nd ed., 1913, and Noth, ibid., 3rd ed., 1936; *La Bible du Centenaire*, ii, 1947, p. 32. Houbigant (*Biblia hebraica cum notis criticis*, ii, 1753, p. 65) secured this meaning by reading ויצר with the simple transposition of two letters (cf. Josh. xvii. 15). Cooke (*The Book of Joshua*, 1918, pp. 186 f.) reads וַיָּצִיקוּ. Others, however, retain M.T. and render 'ging für sie (ihnen) verloren.' So Kautzsch, in *H.S.A.T.*,

to the Philistine incursion into Palestine, which dislodged the Amorites, who in turn pressed the Danites.[1] Moreover, Josh. xix. 43 says that Ekron and Timnah once belonged to Dan. The former became one of the five principal cities of the Philistines, while according to Jg. xiv. 1 the latter was occupied by the Philistines in the time of Samson. There is therefore some indication that it was due to Philistine pressure that part of the tribe of Dan withdrew. This does not mean, however, that the migration of Dan followed immediately on the Philistine entry.[2] That the Philistines took some time to extend their hold is indicated by the fact that it was not until more than a century and a quarter after their entry that we find them pressing into the central highlands in the time of Eli. This would seem to imply that they had taken the whole of the twelfth century to extend their hold along the whole of the coastal plain, and the migration of Dan might have taken place at almost any time within that century. We may, perhaps, with the greatest probability place it about the middle of the century, shortly after the defeat of Sisera, when Canaanite prestige stood low.[3] It is unlikely to have been earlier than the middle of the century, since Philistine pressure was not

3rd ed., i, 1909, p. 332, followed by Holzinger, ibid., 4th ed., i, 1922, p. 358; Eissfeldt, *Hexateuch-Synopse*, 1922, p. 283*; Schulz, *Das Buch Josue*, 1924, p. 63; Noth, *Das Buch Josua*, 1938, p. 92 (who now declares the change he formerly made to be unnecessary).

[1] Cf. Peake, *D.B.* i, 1898, p. 549a; Lods, *Israël*, 1930, p. 390 (E.Tr., 1932, p. 336).

[2] T. H. Robinson holds that the tribe of Dan could not have been on the coast at any time after the Philistine arrival (*History of Israel*, i, pp. 78 f.), and therefore assumes that the Philistines secured immediate control of the whole seaboard. He is also doubtful if Asher could have had any foothold on the coast after this time. He bases on this assumption what he calls a decisive argument for the dating of the Exodus. Since the Danite migration was the result of the Philistine entry, and since the battle of Taanach preceded that migration, therefore the battle of Taanach must have preceded the Philistine entry. The argument is a complete *non sequitur* unless the Philistine control of the seaboard was instantaneous, and the Danite migration immediate. This is a most unlikely assumption, and it is more likely that Albright is right when he says: 'There is no proof that the southern part of the plain of Sharon, around Lydda and Jaffa, which is assigned in the lists of Joshua to Dan, was occupied by the Philistines until comparatively late in the period of the Judges, when they began to expand northward' (*B.A.S.O.R.*, No. 62, Apr. 1936, p. 27). Cf. Ricciotti (*Storia d'Israele*, 2nd ed., i, 1934, p. 306; French Tr., i, 1939, p. 315) who says that about 1100 B.C. the Philistines began to expand and came into contact with the Israelites.

[3] Cook (*Notes on Old Testament History*, 1907, p. 41) suggested that the migration did not take place until after the time of David.

immediately effective, and during the period of Sisera's power
we should less expect this migration than later, even though it
would not be impossible at that time.

Here, then, in the middle of the twelfth century, we find the
grandson of Moses alive. At the time of his installation as Micah's
priest he is said to have been a young man,[1] but we have no idea
how long he had been with Micah before he was kidnapped
with the image he kept. In any case this tradition is at variance
with 1 Kgs. vi. 1, which would put the death of Moses at about
1400 B.C., and would be inconsistent with the survival of his
grandson some 250 years later. Moreover, the father of Micah's
priest is said to have been born before the Exodus,[2] or some 300
years before the migration of the Danites.[3]

Once more we find the effort to turn this difficulty by the
familiar device of supposing that the genealogy is not a firm one
and that links have been omitted.[4] But a genealogy that jumped
three centuries without a link could scarcely establish any
descent. The only conceivable point of recording this genealogy
was to show the connexion of Jonathan with Moses, and the
assumption of such a gap robs it of this point.[5] Moreover, there
is no reason to doubt the completeness of this genealogy save an
assumed date for the Exodus which cannot be squared with it.
If this were the only item of evidence which was out of harmony
with it, it might be allowable to explain it away. But when, as
we have seen, there are so many items of Biblical evidence which
are inconsistent with it, the case is different, and the cumulative
improbability that all must be dealt with violently in the interests
of 1 Kgs. vi. 1 becomes much greater.[6]

That the 480 years of this verse are not easily reconciled with
the framework of the book of Judges and the supplementary

---

[1] Jg. xvii. 7.   [2] Ex. ii. 22.
[3] The position is not materially altered on the view that the Exodus took
place in the fifteenth century B.C., wherever in the twelfth century the migration of the Danites is placed. If it is put between the arrival of the Philistines
and the victory over Sisera, the '300 years' could only be reduced to about
275 years, while if the migration is put after the battle, the case is so much the
worse.   [4] Cf. T. H. Robinson, *History of Israel*, i, p. 156 n.
[5] Cf. Fernández, *Biblica*, xv, 1934, p. 263: 'Pero, como Gersom era cierta-
mente hijo inmediato de Moisés, como se desprende de Ex. 2, 22; 18, 3
[*sic*, for 18, 30, i.e. Jg. xviii, 30], parece natural que en el mismo sentido inter-
pretemos la voz, cuando se trata de la filiación de Jonatán respecto de
Gersom.'
[6] Burney (*Israel's Settlement in Canaan*, p. 92 n.) pertinently asks what is the
importance of maintaining a chronology that wrecks the historicity of the
narratives.

figures found elsewhere to cover the rest of the period between the Exodus and the founding of the Temple is well known. Many attempts to harmonize the figures have been made, and none is wholly satisfactory. The chronological data given in the book of Judges are as follows:

Israel serves Cushan-rishathaim[1]	8 years
Deliverance by Othniel; the land rests[2]	40 ,,
Israel serves Eglon[3]	18 ,,
Deliverance by Ehud; the land rests[4]	80 ,,
Oppression by Jabin[5]	20 ,,
Deliverance by Deborah and Barak; the land rests[6]	40 ,,
Oppression by Midian[7]	7 ,,
Deliverance by Gideon; the land rests[8]	40 ,,
Abimelech reigns over Israel[9]	3 ,,
Tola judges Israel[10]	23 ,,
Jair judges Israel[11]	22 ,,
Oppression by the Ammonites[12]	18 ,,
Jephthah judges Israel[13]	6 ,,
Ibzan judges Israel[14]	7 ,,
Elon judges Israel[15]	10 ,,
Abdon judges Israel[16]	8 ,,
Oppression by the Philistines[17]	40 ,,
Samson judges Israel[18]	20 ,,

It will be seen that the total for the period of the Judges is 410 years. To cover the period from the Exodus to the founding of the Temple we must add to these:

Period of the Wandering in the Desert[19]	40 years
Period of Joshua and the Elders[20]	x ,,
Eli judges Israel[21]	40 ,,
Samuel judges Israel[22]	$20+y$,,
The reign of Saul[23]	z ,,

[1] Jg. iii. 8. [2] Jg. iii. 11. [3] Jg. iii. 14. [4] Jg. iii. 30.
[5] Jg. iv. 3. [6] Jg. v. 31. [7] Jg. vi. 1. [8] Jg. viii. 28.
[9] Jg. ix. 22. [10] Jg. x. 2. [11] Jg. x. 3. [12] Jg. x. 8.
[13] Jg. xii. 7. [14] Jg. xii. 9. [15] Jg. xii. 11. [16] Jg. xii. 14.
[17] Jg. xiii. 1. [18] Jg. xv. 20, xvi. 31. [19] Num. xxxii. 13.
[20] Jg. ii. 7. No length of time is here stated. [21] 1 Sam. iv. 18.
[22] 1 Sam. vii. 2, 15. How much more of the period of Samuel followed the events of this chapter is not stated.
[23] 1 Sam. xiii. 1 in the Hebrew text says that Saul reigned two years only. But the Hebrew שׁתי שׁנים is unusual, and שׁנתים would be expected if this were intended. Keil and Delitzsch proposed to read 'twenty-two years', but thought to secure this by supposing the numeral כ had fallen out (cf. *Biblical Commentary on the Books of Samuel*, E.Tr., 1866, pp. 123 f.). Against this Driver brings the observation that there is no evidence that the letters of the alphabet

David's reign[1] . . . . 40 years

Four years of Solomon's reign[2] . . . . . 4 „

Here we have a total of $144+x+y+z$ years, or a total from the Exodus to the founding of the Temple of 554 years, in addition to the period of the Settlement, the reign of Saul, and part of the judgeship of Samuel. This is far in excess of the figures of 1 Kgs. vi. 1, and far in excess of any that could be seriously entertained.[3]

The first question that has to be asked is whether the compiler of the book of Judges designed his figures to yield a total of 480 for the period from the Exodus to the foundation of the Temple, or whether the author of 1 Kgs. vi. 1 arrived at his figure by the study of the figures before him. The former is hard to believe.[4] The framework of the book of Judges reveals the hand of a member of the Deuteronomic school by its close relation of the fortunes of Israel to her religious loyalty or disloyalty. The framework of the book of Kings also reveals the hand of a member of the Deuteronomic school by its application of the test of the attitude of the kings to the centralization of worship in Jerusalem in all its judgements. In both frameworks we find chronological data. There is no reason to suppose that the figures given in the books of Kings were governed by a theory as to the total they should yield, and it is improbable that those given in the book of Judges were governed by a theory. Had they been, it might have been expected that they would more easily have yielded the required total.

Moreover, it is widely held that 1 Kgs. vi. 1 did not come from the hand of the compiler of the books of Kings, but was subsequently added. The LXX transfers this verse into the middle of a rearranged form of verses 31 f. (E.V. 17 f.) of the previous

were used for numerals in Hebrew MSS. anciently enough to satisfy this view (*Notes on the Hebrew Text of the Books of Samuel*, 2nd ed., 1913, p. 97), and we should have to read עשרים ושתים שנה. This is, of course, an unsupported conjecture. In Acts xiii. 21 we find a reign of forty years ascribed to Saul.

[1] 1 Kgs. ii. 11.   [2] 1 Kgs. vi. 1.

[3] Houbigant (*Biblia hebraica cum notis criticis*, ii, 1753, pp. xxix ff.) allowed 40 years for x and by making Eli's period and Samuel's in part concurrent reduced $y+z$ to 5 years. He also reckoned but 3 years of Solomon's reign, thus yielding a gross total of 598 years. By reducing Ehud's period to 20 years, and ignoring the period of Ammonite and Philistine oppression, this was condensed to 480 years.

[4] Cf. J. S. Griffiths, *The Exodus in the Light of Archaeology*, 1923, p. 63, where it is rightly said that there is not a particle of evidence that the author of the book of Judges supposed that 480 years separated the Exodus from the founding of the Temple.

chapter, reading 'four hundred and fortieth' instead of 'four hundred and eightieth', and then brings vi. 37, 38a to replace vi. 1 here. Wellhausen held that the LXX represents the original text,[1] but Jack objects that there is ample evidence that the LXX, which has many chronological differences from M.T., is not to be easily accepted as superior, and here Aquila and Symmachus, as well as the Peshitta, all support the M.T.[2] He does not, however, deal with Wellhausen's arguments, which are that vi. 37, 38a break the connexion between vi. 36 and vii. 1 ff., and that vi. 1 is superfluous in a narrative which contained vi. 37, 38a; and also that a different hand is revealed in that vi. 1 has חדש where vi. 37 has ירח. Jack might, indeed, have observed that if vi. 37, 38a do not seem in place that is no evidence that they must have stood where vi. 1 now stands, and Stade, who holds that vi. 1 is not original, has pointed out that they are scarcely in place where they stand in LXX.[3] Nor can the use of the word חדש be seriously advanced against the originality of vi. 1.[4] It is often noted that Josephus gives the period from the Exodus to the founding of the Temple as 592 years.[5] But this again is not serious evidence here. For it cannot be supposed that 1 Kgs. vi. 1 was added so late as the time of Josephus, and hence if Josephus gives a different figure it cannot be concluded that it was because he found none in the text.

A further alleged count against the originality of 1 Kgs. vi. 1 is the consideration that the sum of the lengths of the reigns of the kings of Judah from the fourth year of Solomon to the destruction of Jerusalem, as given in the books of Kings, gives the total of 430 years. If to this fifty years be added, to cover the period from the destruction of the Temple to its rebuilding after the Exile, we again have a total of 480 years. More than one writer has claimed that this cannot be accidental, and has supposed that 1 Kgs. vi. 1 was inserted by an editor who wished

[1] Cf. Bleek's *Einleitung in das Alte Testament*, 4th ed., revised by Wellhausen, 1878, p. 232, and *Composition des Hexateuchs*, 3rd ed., 1899, pp. 264 f. See also Benzinger, *Die Bücher der Könige*, 1899, p. 30.
[2] Cf. *The Date of the Exodus*, 1925, pp. 202 f.
[3] Cf. *Z.A.W.* iii, 1883, p. 135. See also Kittel, *Die Bücher der Könige*, 1900, p. 46.
[4] The word ירח is used but four times in the books of Kings, of which two are found in 1 Kgs. vi. 37 f., whereas חדש is found far more frequently. We can hardly appeal to ירח, therefore, as a test of the compiler's authorship.
[5] Cf. *Antiquities*, viii. iii 1 (viii. 61), and x. viii. 5(x. 147). Elsewhere Josephus gives the period as 612 years. So *Against Apion*, ii. 2 (19), and *Antiquities*, xx. x. 1 (xx. 220).

artificially to equate the period between the Exodus and the
founding of the Temple with that between the founding of the
first and the second Temples.[1] In that case it must have been
added after the founding of the second Temple.

This is scarcely cogent. For attention is not drawn to the second
period of 480 years, as it might have been expected to be in a
marginal gloss which was afterwards incorporated in the text, if
that gloss were made specifically to equate an earlier period
with it. Anachronisms are found elsewhere in the Bible, so that
there is no reason to suppose that the copyist who incorporated
the supposed gloss in the text would have omitted the reference
to something that lay beyond the period covered by the books
of Kings if he had found it there. I do not find the case against
the originality of 1 Kgs. vi. 1, therefore, to be at all compelling.[2]

Nor have we disposed of the problem when we have decided
the origin of this verse. From whatever hand it came we have
to ask on what the writer based his estimate. Many have supposed that he based it on a careful study of the chronological
data found in the Bible and set out above, and that we can
recover the clue to his treatment of it. The various efforts which
have been made to recover it give ample evidence of the ingenuity
of modern writers to manipulate the figures, but inspire no confidence in their basic assumptions. It may suffice if we examine
four of the many attempts which have been made.

Moore supposes that the periods of oppression are not included
in the total.[3] In this he was following Nöldeke,[4] who secured the

---

[1] Cf. Stade, *Geschichte des Volkes Israel*, i, 1887, pp. 88 ff.; Burney, *Notes on
the Hebrew Text of the Books of Kings*, 1903, pp. 59 ff.; Gampert, *R.Th.Ph.*,
N.S. v, 1917, pp. 246 f. Jack here agrees that 'the coincidence between the two
periods, it must be admitted, cannot be accidental, and marks the Biblical
chronology as artificial and the statement in 1 Kings vi. 1 as probably a post-
exilic insertion' (*The Date of the Exodus*, p. 204).

[2] Cf. Dussaud, *Les Origines cananéennes du sacrifice israélite*, 2nd ed., 1941,
pp. 347 f. I am in agreement with Dussaud in his rejection of the objections
which have been raised against the originality of this verse. I do not think his
reference to temple archives as a repository of chronological tradition is very
relevant here, however. Obviously the new Temple of Solomon would have
no archives that dated from the Exodus. No earlier Temple in Jerusalem
would be interested in the Exodus of the Israelites, and there is no reason
whatever to connect this figure with the archives of any other shrine.

[3] Cf. *Judges*, 2nd ed., 1898, pp. xxxvii ff. Similarly Cornill, *Introduction to
the Canonical Books of the Old Testament*, E.Tr., 1907, p. 169; Lagrange, *Le
Livre des Juges*, 1903, pp. xlii f. Cf. too Ruffini, *Chronologia V. et N.T. in aeram
nostram collata*, 1924, pp. 24 ff.

[4] Cf. *Untersuchungen zur Kritik des Alten Testaments*, 1896, pp. 192 f. This idea

total of 480 by the simple omission of these periods, reckoning
Abimelech as an oppressor, and then adding forty years to cover
the period of Joshua and the reign of Saul, and accepting the
twenty years of 1 Sam. vii. 2 as the complete period of Samuel.
Moore makes some variations in this, while accepting the basic
assumption that the periods of the oppressors are to be omitted.
He supposed that the round figures attributed to most of the
judges were held to include the oppressions that preceded their
deliverance, so that the period of each judge was reckoned from
the end of the period of the previous judge. By treating the
period of Abimelech in the same way, and by the assumption
that the period of Saul, who was regarded as a usurper by the
later school, is similarly incorporated, a considerable reduction
in the total is effected. Further, the LXX text of 1 Sam. iv. 18
ascribes to Eli a judgeship of twenty years, instead of the forty
years of the M.T. The predominance of the numbers twenty,
forty, and eighty in the table has been frequently noted, and it
is then observed that when the years of the Minor Judges, of
whom we are told nothing but their names, are added together
and combined with the six years of Jephthah and the four years
of Solomon, we have a further total of eighty years. We now
have:

Period of Wandering in the Desert	.	.	40 years
„ Joshua and the Elders .	.	.	*x* „
„ Othniel . . .	.	.	40 „
„ Ehud . . .	.	.	80 „
„ Deborah and Barak .	.	.	40 „
„ Gideon . . .	.	.	40 „
„ Samson . . .	.	.	20 „
„ Eli . . .	.	.	20 „
„ Samuel . . .	.	.	*y* „
„ David . . .	.	.	40 „
Periods of Jephthah and the Minor Judges, and four years of Solomon	.	.	80 „

This now yields a total of 400 years, with a remaining eighty
years to be divided between *x* and *y*, of which *y* is known to be
something over twenty years. It is probable then that we should
attribute to each of these forty years.[1]

is much older than Nöldeke, of course. It figures in Houbigant, *Biblia
hebraica cum notis criticis*, ii, 1753, p. xxi, as 'calculus communis'. The only
differences from the scheme of Moore (see below) are that there Joshua is
assigned 17 years and Abimelech's 3 years are reckoned, while Eli's period is
computed at 40 years.

[1] Cf. Moore, op. cit., p. xlii.

Against this it is to be observed that it is hard to see how the eighteen years of the Ammonite oppression can be held to be included in the six years of Jephthah's judgeship, and quite improbable that statements that the land had rest were intended to include the periods when the land did not have rest but oppression. Further, it is frequently noted that the formula for the Minor Judges is different from that of the others, and that we are told nothing of any oppression from which they effected deliverance. Nor is their judgeship related in any way to the religious state of the nation and the misfortunes that disloyalty had brought. Hence it has commonly been thought that they were introduced into the text by a later hand, in order to make up the number of the Judges to twelve, to agree with the number of the tribes of Israel. It has then to be noted that Shamgar, of whom one exploit is recorded, is furnished with no chronological datum.[1] Nöldeke, who included the periods of the Minor Judges in the reckoning which he supposed to lie behind 1 Kgs. vi. 1, believed that these were later additions to the text,[2] and Moore seems to follow him.[3] In that case we have a Deuteronomic book of Judges, compiled apparently after the publication of Deuteronomy in 621 B.C., and a Deuteronomic book of Kings, completed soon after 561 B.C. We then have an insertion in the book of Judges which is either basic to a verse in the Deuteronomic book of Kings, or to a later insertion in that book. If the insertions in

[1] Cf. Jg. iii. 31.

[2] Cf. op. cit., pp. 189 f. Steuernagel (*Lehrbuch der Einleitung in das Alte Testament*, 1912, pp. 288 f.) similarly finds the Minor Judges to be additions to the text, and also Abimelech. He then adds the years of the Major Judges to yield 226 years (Othniel 40, Ehud 80, Barak 40, Gideon 40, Jephthah 6, and Samson 20 years), the years of oppression to yield 91 years (Aram 8, Moab 18, Canaan 20, Midian 7, Ammon 18, Philistines 20—the remainder of the 40 years of Philistine oppression being concurrent with Samson's judgeship), the years of Moses (40 years), Joshua (x years), Samuel and Saul (y years), David (40 years), and Solomon (3 years) to yield a total of $83+x+y$ years. In all, therefore, we have $400+x+y$ years, leaving 80 years to be distributed between x and y.

[3] Cf. op. cit., p. xxviii. Pfeiffer (*Introduction to the Old Testament*, 1941, p. 332) holds that the Minor Judges did not figure in the Deuteronomic book of Judges, but says there is no reason for assuming that they did not figure in JE. It would be equally true to say that there is no reason to assume that they did. If the Minor Judges were subsequently added to the Deuteronomic book of Judges, we have no means whatever of knowing whence they were taken. Some earlier writers, indeed, had held that the Deuteronomic editor of Judges had excluded the Minor Judges from his work, and that a later hand had restored them. So Gautier, *Introduction à l'Ancien Testament*, 3rd ed. i, 1939, p. 245. On this view cf. Eissfeldt, *Die Quellen des Richterbuches*, 1925, p. 116.

the book of Judges were made with a chronological purpose and the figures were either freely added to give some sort of verisimilitude or already found in some older traditions which were used, it would be surprising if they just happened to yield the round figures which the author of 1 Kgs. vi. 1 found. If there is any significance in the fact that the years of the Minor Judges and Jephthah together with the four years of Solomon make up eighty years, then whoever added them may be presumed to have had some purpose in mind in adding them. It should be noted that on the theory outlined above these figures require for their interpretation a figure in another book—the fourth year of Solomon—which is nowhere referred to in the book of Judges. These additions could therefore have been made only by the author of 1 Kgs. vi. 1, since only in that verse is any conceivable purpose to be found along the lines of this theory. Yet no evidence is offered that these additions were by the author of 1 Kgs. vi. 1, and the forced and unnatural interpretation that has to be given to other items in the chronology to make it fit the Procrustean bed of the 480 years, including the resort to the LXX text of 1 Sam. iv. 18 for no apparent reason save that it serves the purpose of the theory, makes the whole case quite unconvincing. It seems far more likely that the verses about the Minor Judges were added later, and that there is no special significance in the fact that their years add up to a total of seventy.

A different approach is made by Gampert.[1] He accepts the figure of 1 Sam. vii. 2 as covering the whole of the period of Samuel, but otherwise starts with all of the figures noted above, save that for Solomon he reckons his three completed years only. This reduces the total to 553 years, together with the period of Joshua and the reign of Saul. These last two he eliminates altogether, Saul because he supposes his reign to be included in the judgeship of Samuel, and Joshua because he was regarded as the mere attendant of Moses and the executor of his orders. He then observes that if the Minor Judges and Abimelech are ignored, the saving of seventy-three years reduces the total to 480 years. On this view the verses relating to the Minor Judges may be presumed to have been added to the text of Judges subsequently to the writing of 1 Kgs. vi. 1. But why the years of Abimelech are omitted is not clear unless it is that the exigencies of the theory required it. For the story of Abimelech cannot be presumed to have been added by the same hand as the notices of the Minor Judges. Even more glaring is the omission of the

[1] Cf. *R.Th.Ph.*, N.S. v, 1917, pp. 241-7.

period of Joshua, who could hardly have been overlooked in any chronology of the period.[1]

But having explained how the author of 1 Kgs. vi. 1 arrived at his figure by careful calculation from the data of the earlier books, Gampert goes on to claim[2] that his hypothesis confirms the view of Wellhausen that that figure was a round calculation of a period of twelve generations of forty years each, and that it rested on the succession of the High Priests.[3] Gampert objects to the view that it rests on twelve generations of national leaders, at which we shall look below, since Joshua and Samuel would have to be included there, and his use of the figures of the earlier books requires him to ignore these leaders. For the list of High Priests we have to turn to the Chronicler. In 1 Chron. v. 27–41 (E.V. vi. 1–15) and vi. 35–8 (E.V. vi. 50–3) we are given the lists of the High Priests from Aaron to the time of Solomon, and then on to the time of the fall of Jerusalem. Here it is observed that from Aaron to Jehozadak, who was High Priest at the time of Nebuchadrezzar's capture of the city, there were twenty-three generations, and if Joshua, the son of Jehozadak, who was High Priest at the time of the Return is added, we have twenty-four generations. In 1 Chron. v. 36 (E.V. vi. 10) we are told that the second Azariah exercised the priestly office in Solomon's Temple, but Gampert thinks this should be transferred to the first Azariah, since it was he who was High Priest in the time of Solomon.[4]

Here we have to ask why the writer of 1 Kgs. vi. 1 should have troubled to make the laborious calculation Gampert first supposes, unnaturally eliminating Abimelech and Joshua, if he was really resting on a rough and ready calculation of twelve generations of High Priests at forty years to the generation. If he really worked with exact figures it is gratuitous to assume he worked

[1] Bentzen (*Indledning til det Gamle Testamente*, I. i, 1941, p. 84) has a scheme with some features in common with Gampert's, but avoiding some of its embarrassments. To the 410 years of the framework of the book of Judges he adds 40 years for the wandering in the wilderness, &c., and 40 for David; and he reckons only the three completed years of Solomon. This gives a total of 533 years, in addition to the periods of Joshua, Samuel, and Saul. By ignoring the 73 years of the Minor Judges, reducing the period of Eli to 20 years with the LXX, and holding the 40 years of the Philistine domination to be concurrent with the periods of Samson and Eli, he reduces the total to 400 years, plus the periods of Joshua, Samuel, and Saul.   [2] Loc. cit., p. 246.

[3] Cf. *Prolegomena to the History of Israel*, E.Tr., 1885, p. 230.

[4] In this he is almost certainly right. Cf. Elmslie, *The Books of Chronicles*, 1916, p. 40. This was recognized by the older commentators; also cf. Zöckler, *The Books of Chronicles*, E.Tr., 1876, p. 69; Benzinger, *Die Bücher der Chronik*, 1901, p. 21.

with round figures; if he worked with round figures, it is gratuitous to suppose that he worked with exact figures. Moreover, the
view that he worked with these High Priestly names is held to
confirm the supposition that the author of 1 Kgs. vi. 1 could not
have written the verse until after the Return from the Exile.
But there is not the slightest reason to suppose that the author of
1 Kgs. vi. 1 had access to the books of Chronicles, or that he had
independent knowledge of the High Priestly genealogy.[1] I am
therefore just as unconvinced that the succession of High Priests
had anything to do with the verse as I am that it rested on a
forced interpretation of the chronology given in the earlier books.

Garstang presents a scheme[2] which has some features in common with that of Gampert, but which is freed from some of the
embarrassments of the latter's. He ignores the Minor Judges,
whose insertion he attributes to the hand of P, but retains Abimelech. Further, he reduces the eighteen years of the Ammonite
oppression, mentioned in Jg. x. 8, to one year, on the ground
that the eighteen years of oppression applied only to the Israelites who lived on the east of the Jordan. The period of Samson
he reckons concurrently with the period of the Philistine oppression, and for the period of Eli he halves the figure of the Hebrew
text by following the reading of the LXX in 1 Sam. iv. 18. By
these devices he saves 127 of the 554 years of the reckoning given
above, thus reducing it to 427. The period of Joshua and the
Elders he estimates at forty years, and the reign of Saul at fifteen
years; while for the period of Samuel he accepts the figure of
1 Sam. vii. 2, and hence does not add anything to its twenty
years. By adding 55 years to the 427, therefore, he arrives at
a total of 482 years, which is very close to the 480 years of
1 Kgs. vi. 1.

This is all very ingenious and unconvincing. There is no
reason that would be likely to strike an ancient computer to
treat the years of Samson's judgeship differently from those of
the others, and the same is true of the years of the Ammonite
oppression. Moreover, it is improbable that Garstang would have
preferred the LXX in 1 Sam. iv. 18, unless it had been convenient
for his calculation.[3] The fact that Eli is represented as a very

[1] Jack (op. cit., p. 206) shows that the genealogy given by the Chronicler
here is completely unreliable, as also are others of his genealogies. We therefore cannot assume that the author of 1 Kgs. vi. 1 worked with this list unless
he had the Chronicler's work before him.

[2] Cf. *Joshua–Judges*, 1931, pp. 55 ff.

[3] S. R. Driver (*Notes on the Hebrew Text of the Books of Samuel*, 2nd ed., 1913,
p. 48) does not think this an important enough reading of the LXX to record.

old man at the time of his death surely favours the forty years of the Hebrew text rather than the twenty years of the Greek text.

One other scheme of harmonization may be mentioned. This was presented by Fruin,[1] and while it is less artificial than that of Moore, it is heavily handicapped by embarrassments. Fruin thinks that no allowance was made for periods for which no figure was recorded, and hence he reckons nothing for the period of Joshua. But he also disregards the forty years of Eli's judgeship, and the period of Samuel's judgeship, for which partial figures are recorded. Further, he thinks the reference to eighteen years of Ammonite oppression mentioned in Jg. x. 8 is secondary, since Heshbon is said to have been taken in the fortieth year from the Exodus, and the judgeship of Jephthah is ascribed to a date 300 years later than this. By adding up all the figures for the oppressions and the Judges, including the Minor Judges Tola and Jair, but omitting the Ammonite oppression, he reaches a very close approximation to the 300 years. To Saul he attributes precisely the two years specified in the Hebrew text of 1 Sam. xiii. 1. By these means he reduces the $554 + x + y + z$ of the reckoning given above by $76 + x + y + z$. This yields a total of 478 years, to which he adds two for Ishbosheth,[2] and so arrives at the figure of 1 Kgs. vi. 1.

This theory attributes to the author of 1 Kgs. vi. 1 a very wooden use of his sources, since the period of Joshua is reduced to vanishing point, and an arbitrary use of his sources at other points, since Eli and Samuel also reach vanishing point, despite the record that we have. Moreover, if he had used his sources intelligently he would have recognized that the two years of Ishbosheth's reign must have been concurrent with part of David's Hebron period. The result is therefore again quite unconvincing.[3]

---

[1] Cf. *N.T.T.* xxiii, 1934, pp. 316–25. [2] Cf. 2 Sam. ii. 10.

[3] A highly ingenious suggestion is that of Petrie (*Egypt and Israel*, 1911, pp. 54 f.). This view reduces the period of the Judges to a total of about 120 years by supposing that we have parallel histories, relating to the north, east, and west of the land, combined. The northern history covered Cushan-rishathaim's oppression (8 years), Othniel's period (40 years), Jabin's oppression (20 years), Deborah's period (40 years), and Elon's judgeship (10 years), or 118 years in all. The eastern history covered Eglon's oppression (18 years) Ehud's period (80 years) with part of which Jair's judgeship (22 years) was made concurrent, the Ammonite oppression (18 years), and Jephthah's judgeship (6 years), or 122 years in all. The western history covered the Midianite oppression (7 years), Gideon's period (40 years), Abimelech's rule (3 years), Tola's judgeship (23 years), Abdon's judgeship (8 years) reckoned concur-

The fundamental assumption of all these schemes seems to be quite unwarranted, and the variety and mutually inconsistent character of the views to which it has given rise[1] ought to suggest that it should not be taken for granted. It seems to me most improbable that the author of 1 Kgs. vi. 1 made any elaborate calculation, and the round figures of his total suggest that he worked with round figures.[2] But there is no reason to suppose that he worked with the High Priestly genealogy, for we have no evidence that he had access to it. On the other hand, if he had any access to the books of Joshua, Judges, and Samuel, he must have known of the succession of national leaders from the Exodus to Solomon. It has already been said that there is reason to suppose that the notices of the Minor Judges are secondary, as Garstang and many others have held, and in any case they do not stand out in the tradition as great national leaders. The

rently with Ibzan's judgeship (7 years), the Philistine oppression (40 years) which is held to include Samuel's judgeship (20 years), or 121 years in all. These histories are held all to have ended with Saul's election to the throne in 1030 B.C. Hence Gideon is made to precede Othniel and Ehud, and Othniel with great improbability is connected with the northern history. He is apparently held to have marched against the northern foe through the area which Gideon was peacefully judging. Similarly Deborah is made contemporary with Tola and her rallying of the central tribes against Sisera is held to have been during the period of rest that Tola gave to this part of the land, while her deliverance is represented as belonging wholly to the northern history. Other improbabilities belong to this scheme, which can hardly be accepted. That there was overlapping between the periods of the Judges, and that they were local rather than national heroes is commonly held, and Ruffini (*Chronologia Veteris et Novi Testamenti*, 1924, p. 27) thinks the reference to Philistines and Ammonites in Jg. x. 7 points to the fact that the periods of Jephthah and Samson synchronized. But the view of Petrie goes much beyond the common view.

[1] Cf. Gautier, *Introduction à l'Ancien Testament*, 3rd ed., 1939, i, p. 244: 'les chronologistes, tous animés du désir d'atteindre un même but, diffèrent quant aux moyens à employer. Ils s'ingénient à faire rentrer les unes dans les autres les durées assignées aux divers juges et usent largement de l'hypothèse de carrières simultanées et parallèles; ils aboutissent ainsi, fatalement, au résultat voulu.'

[2] Cf. Barnes, *The First Book of the Kings*, 1911 ed., p. 46: 'It would be unsafe to take the 480 years as the basis of any exact calculations.' It may be noted that Nöldeke (op. cit., pp. 188 ff.) similarly took the figures of 1 Kgs. vi. 1 to be round figures resting on a rough calculation of twelve generations of forty years each, and so rendered quite unnecessary and irrelevant his effort to make this agree with the figures given in the book of Judges. Similarly with many of those who have followed Nöldeke. Cf. too Höpfl, *Introductio specialis in Vetus Testamentum*, 5th ed., 1946, p. 141: 'Numeris in Jdc vix valor strictae chronologiae competit, cum in genere iuxta certum schema positi sint: 80, 40, 20, i.e. numeri rotundi.'

H

leaders who might be expected to be recalled are: Moses, Joshua, Othniel, Ehud, Deborah and Barak, Gideon, Jephthah, Samson, Eli, Samuel, Saul, and David.[1] Here we have twelve[2] leaders to whom an average of forty years each might be attributed to yield the 480 years, without the expenditure of midnight oil and improbable ingenuity. But if this view is correct, the 480 years cannot be used as a serious chronological computation.[3] Nevertheless, as will be said later, it is not wholly without approximation to historical fact.

Reference has been made already to Jg. xi. 26, which places the judgeship of Jephthah 300 years[4] after the period of Sihon's defeat in the fortieth year after the Exodus from Egypt.[5] This must be understood to be in round figures, and must not be pressed exactly. If the Minor Judges Tola and Jair are omitted, the period from Joshua to Jephthah according to the reckoning of the book of Judges is 274 years, and if to this a reasonable figure is allowed for the period of Joshua, it will be seen that we have a fairly close approximation to the figure of Jg. xi. 26.[6] When we submit this to archaeological control, however, we are confronted by objections. Burrows places the exploits of Jephthah at *circa* 1100 B.C.,[7] while Cook places them somewhat later.[8] This would bring the victory over Sihon to somewhere in the fourteenth century B.C. Here the evidence adduced by Glueck, showing that there was a long break in the history of settled life on the east of the Jordan, has to be remembered. In the light of this

---

[1] So Nöldeke, op. cit., p. 190; Budde, *Das Buch der Richter*, 1897, p. xix; Cornill, *Introduction to the Canonical Books of the Old Testament*, E.Tr., 1907, p. 169; Burney, *Israel's Settlement in Canaan*, pp. 4 f., and *The Book of Judges*, p. liv.

[2] Counting, for this purpose, Deborah and Barak as one.

[3] Cf. Burney, *The Book of Judges*, p. liii: 'These and similar calculations can only, however, possess a relative importance; since it is evident that the author of the statement in 1 Kgs. 6[1] must have been employing an artificial method of reckoning.'

[4] L. Desnoyers, *Histoire du Peuple hébreu*, i, 1922, p. 411, holds that the figure in this verse is a later insertion. Cf. Moore, *Judges*, 1898, p. 297; Cooke, *The Book of Judges*, 1918, p. 121; Burney, *The Book of Judges*, 1920, p. 304.

[5] Cf. Dt. i. 3 f.

[6] Garstang (*Joshua–Judges*, 1931, pp. 57 f.) brings the figure to 298 by reducing the period of Ammonite oppression to 1 year, and allowing 40 years for Joshua and the Elders, and by carrying down his reckoning to the second year of Jephthah.

[7] Cf. *What Mean these Stones?* p. 73.

[8] Cook holds that the Jephthah story once stood in immediate connexion with the story of Saul's victory over the Ammonites (cf. *Critical Notes on Old Testament History*, 1907, p. 24; and *C.A.H.* ii, p. 372).

evidence, it is held that the victory over Sihon cannot have been won so early.[1] De Vaux, however, who substantially accepts Glueck's evidence, says that while most of the area west of the Jordan may have had but nomad peoples in the fourteenth century B.C., there is evidence that Heshbon was a small settled area at that time.[2] According to the Biblical traditions, Sihon was contemporary with Og, king of Bashan, who is placed in the Iron Age.[3] Yet the fourteenth century lies before the Iron Age. Against this it has to be remembered that iron is clearly indicated as a rare metal in the days of Og, and it has been noted above that there are some references to iron in the Amarna letters of the fourteenth century B.C. The archaeological evidence against a victory over Sihon in the fourteenth century B.C. is not therefore compelling.[4]

From all this it will appear that the chronology of Ex. xii. 40 and 1 Kgs. vi. 1 has many difficulties to encounter on any view of the history that may be adopted. The full acceptance of that chronology, putting Jacob's descent into Egypt in 1877 B.C., and assigning Abraham to the first part of the twenty-first century B.C., is so improbable that it could find few serious defenders to-day.[5] It would involve the complete loosing of Abraham from any connexion with Ḥammurabi, and the jettisoning of far more

[1] Cf. *A.A.S.O.R.* xviii–xix, 1940, pp. 242–51.
[2] Cf. *Vivre et Penser*, i (replacing *R.B.* l, 1941), pp. 19–25, 33–5. Cf. also Noth, *Z.A.W.*, N.S. xix, 1944, pp. 37 f. note. Albright (*B.A.S.O.R.*, No. 90, Apr. 1943, pp. 17 f. n.) says: 'Glueck's negative conclusions in the area under discussion'—i.e. East of the Jordan—'may have to be modified somewhat. . . . I am inclined to think that the situation brought to light by Glueck's exploration is due to the fact that occupation became concentrated in fortified towns and castles during the Hyksos period, instead of being distributed through unwalled settlements. Sherds belonging to the 17th–15th centuries would be buried in the accumulating debris inside the walls and would seldom appear on either surface or slopes of a site. The relative paucity of sherds would then find a simple explanation—the decrease of public security in the Hyksos age.' Harding (*P.E.Q.* 1948, pp. 118 f.) reports the finding of a tomb group of the Hyksos period in Amman, and notes that this may have bearing on Glueck's conclusions. It would seem to be entirely consistent with the above quoted view of Albright.
[3] Cf. Dt. iii. 11.
[4] Cf. Bergman, *J.P.O.S.* xvi, 1936, p. 249, where the date of Jg. xi. 26 is held to be accurate.
[5] It has found one recent defender in J. McK. Adams. Cf. *Ancient Records and the Bible*, 1946, pp. 174 f., 187 ff. Adams makes Abraham contemporary with Ḥammurabi, and surprisingly states (p. 190) that 'the generally accepted date for the great Babylonian lawgiver' is 2132–2081 B.C. This was scarcely true in 1946, or for some years before that.

Biblical evidence than the two verses to which it would cling. On the other hand, if Abraham is loosed from Ḥammurabi, but placed in the twentieth century, with the Descent into Egypt in the Hyksos period and an Exodus in the thirteenth century B.C., as they are by Burrows and Wright, we are faced with the assumption that the Biblical chronology wrongly dated the Exodus, but correctly remembered the duration of long periods stretching back to far more ancient times. We are also faced with the difficulties already noted, of the assumed false connexion of Joseph's Pharaoh with the Heliopolitan worship, and the relative location of Goshen and the court.

Moreover, it has often been noted that there are inner inconsistencies within the Biblical traditions of the Conquest. Thus, Josh. x attributes to Joshua the complete conquest of all the southern part of the land,[1] afterwards occupied by Judah, and the annihilation of the population of Makkedah, Libnah, Lachish, Gezer, Eglon, Hebron, and Debir.[2] On the other hand, there are scattered notes in the book of Joshua which are in disagreement with this. Josh. xvi. 10 says that the population of Gezer was not annihilated but remained in occupation. Further, the conquest of Debir, which in Josh. x. 38 f. is attributed to Joshua, is attributed to Othniel in Josh. xv. 17. But Othniel is represented in the book of Judges as the first of the Judges, belonging to the age that followed Joshua, and Jg. i. 13 repeats the story of the capture of Debir, but places it after the death of Joshua.[3] Similarly the capture of Hebron is ascribed to Caleb in Josh. xv. 14, and in Jg. i. 10 to Judah after the death of Joshua.

It has been commonly held that the latter part of Josh. x is unhistorical in attributing all these conquests to Joshua, and this view has been maintained by Elliger[4] and Noth.[5] Wright has contested this view, and has maintained that if the Exodus lay in the thirteenth century B.C. the general picture presented by this chapter is in harmony with the evidence of archaeology, and that it may therefore be accepted.[6] He argues for the historicity

---

[1] Josh. x. 40–2.   [2] Ibid. 28–39.

[3] Cf. Jg. i. 1. But it is probable that the indication of date is editorial. The death of Joshua is recorded in Jg. ii. 8, but that verse probably was not drawn from the same sources as the material of chapter i, so that it can no more be taken as the sequel to the events of chapter i (as by Jack, *The Date of the Exodus*, 1925, p. 71) than i. 1 can be taken as their antecedent.

[4] Cf. *P.J.B.* xxx, 1934, pp. 47–71.

[5] Cf. ibid. xxxiii, 1937, pp. 22–36, and *Das Buch Josua*, 1938, pp. 34 ff.

[6] Cf. *J.N.E.S.* v, 1946, pp. 105–14.

of Josh. x, and also for that of Jg. i, and finds no difficulty in believing that the work which Joshua did so completely, according to Josh. x, needed to be done all over again immediately after his death. This is a surprising thesis. If Joshua had destroyed all that breathed from Kadesh-Barnea to Gibeon,[1] there would seem not to have been many for the tribes of Judah and Simeon to attack, and even if this is treated as an exaggerated statement, it is hard to suppose that a systematic conquest, such as is indicated in Josh. x, was so ephemeral.[2] Wright accepts the evidence of archaeology that there was a long period of disturbance and local fighting, precisely as the book of Judges indicates.[3] But surely this means that there cannot have been any systematic conquest at the very beginning of the period. It would seem to be more likely that Josh. x ascribes to Joshua a systematic conquest in a single campaign, when the historical truth which underlies it is rather a series of local encounters spread over a long period. Joshua's routing of the armies that assembled at Aijalon may then be accepted as historical, but the truth so far as the conquest of Judah is concerned should be sought in the scattered fragments in Numbers, Joshua, and Judges.

We have two accounts of the destruction of the place in south Judah to which the name Hormah was given. The one says that this took place in the time of Moses, while the other says it took place after the death of Joshua. Both of these traditions are unlikely to be true. In Num. xxi. 1–3 we read that when the children of Israel left Kadesh-Barnea they were attacked by the king of Arad. They vowed that they would put the enemy cities to the ban, and in fulfilment of this vow they destroyed it and called the name of the place Hormah. In Jg. i. 16 f. we read that the tribes of Judah and Simeon went from the city of palm-trees[4] to Arad, where they smote the Canaanites who inhabited

---

[1] Cf. Josh. x. 40–2.
[2] Cf. Jack, *The Date of the Exodus*, 1925, p. 71: 'We cannot conceive that the Israelites, having gained complete possession of the land and exterminated their enemies, were after Joshua's death driven back upon Jericho and began a second series of campaigns which restored the country by degrees to them.'
[3] Cf. *J.N.E.S.*, loc. cit., p. 113.
[4] The city of palm-trees is commonly understood to be Jericho. But Simpson (*The Early Traditions of Israel*, 1948, p. 324) suggests that it is Tamar, 85 miles south of Arad, while Meek (*Hebrew Origins*, 1936, p. 37 n.) would identify it with Beersheba. Against Garstang's argument (*Joshua–Judges*, 1931, p. 215) that the movement was upwards and hence must have been from Jericho, he refers to Num. xiii. 18, 21 f., xiv. 40 ff., where the verb is used for movement from the south.

Zephath and called the place Hormah. Each of these accounts has been edited to reflect some aspect of the dominant tradition, and each is most significant in what it preserves that is out of harmony with that tradition. The second account indicates that this attack was not made by the united tribes, but by Judah and Simeon, with some Kenite elements. The first indicates that it was made from the south and in the age that preceded the time of Joshua.[1] It is most improbable that a successful campaign would have been followed by a withdrawal,[2] and it is most likely that we have here reflected the beginning of a movement by some of the tribes into the south in an age quite separate from that of Joshua.[3] The accounts of the conquest of Hebron and Debir by Judah and Caleb may then be further stages in this movement, and may be loosed altogether from any connexion with Joshua.[4]

That Judah entered the land from the south is rendered probable by the isolation from the northern tribes which marked it in early times. In the Song of Deborah Judah is not mentioned for praise or blame, and neither is Simeon. If these tribes were in the stream of the common life of the twelve tribes, this would be surprising, and still more so if, as is sometimes claimed, they belonged to an amphictyony, or religious confederation, pledged to support their fellow tribes in need, and including all the Israelite tribes. In that case they would have been cursed for their breach of loyalty to the amphictyony, as Meroz, upon

---

[1] Paton (*B.W.* xlvi, 1916, pp. 178 ff.) concludes that JE in Joshua is more trustworthy than D and P, that Jg. i is more trustworthy than JE in Joshua, and that Num. xv. 44 f. and xxi. 1–3 give a more trustworthy account than Jg. i.

[2] Cf. Tonneau, *R.B.* xxxv, 1926, p. 592: 'S'ils avaient pu forcer le passage à Sephat rien ne les eût empêchés de poursuivre leur route et d'arriver directement en Canaan par le sud.' Cf., too, Cook, *Critical Notes on Old Testament History*, 1907, pp. 38 ff., 81 f., esp. p. 39: 'It is irresistible to avoid the conclusion [*sic*, apparently for 'to reach the conclusion'] which several critics have reached, that after the events at Kadesh some clans actually succeeded in making their way into Judah.'

[3] Cf. Burney, *Israel's Settlement in Canaan*, pp. 28 ff. See also Steuernagel, *Die Einwanderung der israelitischen Stämme in Kanaan*, 1901, pp. 75 ff., where Num. xiv. 43, 45, xxi. 1–3, Jg. i. 16 f., are brought together and treated as fragments of an account of an attack on Judah from the south. This is dated (p. 123) *circa* 1400 B.C., while the occupation of the mountains of Ephraim is dated *circa* 1385 B.C. Kennett (*Old Testament Essays*, 1928, pp. 25 f.) opposes the view that Judah advanced from the south.

[4] Josh. xv. 13–19; Jg. i. 10–15. Steuernagel (op. cit., pp. 74 f.) brings Num. xiii. 22, 28 into association with Josh. xv. 13 f., and holds that Caleb is referred to in both.

whom there clearly rested some obligation, was cursed.[1] Even Reuben and Gilead and Dan and Asher are not cursed, though there is reproach, implying that some bond was recognized between these tribes and those that rallied to Deborah and Barak, though not the bond of a sacred oath. Yet Judah and Simeon are unmentioned. But Judah, at least, was not entirely outside the stream of the common life of the Israelite tribes, though not wholly within it. We read in particular of Levites, in the period of the Judges, maintaining relations with Judah[2] and with others of the tribes in a way that was quite different from relations with the Jebusites.[3] It is therefore probable that Judah does not figure in the Song of Deborah because geographical and other conditions made it impracticable to expect any contingents from the south to come to Mount Tabor; and this would hold even more for Simeon.

Jerusalem was still a Jebusite stronghold. It is true that Jg. i. 8 says the tribe of Judah smote the city with the edge of the sword and set fire to it. But Jg. i. 21 states that the tribe of Benjamin failed to capture it, and the Jebusites remained in the city, while Jg. xix. 11 f. represents it as still a Jebusite city, until David captured it and made it his capital.[4] We also read that Gezer remained in Canaanite hands in the period of the Judges,[5] and it does not seem to have become an Israelite city until the days of Solomon.[6] There would seem to have been an unconquered belt of the country separating Judah from the northern tribes, and this would make it quite impracticable for Judah to march against Sisera.

There was also a belt of unconquered cities in the Vale of Esdraelon, stretching from Beth-shan to the coast. But it was against the Canaanites of this belt, under the leadership of Sisera, that the attack of the Israelites was directed. The tribes to the north and south of that belt gathered under the leadership of Deborah and Barak to break the power that was crushing them one by one. For contingents from the tribe of Judah to march to Mount Tabor, leaving hostile cities between them and their homes, would be to invite attack on those homes in their absence. In a later age central and southern tribes could unite against the Philistines without fear of embarrassment from Gezer or Jerusalem or any other Canaanite city. For the Philistines menaced Canaanite and Israelite alike. But Sisera was no menace

[1] Jg. v. 23.
[2] Cf. Jg. xvii. 7, xviii. 3, xix. 1.
[3] Jg. xix. 11 f.
[4] 2 Sam. v. 6 ff.
[5] Jg. i. 29.
[6] 1 Kgs. ix. 16.

to Jerusalem, while a Judah that was steadily pressing north-wards was. It therefore seems highly probable that Judah did not extend its power southwards from Jericho, as the book of Joshua declares, but from the south northwards, and that its conquest began before the time of Joshua and the capture of the central highlands.

The attack would then be from the neighbourhood of Kadesh-Barnea. There is some reason to suppose that this place figured even more largely in the traditions of the southern tribes than it does in the present Pentateuch. When the Israelites came out of Egypt we read that after crossing the Red Sea they went three days' journey into the wilderness without finding water.[1] We are not told the name of the place they then reached, but it seems probable that it was Kadesh. For they came to a place called Marah, where were some bitter waters which Moses sweetened,[2] and we read that after the sweetening of the waters God made for them statutes and ordinances, and there he tested them.[3] This would seem to refer to the testing which took place at Massah,[4] which means 'testing'. But Massah is identified with Meribah,[5] and Meribah is elsewhere located at Kadesh.[6] It would appear that all of these traditions gathered originally around Kadesh, where there is known to have been a sacred spring, called En-mishpat,[7] with other springs in the neighbour-hood, and these would seem to be the ones referred to in these traditions. Lods says: 'Situated at the junction of several of the desert trails . . . it has four main springs, distant from one another from one to three hours' journey. The most abundant of them, Ain-el-Qedeirat, flows out of a rock in three jets, each as thick as a man's arm, and forms a stream by whose bank grow shady acacias and luxuriant vegetation.'[8]

---

[1] Ex. xv. 22.   [2] Ibid. 23.   [3] Ibid. 25.
[4] Ibid. xvii. 1–7.   [5] Ibid. 7.

[6] Num. xx. 13, xxvii. 14; Dt. xxxii. 51. On the other hand, Ex. xvii. 6 f. would appear to associate Massah and Meribah with Horeb. But it is prob-able that there was some conflation here, and that these two verses come from separate sources. Cf. Driver, *The Book of Exodus*, 1918, p. 157; Beer-Galling, *Exodus*, 1939, pp. 90 f.

[7] Gen. xiv. 7. Cf. 'the waters of Meribah', Num. xx. 13, 24; Dt. xxxiii. 8; Ps. lxxxi. 8 (E.V. 7), xcv. 8, cvi. 32; and 'the waters of Meribah of Kadesh', Num. xxvii. 14; Dt. xxxii. 51; Ezek. xlvii. 19, xlviii. 28.

[8] Cf. *Israel*, 1932, p. 176 (= *Israël*, 1930, pp. 199 f.). Lods here follows a common identification of the site of Kadesh at 'Ain Qadīs. So Abel (*Géo-graphie de la Palestine*, i, 1933, p. 306), Noth (*Die Welt des Alten Testaments*, 1940, p. 45), and Davis-Gehman (*The Westminster Dictionary of the Bible*, 1944, p. 340a). Cf. also Engnell, *S.B.U.* i, 1948, cols. 1171 f.; and Mowinckel,

It is therefore probable, as has frequently been recognized,[1] that in the earliest tradition the Israelites who came out of Egypt were said to have proceeded straight to Kadesh,[2] which they reached three days after leaving the pursuing Pharaoh behind. This is then probably to be brought into association with the request of Pharaoh to allow them to go three days' journey into the wilderness to sacrifice to Yahweh.[3] It would then follow that Kadesh was associated with Yahweh before the Israelites arrived there.[4]

In the form in which the Pentateuch now stands, however, the tribes are said to have gone to Horeb, or Sinai, which was far from Kadesh, and only to have come to Kadesh subsequently. In the book of Deuteronomy we are told that Kadesh was eleven days' journey away from Sinai.[5] The reference to Kadesh in the passages mentioned was suppressed, giving the impression that all these incidents took place on the way to Sinai or Horeb, and again all at Kadesh later. Yet it is to be noted that thirty-eight of the forty years of the wilderness period are said to have been spent at Kadesh.[6]

From Kadesh the spies were sent into the land, and according to the J account they proceeded no farther than Hebron, and the minority report was given by Caleb alone.[7] This account would therefore seem to be connected with a movement from Kadesh into the district occupied by Judah, with whom, as has been noted, Calibbite elements were associated.

It is likely, therefore, that two accounts of what happened after the Israelites came out of Egypt have been combined.[8]

Norsk Geografisk Tidsskrift, ix, 1942, pp. 5 ff., where, however, the Biblical Kadesh is recognized to be a district rather than a place. So, too, de Vaux, *R.B.* xlvii, 1938, pp. 89 ff.; cf. earlier Savignac, *R.B.* xxxi, 1922, pp. 55 ff. Phythian-Adams (*The Call of Israel*, 1934, pp. 187 ff.) would locate it at Petra, and is followed by Elmslie (*How came Our Faith*, 1948, pp. 104 n., 212).

[1] Cf. Wellhausen, *Prolegomena zur Geschichte Israels*, 4th ed., 1895, p. 348; Smith, *Old Testament History*, 1911, pp. 61 f.; Hölscher, *Die Profeten*, 1914, pp. 112 f.; Cook, *C.A.H.* ii, 1924, p. 361; Sellin, *Geschichte des israelitisch-jüdischen Volkes*, i, 2nd ed., 1935, pp. 65 ff.; Simpson, *The Early Traditions of Israel*, 1948, pp. 436 f.

[2] Cf. Jg. xi. 16.   [3] Ex. v. 3; cf. iii. 18, viii. 23 (E.V. 27).

[4] Cf. Mowinckel, *Norsk Geografisk Tidsskrift*, ix, 1942, pp. 21 f.

[5] Dt. i. 2.   [6] Cf. ibid. 46, ii. 1, 14.

[7] Num. xiii. 22, 26, 30, xxxii. 8; Dt. i. 19 ff. Simpson (*The Early Traditions of Israel*, 1948, pp. 34 f.) says that the E document does not mention Kadesh or Hebron.

[8] Cf. Mowinckel, *Norsk Geografisk Tidsskrift*, ix, 1942, pp. 14 ff., where it is held that the Sinai and law-giving traditions have been interpolated in a

According to the one they proceeded straight to Kadesh, and
there offered sacrifice to Yahweh and received his statutes. They
remained there for thirty-eight years and then advanced northwards into the territory occupied by Judah. According to the
other, they proceeded to the sacred mount of Sinai or Horeb,
where they received the divine ordinances, and had a two years'
period of wandering in the wilderness.[1]

It has to be remembered that while the J narrative displays a
special interest in the traditions of Judah and the E narrative in
those of Ephraim, both are corpora of traditions of all the tribes.
Both appear to have been compiled after the traditions had been
fused in the period of the early monarchy. Hence both represent
all the tribes as having together passed through all the major
experiences recorded. Lods observes that we need not infer from
the fact that in the J tradition Kadesh was the original home of
the Mosaic legislation that in this form of the tradition Sinai had
no place, and he suggests that in its earliest forms the J tradition
described a short visit to Sinai in the course of a long stay at
Kadesh.[2] This is likely, indeed, for Sinai certainly figures in the
J tradition. But this does not mean that the group that sojourned
for so long at Kadesh actually paid a visit to Sinai. We have to
distinguish between the history behind the tradition and the
tradition as it is modified by combination with the traditions of
the various tribes. If the tribes all came out of Egypt and were
all led by Moses, they cannot have gone first to Kadesh and also
have gone first to Sinai or Horeb, and one of these traditions
would have to be pronounced false. But if some of the tribes came
out of Egypt and some did not, and if some were led by Moses
and some were not, then it is equally possible that some went to
Kadesh and some did not, and that some went to Sinai or Horeb
and some did not. We can no more conclude that all the tribes
went to Sinai or Horeb because both J and E have traditions
of a visit to that mountain, than we can conclude that all the
tribes were led by Moses because both J and E represent him as
the leader. We need not discuss whether Sinai is to be equated

Kadesh tradition. Cf., too, Meinhold, who says (*Der Dekalog*, 1927, p. 8):
'Die älteste der 4 zum Pentateuch verarbeiteten Schriften . . . weiss nichts von
einem Bundesschluss, einer Gesetzgebung am Sinai.'

[1] Cf. Paton, *B.W.* xlvi, 1916, p. 88: 'One of the most remarkable features
of the story of the wanderings is the inability of the documents to combine the
story at Kadesh with the story at Sinai.'

[2] Cf. *Israël*, 1930, pp. 201 ff. (E.Tr., 1932, pp. 177 f.). Simpson (*The Early
Traditions of Israel*, 1948, pp. 441 f.) holds that the story of Moses's visit to
Sinai is unhistorical, and that it is a purposeful fiction.

with Horeb or not.[1] What is certain is that Sinai takes the place in the J tradition that is taken by Horeb in the E and D traditions.

Here it should be remembered that if all the tribes had come out of Egypt together it would be surprising for some of them to forget the goal of their first journey and the place where they had a rendezvous with Yahweh. On the other hand, if the two groups really had separate experiences, it would not be surprising for each group to impress upon its form of the combined traditions of the whole its own special memories. This would mean that we do not have to choose between the two separate forms of the tradition which can be found behind the present conflation. The conflation is unhistorical, but the separate traditions may be accepted as genuinely historical. Our only difficulty is to disentangle them. In particular we have to decide which of the groups came out of Egypt and which of them was led by Moses. Here scholars of eminence are not agreed, and it may be granted that the decision is not simple. But all that I am concerned at the moment to stress is that the Biblical traditions are not simple, whether we look at their chronology or their content.[2] The chronology of Ex. xii. 40 and 1 Kgs. vi. 1 finds itself in conflict with a whole series of data, as we have seen; and the Kadesh and Sinai or Horeb traditions equally find themselves in conflict, as also do the traditions of the entry into the land. The story of an advance from the south of a group consisting of some only of the tribes and of the scattered attack of the various tribes each acting singly or in local groups finds itself in conflict with the story of an advance by all the tribes across the Jordan at Jericho with the spread over the land from that - point. And if we resolve the attack across the Jordan into the

[1] T. H. Robinson (*History of Israel*, i, 1932, p. 83) notes that in one tradition the sacred mount appears to have been situated in the neighbourhood of Kadesh. Cf. Mowinckel, *Norsk Geografisk Tidsskrift*, ix, 1942, pp. 17 ff., esp. p. 20. The problem of the location of Sinai, and of its relation to Horeb, is not a simple one, and while not a little of the evidence points to the neighbourhood of Kadesh, this is not the whole of the evidence. Cf. Pedersen, *Israel I–II*, 1926, pp. 501 f. Nielsen (*The Site of the Biblical Mount Sinai*, 1928) argued for the location of Mount Sinai at Petra.

[2] Cf. Cook, *The Old Testament: a Reinterpretation*, 1936, p. 59: 'When one examines the traditions in Gen. xii–l, it is found that most of them imply an entrance, a settlement, and a continuous occupation once and for all. That is to say, the Old Testament blends two quite distinct views of the origin of Israel: (a) the one in Genesis knows of the patriarchs settling in Canaan, of their Aramaean connections, and of a definitive conquest; the other (b) traces the national history back to Moses and the Exodus, when Israelites entered and conquered the land of their forefathers for the first time.'

attack of a single group of the tribes, we have to consider its age relatively to the attack from the south. Moreover, when we have separated a Kadesh tradition from a Sinai or Horeb tradition we have to consider their relation to one another and the relation of both to the Yahwism which all the tribes recognized as their religion.

LECTURE III

SYNTHESIS

IN the preceding lectures we have surveyed the non-Biblical and the Biblical evidence which has to be taken into account in framing a self-consistent and satisfying view of the history and chronology of our period. My aim has been, not to select just those items of evidence which are convenient for my own theory and to ignore the rest, as has been far too common in discussions of this problem, but to include every variety of evidence in order that the full complexity of the problem might appear. Any simple view of a fifteenth-century Exodus of all the tribes under Moses and Joshua is out of the question. It can claim the support of Garstang's dating of the fall of Jericho, but it is not supported by Palestinian archaeology as a whole, which, as Albright says, shows that the main wave of destruction fell in the thirteenth century.[1] It can claim the support of 1 Kgs. vi. 1, but it is not supported by a considerable amount of other Biblical evidence, at which we have looked. It has never been supported by Egyptologists, and so far as I am aware, its holders have never attempted to relate it seriously to the Egyptian evidence.[2] On the other hand, any simple view of a thirteenth-century Exodus of all the tribes is equally out of the question. It can claim the support of Ex. i. 11 and of the relevance of Egyptian conditions at the time of the Exodus, but it has to deny or explain away the earlier Egyptian references to Asher, and to overpress the philological difficulties in the equation of Ḫabiru and Hebrews so as to dissociate the Amarna letters entirely from the Biblical history, and it is embarrassed by the Merneptah stele. It is significant that Meek and Albright, no less than many older scholars, hold that there was a double entry into Palestine, even though their account of that double entry differs materially from that represented by Burney. But, as I hope I have made plain, it is not merely a question of the date of the Exodus and of the movements into Palestine, but of relating the entries to one another and of explaining how all the tribes came to be Yahweh-worshipping and why they thought of themselves as related to

[1] Cf. *Haverford Symposium*, p. 23.
[2] Garstang has attempted to relate the consequent history to Egyptian history, but what is in mind here is the attempt to show that Thothmes III carried out building enterprises and established his court in the immediate neighbourhood of the Israelite settlements.

one another. The Descent into Egypt and the Exodus must be
considered together in any satisfying view. That is why the
subject of these lectures is 'From Joseph to Joshua', and not
merely 'The Date of the Exodus'.

The view which I put forward some years ago, and by which
I still stand, with but minor modifications, does violence to no
archaeological evidence known to me, save that it shares the
embarrassment of Ai with every view. At the same time it
utilizes more of the Biblical evidence than any other view. It can
scarcely be gainsaid that the Biblical traditions have been edited.
Yet it is likely that they preserve historical material, and are not
to be dismissed as negligible.

I find the entry of the Hebrew tribes into Palestine to be
reflected in the Amarna letters. This is not on the ground of the
philological equation of the names Ḥabiru and Hebrews, which
I hold to be probable but not certain. Still less is it because I fail
to recognize that the Ḥabiru of the Amarna letters were but a
part of the Ḥabiru of the ancient world, or wish to impose upon
the use of the name in one locality a nuance which it came to
have in another. In Nuzu the Ḥabiru were socially depressed
classes, but in Palestine they were *ḥabbatu*, or plunderers, seeking
to get possession of lands and townships. In view of the now
recognized interchange between Ḥabiru and SA-GAZ, and therefore of the close association between the aggressive elements
referred to variously under these names, we may say that there
is evidence of their activity in the south and in the north, but
that the only place in the centre of the land where there is
evidence of their activity is Shechem. There is, however, evidence
that Megiddo was under some pressure from Labaya, of Shechem,
who had joined the enemy.[1]

This does not seem to me to support the view of Meek,[2] that
the entry of the Joseph tribes is reflected in the Amarna letters,
or the view of Albright,[3] that those tribes were already in posses-

[1] Cf. TA 242–6 (Knudtzon, *Die El-Amarna Tafeln*, i, p. 786–97).

[2] Cf. *B.A.S.O.R.*, No. 61, Feb. 1936, pp. 17–19. Cf. also Luckenbill,
A.J.Th. xxii, 1918, pp. 40 f.

[3] Cf. *B.A.S.O.R.*, No. 58, pp. 10–18. See also *J.P.O.S.* i, 1921, p. 66, where
Albright suggested that the central highlands had been continuously occupied
from the time of Abraham, whom he then placed at the beginning of the
Hyksos period. He thus put the Amarna age fighting between the settlement
of the Joseph tribes and the settlement of Judah. In *B.A.S.O.R.*, No. 35, Oct.
1929, p. 6, Albright said: 'If the Hebrews attacked and destroyed many of
the Canaanite towns of Central Palestine in the sixteenth and fifteenth centuries B.C., but did not settle down themselves until the thirteenth and

sion of the centre of the land at the very beginning of the Amarna age. It is unjustified to base on silence the assumption that all the cities of this part of the land had fallen,[1] and, since the known areas of disturbance were chiefly in the north and in the south, it seems more probable that there were attacks from the north and from the south[2] and that neither thrust penetrated effectively into the centre. This is as we should expect. For it would be surprising for attacks made from these directions to be swiftly effective in the centre of the land, without a consolidated hold on the districts through which they came.

So far as the southern thrust of the Amarna age is concerned, I relate it to the Biblical tradition of an entry into Palestine from the south before Joshua's attack. The tradition of that attack only survives in traces in the Bible, but it fits well into the picture of the Ḥabiru activity.[3] It was probably, as we have seen, an attack made from Kadesh-Barnea, after a sojourn there of thirty-eight years, and its first notable victory was at Hormah,

twelfth, the archaeological situation would be fully explained.' It is hard to believe that they waited so long to occupy what they had conquered.

[1] Böhl (*Kanaanäer und Hebräer*, 1911, p. 93) suggests that the reason why we have no Amarna letters from Bethel, Hebron, Beersheba, Shiloh, and Gibeon is that these cities were already occupied by the Israelites in the Amarna age. Powis Smith (*A.J.S.L.* xxxii, 1915–16, p. 85) extends this argument from silence to include Jericho and Mizpah as well as these other cities. Similarly, Jack (*The Date of the Exodus*, 1925, p. 157) thinks the Israelite occupation of Hebron, Beersheba, Bethel, Gibeon, and other important centres is the correct inference from silence. Again Meek (*Hebrew Origins*, 1936, p. 20; cf. *A.J.Th.* xxiv, 1920, p. 211) concludes from the absence of letters from Jericho, Shechem, Gibeon, Mizpah, and Shiloh that all of these places were already occupied. On the other hand, however, Meek states (*Hebrew Origins*, p. 25; cf. *B.A.S.O.R.*, No. 61, Feb. 1936, p. 19) that Jericho was captured shortly after 1400 B.C. and that the invaders 'then gradually extended their conquests into the highlands of Ephraim, capturing Bethel in the west *c.* 1300 or slightly later' and emphasizes (*B.A.S.O.R.*, loc. cit., p. 17) that the newcomers 'must have continued over a period of a century or more before they made any considerable portion of the land their own'. I am in some difficulty to harmonize this insistence on the gradualness of the conquest with the claim that the absence of letters from so many cities in the Amarna age is accounted for by the fact that they were 'in the hands of the invading Habiru by that time'. [2] Cf. Jack, *The Date of the Exodus*, pp. 144 f.

[3] Cf. Jack, ibid., p. 143: 'When we find the name Ḥabiru in the Amarna Letters about 1400–1370 B.C., as the designation of a large body of people invading Palestine from the south, attacking and capturing cities, and taking possession of the land, and when we remember on Biblical grounds that the date coincides with the entry of the Israelites who proceeded north from Kadesh-Barnea and overran the land, we can have no difficulty in concluding who these invaders were.'

which was put to the ban. According to Jg. i Judah and Simeon carried out this incursion, together with certain non-Israelite elements, including Kenites and Calibbites.[1] There is reason, as we have seen, to suppose that Levi, too, was associated with this attack, though since Levi failed to secure any territorial unity its name has been allowed to fall out.[2] Reuben, too, was probably associated with it. It is surprising to find no mention of Reuben in Jg. i, though the ancestor of the tribe is said to have been the eldest son of Jacob.[3] It has recently been argued anew by Noth that Reuben was once west of the Jordan, and crossed to the east.[4] It is therefore likely that Reuben belonged to the group of tribes that moved northward from Kadesh. It is probable that this group of tribes soon separated and that each tried to establish itself in some district of the land, Judah steadily working her way northwards and not advancing more rapidly than she could consolidate her gains, Simeon and Levi more adventurously pressing on farther north but failing to secure any permanent settlement, and Reuben pressing on and reaching the east of the Dead Sea where she secured some foothold.[5]

In the Amarna age there was activity in the north as well as in

---

[1] Jg. i. 3, 17; i. 12, 16. Cf. also 1 Sam. xxvii. 10, xxx. 26 ff. for the evidence of the association of Kenites with Judah.

[2] Cf. Kennett, *Old Testament Essays*, 1928, pp. 27 f., where it is held that the non-mention of Levi in Jg. i is not surprising in view of the fact that it did not assume its present shape until after Levi was regarded as set apart for service at the sanctuary.   [3] Gen. xxix. 32; xxxv. 23.

[4] Cf. *Z.A.W.*, N.F. xix, 1944, pp. 14 ff. So, earlier, Steuernagel, *Die Einwanderung der israelitischen Stämme in Kanaan*, 1901, pp. 15 ff., Burney, *Israel's Settlement in Canaan*, pp. 50 f., and Lods, *Israël*, 1930, p. 384 (E.Tr., 1932, pp. 331 f.). Following Steuernagel, Burney also held that Naphtali once occupied a position in the neighbourhood of the southern Dan (op. cit., p. 23; cf. Steuernagel, op. cit., pp. 28 f.) and that Issachar and Zebulun may once have been located in central Palestine (op. cit., pp. 51 ff.; cf. Steuernagel, op. cit., pp. 12 ff.). Noth (*Das System der zwölf Stämme Israels*, 1930, pp. 77 f.) denies this, however. In *Z.A.W.*, N.F. xix, 1944, pp. 13 f. Noth argues for the association of Gad with Reuben. Several scholars have held that eastern Manasseh was once west of the Jordan and then migrated eastwards (so Budde, *Das Buch der Richter*, 1897, pp. 12 f.; Moore, *Judges*, 1898, pp. 150 f.; Gressmann, *Mose und seine Zeit*, 1913, pp. 316 f.; Burney, *The Book of Judges*, 1920, pp. 49 ff., 134 f., and *Israel's Settlement in Canaan*, pp. 32 ff.; Noth, *Das System der zwölf Stämme Israels*, 1930, p. 36, and *Die Welt des Alten Testaments*, 1940, p. 58; Lods, *Israël*, 1930, p. 384 (E.Tr., 1932, p. 332)), but Segal (*P.E.F.Q.S.* 1918 pp. 124 ff.) opposes this view, and so Bergman (*J.P.O.S.* xvi, 1936, p. 248) and Simons (in *Orientalia Neerlandica*, 1948, pp. 191 ff.).

[5] Meek (*Hebrew Origins*, 1936, p. 39) holds that Reuben was *expelled* from the southern group.

the south,[1] and apparently by groups working separately and independently from those in the south. The brief story of the Conquest given in Jg. i represents the tribes as going up separately to win homes for themselves, with the exception of Judah and Simeon, who went up together. If the northern tribes were pressing in, either singly or in small groups, simultaneously with those in the south, we should have comparable conditions. The Egyptian references to Asher in the reigns of Seti I and Rameses II would be provided for, and there would be no need to stress the element of doubt about this evidence. Similarly, the questionable references to Asher and Zebulun in the Ras Shamra texts would cause no embarrassment. It has been already said that it is very improbable that these references really stand in those texts, but this is not due to the necessities of my view. I believe that Zebulun and Asher were already in the land in the fourteenth century B.C., whether they are mentioned in the Ras Shamra texts or not, and the evidence of those texts can be considered entirely without prejudice. Further, the occupation by Dan of places that were afterwards occupied by the Philistines would be accounted for, since this movement long preceded the coming of the aliens and non-Semites who ultimately gave their name to the land. Finally, the complete and acknowledged lack of agreement between the Biblical account of Joshua's invasion and the picture presented in the Amarna letters would be fully accounted for. For I differentiate the Amarna age attack from Joshua's and place it in an earlier age.

I connect the Amarna age rather with the age of Jacob. Here we have some surviving fragments of Biblical tradition to help us. The only place in the centre of the land where the Ḥabiru are known to have been active is Shechem, of which they appear to have gained possession. If this is connected with the incident recorded in Gen. xxxiv,[2] then Simeon and Levi were involved, and it is on this account that I suppose that Levi, while still a secular tribe, was associated with the advance northwards, and that Simeon and Levi adventurously pressed on ahead of Judah. These two tribes gained possession of Shechem by an act of

---

[1] We read of the SA-GAZ being at Gebal (TA 68: 12 ff.; Knudtzon, *Die El-Amarna Tafeln*, i, pp. 360 f.), Beirut (TA 118: 24 ff.; Knudtzon, op. cit. i, pp. 514 f.), cities dependent on Sidon (TA 144: 24 ff.; Knudtzon, op. cit. i, pp. 602 f.), and possibly at Ashtaroth and Boṣra in Transjordan (TA 197: 10 ff.; Knudtzon, op. cit. i, pp. 726 f.; cf. ii, p. 1292).

[2] Cf. Burney, *Israel's Settlement in Canaan*, pp. 37 ff.; Barton, *J.B.L.* xlviii, 1929, pp. 147 f.

I

treachery, which brought down on them a curse, and they were condemned to be 'scattered in Israel'. This would indicate that they did not retain their hold on Shechem, and indeed we know they did not. Simeon acquired some territorial hold in the south of Judah, until it was absorbed in the tribe of Judah; Levi failed to achieve any territorial status at all as a secular tribe. The antiquity of this Biblical tradition is guaranteed by the fact that Gen. xlix. 5–7 must antedate the assumption of a priestly function by the Levites, and hence go back to a time earlier than the age of Moses' grandson. For Micah's satisfaction at having a Levite for his priest[1] shows that Levites were already assuming a functional character. Yet in the verses from the Blessing of Jacob there is no hint of a functional character, but when it was written there was only the expectation that Simeon and Levi would share a common fate.

By this Shechem incident we are therefore led to place Jacob in the Amarna age. If we place his entry at the beginning of the Amarna age, circa 1400 B.C., the interval between him and an Abraham who lived in the seventeenth century would be rather longer than the Biblical chronology would allow, and that is already more than is probable for two generations. On the other hand, it would be much less than some have supposed, for in the days when Abraham was believed to belong to the twenty-first century B.C. it was common to bring Jacob into the Hyksos period.[2] Moreover, though it is now apparently securely established that Hammurabi belonged to the eighteenth or seventeenth century B.C., the equation of Amraphel with Hammurabi is not beyond doubt,[3] and without it we are left without secure

[1] Jg. xvii. 13.

[2] Garstang claimed that his excavations at Jericho established the 'basic probability' of the Biblical chronology which placed Abraham's departure from Harran in 2092 B.C., and Jacob's entry into Egypt in 1877 B.C. (*The Heritage of Solomon*, 1934, p. 151 n.). But as he placed Jacob's entry in the Hyksos period (ibid., p. 151), which began not earlier than 1730 B.C., and dated Abraham circa 2000 B.C. (ibid., p. 145: 'shortly before the accession of Hammurabi'; p. 62, where Hammurabi is dated circa 2000 B.C.), he lengthened the interval between Abraham and Jacob to approximately the same period as my view would require—if Abraham is made contemporary with Hammurabi, according to the newer dating—and also reduced the Sojourn in Egypt to little more than half of the time assigned in the Biblical chronology.

[3] Albright, while dating both Hammurabi and Abraham in the seventeenth century, does not make them contemporaries, but places Abraham later than Hammurabi. (For his subsequent abandonment of this view, cf. *supra*, p. 64 n.)

clue to the age of Abraham.[1] While I recognize that there is some difficulty in accommodating the Biblical tradition here, it is at a point to which little attention has been paid in most discussions of Biblical chronology and it will be remembered that Albright has narrowed the interval between Abraham and Jacob to vanishing point, or even, on his latest views, seemed to reverse their order and put Abraham a century after Jacob.[2]

In the Biblical account the Shechem incident is placed before the Descent into Egypt. We find in that age two separate groups, one in the neighbourhood of Hebron and one at Shechem, but in touch with one another. Joseph is sent by his father from Hebron to his brethren in the Shechem area,[3] and since Hebron lay in the area of Judah's activity, this would be consistent with the view that Judah, Simeon, and Levi advanced together from the south, while Simeon and Levi pressed farther north. It would accord with the conditions of the Amarna age, when there was Ḥabiru activity south of Jerusalem and also in the Shechem area.

In the Biblical tradition of that age, while Simeon and Levi have bands of followers and are able to attack towns, Joseph appears as a single individual. There is therefore no tribe of Joseph at this stage. Neither is there any tribe of Benjamin. For at an even later stage in the story Benjamin is represented as still a boy at home, who is not with his brothers. This again harmonizes with our lack of evidence of activity in the Amarna age in the Josephite or Benjamite area of Palestine with the exception of the Shechem incident, which is rather to be connected with Simeon and Levi than with the tribes that later occupied this area.

As against this view that there was no tribe of Benjamin in the Amarna age, it should be noted that in Mari texts there is evidence of a tribe of Benjamin at an earlier date, with qualities which have been compared with those of the Biblical Benjamites.[4] It is improbable, however, that this can be the Biblical

[1] Cf. what I wrote in B.J.R.L. xxii, 1938, p. 285: 'For myself, I am not disposed to try to fix the age of Abraham. I would merely urge that there is no strong evidence to point to the age of Ḥammurabi, and that the evidence of Gen. xiv. 1 is both obscure in itself, and of doubtful value even if it were clear. . . . We have no means of knowing, therefore, how far the Amarna age was from the age of Abraham.'

[2] For his most recent positions on this question, restoring the Biblical order, cf. supra, p. 64 n. [3] Gen. xxxvii. 12–15.

[4] Cf. Dossin, in Mélanges Syriens (Dussaud Festschrift), ii, 1939, pp. 981–96. In an unpublished paper (cf. J.B.L. lxvi, 1947, p. xxviii) A. Parrot, the distinguished excavator of Mari, argued for a connexion with the Biblical

tribe. Dossin calls it an Amorite tribe, and assigns its activities to *circa* 2000 B.C. This date would suffice to dissociate it from the Biblical Benjamites. Moreover, in the Biblical tradition that Benjamin alone of all the sons of Jacob was born in Palestine we find a complete lack of any memory of non-Palestinian activities of this tribe.

Since the carrying of Joseph into Egypt is represented as taking place while some of the Israelites were in the vicinity of Shechem, this would appear to point to the Amarna age for the background of the Joseph story. That age would provide a more satisfactory background for it than any other age of which we have knowledge.[1] No Pharaoh would be more ready to welcome ministers from unusual sources than Ikhnaton, and more than one indication in the Joseph story points to this age. It has been already said that a whole series of considerations tells against the commonly assumed Hyksos setting for the Joseph story. We may now observe that there are positive reasons for looking to the age of Ikhnaton for its setting.[2]

Benjamites, and Alt (*P.J.B.*, xxxv, 1939, p. 52) reckons with the possibility of this connexion. So, too, Mendenhall, *B.A.* xi, 1948, p. 16. But the name is one which could easily become attached to more than one group of men; and in the Mari texts its counterpart, Benê-sim'al, is to be found (cf. Dossin, loc. cit., p. 983). Danell (*Studies in the Name Israel in the Old Testament*, 1946, p. 33) is more cautious about this identification, while Albright (*J.B.L.* lviii, 1939, p. 102) definitely rejects it. So too Dougherty, *Scripture*, iii, 1948, p. 100. Similarly de Vaux (*R.B.* liii, 1946, p. 344) says: 'On a noté aussitôt que les Benê-Yamina portaient le même nom que les Benjaminites, qui seront une tribu israélite, mais cette appellation commune n'indique aucun rapport historique.'

[1] Cf. Cook, *C.A.H.* ii, 1924, p. 357: 'People were being sold for food to Yarimuta; and were actually fleeing for refuge to Egypt, where Syrian (Palestinian) officials, like Yankhamu and Dudu, could hold high positions.'

[2] Amongst those who have assigned the entry into Egypt to the Amarna age are Wood (*J.B.L.* xxxv, 1916, pp. 166 f.), Meek (*A.J.Th.* xxiv, 1920, p. 210; *Hebrew Origins*, 1936, p. 28), Burney (*Israel's Settlement in Canaan*, pp. 87 ff.), Kittel (*Geschichte des Volkes Israel*, i, 5th and 6th ed., 1923, p. 366), and Schmidtke (*Die Einwanderung Israels in Kanaan*, 1933, p. 66). Some older writers also argued for this age, but sought to support their case by emended texts, and instead handicapped it. So Cheyne (*O.L.Z.* iii, 1900, cols. 151 f.) proposed the reading אביר כונאתן = 'mighty one of Ikhnaton', or (*E.B.* ii, 1901, col. 2594) חבר כונאתן = 'friend of Ikhnaton' for אברך ונתון אתו in Gen. xli. 43 (cf. Müller's criticism, *O.L.Z.* iii, 1900, cols. 325 f., and Cheyne's reply, *O.L.Z.* iii, 1900, cols. 464 f.); while Marquart (*Philologus*, Supplementband vii, 1899, p. 677) proposed צפתן for צפנת in Gen. xli. 45, and equated the last syllable with Aton, and further suggested that the name of Joseph's wife was connected with the name borne by Ikhnaton's second daughter, who married Tutankhamen, and hence for אסנת read ענחסאתן. Cf. Winckler, in

Pharaoh Ikhnaton ascended the throne as Amenhotep IV, with his capital at Thebes, and with the Theban priesthood wielding great influence in the affairs of state.[1] The new king, who is thought to have been brought up at Heliopolis,[2] was a devotee of the Aton worship,[3] which seems to have already gained in prestige before his accession.[4] Soon the Pharaoh exalted the Aton worship, and proclaimed Aton to be the sole god. He broke with the Theban priests and with all that they stood for and confiscated their revenues.[5] He changed his name from Amenhotep to Ikhnaton, and in order to get away from the influence of the Theban priesthood, which must have exerted all its influence against his religious revolution, he built a new capital, called Akhetaton, to which the government was trans-

Schrader–Winckler–Zimmern, *Die Keilinschriften und das Alte Testament*, 3rd ed., 1903, p. 211.

[1] Cf. Breasted, *History of Egypt*, 1906, p. 362: 'One of Amenhotep III's High Priests of Amon had also been chief treasurer of the kingdom, and another, Ptahmose, was the grand vizier of the realm; while the same thing had occurred in the reign of Hatshepsut, when Hapuseneb had been both vizier and High Priest of Amon. . . . Indeed, the fact that such extensive political power was now wielded by the High Priests of Amon must have intensified the young king's desire to be freed from the sacerdotal thrall which he had inherited.' Cf. also id., *C.A.H.* ii, 1924, pp. 112. Similarly Weigall, *The Life and Times of Akhnaton*, 1923, p. 16: 'At Thebes the priesthood of Amon formed an organization of such power and wealth that the actions of the Pharaoh had largely come to be controlled by it.' Cf. White, *J.A.O.S.* lxviii, 1948, pp. 97 f.

[2] Cf. Steindorff and Seele, *When Egypt ruled the East*, 1942, pp. 201, 204.

[3] Breasted calls him 'the first *individual* in human history' (*History of Egypt*, 1906, p. 356) and paints an idealistic picture of him. He says (*Development of Religion and Thought in Ancient Egypt*, 1912, p. 339): 'Until Ikhnaton the history of the world had been but the irresistible drift of tradition. All men had been but drops of water in the great current. Ikhnaton was the first individual in history.' Others rate him rather less highly. Cf. Wardle, *Z.A.W.*, N.F. ii, 1925, pp. 203 ff. Mercer denies that he was a monotheist (*J.S.O.R.* x, 1926, pp. 14 ff.), as is claimed by Breasted and others (cf. Peet, *M.E.O.J.* ix, 1921, pp. 39 ff.). White (*J.A.O.S.* lxviii, 1948, pp. 91 ff.) goes much farther in depreciating Ikhnaton, and holds that he originated virtually nothing (p. 102). The movement towards monotheism is said to have been centuries old when he ascended the throne, and the tension between the temporal and the ecclesiastical powers already existed. Cf. Baikie, *The Amarna Age*, 1926, p. 313.

[4] Cf. ibid., p. 204; also Peet, *M.E.O.J.* ix, 1921, pp. 42 f. But cf. Roeder, *Preussische Jahrbücher*, clxxxii, 1920, p. 72.

[5] Cf. Speleers, *Supplément au Dictionnaire de la Bible*, ii, 1934, col. 815: 'Son fanatisme le poussa à persécuter le clergé d'Amon et produisit des résultats désastreux pour celui-ci, qui y perdit ses privilèges et ses biens; temples et sanctuaires tombèrent en ruines; le culte d'Amon fut même aboli et ses desservants furent remplacés par ceux d'Aton.'

ferred. Large endowments were given to the Aton worship. This
was the worship of the solar disk, but that it was intimately connected with the old solar worship of Heliopolis is agreed by all
writers.[1] Moreover, the title the Pharaoh assumed for himself
was identical with that borne by the High Priest of Heliopolis.[2]

Clearly a Pharaoh who had broken with the Theban priesthood which hitherto had supplied many of the chief officers of
the state would be forced to look round to find talent where he
could to carry on the administration. To this *a priori* consideration we may add that he is known to have employed Semites in
high office.[3]

The Amarna letters give evidence of the weakening of the Egyptian grip on Palestine, and Ikhnaton is often depicted as a weak
dreamer who let his empire fall to pieces while he was immersed
in his religious changes. This is not a very convincing picture.
In the first place, it should be remembered that the weakness in
Palestine did not begin with the accession of Ikhnaton, but was
already manifest under his predecessor.[4] In the second place, it
is to be observed that there was no sign of weakness in Egypt
during the reign of Ikhnaton. The powerful Theban priesthood
must have been bitterly opposed to his policy, and the fact that
within a few years of the death of Ikhnaton it was all reversed
and Amon was once more restored to his position, and his priests
to their privileges,[5] is sufficient indication that the reform had

[1] Cf. Breasted, *History of Egypt*, 1906, p. 360; G. Roeder, *Preussische Jahr-
bücher*, clxxxii, 1920, p. 72; Peet, *M.E.O.J.* ix, 1921, pp. 42 f.; Baikie, *History
of Egypt*, ii, 1929, pp. 359 ff.; Erman, *Die Religion der Ägypter*, 1934, pp. 114 f.;
Steindorff and Seele, *When Egypt ruled the East*, 1942, pp. 204 f.; Drioton and
Vandier, *Les Peuples de l'Orient méditerranéen*, II. *L'Égypte*, 1946, p. 452;
Leeuwenburg, *Echnaton*, 1946, pp. 71 f.

[2] Cf. Breasted, op. cit., p. 360.

[3] e.g. Dudu and Yanḥamu, with each of whom Joseph has been improb-
ably identified (cf. Cheyne, *E.B.* ii, 1901, col. 2591; Procksch, *Genesis*, 1924,
pp. 406 f.; Barton, *Archaeology and the Bible*, 6th ed., 1933, pp. 366–8; Marquart, *Philologus*, Supplementband vii, 1899, p. 680; Winckler, *Abraham als
Babylonier, Joseph als Ägypter*, 1903, p. 31). See also Burney, *Israel's Settlement in
Canaan*, p. 88. Heyes (*Bibel und Ägypten*, 1904, pp. 233 f.) rejected the view that
Yanḥamu is Joseph.

[4] Cf. Baikie, *The Amarna Age*, 1926, p. 354: 'It is scarcely fair to lay upon
the shoulders of Akhenaten, as is so often done, the whole blame for the loss
of the Egyptian empire in Asia. . . . The process which destroyed the empire
was no new thing; it had been going on for years before Akhenaten had anything to do with the matter, and nothing would have stopped it but a vigo-
rously aggressive policy.'

[5] Indeed they greatly increased their power. Cf. Speleers, *Supplément au
Dictionnaire de la Bible*, ii, 1934, cols. 815 f.: 'Le culte d'Amon retrouva son

taken no deep root and had no real place in the people's affec-
tions. Yet during the reign of Ikhnaton the opposition, whether
open or concealed, could not affect his course. No weakling
could carry through such a revolution, affecting religion, where
change is always made with difficulty and in the face of great
resistance. Ikhnaton must have been a man of inflexible will,
and he must have had officials of strength and ability on whom
he could rely to impose his will on the nation. If his administration was weak in Palestine, it was because it chose to be. In
Egypt it was rigid and strong. Such a position would be readily
intelligible if Joseph were the chief minister of Ikhnaton. The
charges of treachery made in some of the letters would not reach
the ears of the Pharaoh, or would be offset by the counter-
charges, and the support said to be given to the enemy by some
of the Pharaoh's own officials would be more easily understandable if those officials knew that they had the connivance of the
Pharaoh's chief minister.

It has already been observed that the connexion between
Ikhnaton's religion and the temple of Heliopolis is generally
acknowledged. When we read, therefore, that the Pharaoh gave
Joseph the daughter of the priest of Heliopolis to wife, we recognize that in no age would this have been a greater honour than
in that of Ikhnaton.[1] In the Hyksos period, as has been said, it
would have been anything but an honour.

Moreover, geographical conditions are in favour of this age.
In the Hyksos period the capital was Avaris, which is probably
to be identified with Pi-Ramesse, as has been said, and this again
with Tanis. The Biblical traditions, which locate the wonders
that preceded the Exodus in the fields of Zoan, or Tanis, thus
place the land of Goshen, or Rameses, in the immediate neighbourhood of Avaris. It has been noted[2] against my view that the
distance of Goshen from Thebes is so great that Joseph could
hardly have spoken of his father as near, when he was in Goshen.[3]
Against this, it is to be noted that the capital in Ikhnaton's

ancienne vogue et sa prospérité ne cessa plus de se développer; l'inventaire
contenu dans le Pap. Harris (époque de Ramsès III) en dit long sur les
fabuleuses richesses d'Amon et de sa famille divine. La prépondérance incon-
testée de son culte permit bientôt à son clergé de prendre la place des nobles
féodaux du moyen empire; aussi, au cours de la XIXᵉ dynastie, le clergé
formait déjà un véritable état dans l'État.'

[1] Borchardt (*Z.Ä.S.* xliv, 1907–8, pp. 97 f.) adduces evidence that his
maternal uncle was High Priest of Heliopolis.

[2] Cf. Wright, *B.A.S.O.R.*, No. 86, Apr. 1942, pp. 34 f., and my reply ibid.,
No. 87, Oct. 1942, p. 40.   [3] Gen. xlv. 10.

reign was not Thebes, but Akhetaton, lower down the Nile.
Moreover, it is possible that the Pharaoh had a residence also
at Heliopolis. Weigall says that he had a palace there,[1] but of
this I can find no independent confirmation. In view of the
manifest interest of the Pharaoh in Heliopolis, and the suggestion that he may have been brought up there, it is possible that
he had a residence there. Even if the court was not there, it is
possible that Joseph was resident there, for Drioton and Vandier
say that in the time of the XVIIIth Dynasty Egypt had two
viziers, one resident in Thebes and one resident in Heliopolis.[2]
The Theban vizier was doubtless at Akhetaton in the time of
Ikhnaton, and Joseph might well have been at Heliopolis, with
charge of Lower Egypt and Palestine.[3] If the court was for any
part of the year at Heliopolis, or if Joseph lived there, the
reference to the land of Goshen, where Joseph's kindred dwelt,
as near to him while still far enough from the court to avoid the
risk of offence to the courtiers by the sight of shepherds, would
be easily intelligible, while even if Joseph resided at Akhetaton,
Goshen could still be thought of as near compared with Palestine. The conditions are therefore very much more appropriate
than in the Hyksos period. For if Goshen was in the immediate
neighbourhood of the court, the courtiers would not be protected
from the offensive sight of the shepherds, while it is highly improbable that the Hyksos court would study the susceptibilities
of the Egyptians—and still less so if, as Albright supposes, the
Hebrews formed part of the conquering Hyksos armies.

I find, then, a substantial historical value in the Joseph story.
It is probable that not every element is to be taken literally, since
such a story tends to draw to itself accretions, just as the Joshua
story has done.[4] It is often supposed that the story of Potiphar's

---

[1] Cf. *The Life and Times of Akhnaton*, 1923, p. 166.   [2] Cf. op. cit., p. 334.

[3] In this case, however, Gen. xli. 41 would have to be regarded as inexact,
since there Joseph is said to have been put in charge of the whole land of
Egypt.

[4] I am not, therefore, persuaded by Reicke's attempt (*S.E.Å.* x, 1945,
pp. 6 ff.) to prove that the Joseph story is a cult legend of the Adonis-
Tammuz-Osiris type. He adduces a large number of parallels between the
Biblical story and the Ras Shamra texts, which are held to be mythical texts
related to the cult. Here it seems to me that Bentzen supplies the key when he
speaks of the Israelite historification of cultic myth (cf. *J.B.L.* lxvii, 1948,
pp. 37 ff.). By this he means that at the Israelite feasts, instead of mythological texts being recited, texts in which the old myths had been recast
in terms of history were used. This view would allow full value for all
the parallels that Reicke notes without dissolving the history into myth
(cf. *Studia Theologica*, i, 1947, p. 186). Cf. also Riesenfeld, *The Resurrection in*

wife is fiction because of its similarity to the Egyptian 'Tale of the Two Brothers'.[1] But this hardly follows. History is often the account of things that have happened but once, while stories may recount what has happened more than once. Potiphar's wife was probably not the only woman of her kind, and the author of the 'Tale of the Two Brothers' may have based his story on her like.

On the other hand, the story of the revolution in land tenure which is attributed to Joseph is probably a reflection of conditions which antedated the reign of Ikhnaton, though even here it may contain some partial memory of things that happened in that age. We read that Joseph appropriated all lands for the Pharaoh in return for grain, save that to the priests Pharaoh gave a portion.[2] Breasted says it was in the time of Ahmose I, the Pharaoh who drove out the Hyksos in 1580 B.C., that this system was introduced.[3] He suggests that it was the work of Ahmose that is reflected in the Biblical story, where it is transferred to Joseph.[3] That Joseph can have belonged to the time of Ahmose I is quite out of the question. The hated Asiatic Hyksos had just been driven out, and their triumphant ejector would hardly be the man to install a Semite as his chief minister. We cannot, however, rule out the possibility that in the Hebrew tradition a system of land tenure which was known to hold in Egypt was wrongly attributed to Joseph. It may, however, rest on some confusion between the system of Ahmose I and what Ikhnaton did.[4] For though Ikhnaton did not carry through any general

Ezekiel xxxvii and in the Dura-Europos Paintings, 1948, p. 14: 'When studying the Old Testament we must never overlook the fact that historical events are reflected in the cult, just as the cult leaves its mark upon the recording of history in the books of the Bible.' Pedersen holds a somewhat similar view with regard to what he calls the 'Passover Legend', which he finds to be a cultic text based on history, though he thinks the history which lies behind the legend can no longer be recovered. Cf. *Israel III–IV*, 1940, pp. 728 ff., and *Z.A.W.*, N.F. xi, 1934, pp. 161 ff. Dahl (*Studia Theologica*, i, 1947, pp. 72 f.) would seem to allow greater historical value to the events which were commemorated in the cult.

    [1] Cf. Erman, *The Literature of the Ancient Egyptians*, E.Tr. by Blackman, 1927, pp. 150 ff., for this tale.
    [2] Gen. xlvii. 20–6.
    [3] Cf. *History of Egypt*, 1906, p. 229.
    [4] Cf. Schäfer, *Z.Ä.S.* lv, 1918, p. 31 n.: 'Die Worte des Königs (Amenophis IV) in seiner grossen Inschrift scheinen mir von ausserordentlicher Wichtigkeit noch in anderer Beziehung, nämlich für unsere Kenntnis von den Grundeigentumsverhältnissen im alten Ägypten. Denn offenbar werden von ihm diejenigen aufgezählt, die Grundeigentumsrecht im Staate überhaupt bean-

confiscation of property, so far as is known, he did appropriate the estates of the priests with the exception of the priesthood of Aton, whose property he greatly increased by his benefactions.[1] It is true that in the Bible we are expressly told that the Pharaoh did not dispossess the priests, but since it goes on to add that they had a portion which the Pharaoh gave them, it would suggest that the revenues which were undisturbed were those which the Pharaoh had bestowed. The priests of the worship which was proscribed were no longer recognized as priests.

In the Biblical account Joseph is later joined by seventy of his kinsmen with their wives and dependants. It was thus a very small group which went into Egypt. While it is represented as including the ancestors of all the twelve tribes, this may well be due to a desire to ascribe a common history to all the tribes, and to represent them as all coming out of Egypt into Palestine together.[2] It should be remembered that Simeon and Levi alone are represented as being powerful enough to attack a whole city at an earlier stage, so that it is clear that at that time they must have been tribal units, rather than two of twelve divisions of a total of seventy,[3] and the total number of the twelve tribes—or such of them as had tribal existence at the time—must have been far in excess of seventy. It seems likely that it was principally

spruchen können. Das sind, ausser dem Könige selbst, nur die Götter und die Fürsten. Das 'Niemand' betont noch einmal die Ausschliesslichkeit der Aufzählung. In der Erwähnung der 'Fürsten' könnten die letzten den alten Gaufürsten noch gebliebenen Grundrechte stecken. Diese Auffassung der ganzen Stelle passt ausgezeichnet zu dem, was der Erzähler der Josephgeschichte 1 Mos. 47, 20, 22 über Ägypten erfahren hat. Nach ihm haben dort nur der König und die Tempel (die ausserdem noch Lieferungen vom Könige erhalten) Rechtsansprüche auf Grundeigentum. Das schien ihm so verwunderlich gegenüber heimischen Verhältnissen und so klug, dass er die Herbeiführung dieses Zustandes für seinen Urvater in Anspruch nahm. Die 'Fürsten' werden nicht erwähnt. Deren Rechte mögen in den fast fünfhundert Jahren seit Amenophis dem IV geschwunden sein, wenn man nicht annehmen will, dass sie auf die 'Krieger' übertragen sind, die Diodor 1, 73 an dritter Stelle (König, Priester, Krieger) nennt. Vielleicht aber darf man die Erzählung in der Genesis überhaupt nicht so scharf in alle Einzelheiten pressen.' Also Gressmann, in ΕΥΧΑΡΙΣΤΗΡΙΟΝ (Gunkel Festschrift), i, 1923, p. 29.

[1] Cf. Breasted, op. cit., p. 362; Speleers, loc. cit., col. 815; Moret, Rois et Dieux d'Égypte, 1923 ed., p. 59.

[2] Gressmann (in ΕΥΧΑΡΙΣΤΗΡΙΟΝ (Gunkel Festschrift), i, 1923, pp. 7 ff.) finds traces in the Old Testament of a tradition that Jacob died in Canaan.

[3] On the critical problems of Gen. xxxiv and the objection to the chapter on the ground of the representation of the slaughter as carried out by Simeon and Levi as two individuals, cf. Pedersen, Israel I–II, 1926, pp. 521 ff.

some of the Levites[1] and perhaps Simeonites, who were scattered after the treachery at Shechem, who joined Joseph in
Egypt. Simeon and Levi[2] were 'scattered in Israel', and in that
case it would be natural for them to fall back on Judah, if they
had entered the land in alliance with Judah. Simeon found a
territorial home in the south of Judah, until it disappeared as a
separate tribe.[3] Some of the Levites may have similarly fallen
back on Judah, and we find later evidence of Levite settlements
there.[4] But a small group of others may have sought refuge in
Egypt, and included amongst them an ancestor of Moses, whence
we can reasonably infer that there were some Levites,[5] while the
tradition that Simeon was held a prisoner by Joseph[6] may perhaps suggest that there were some Simeonites amongst them. In
that case, however, the Simeonites seem to have been absorbed
during the Sojourn in Egypt, and not to have emerged as a
separate tribe under the leadership of Moses. Just as the
Simeonites who settled in the south of Judah seem to have
become absorbed and to have lost their tribal unity, so these
elements that went into Egypt appear to have lost their identity
as a tribe. On the other hand, the Levites seem to have preserved
their distinctness, and Levites as well as the Joseph tribes came
out of Egypt. In this way the Levite connexions with both waves
of immigration may be easily explained.

We should not omit to observe that Meek disputes this whole
reading of the Shechem story of Gen. xxxiv, and instead offers a

[1] Meek (*Hebrew Origins*, 1936, pp. 31 f.) holds that only the Levites were
in Egypt, while Waterman (*A.J.S.L.* lv, 1938, pp. 33 ff.; cf. *J.A.O.S.* lvii,
1937, pp. 375 ff.) denies that the Levites were ever in Egypt (cf. Meek's reply,
A.J.S.L. lvi, 1939, pp. 117 ff.).

[2] Haldar (*Associations of Cult Prophets among the Ancient Semites*, 1945, p. 96)
resorts to the suggestion that in Gen. xlix. 5–7 the Levites referred to are
priests who were associated with the tribe of Simeon. This is very forced and
unconvincing, since there is nothing to suggest that while the whole of
Simeon is referred to, only a portion of the Levites is meant. Yet if Levites
simply meant priests, as Haldar holds, they could hardly be confined to the
priests of a single tribe.

[3] Cf. Albright, *J.P.O.S.* iv, 1924, pp. 149–61; Alt, ibid. xv, 1935, pp. 303 ff.

[4] Jg. xvii. 9. In Jg. xix. 1 we read of another Levite who took a concubine
from Bethlehem-judah.

[5] Waterman (*A.J.S.L.* lv, 1938, p. 34) denies that Moses was a Levite, but
thinks the Levites championed Moses against a rival cult (*J.A.O.S.* lvii, 1937,
p. 378). He holds that Moses was really an Edomite. Meek opposes this with
convincing reasons to accept the tradition that he was a Levite (*A.J.S.L.* lvi,
1939, pp. 113 f.). Paton (*J.B.L.* xxxii, 1913, pp. 29 f.) would make Moses an
Ephraimite, but Meek's arguments would apply equally here.

[6] Gen. xlii. 24.

choice of two alternative readings of it.[1] The one alternative is
that it had nothing to do with either Shechem or the Canaanites,
but that its historical basis was a conspiracy against Judah
within the southern confederacy by Simeon and Levi, which
took place at Kadesh long after the Amarna age.[2] This assumes
so drastic a rewriting of the incident that it is hard to see what is
left. It is now transferred to the age of Moses, and to a totally
different locality,[3] and the reference to circumcision and to a covenant with Canaanites is meaningless. Moreover, the sequel must
also be rewritten. For Meek would still connect the incident with
the curse of Gen. xlix. 5–7,[4] but instead of the dispersion in
Israel which was there predicted he finds the real issue to be
absorption into Judah, in place of the alliance that had gone
before.

The second alternative which Meek offers is the supposition
that the incident had nothing to do with Simeon and Levi, but
had to do with Shechem in the Amarna age, when an alliance
was concluded between Shechem and the Ḥabiru.[5] On this view
the story could offer no explanation of the scattering of Simeon
and Levi, since it was concerned with an incident that happened
long before they entered the land, and with a locality which
was far from their settlement.

Neither of these views seems very convincing, and it is hard to
see how the present story ever came into existence on the basis of
either supposition. I therefore prefer to take the view which I
have outlined, and to find a much greater substance of history
in the story of Gen. xxxiv, relating it to the age of Jacob and to
the Amarna age, to Shechem and the Canaanites on the one
hand, and to Simeon and Levi on the other, and seeing here the
explanation of their failure to retain their hold on the Shechem
area.

[1] Cf. *Hebrew Origins*, 1936, pp. 122 f.
[2] For Meek places the entry of the southern tribes under Moses later than
the entry of the Joseph tribes under Joshua.
[3] Waterman (*A.J.S.L.* lv, 1938, p. 35) maintains that the story is a tradition transferred from Hormah to Shechem, though it is hard to see what
motive for its transfer could be found.
[4] Waterman would also connect it with Gen. xlix. 5–7, but thinks Levi
was not original to either context (*A.J.S.L.* lv, 1938, p. 35). No adequate
reasons for this view are provided, and the treatment seems to be arbitrary.
Möhlenbrink (*Z.A.W.*, N.F. xi, 1934, p. 228) also thinks Gen. xxxiv originally
referred only to Simeon. He connects Gen. xxxiv and xlix but thinks these
have nothing to do with the Levite priests.
[5] i.e. with the Joseph tribes, on Meek's view. See below, pp. 140 ff.

Many writers have emphasized the fact that Shechem probably played a larger part in Israel's early traditions than a simple
reading of the Biblical story would suggest. Burney suggested
that Gen. xlviii. 22 was aetiological[1] and was intended to show
why Shechem had become Josephite after once belonging to
another section of the Israelite people. In that verse we read,
'Moreover, I have given thee one shoulder above thy brethren',
where the word for shoulder was probably originally intended
to be read as the name of Shechem.[2] It is quite undeniable that
in the Biblical account Shechem was once occupied by Simeon
and Levi and later became an Ephraimite city.

Other writers emphasize the significance of the Shechem tradition in early Israel.[3] In Josh. xxiv we read that the twelve tribes
of Israel assembled at Shechem[4] and there solemnly pledged
themselves to their God in the days of Joshua, and we learn
from the book of Judges that there was a sanctuary in Shechem
dedicated to Baal-berith,[5] or El-berith.[6] Great significance is
attached to this by many writers, who hold that the Shechem
covenant is the oldest Israelite covenant, certainly older than the
covenant of Sinai or Horeb.[7] It is suggested that Shechem was

---

[1] Cf. *Israel's Settlement in Canaan*, p. 43.

[2] In the M.T. the numeral is masculine in form, אחד, whereas in the
Samaritan text it is feminine, as would be expected with the name of a city.
It should be noted, however, that in the M.T. the vocalization אַחַד is that
of the feminine form, אַחַת. The LXX and the Targum of Pseudo-Jonathan
both found the name of the city of Shechem here. Cf. Brinker, *The Influence
of Sanctuaries in Early Israel*, 1946, p. 146; Robertson, *B.J.R.L.* xxx, 1946–7,
p. 102.

[3] Cf. Meyer, *Die Israeliten und ihre Nachbarstämme*, 1906, pp. 542 ff.;
Luckenbill, *A.J.Th.* xxii, 1918, pp. 41 ff.; Meek, *Hebrew Origins*, 1936,
pp. 26 ff.; Robertson, *B.J.R.L.* xxx, 1946–7, pp. 95 ff.

[4] In Josh. xxiv. 1, 25, LXX and the Arabic version read Shiloh for Shechem.
This is accepted by Poels (*Examen critique de l'Histoire du Sanctuaire de l'Arche*,
i, 1897, pp. 69 f.), who thinks that an original שלם has been corrupted to
שכם and that שלם is an alternative form of שילה. This does not seem very
likely, and the reading of M.T. is to be preferred.

[5] Cf. Jg. viii. 33, ix. 4.   [6] Jg. ix. 46.

[7] Cf. Meek, *Hebrew Origins*, 1936, pp. 26 f.: 'It is not surprising to find
scholars suggesting that Shechem was the original home of the Hebrew Torah
as against Sinai-Horeb or Kadesh, in that the Shechem story is manifestly
the earlier. Indeed a goodly number . . . would go so far as to suggest that the
Book of the Covenant (Exod. 20:22–23:19), in whole or in part, originally
stood in Joshua 24, constituting the "Book of the Law of God" mentioned in
verse 26.' Similarly Luckenbill (*A.J.Th.* xxii, 1918, pp. 41–3) holds that
Gerizim and not Sinai was the original Mount of the law. Cf. also Sellin,
Oriental Studies (Haupt Festschrift), 1926, pp. 124 ff., and *Geschichte des*

the amphictyonic sanctuary of a confederacy of Israelite tribes,[1] or even that it was already a pre-Israelite centre, whose covenant antedated the Israelite entry and was taken over by them.[2] On this view the 'Israelite' patriarchs were really Canaanite heroes who were adopted by the Israelites.[3]

That Hebron was an amphictyonic sanctuary for the confederacy of tribes that entered from the south is probable enough,[4] though there seems less evidence that Shechem was such a sanctuary in the days of Joshua for the tribes that entered the land under his leadership. His capture of Shechem is unrecorded, and long after his death the city is still in Canaanite hands. It is therefore hardly likely to have been the centre of an Israelite amphictyony at that time.[5] On the other hand, we have the

israelitisch-jüdischen Volkes, i, 2nd ed., 1935, pp. 97 ff., where it is argued that the Sinai and Shechem covenants belong to two different groups, and that Joshua was the real founder of the national religion.

[1] Cf. Danell, *Studies in the Name Israel in the Old Testament*, 1946, p. 46: 'Shechem, which was originally Joseph's sanctuary, came to be the amphictyonic centre of Israel during the time of Joshua if not before.' Nyberg (*A.R.W.* xxxv, 1938, p. 367) says: 'Tatsächlich ist auch Sichem in der Zeit vor der Eroberung Jerusalems eine Art politische Zentralstelle für die israelitischen Stämme gewesen.' Noth (*Das System der zwölf Stämme Israels*, 1930, pp. 107 f.) holds that there was a twelve-tribe amphictyony based on Shechem, and that Judah belonged both to this and to a Hebron amphictyony, which was partly Israelite and partly non-Israelite (for the latter cf. too *P.J.B.* xxx, 1934, pp. 30 f.). Meek, however (*Hebrew Origins*, 1936, pp. 25, 139), thinks the Shechem amphictyony was originally only for the Joseph tribes. The thought of an Israelite amphictyony, after the pattern of a Greek amphictyony, is found already in Sayce, *P.S.B.A.* xi, 1888–9, p. 347. Cf. also Alt, *Die Staatenbildung der Israeliten in Palästina*, 1930, p. 11, and Noth, *Die Gesetze im Pentateuch*, 1940, pp. 70 ff.

[2] Cf. Simpson, *The Early Traditions of Israel*, 1948, p. 648: 'The idea of a covenant between Jahveh and Israel is a derivation from the pre-Israelite cult of Baal-berith of Shechem.'

[3] Cf. Weill, *R.H.R.* lxxxvii, 1923, p. 69: 'On arrive aisément à cette idée que les conquérants israélites ont trouvé dans le pays Jacob et Joseph, Isaac aussi sans doute, noms de lieux ou de tribus, figures religieuses ou héroïques dans les traditions cananéennes, et se sont approprié ces ancêtres.'

[4] It is also quite certain that this confederacy included non-Israelite elements, since we are expressly told of Kenites and others who accompanied Judah. It seems probable that Kadesh was an older amphictyonic centre for this group, as Mowinckel (*Norsk Geografisk Tidsskrift*, ix, 1942, pp. 13 f.) has argued. Mowinckel connects with this amphictyonic centre Kenites, Kenizzites, Jerachmeelites, Simeonites, Levites, and Judahites, though he holds that Simeon and Judah were settled farther north. On the contrast between the pre-Israelite city-states and the Israelite tribal organization cf. Alt's important study, *Die Landnahme der Israeliten in Palästina*, 1925.

[5] Cf. Pedersen, *Israel III–IV*, E.Tr., 1940, p. 85: 'It is possible that the

account of the much earlier covenant between Simeon and Levi
on the one hand and Shechem and Hamor on the other, and it
may well be this covenant which was perpetuated in the name
of the deity of El-berith or Baal-berith.[1] It is to be noted that the
capture of Shechem by Simeon and Levi is ascribed to Jacob in
the already quoted Gen. xlviii. 22, and elsewhere the building of
an altar at Shechem is attributed to Jacob.[2] There is, therefore,
a curious duplication, in that the building of an altar at Shechem
is attributed to both Jacob and Joshua,[3] and the establishment
of a covenant at Shechem is attributed to the age of Jacob and
to the age of Joshua.[4] Moreover, in Gen. xxxv. 2 ff. we read of
the putting away of strange gods at Shechem in similar duplica-

prominence given to Shechem is due to conditions which developed in
the monarchical period.' Noth (op. cit., pp. 35 f.) says the *terminus a quo* for the
twelve-tribe group is the Song of Deborah. Mowinckel, however, maintains
that the twelve-tribe system is post-Davidic, and that in the period of the
Judges a ten-tribe system was formed (cf. *Zur Frage nach dokumentarischen
Quellen in Josua 13–19*, 1946, p. 22).

[1] Cf. Ryder Smith, *J.T.S.* xlvii, 1946, p. 37.
[2] Gen. xxxiii. 20. In Gen. xxxiii. 18, R.V., with a slight change in the
vocalization, renders 'Jacob came in peace to the city of Shechem', instead
of M. T., 'Jacob came to Shalem, a city of Shechem'. The change may have
been deliberately made to point to Jerusalem (so Brinker, *The Influence of
Sanctuaries in Early Israel*, 1946, p. 145). Poels, however, prefers to restore the
tautologous 'Jacob came to Shechem, the city of Shechem' (*Examen critique
de l'Histoire du Sanctuaire de l'Arche*, i, 1897, p. 70). Nyberg defends the M.T.
(*A.R.W.* xxxv, 1938, pp. 357, 367 f.) and holds that Shalem is to be identified
with Shechem, and so Mackay (*P.E.Q.* 1948, p. 122).
[3] Josh. viii. 30, where the altar is said to have been on Mt. Ebal, where we
should almost certainly read Gerizim, as also in Dt. xxvii. 4, where the
Samaritan text has Gerizim. That these two passages are connected is certain,
since Joshua's building of the altar is said to have been in fulfilment of the
injunction given in the other passage.
[4] In Gen. xxxiv we have the covenant in the age of Jacob, and in Josh.
xxiv. 25 the covenant of Joshua. The covenant of Gen. xxxiv was accompanied by the circumcision of the Canaanites. Brinker (op. cit., pp. 143 ff.)
holds that the Gilgal where Joshua is said to have circumcised the Israelites
(Josh. v. 2) is to be located near Shechem, and also connects Gen. xvii,
which tells of Abraham's covenant and circumcision of his household, with
Shechem. No place is specified in the text of the latter passage, however. If
Brinker is right in these suggestions, the persistence of circumcision and
covenant in the traditions attached to this place is remarkable. Brinker holds
that the story of Joshua's circumcision of his followers immediately before a
critical battle is most improbable, and it is much more likely that a single
ancient tradition has been reapplied than that we have repeated incidents.
Especially is this so in relation to the building of the altar. For if Jacob had
already built one to his God, there would be no more need for Joshua to
build another than there was at Bethel.

tion of what is recorded in Josh. xxiv.[1] On the other hand, the
story of Josh. xxiv would hardly account for the later references
to El-berith or Baal-berith, since the Israelite God Yahweh does
not figure in this name. In a covenant made between Simeon
and Levi and Canaanite elements anterior to the days of Moses,
and therefore before the Israelites had made Yahweh their God,
the name El-berith would be more natural.[2] It is therefore probable that the story of Josh. xxiv represents the transfer to
Joshua of an older tradition of a covenant between Israelites and
Canaanites, but in an appropriately altered form. For here it is
given relevance to all the Israelite tribes,[3] and is brought into
association with the God Yahweh whom Moses had given them.
In its present form it recounts the renewal of the loyalty pledged
at Sinai.[4] But if this is the oldest covenant, as so many scholars
hold, it is more likely that it should be connected with the covenant with the Canaanites made in the Amarna age. It seems to
me wholly improbable that the Mosaic covenant is a later invention on the basis of the Shechem covenant, which is then
regarded as re-edited to make it a reflection of its own shadow.
The work of Moses is too significant to be so lightly dismissed.
On the other hand, for Joshua to gather to himself traditions relating to the Conquest and Settlement in which he had no part
is less surprising.[5] We may, then, with some probability find
evidence of temporary Hebrew dominance in Shechem in the

[1] Steuernagel (in *Festschrift Georg Beer*, 1935, pp. 62 ff.) draws attention to
this, though unlike the present writer he regards the divine name Yahweh as
original to the Joshua passage.

[2] May (*J.B.L.* lx, 1941, p. 119) thinks that the name El-berith may go
back to the patriarchal period. It should be added that he accepts the
association of Joshua with Shechem and thinks it most significant. Its significance, however, he interprets as the adoption of Canaanite legislation
as the basis for Hebrew society. This is scarcely a natural interpretation
of Josh. xxiv, though it could more easily be connected with the story of
Gen. xxxiv.

[3] Whatever view is taken of the date of the Exodus, it is most improbable
that Joshua led the united tribes of Israel, and to this extent the tradition of
this chapter has almost certainly been edited. It is the less difficult, therefore,
to suppose that it has been edited in others.

[4] Simpson (*The Early Traditions of Israel*, 1948, p. 648) observes: 'If the
Sinai-Horeb tradition were the earlier, it would be difficult, in view of the
consistent recognition of the definitive character of the work of Moses, satis-
factorily to account for the rise of the Shechem tradition with its necessary
implication that the covenant of Sinai-Horeb somehow needed to be supplemented.' It may be noted that Josh. xxiv. 25 says that Joshua set a statute and
an ordinance for Israel in Shechem. This was surely a little superfluous after
the work of Moses. [5] Cf. *supra*, p. 43.

Amarna age, followed by a Hebrew withdrawal, and the reversion of the city to Canaanite control until after the age of Joshua.[1] The historical events that are reflected in the traditions then belong to the period of the Descent into Egypt, and point to the Amarna age for that Descent.

The references to Ḥabiru in the Amarna letters and to ʿAperu in Egyptian sources provide no embarrassment to this view. The earliest reference to the ʿAperu in Egypt comes from the reign of Amenhotep II, and is to captives in war.[2] It is quite clearly not to any group that could be identified with the Hebrews who went into Egypt in the time of Joseph in accordance with the Biblical account, for they were not prisoners of war. On the other hand, on the view which I have presented, the Israelites who entered Palestine in the Amarna age were part of a much wider group of Ḥabiru, some branches of whom were in or near the Egyptian empire in the time of Amenhotep II, and therefore well able to be involved in some clash with his troops. If the Hebrews who went into Egypt were part of the Ḥabiru of the Amarna letters—themselves only one of the groups of Ḥabiru now known to have existed—we could understand the name ʿAperu appearing in Egypt at the end of the same century in the reign of Seti I[3] as the name of a group of people set to task-work for the Pharaoh. As de Vaux observes: 'As the Hebrews of the patriarchal age led the same life as the Ḥabiru of the cunei-form documents, so the Hebrews of the Sojourn in Egypt shared the condition of the ʿApiru of the Egyptian documents.'[4]

The Pharaoh of the Oppression would then be Rameses II. This is correctly reflected in the tradition that the name of one of the cities on which the Israelites were employed was Raamses. His known extensive building activity in the Delta region makes him a suitable Pharaoh, quite apart from the

---

[1] I find this view preferable to that of Sellin, who argued (*Wie wurde Sichem eine israelitische Stadt?* 1922) that Shechem first became Israelite in the twelfth century B.C. in the time of Abimelech, and that in Jg. ix we have two accounts of this combined, an older and historical account, dating from about 1000 B.C., and a later and legendary account, which is connected with Gen. xlviii. 22, xlix, 5-7, and xxxiv, where we have a dating back of the Abimelech episode. In that case it is hard to see why Simeon and Levi came into the story. [2] Cf. *supra*, p. 47.

[3] Cf. Gunn, *apud* Speiser, *A.A.S.O.R.* xiii, 1933, p. 38 n.; de Vaux, *Z.A.W.*, N.F. xv, 1938, p. 229. On Seti I's Beth-shan inscription cf. Rowe, *The Topography and History of Beth-shan*, 1930, pp. 29 f. It has been noted above that one text speaks of ʿAperu in the time of Thothmes III, but this is not a contemporary text or an historical text. [4] Cf. *Z.A.W.*, N.F. xv, 1938, p. 233.

K

preservation of his name in the name of this city. Moreover, as has been said, we are told elsewhere in the Bible that the Israelites dwelt in the fields of Zoan, or Tanis, which is probably to be identified with Pi-Ramesse or Raamses, giving an independent confirming tradition. These passages cannot be simply dependent on Ex. i. 11, since there Zoan is unmentioned and here Raamses is unmentioned, and it is only the probability that Tanis is to be equated with Pi-Ramesse, which the work of the last two decades has shown to be probable, which unifies the traditions of these Biblical sources. Further, the content of the tradition of the Exodus makes it plain that the court was in the immediate neighbourhood of the Israelites; and the content of the tradition is always a safer guide than a chronology which has been attached to it centuries later. In the time of Rameses II the court did reside at Pi-Ramesse, but in the time of Thothmes III it did not. Indeed, by this test of the geographical relationship to the location of the court the Ramesside period is the only possible period for the oppression,[1] unless the whole Biblical tradition is dismissed as a fiction in the interests of the reliability of 1 Kgs. vi. 1, or the tradition that placed Israel in the fields of Zoan is discredited. The Hyksos court resided at this spot, but the Hyksos period can scarcely be identified with the period of the Oppression.[2] But from the Hyksos period to the Ramesside

[1] Cf. de Vaux, ibid., p. 236: 'En effet les récits bibliques sur la fin du séjour en Égypte supposent une époque où les Pharaons résidaient dans le Delta et y entreprenaient de grandes constructions: ces conditions ne furent réalisées que sous la xixe dyn. égyptienne.'

[2] It is well known that Josephus followed Manetho in identifying the Exodus of Israel with the expulsion of the Hyksos (*Contra Ap.* i. 16 (103)). This view has found some defenders in modern times. Thus Niebuhr (in Helmolt's *The World's History*, E.Tr. iii, 1903, pp. 627 f.) says: 'It is clear that we have here [i.e. in the account of the expulsion of the Hyksos] a description of the biblical exodus of Israel from Egypt, as seen from another point of view. Criticism is as yet unable to decide whether Manetho related the story as it stands; at any rate it entirely rejects that part of Josephus's version which identifies the Shasu with the Israelites. Hence other scholars have come to the conclusion that the Israelites were never in Egypt at all. In fact it is necessary either to adopt the latter conclusion or to accept the identification of the Hebrews with the Shepherds of Manetho as correct in its main features.' Hall (*The Ancient History of the Near East*, 7th ed., 1927, pp. 213 n., 408 n., *P.E.F.Q.S.* 1923, pp. 125 f., and *C.A.H.* i, 2nd ed., 1924, p. 311) and Gardiner (*J.E.A.* v, 1918, pp. 36 ff., xix, 1933, pp. 122 ff.) also followed Josephus. Most writers reject this view, however, on the double ground that though it would be entirely credible for expulsion to be converted into successful escape in the traditions, it is quite incredible that a people who had lived in Egypt as masters would have invented the story that they had been slaves,

period the Hyksos capital of Avaris was not the seat of the court.

Albright earlier held that the Oppression may well have lasted for ten years or even less,[1] and that the Exodus took place *circa* 1290 B.C. When I noted that this did not seem long enough to satisfy the Biblical conditions,[2] and would allow no basis of history for the Moses story, he replied that he placed the beginnings of the Oppression under Seti I.[3] This represented a change in his position which he had not hitherto published, and a definite improvement. For it is stated in the Biblical tradition that the Exodus did not take place in the reign of the Pharaoh who began the Oppression.[4] According to the Biblical account, Moses was born after the Oppression began, and was eighty years old at the time of the Exodus.[5] This is almost certainly an exaggerated age, but since Moses was clearly a full-grown man at the time of his flight from Egypt, and lived with Jethro for some years before returning to lead his brethren out, we must allow him to have reached a reasonably advanced age at the time of the Exodus, probably not less than fifty years, and possibly nearer sixty. Stories similar to that of his birth and nurture at the Pharaoh's court are told of Sargon and others,[6] and it may well be that folk-lore has contributed something to the story. But even if all historical value be denied to this, there is no reason to deny that Moses slew an Egyptian through sympathy with his oppressed brethren, and was forced to flee. Without this it would

and that the period of wandering in the wilderness would have to be greatly stretched to cover the time between the expulsion of the Hyksos in 1580 B.C. and an entry into Palestine either in the Amarna age or in the late thirteenth century B.C. (cf. Mallon, *J.P.O.S.* v, 1925, pp. 85 ff.). Such a theory would allow historical validity only to the statements that Israel was once in Egypt and came out; it would deny historical validity to everything else in the Biblical story—the forced labour, the work of Moses, the corollaries for religion of the deliverance. When the persistence of Israelite memory of the Egyptian taskmaster, and the strength of the tradition that the whole religious life of the nation took its rise in a deliverance of which it was but a spectator is remembered, it is hard indeed to feel that it is utterly without foundation. Moreover, in Manetho's story the expelled Hyksos founded Jerusalem, whereas in Israelite records we find that Jerusalem continued to be a Jebusite, non-Israelite city until the time of David.

[1] Cf. *B.A.S.O.R.*, No. 58, Apr. 1935, p. 10 n.
[2] Cf. *B.J.R.L.* xxii, 1938, pp. 274 f.; *B.A.S.O.R.*, No. 89, Feb. 1942, p. 29.
[3] Cf. ibid., p. 29 n. (Editor's note).
[4] Ex. ii. 23.
[5] Ex. vii. 7.
[6] Cf. Gruffydd, *Z.A.W.*, N.F. v, 1928, pp. 260–70.

be impossible to understand his coming to Egypt from the desert to lead the Israelites out.[1]

In the Biblical story the oppressor's court was hard by the Israelite dwellings at the time when Moses was born, and the Exodus took place under a succeeding Pharaoh, whose court was similarly close to them. It is known that Seti I began the operations in the Delta region which Rameses II continued, and if the Oppression belongs to the Ramesside period it is highly probable that it began in his reign. There is less evidence, however, that the court of Seti I resided at the place which became known as Pi-Ramesse. Montet, indeed, states that Rameses chose the site for the city,[2] but Steindorff and Seele state that Seti I re-established the city of Avaris-Tanis.[3] It is, however, probable that the operations at Pi-Ramesse, though begun in the reign of Seti I, were carried out under the direction and authority of Rameses II.[4] There is reason to believe that Merneptah, the successor of Rameses II, did continue to live at Pi-Ramesse,[5] and, in the absence of any evidence that Seti I lived there, the birth of Moses under Rameses II and an Exodus under Merneptah would seem to fit the Biblical account better than birth under Seti I and an Exodus under Rameses II, just as the length of the reign of Rameses would better accord with the Biblical tradition. If, however, Ex. ii. 23 is set aside, the Exodus could be placed in the latter part of the reign of Rameses II.[6]

We have to ask, therefore, what compelling reasons there are

[1] Waterman (*A.J.S.L.* lv, 1938, p. 39) holds that there is no reason to associate Moses with Egypt at all, and Simpson (*Revelation and Response in the Old Testament*, 1947, p. 34) takes a similar view. Meyer (*Die Israeliten und ihre Nachbarstämme*, 1906, p. 51 n.) went even further, and questioned the historicity of Moses altogether.   [2] Cf. *Le Drame d'Avaris*, 1941, p. 123.

[3] Cf. *When Egypt ruled the East*, 1942, p. 256.

[4] Cf. Seele, *The Coregency of Ramses II with Seti I and the Date of the Great Hypostyle Hall at Karnak*, 1940. Seele establishes the reliability of the claim of Rameses to have been associated on the throne with Seti I, and argues that he was in charge of building operations at Karnak and elsewhere. He says: 'Ramses so explicitly emphasizes his authority over building operations that I am disposed to believe that he actually exercised a considerable amount of personal control over the planning and execution of such works. It is not impossible that the period of the coregency saw Seti I for the most part absent from Egypt on various military campaigns, while Ramses remained at home to administer affairs of state.' Drioton and Vandier formerly followed Breasted in holding this claim to coregency to be a fiction (op. cit., p. 372), but Vandier has now withdrawn this and accepted Seele's arguments as convincing (ibid., pp. 652 f.).

[5] Cf. Montet, op. cit., p. 146.

[6] It is placed there by de Vaux (*Z.A.W.*, N.F. xv, 1938, p. 237).

to doubt the Biblical traditions. If extra-Biblical evidence is fatal
to the acceptance of those traditions they must be given up; but
we may reasonably ask whether it is really fatal. It is claimed
by Albright and his followers that the archaeological data best
fit an Exodus *circa* 1290 B.C., and an entry into Palestine *circa*
1250 B.C. Against this it is to be observed that there is no archaeological evidence for the date of the event of the Exodus. There is
evidence relevant to the determining of the period of the Oppression and the period of the entry into Palestine, but there is no
archaeological evidence that a period of forty years separated
the Exodus from the entry into Palestine. Moreover, we have
already seen that the Biblical evidence is here not without difficulties. Thirty-eight of the forty years are said to have been
spent at Kadesh, and only two years in the rest of the wanderings. Moreover, it has already been seen that the Kadesh tradition is probably distinct from the Horeb–Sinai tradition, and the
Kadesh tradition belongs to the story of the earlier incursion
into Palestine that preceded the Amarna age. That tradition is
combined with the wandering after the Exodus to harmonize
the two traditions in a single account, and to represent all the
tribes as entering together at a single time. It is probable that
the thirty-eight years is a specious precision, to yield a total of
forty years for the Wilderness period, and that the two years for
the remainder of the period is more reliable.[1] In any case, when
the Kadesh Sojourn is subtracted, we are left with a very short
period from the Exodus to the entry into Palestine for the group
that came out of Egypt. Hence, for an entry *circa* 1250 B.C. an
Exodus substantially later than 1290 B.C. would suffice. I would
emphasize that while my view seems to differ substantially from
Albright's in the date of the Exodus, it differs slightly in the date
of the entry into Palestine. And it is here that archaeological
evidence is most relevant. For, whereas Albright places the entry
into Palestine *circa* 1250 B.C., I have hitherto placed it *circa*
1230 B.C.[2] The margin of difference is here very slight, and the
archaeological datings cannot by their nature be so precise as to
fix the time absolutely. Albright himself has said: 'The available

[1] Cf. Steuernagel, *Die Einwanderung der israelitischen Stämme in Kanaan*, 1901,
pp. 74 f.: 'Das bedeutet aber nichts anderes, als dass es ein Irrtum ist,
anzunehmen, dass zwischen Num. 13 und Jud. 1 eine grosse Lücke klafft, in
die man einen Bericht über eine Wanderung durch das Ostjordanland nach
Art des elohistischen einschalten könnte. Dieser hat in J keinen Platz; und
es ist nicht ein unglücklicher Zufall, dass uns ein solcher nicht erhalten ist.'
[2] Cf. *B.A.S.O.R.*, No. 85, Feb. 1942, p. 30.

evidence proves that the main wave of destruction fell in the thirteenth century and that the reoccupation of the more important towns must be dated between 1250 and 1150 B.C.',[1] and the substitution of 1230 for 1250 in this statement would hardly be regarded as a vital modification.[2] It may be noted that Bergman, who agrees with Albright in placing the Exodus early in the thirteenth century B.C., places the crossing of the Jordan not earlier than 1240 B.C.[3] It should be added that to place the Exodus in the latter part of the reign of Rameses II, *circa* 1250 B.C., and the entry into Palestine some two years later, discarding Ex. ii. 23, would not be a serious modification of my view, though I am not persuaded that it is archaeologically demanded.

It is to be noted that an Exodus in 1290 B.C. would mean that Moses returned to Egypt within a very few years of his flight and during the reign of the Pharaoh from whom he had fled—unless his flight is pushed back to the reign of Seti I, and it is denied that he could have been born after the beginning of the Oppression. An entry into Palestine *circa* 1250 B.C. is conceivable enough, since the activity of Rameses II in Palestine and Syria belongs to the earlier part of his reign, and in his old age his strength was failing, though an entry at the beginning of Merneptah's reign is equally conceivable. Merneptah's grip on Palestine was much weaker and his famous stele would, by its very claim to have made a punitive raid into Palestine, seem to indicate that there was some disorder there at the time. But an Exodus from Egypt early in the reign of Rameses II, when he was at the height of his power, seems less probable than towards the end, when he was less effective, or at the beginning of the reign of Merneptah.

A further consideration would seem to tell against an Exodus *circa* 1290 B.C. If the Descent into Egypt is correctly located by me in the Amarna age, the four generations of the Biblical tradition would seem to carry us down about 120 to 140 years for the Exodus. This is confirmed by the fact that Joseph is represented as living for about seventy years after the Descent into Egypt,[4] and as having died some time before the rise of the oppressing

[1] Cf. *Haverford Symposium*, p. 23.
[2] In *J.P.O.S.* i, 1921, p. 66, Albright observed that a date for the Conquest *circa* 1230 B.C. 'is perhaps as close to accuracy as we will ever get'.
[3] Cf. ibid. xvi, 1936, p. 251.
[4] It is probable that this should be reduced somewhat and that the total of 110 years ascribed to Joseph, like the 120 years ascribed to Moses, is exaggerated.

Pharaoh, after whose oppression began Moses was born. It is to be observed that the Biblical tradition—apart from the chronology of Ex. xii. 40—would not suggest a long interval between the death of Moses and the rise of the oppressing Pharaoh. No reader would suppose that between Ex. i. 6, which states that Joseph and all who belonged to his generation died, and i. 8, which tells of the rise of the oppressor, a period of three centuries lay. At the same time some interval is implied. Eerdmans, who places the Descent and the Exodus much later than others,[1] allows but seventy years in all for the Sojourn in Egypt.[2] This seems quite

---

[1] Cf. *Alttestamentliche Studien*, ii, 1908, pp. 67–76, and *The Religion of Israel*, 1947, pp. 13–17. Eerdmans distinguished the Hebrews from the Israelites, and held that the former were in Egypt for four centuries while the latter only entered Egypt *circa* 1210 B.C. and suffered oppression under the twentieth Egyptian dynasty. This provided no long reign such as is indicated in the Biblical tradition, and despite the brevity of the Sojourn which he is compelled to postulate, Eerdmans has to reduce the period of the Wandering, Settlement, Judges, and the reign of Saul to not much more than a century. This seems unduly short. Moreover, either the entry would have to be entirely loosed from the fall of Jericho, or that event would have to be placed later than any archaeologist has yet suggested. Further, Eerdmans's claim to identify Joseph is not convincing. For that identification he relies on the Harris Papyrus (*Alttest. Studien*, p. 68; *The Religion of Israel*, p. 14), where we read: 'From the abundant years of the past we had come to other times. The land of Egypt was in chiefships and in princedoms; each killed the other among noble and mean. Other times came to pass after that; in years of scarcity Arisu, a Syrian, was to them as chieftain. He made the whole land tributary to himself alone. He joined his companions with him, and seized their property. And they treated the gods in the same manner as they treated the people; offerings were not presented in the shrines of the temples.' (Cf. Petrie, *History of Egypt*, iii, 1905, pp. 134 f.; or Breasted, *History of Egypt*, 1906, p. 474; *C.A.H.* ii, 1924, pp. 171 f.) This merely offers a point of connexion with one element of the Biblical tradition, and that by no means complete. For if Joseph had been master of Egypt in his own name and by the might of his arm, the Biblical tradition, that represents him as merely the minister of Pharaoh, would be surprisingly inaccurate. No effort is made to establish any substance of history for the tradition of Joseph's marriage or for the tradition of the building of Pithom and Raamses at the time of the Oppression. Moreover, Breasted describes the period that followed the death of Merneptah until the reign of Rameses III (1215 B.C. to 1198 B.C., within which the administration of Joseph would fall) as a period of unsettlement which led to complete anarchy, and finds the above quoted Harris Papyrus to refer to five years of usurpation. This is quite other than the Biblical tradition of fourteen years of strong and wise government under Joseph, and the last vestige of relevance falls from the theory.

[2] Cf. *The Religion of Israel*, p. 17, where the Exodus is placed at 1140 B.C. In *Alttest. Studien*, loc. cit., p. 68, he had put it *circa* 1130 B.C. Gressmann (*Mose und seine Zeit*, 1913, pp. 404 f.) allowed but fifty years for the Sojourn

inadequate for a normal four generations, and the same consideration would bring us much below 1290 B.C., if the Descent into Egypt belonged to the reign of Ikhnaton.

It is to be observed that if Joseph went into Egypt in the earlier part of the reign of Ikhnaton, and the descent of the group that later went down into Egypt is assigned to the end of Ikhnaton's reign, after the seven good years and part of the seven years of famine,[1] the period between the Descent and an Exodus *circa* 1230 B.C. would be about 130 years.[2] The most intractable of the Biblical genealogical data would still be that of Moses through his mother. It is to be noted, however, that whereas it would be quite impossible to suppose that a Moses who was eighty years old at the time of the Exodus was the son of a half-sister of one who had gone down into Egypt 430 years before, it would not be entirely incredible on this chronology. Since Jochebed is said to have been born to Levi after the Descent into Egypt,[3] and since she married the son of Kohath,[4] who may himself have been quite young at the time of the Descent, she was probably born to Levi some years after the Descent. She was presumably the half-sister of Kohath, since she married his son, and it is possible that Levi took a young wife in his old age and begat Jochebed by her. It is not inconceivable that she was born thirty years after the Descent. Similarly, it is not impossible that she was in the thirties when Moses was born, since he was not her first-born. Moreover, as has been said, the content of the Mosaic tradition would imply that he was no longer a young man at the time of the Exodus. He is likely to have been in the fifties, even if we reduce substantially the eighty years ascribed to him in Ex. vii. 7,[5] and not inconceivably nearer sixty. We therefore reach

in Egypt, while Simpson (*The Early Traditions of Israel*, 1948, pp. 427 f.) says it was 'hardly long enough for Moses to grow from infancy to maturity'. Montet, on the other hand, goes to the opposite extreme, and says the 430 years of Ex. xii. 40 is too short a period for the Sojourn in Egypt, to which he assigns 500 or 600 years (cf. *Mélanges Hartwig Derenbourg*, 1909, p. 51).

[1] Gressmann (in ΕΥΧΑΡΙΣΤΗΡΙΟΝ (Gunkel Festschrift), i, 1923, p. 29) held that the most ancient tradition knew but two years of famine.

[2] Feigin (*Missitrei Heavar*, 1943, p. 330) holds that the Sojourn lasted for 143 years, basing himself partly on the four generations of the genealogies and partly on the ease of emending the text of Ex. xii. 40 to yield this figure. He assigns the Exodus to the year 1379 B.C. (ibid.).

[3] Num. xxvi. 59. [4] Ex. vi. 18, 20.

[5] The life of Moses is divided in the tradition into three periods of forty years each, in Egypt before his flight, with Jethro, and in the wilderness after the Exodus. This is almost certainly an artificial scheme, so that smaller

a total of upwards of 120 years without straining credibility, and
the nearer we approach the Biblical figure of eighty for Moses at
the time of the Exodus the easier the case becomes.[1]

At whatever point in the thirteenth century the fall of Lachish
and Debir should be located, no difficulty is created for my dating of the two incursions into Palestine. For on my view Judah
entered the land in the fourteenth century B.C., and was therefore there in ample time for the extension of its hold on the south
at any time in the thirteenth century. Nor does the reference to
Israel on the stele of Merneptah provide any difficulty. It has
been suggested that that reference is a boastful perversion of
the Pharaoh's failure to prevent their leaving Egypt.[2] When the
Israelites disappeared into the desert, Merneptah could boast
that they had been wiped out. While this is possible, there is no
need to resort to it. The reference could be to the Amarna age
group, though the fact that they do not appear to be a settled
group is against this.[3] Also, for what it is worth, the fact that the
name Israel is here used is perhaps against it.[4] But since on my
view those whom Moses led out of Egypt need not be supposed
to have spent long in the wilderness, but to have entered Canaan
about two years after their departure from Egypt, an Exodus
early in Merneptah's reign would leave it possible for this group
to be in Palestine in time for inclusion on the stele.[5] It is

numbers may with probability be substituted, and especially for the last of
these three periods.

[1] Cf. *supra*, p. 71, where it has been said that the *maximum* period which
would satisfy the Biblical data in this matter is 160 years. It will be seen that
the period my view requires falls well within this maximum.

[2] Cf. Montet, *Le Drame d'Avaris*, 1941, p. 149.

[3] Paton (*The Early History of Syria and Palestine*, 1902, p. 134) supposed that
the reference was to the portion of Israel which did not go down into Egypt,
and which had inhabited the region between Egypt and Canaan. But the
main reasons for supposing that all the tribes did not go down to Egypt are
the historical evidences of their presence in Palestine during the period of the
Sojourn; and there is no reason to suppose that Israelite tribes were in the
region suggested throughout the period of the Sojourn in Egypt. Barton
(*Semitic and Hamitic Origins*, 1934, p. 87) held the reference in the Merneptah
stele to be to the Leah tribes which had not gone into Egypt, but which had
entered Palestine in the Amarna age and had steadily pushed in among the
peoples already there and gradually absorbed them. Cf. Chaine, *Le Livre de la
Genèse*, 1948, p. 457: 'Il faudrait alors admettre que tous les Hébreux ne sont
pas allés en Égypte; des clans ont bien pu demeurer dans le pays de Kanaan.
C'est déjà l'hypothèse suggérée par la stèle de Mérenptah qui nomme Israël à
une époque où les Hébreux de l'Exode n'étaient pas encore installés en
Kanaan.'   [4] Cf. *supra*, pp. 55 f.

[5] The stele is dated in the fifth year of Merneptah. That Pharaoh's acces-

improbable, however, that the Israelites suffered any major ills at the hand of Merneptah, to whatever date the Exodus is ascribed.

Mercer, who ascribes the Exodus to the reign of Merneptah, holds that shortly after that event Judah with its associates Caleb, the Kenites, and the Jerachmeelites, invaded Canaan from Kadesh by way of Hebron, and that so soon as Merneptah realized that the Hebrews who formerly dwelt in Goshen had escaped, he planned to attack them.[1] This seems an improbable view. For the stele of Merneptah shows that his foray was on a much more catholic scale than one simply, or even primarily, directed against Judah.

An Exodus at the beginning of the reign of Merneptah would leave it possible for the group that came out of Egypt to take Jericho well within the period to which Vincent ascribes its fall, but if Garstang's date or any of Albright's dates is correct, then it would be necessary, with Albright and his school, to loose the fall of that city from the group that Moses led and to ascribe it to the older immigrants.[2] On the other hand, the fall of Bethel within the thirteenth century would provide no difficulty whatever. These are the broad limits given for the fall of that city by Albright[3] and Burrows,[4] though Albright earlier gave the first

sion is commonly dated 1225 B.C. (so in *C.A.H.*), but Albright follows Borchardt's chronology (cf. *Z.Ä.S.* lxx, 1934, pp. 97 ff.) and dates it in 1235 B.C. (cf. *B.A.S.O.R.*, No. 58, Apr. 1935, p. 18; No. 74, Apr. 1939, p. 21), while Steindorff and Seele (*When Egypt ruled the East*, 1942, p. 275) date it in 1232 B.C. An Exodus at the beginning of Merneptah's reign, followed by two years of wandering, would bring the entry into Palestine of those who came out of Egypt still early in the same reign, and would account for the fact that they appear to be an unsettled people.

[1] Cf. *A.Th.R.* v, 1922–3, p. 107. Griffiths (*The Exodus in the Light of Archaeology*, 1923, pp. 49 ff.) connects the events recorded in Merneptah's stele with Num. xiv. 40 ff. and Dt. i. 41 ff., and thinks Merneptah was claiming a victory which was won by tribes under his suzerainty. This is improbable, since it leaves unaccounted for the context in the inscription, which tells of the chastisement of other peoples in Palestine and Syria. Griffiths locates the Exodus in the second year of Merneptah's reign.

[2] Cf. Dhorme, *R.H.R.* cviii, 1933, p. 88: 'Les ruines de Jéricho, c'est là ce qui a frappé les imaginations. Elles existaient avant l'arrivée des Hébreux. L'époque d'el Amarna, marquée par les guerres incessantes entre les villes palestiniennes, avait connu sans doute la catastrophe dans laquelle les remparts ont été démantelés.' Cf. also Watzinger, *Z.D.M.G.* lxxx, 1926, pp. 134 f.

[3] Cf. *From the Stone Age to Christianity*, 2nd ed., 1946, p. 212; *B.A.S.O.R.*, No. 56, Dec. 1934, p. 11; No. 74, Apr. 1939, p. 17.

[4] Cf. *What Mean these Stones?* 1941, p. 76.

half of that century.[1] The archaeological evidence is not here precise,[2] however, and the difference between Albright's narrower limits and the date *circa* 1225 B.C. that my view would suggest for the fall of Bethel is hardly a serious one, while the broader limits he more recently allows would remove all difference.

So far as Ai is concerned, its evidence no more embarrasses my view than it does any other, and if any one of the various ways suggested to get round the difficulty is accepted it would apply just as well on my dating as on any other. The capture of Ai ascribed to Joshua cannot be identified with the archaeologically ascertainable destruction of the city.

Nor would Jg. xi. 26 provide any difficulty, if archaeology will allow the possibility of Heshbon having been conquered in the fourteenth century B.C. For on my view Gad and Reuben belonged to the earlier wave of immigration, and did not go down into Egypt, and therefore a Gileadite could well refer to the occupation or conquest of this region in that century. If, on the other hand, archaeology will not allow the possibility of Heshbon having been conquered in the fourteenth century B.C.,[3] then it is archaeology and not the exigencies of my view which raises difficulties against Jg. xi. 26, and we should have to suppose that an incident which really belonged to the second wave was here dated in the time of the first.[4]

As little would 1 Kgs. vi. 1 provide any serious difficulty. For if the group that entered Palestine in the Amarna age had been in the neighbourhood of Kadesh for anything like forty years before that—and the Biblical tradition assigns thirty-eight years to the stay at Kadesh—then they must have reached Kadesh not far from 480 years before the founding of the Temple. That figure is doubtless a round one, and not to be taken exactly, but it would not be unduly wide of the mark. The combining

[1] Cf. *B.A.S.O.R.*, No. 57, Feb. 1935, p. 30; No. 58, Apr. 1935, p. 13.
[2] In his latest pronouncement (*The Archaeology of Palestine*, 1949, pp. 108 f.) Albright says: 'At present the evidence points to a date in the early thirteenth century for the fall of Bethel . . .; it must, however, be frankly confessed that our evidence against a date somewhat later in the thirteenth century . . . is mainly negative.'
[3] It has been observed above (p. 99) that the archaeological evidence does not seem to be conclusive against this date.
[4] Noth (*Z.A.W.* lx, 1944, pp. 37 ff.) suggests that Sihon was not conquered at the time of the entry of Reuben and Gad but subsequently. He thinks Reuben first settled west of the Jordan, while Gad settled in the region of Jaazer, but that later Reuben joined Gad and they together enlarged their territory at the expense of Sihon.

of the two streams of tradition, and the representation of all the tribes as entering the land together after the Exodus from Egypt, would then be responsible for the arrival at Kadesh of the earlier wave being synchronized with the Exodus of the later.[1]

It will be seen that on this view the Israelites who went into Egypt were part of those who entered Palestine in the Amarna age. Their recognition of a common ancestry with those who did not go into Egypt was not therefore an idle fiction but had substance, and my view brings into relation with one another the various elements of the problem. A separate history of a little more than a century and a quarter would be long enough to account for the measure of distinctness which always existed between Judah and the Joseph tribes, and the potential friction between them, without being long enough to obliterate the consciousness that they were of common stock. Moreover, this view explains the connexion of Levi with both waves of immigration.

That the Joseph tribes and Judah entered into the possession of their territory in different periods is agreed by a very long line of modern scholars. Some recent scholars have inclined to share with Meek and Albright the view that the Joseph tribes settled first and Judah later. It is, therefore, necessary briefly to examine this view, and to show what advantages the view I adopt has over it. And since the views of Meek and Albright differ in some important respects, they must be separately traversed.

Meek finds the Amarna letters to reflect the campaigns of

[1] J. Coppens (in *Apologétique*, 1948, p. 1003 n.) does not commit himself to a date for the Exodus. He says: 'La question reste toujours incertaine; *lis sub judice est*. Nous devons toutefois à la vérité d'ajouter qu'en ces dernières années, l'hypothèse d'une date plus récente, située au cours du xiiie siècle, gagne du terrain. Elle peut en appeler à de nouveaux arguments: 1° le fait que la date d'Hammurabi est rajeunie de deux siècles nous invite à rajeunir dans la même mesure toute la chronologie israélite: ce qui nous ramène pour l'Exode du xve au xiiie siècle; 2° les traditions sur l'Exode supposent la présence d'Édom, Moab, et Ammon en Transjordanie. Or, d'après les résultats des explorations de M. N. Glueck en Transjordanie, ces peuples n'y ont pas fixé leur demeure avant le xiiie siècle; 3° parmi les villes détruites par Israël lors de son entrée en terre de Canaan, figure certainement Lachish (Tell ed Duweïr). Or, les fouilles entreprises sur le site par la Wellcome-expedition . . . ont établi que la ville fut détruite et saccagée vers 1230; 4° enfin, les fouilles de M. Montet dans le delta égyptien, notablement à Tanis . . . confirmeraient, elles aussi, la chronologie récente.' Against this Coppens sets the dating of the fall of Jericho *circa* 1300 B.C., which does not permit the assignment of the Exodus to the reign of either Rameses II or Merneptah. (For this note I am indebted to Monsignor J. M. T. Barton, the work of Coppens not having been directly accessible to me.)

Joshua,[1] and holds that the Exodus under Moses took place a
century later and that the tribes he led were those that entered
Judah from the south *circa* 1200 B.C.[2]

It has already been said that we cannot safely argue from
silence that in the Amarna age the Ḥabiru had captured and
occupied the central highlands, on the ground that no letters
come from that part of the country. Shechem is the only city of
which we have certain evidence of their occupation. Moreover,
the move from the south into Judah is located by Num. xxi. 1–3
earlier than the entry by way of Jordan, while Jg. i. 1 states
categorically that Judah went up first against the Canaanites.
Further, the sons of Leah are represented as older than the sons
of Rachel, and already play a part in affairs while Joseph and
Benjamin are children. Ephraim and Manasseh are said to have
been born in Egypt, and until there is evidence that both the
Amarna age Ḥabiru and the tribes whom Moses led had come
out of Egypt, the Biblical evidence must be seen to point clearly
to the Joseph tribes as having come out of Egypt rather than the
group associated with Judah, if these are distinguished. Yet once
more, it has already been noted that in the Biblical tradition
that Simeon and Levi were in the neighbourhood of Shechem
long before the Exodus under Moses, and that Simeon entered
the land along with Judah, we have a further item of Biblical
evidence pointing to the priority of the entry of the southern
group over the entry of the Joseph group. Again, Gen. xxxviii has
been seen to suggest that Judah had been permanently resident
in Palestine from before the Descent into Egypt.[3] On the other
hand, there is no Biblical evidence whatever to point to an entry
of the Joseph tribes before the entry of Judah.

Nor does the matter rest there. On Meek's view Joshua is to
be placed more than a century before Moses—again in com-

[1] Cf. *supra*, p. 40 n.
[2] Cf. *A.J.Th.* xxiv, 1920, pp. 209–16; *B.A.S.O.R.*, No. 61, Feb. 1936,
pp. 17–19; *Hebrew Origins*, 1936, chap. i. Luckenbill had earlier presented
this view more generally than Meek, but in substantial agreement with Meek
and Albright. He maintained that the conquest of central Palestine by *Israel*
took place in the Amarna age, while one or more of the *southern* tribes
sojourned in Egypt in the days of Rameses II (*A.J.Th.* xxii, 1918, pp. 40 f.).
Similarly, Powis Smith had argued that there were Hebrews in Canaan at
least as early as *circa* 1400 B.C., but without defining which group he supposed
to have been there (*A.J.S.L.* xxxii, 1915–16, pp. 81 ff.). Elsewhere, however
(*A.J.S.L.* xxxv, 1918–19, p. 16), he says: 'The northern clans had settled in
Ephraim for many generations before the clans from Egypt and the Negeb
moved into Judah.'
[3] Cf. Robinson, *History of Israel*, i, 1932, p. 170.

plete conflict with the Biblical traditions.[1] There Joshua is depicted as an attendant on Moses, who became the Israelite leader when Moses died.[2] His association with the Ark is not something extraneous to the tradition, but intimately belonging to it, and since the Ark is later found in Ephraimite territory at Shiloh, and is never represented as brought into the territory of Judah until the time of David—when it was brought into the quondam Jebusite city that became his capital, and subsequently the capital of the southern kingdom after the Disruption—there seems little reason to doubt it. Yet it is equally impossible to dissociate the Ark from Moses, or to suppose that the story of its making is either free invention or a transfer to Moses of something that Joshua did. For in relation to a Joshua who was, *ex hypothesi*, never at Horeb or Sinai, and who was merely the leader of the Amarna age Ḥabiru and of completely unknown past, the Ark is left entirely without explanation or *raison d'être*.

It is to be observed that the Song of Deborah, in its opening verses, preserves the memory of the mount of Yahweh. That song is quite certainly very ancient, and equally certainly of northern origin. If Meek's view is correct, and the Joseph tribes were not with Moses at the sacred mount, it is hard to see why Deborah should sing in these terms. Further, in a later age we find Elijah repairing to the sacred mount from the northern kingdom, while Amos and Hosea, both of whom prophesied to the northern kingdom, knew of the tradition that Ephraim had come out of Egypt.[3] All this would be readily intelligible if the Joseph tribes came out of Egypt with Moses and went to the sacred mountain, but is not readily intelligible on Meek's view. Further, Jg. i. 18 states that Judah once occupied what became some of the principal cities of the Philistines. Since on Meek's view Judah's entry

[1] Cf. Danell, *Studies in the Name Israel in the Old Testament*, 1946, p. 44 n.: 'Meek is thus forced to make Joshua older than Moses, which is contrary to a unanimous tradition.'

[2] Möhlenbrink (*Z.A.W.*, N.F. xviii, 1942–3, pp. 14–55) quite differently dissociates the Joshua tradition from the Moses tradition, holding that they were originally independent of one another. The Joshua tradition he connects with Shiloh, while the original Gilgal tradition belonged to the Moses story. Hölscher goes so far as to deny any historical reality to the figure of Joshua. He says (*Geschichte der israelitischen und jüdischen Religion*, 1922, pp. 39 f.): 'Rein mythisch ist wahrscheinlich auch die Gestalt des Kriegshelden Josua, den die Sage mit den Kämpfen um die Eroberung des mittleren Westjordanlandes verbunden hat.'

[3] Cf. Am. ii. 10; iii. 1; ix. 7; Hos. xi; xii. 10 (E.V. 9); xiii. 4. This consideration is noted by Danell, *Studies in the Name Israel in the Old Testament*, 1946, p. 45.

did not long antedate the Philistine entry, this is less easily provided for than on the view that Judah and Simeon entered in the Amarna age.

Yet again, we have to consider the religious development of Israel. The J document of the Pentateuch ascribes the beginnings of Yahwism to the childhood of the human race, and knows no moment of its introduction to Israel by Moses, while the E document dates its introduction to Israel in the time of Moses. In this Meek agrees. He says: 'According to J, our oldest and probably most reliable source, it was not a new god at all but a god long known to the Hebrews, under whose guidance Moses brought the people out of Egypt.'[1] Although he further agrees that E and P represent the name Yahweh as a new name to the Hebrews, first revealed to them by Moses, he is doubtful how far this is to be relied on.[2] For he holds that the cult of Yahweh was of southern origin, and that the Levites were its propagandists, who spread it through the other tribes, until it became the cult of all the tribes.[3] Apparently Meek shares the common view that the J document is of southern origin, while the E document is of northern origin. If the worship of Yahweh antedated Moses, it would be understandable that the southern group, which, *ex hypothesi*, Moses led, should represent its beginnings as lying in the far distant past. But what is not explained is why the northern tribes, which on this theory were not introduced to Yahwism until after the days of Moses, and which never came into any sort of contact with Moses, should have ascribed the beginnings of Yahwism to him.

If, on the other hand, we accept the Biblical traditions that

[1] Cf. *A.J.Th.* xxiv, 1920, p. 212.
[2] Cf. *Hebrew Origins*, 1936, p. 87.
[3] Cf. *A.J.Th.*, loc. cit., pp. 212 f. Cf. also Meek, *A.J.S.L.* xxxvii, 1920–1, pp. 101 ff.; and Skipwith, *J.Q.R.* xi, 1898–9, pp. 239 ff. Skipwith observes: 'There is nothing improbable in the conjecture that the Levite Moses may have adopted as the god of Israel the ancestral deity of the important tribe of Judah. If this hypothesis be entertained it clears up a serious difficulty. Why is the invocation of Jahveh represented in J as beginning with Enosh . . . while in E it is for the first time revealed to Moses? The answer is very simple: J expresses the point of view of Judah, where the worship of Jahveh was in fact immemorial; E that of Ephraim, where tradition could recall its introduction. A stronger confirmation of the hypothesis could hardly be desired' (p. 250). This does not prove that Israel's religion came from Judah, though it may be agreed that it strongly suggests that Judah did not derive its worship of Yahweh from Moses. But by the same token it equally strongly suggests that it was Moses who mediated the worship of Yahweh to the tribes that cherished traditions associating its introduction with him.

associate Moses with Joshua and the Ark, and therefore with
Ephraim, and that represent the Joseph tribes as entering Palestine later than the Leah tribes, we have an intelligible development. In that case the tribes that were not with Moses at the
time of the Exodus were the ones that did not ascribe the beginnings of their Yahwism to him, while those that were with
him did.

To set all this aside on the basis of nothing more definite than
the silence of the Amarna letters on the central highlands is surprising. For, as has been said above, all the archaeological
evidence is consistent with the entry of the Joseph tribes in the
thirteenth century B.C., while the entry of Judah in the fourteenth
century B.C. and gradual pressure northwards has no archaeological evidence against it. On the contrary, as has been observed
above, we have far more evidence in the Tell el-Amarna correspondence of the presence of the Ḥabiru in the south than in the
centre of the land,[1] and while the evidence from excavated sites
does not place the occupation of the Hebrews before the thirteenth century, there is here nothing that needs to be reconciled
with the view I have presented. The Biblical tradition of the
conquest of the centre of the land under Joshua is of a swift
occupation; such fragments of the conquest of the south in
a movement northwards as have survived do not suggest any
swift occupation.

Even more difficult is the form in which Simpson presents[2] an
hypothesis which has much in common with Meek's. He too
supposes that the Joseph tribes entered Palestine more than a
century before the southern tribes, and dissociates Moses wholly
from the former. To neither group did Moses mediate Yahwism,
on this view, since it already existed in a primitive form before
his day. He is thought to have been a priest of Kadesh, who was
never in Egypt and who led no group of Israelites out,[3] but who
later became the leader of the southern tribes after their Exodus
from Egypt, and reformed their Yahwism. Subsequently their
religion received a further enrichment from its contact with the
pre-Yahwistic religion of Hebron.[4] On this view it is passing

[1] Cf. the map in *Supplément au Dictionnaire de la Bible*, i, 1928, cols. 213 f.

[2] Cf. *Revelation and Response in the Old Testament*, 1947.

[3] Ibid., pp. 33 f. Simpson says: 'His relation to the exodus came after the
event, and consisted in drawing out its significance and eliciting from Israel
the proper response.' Cf. Hölscher, *Geschichte der israelitischen und jüdischen
Religion*, 1922, p. 64: 'Die Sage vom Auszug aus Ägypten und vom Unter-
gang der Ägypter im Schilfmeer steht in keiner ursprünglichen Beziehung
zur Gestalt Moses.'					[4] Ibid., p. 49.

strange that the northern group of tribes, which *ex hypothesi* already worshipped Yahweh before the days of Moses and had nothing to do with him, should associate the introduction of the divine name Yahweh amongst them to Moses. If either group had mistakenly supposed that Moses had introduced the worship of Yahweh, it might have been expected to be the southern group, since there was at least a measure of justification for it in that he is held to have given form to their religion.[1]

The course of events as reconstructed by Albright,[2] and generally followed by several writers,[3] has some features in common with that of Meek, while differing from it in important respects. Like Meek, Albright holds that it was the Leah tribes which Moses led, and that the entry into Palestine of the Joseph tribes preceded that of the Leah tribes. He thinks the house of Joseph was already in its home in central Palestine at the beginning of the Amarna age, and that the Amarna letters offer evidence of the growing menace to their neighbours of these tribes, who are identified with the Ḥabiru. The fall of Jericho he places many years after the entry of the Joseph tribes,[4] and the fall of Bethel in the second century after their arrival.[5] Meanwhile the Leah tribes, who entered Egypt *circa* 1720 B.C.,[6] continued in that land until they were oppressed by Seti I[7] and Rameses II. Early in the reign of Rameses, however, they were led out by Moses, who brought about a confederation of the Leah tribes with the Joseph tribes, and with the Concubine tribes, thus uniting all the Israelite tribes in a single confederacy. He was succeeded by Joshua, who in the last third of the thirteenth

---

[1] Ibid., p. 22: 'This was the Jahvism, inarticulate and emotional, to which Moses gave form, making explicit and developing its meaning for life.'

[2] Cf. especially *B.A.S.O.R.*, No. 58, Apr. 1935, pp. 10–18. Many of the individual points have been rediscussed and sometimes modified in subsequent articles, to which reference has been made above. So far as I know, Albright has not modified the general picture, which is here summarized so that it can be seen as a whole.

[3] Cf. Burrows, *What Mean These Stones?* 1941, pp. 271 ff.; Wright, *The Westminster Historical Atlas*, 1945, pp. 39 f., and *The Study of the Bible Today and Tomorrow*, 1947, pp. 84 f.; Finegan, *Light from the Ancient Past*, 1946, pp. 105 ff., 136; Earle, in *The Asbury Seminarian*, i, 1946, pp. 103 f. (but more hesitatingly, and with a final turn towards the Garstang view, for which he admits a strong bias).

[4] Cf. *supra*, p. 13, for Albright's successive modifications of his view on this date.

[5] Cf. *supra*, p. 19, for Albright's statements on the date of this fall.

[6] Cf. *J.P.O.S.* xv, 1935, pp. 225 f.

[7] Cf. *B.A.S.O.R.*, No. 85, Feb. 1942, p. 29 n. (editorial note).

L

century B.C. carried through successful campaigns in the neighbourhood of Gibeon, in Judah, and perhaps also in Galilee.[1]

Here it will be seen that Joshua is placed after Moses, but
he is completely separated from the Ephraimite entry into the
land and from the conquest of Jericho and Bethel-Ai. He is
represented as a leader of the united tribes, with conquests in
the centre, south, and possibly also the north. But how he came
to be the leader, and from what tribe he arose, it is hard to know.
If he was with Moses, then the firm tradition that he was an
Ephraimite and that he led the entry into the Ephraimite territory across the Jordan is worthless; if, on the other hand, he was
an Ephraimite, it is difficult to see how he became the leader of
the tribes Moses led, or what basis there could have been for the
tradition that he led the entry into the land. Moreover, the history of the Ark, and of its association with both Moses and
Joshua, and with the tribe of Ephraim, becomes obscure.[2] It is
true that Albright holds that a confederation was effected bringing the tribes Moses led into association with the Joseph tribes,
who were already west of the Jordan.[3] But he gives no details
as to how he believes it to have been brought about or whether
it was effected before or after the crossing of the Jordan by the
Leah tribes. Of any negotiations with people west of the Jordan
in the time of Moses we hear nothing; nor yet of any crossing of
the river by Moses.

Many of the objections to Meek's view hold also here. It is
true that Albright holds that the Joseph tribes had come out of
Egypt,[4] but he admits that there is no evidence of a double
Exodus from Egypt,[5] and he offers no suggestion of the reasons
for, or manner of, this Exodus of only a part of the Hebrews
who were in Egypt in the fifteenth century B.C. His assignment
of the entry of the Joseph tribes to a date much earlier than that

[1] Cf. B.A.S.O.R., No. 58, Apr. 1935, pp. 17 f.
[2] The oldest tradition concerning the Ark which has come down to us is
in one of the poetic extracts cited by J from an older source (Num. x. 35 f.).
Here the Ark is connected with Moses. In the E source the Ark is not alone
connected with Moses, but with the Ephraimite Joshua who is its attendant
(Ex. xxxiii. 11). In Jg. xx. 27 the Ark is said to have been at Bethel, while in
1 Sam. iii. 3 we find it at Shiloh. Both of these places lay within the borders
of Ephraim.   [3] B.A.S.O.R., loc. cit., p. 17.
[4] Cf. ibid., p. 15 n. Burrows does not follow Albright in this, but says
they came from the north-east (cf. What Mean These Stones? 1941, pp.
271 f.).
[5] Cf. J.B.L. xxxvii, 1918, p. 138: 'The circumstances and date of the first
Exodus are obscure; I do not know of any passages in the Heptateuch which
may have any bearing on the problem.'

of Judah and Simeon, shares with Meek's view the embarrassment of the Biblical evidence that the south was occupied first,
which has been noted above. Moreover, while he refers to the
traditions in the book of Genesis which separate the conquest of
the central area of Palestine from Joshua,[1] he omits to note that
those traditions are especially associated with Simeon and Levi,
whereas on Albright's view Simeon and Levi were in Egypt at
that time. Moreover, the Biblical tradition to which Albright
appeals states that at that time Joseph was still a lad at home,
and therefore not the leader or eponym of an invading host.

Again, it is hard to see how, on Albright's view, the Biblical
traditions of the entry of individual tribes arose. He places the
entry of the Joseph tribes *circa* 1400 B.C., and that of the Leah
tribes *circa* 1250 B.C. But he holds that the movement into Judah
was a movement of the united tribes under Joshua coming from
the north, as represented in the book of Joshua.[2] He maintains
that there was also an independent movement from the south of
Calibbites and related tribes, who were only later incorporated
in Israelite tribes. The Biblical tradition is that Calibbites and
other elements were associated with Judah and Simeon in their
entry.[3] It is true that within the Bible we have inconsistent
accounts, the one associating the entry of Judah with Joshua, and
the other representing it as an independent movement. It is easy
to see how an independent movement could be transferred to
Joshua in accordance with the desire to represent him as the
leader of a united movement of all the tribes, but it is not easy
to see why the entry of Judah and Simeon under Joshua should
be transferred to make it an unhistorical entry with non-Israelite
tribes. It is especially difficult to see why such a transfer should
stand in our oldest account of the Conquest.

The religious development is also as obscure on Albright's
view as on Meek's. Why the Joseph tribes, who on his view were
never with Moses, should associate the beginnings of their Yahwism with that leader, while the Leah tribes, who were with him,
should not, is left completely unexplained.

As against this the view I present is in far closer accord with
the Biblical traditions, while taking full account of all the archaeological evidence. I recognize that in the Biblical traditions we
have combined, in what appears to be a single account, the
reminiscences of a twofold entry into the land. While the traditions are not scientific history, of course, I find in them historical

[1] *B.A.S.O.R.*, No. 58, Apr. 1935, p. 14.
[2] Ibid., p. 17. [3] Cf. Jg. i. 3, 17, 20; Josh. xv. 13.

substance in themselves.[1] They must be controlled by archaeological and extra-Biblical sources where they are available, but
there is nothing in these to throw doubt on the tradition that
Judah and the associated tribes entered the land first, and that
the Kadesh Sojourn was intimately connected with the attack
from the south, or on the view that the Joseph tribes came out
of Egypt under the leadership of Moses at a later date;[2] or on
the tradition that Moses passed on his leadership of the tribes he
led to the Ephraimite, Joshua, who led them across the Jordan
and into the central highlands. Whether the fall of Jericho can
be ascribed to Joshua cannot be determined until there is a firm
agreement amongst archaeologists as to the date of that fall. But
there is no reason to doubt that Joshua was active in the neighbourhood of Bethel. The reasons for doubting his conquest of the
territory occupied by Judah are supplied within the Bible, as
also the reasons for doubting his conquest of Galilee.[3]

So far as the religious development is concerned, the view I
have presented offers no difficulties. Here we must first consider
the question of the source of the Israelite worship of Yahweh. It
has been claimed that this divine name is found at Ras Shamra,
where Yw figures as the son of El.[4] This, however, seems very
improbable,[5] and is in any case of little importance for our purpose, since it is unlikely that the Israelites took over their worship of Yahweh from the people of Ugarit.[6] That the name is

[1] Cf. Bergman, *J.P.O.S.* xvi, 1936, pp. 240 f. where the effect of mixing
traditions of the Mosaic age with those of the earlier Ḥabiru conquest, so far
as Manasseh, Jair, and Machir are concerned, are considered.

[2] Noth (*Das System der zwölf Stämme Israels*, 1930, p. 37) similarly holds that
the Leah tribes settled before the Joseph tribes, agreeing with Steuernagel
(*Die Einwanderung der israelitischen Stämme*, 1901, pp. 50 ff.) save that he prefers
to speak of 'Joseph tribes' rather than 'Rachel tribes' as Steuernagel did.

[3] Cf. *supra*, pp. 42 f., 45, 100 f.

[4] Cf. Dussaud, *R.H.R.* cv, 1932, p. 247; *C.R.A.I.B.L.* 1940, pp. 364 ff., and
Les Découvertes de Ras Shamra et l'Ancien Testament, 2nd ed., 1941, pp. 171 f.;
Bauer, *Z.A.W.*, n.f. x, 1933, pp. 92 ff.; Eissfeldt, *J.P.O.S.* xiv, 1934, pp. 298 f.
(= *Ras Schamra und Sanchunjaton*, 1939, pp. 17 f.); Vincent, *La Religion des
Judéo-Araméens d'Éléphantine*, 1937, pp. 27 f.; Virolleaud, *La Déesse 'Anat*, 1938,
p. 98; Bea, *Biblica*, xx, 1939, pp. 440 f. Lewy (*R.E.S.*, 1938, p. 58) thinks this
Yw was a Ḥurrian deity.

[5] Cf. de Vaux, *R.B.* xlvi, 1937, pp. 552 f.; Albright, *From the Stone Age to
Christianity*, 2nd ed., 1946, pp. 197, 328; Gordon, *Ugaritic Grammar*, 1940,
p. 100; Baumgartner, *Th.R.*, n.f. xiii, 1941, pp. 159 f.; de Langhe, *Un Dieu
Yahweh à Ras Shamra?* 1942.

[6] Cf. Bea, *Biblica*, xx, 1939, p. 441: 'Damit ist allerdings die Frage noch
nicht entschieden, ob dieser *Yw* identisch ist mit dem biblischen *Yhwh*,
Jahwe.'

older than the time of Moses, however, there is little reason to doubt, and it is clearly stated in some of our Biblical sources that this was the case.[1] To find a flat contradiction between Ex. vi. 2 f., which states that God was not known to the patriarchs by the name Yahweh, and passages in Genesis,[2] which represent Him as saying to the patriarchs 'I am Yahweh', is easy. It is less easy to estimate its significance. Obviously both cannot be precisely true. If, however, the Israelite entry into Palestine was in two groups, only one of which was led by Moses, it could well be that he introduced the group he led to the worship of God under the name Yahweh, while the group he did not lead reached its Yahwism independently of him. There could thus be substance in both of the traditions preserved in the Bible, and it is only the attempt to impose a unity on them and to make them tell of a single stream of history that is responsible for the contradiction.

It is improbable that the Israelites had worshipped Yahweh from time immemorial. Had they done so, and had the tribes that came out of Egypt been connected with the tribes that were not in Egypt by blood and faith, there would have been no room for any tradition that Moses mediated Yahwism to them. So far as the tribes that were led by Moses are concerned, it is scarcely to be doubted that he introduced them to the worship of Yahweh as their God. It is true that by syncretism he identified Yahweh with the God their fathers had worshipped, but in so doing he made it clear that Yahweh was a new name by which they were to worship their God.[3] This does not mean that it was a brand-new name for God, first heard on the lips of Moses. The name may not even have been an unknown name to the Israelites in Egypt, though it was not the name they had used hitherto for their own God.

Whence, then, could the name have come? It has long been a common view that Yahweh was the God whose priest Jethro, Moses' father-in-law, was.[4] While this view has been rejected by

[1] Littmann (A.f.O., xi, 1936, p. 162) connects the name with Aryan *Dyāu-s, from which Zeus and Jupiter were derived.
[2] Gen. xv. 7, xxviii. 13.
[3] On the patriarchal religion, cf. Alt, Der Gott der Väter, 1929, where it is argued that each of the patriarchs had his own personal God, who revealed Himself to him.
[4] Holzinger states (Exodus, 1900, p. 13) that this view was first suggested in 1862 by Ghillany, writing under the pseudonym of von der Alm. Its adoption by Stade (Geschichte des Volkes Israel, i, 1887, pp. 130 f., and Biblische Theologie des Alten Testaments, i, 1905, pp. 42 f.) and Budde (Religion of Israel

a number of scholars,[1] and cannot claim to be certain, it seems to me to have all probability on its side. And in the absence of conclusive evidence we can only be guided by probabilities. That Jethro was a priest we are told;[2] but we are not told the name of his God. What we are told, however, is that when Moses came out of Egypt with the Israelites, Jethro came to meet him, and that he was highly elated at the demonstration of the power of Yahweh in the deliverance of Israel. 'Now I know that Yahweh is greater than all gods', he cried.[3] Buber objects[4] that he could hardly have said this if Yahweh were his own God, for no one would make such an implied confession about his own God. But this is scarcely cogent. Whatever belief in the power of Yahweh he might have cherished in the past, this unique demonstration of His power was something that could only have lifted it to a higher degree of knowledge and certainty. Buber supposes[5] that Jethro was so impressed by this demonstration of the power of Yahweh that he forthwith identified his own god with Yahweh, but of that there is no hint in the story. Meek, on the other hand, thinks[6] that Jethro was converted to the worship of Yahweh by this proof of His power. Yet again, not only is there no hint of this, but the sequel gives quite another impression. For Jethro offers sacrifice, and presides at the sacred meal which follows.[7]

to the Exile, 1899, chap. i) brought about its wide acceptance amongst scholars, and it figures in large numbers of works. Cf. especially, W. Vischer, *Jahwe der Gott Kains*, 1929. An important essay by Wensinck in which it is presented was published posthumously: 'De oorsprongen van het Jahwisme', in *Semietische Studiën uit de Nalatenschap von A. J. Wensinck*, 1941, pp. 23–50. See also Schmökel, *J.B.L.* lii, 1933, pp. 212 ff. Noth (*Evangelische Theologie*, 1946, p.309) indicates his adherence to the view, and so does Beer (*Exodus*, 1939, p. 30). Eerdmans (*The Religion of Israel*, 1947, pp. 14 ff.; cf. *The Covenant at Mount Sinai viewed in the Light of Antique Thought*, 1939, and *Alttestamentliche Studien*, ii, 1908, pp. 44 ff.) presented the view with some unnecessary embarrassments.

[1] Meek, *Hebrew Origins*, 1936, pp. 86 ff. (cf. also *A.J.S.L.* xxxvii, 1920–1, pp. 102 ff.) rejects it. So, too, König, *Geschichte der alttestamentlichen Religion*, 1912, pp. 162 ff., Phythian-Adams, *The Call of Israel*, 1934, pp. 72 ff., and Buber, *Moses*, 1947, pp. 94 ff. Volz (*Mose und sein Werk*, 2nd ed., 1932, p. 59) says: 'Ausserdem aber steht die ganze Hypothese auf sehr unsicherem Boden.' Volz himself holds (pp. 59 f.) that before Moses, Yahweh was the god of one of the tribes, who then became the only God of all the tribes.

[2] Ex. iii. 1.   [3] Ibid. xviii. 11.
[4] Op. cit., p. 95.   [5] Ibid., p. 98.
[6] Cf. *Hebrew Origins*, p. 88; *A.J.S.L.* xxxvii, 1920–1, p. 104. Similarly Phythian-Adams, *The Call of Israel*, 1934, p. 73.
[7] Ex. xviii. 12. Cf. Oesterley and Robinson, *Hebrew Religion*, 2nd ed., 1937, p. 148: 'This action is incomprehensible except on the supposition that

Buber here stresses the fact that the sacrifice is offered to Elohim and not to Yahweh,[1] but it can hardly be supposed that the demonstration of the power of Yahweh in the deliverance of the Israelites would lead them forthwith to sacrifice to some other God. Nor is it clear why Jethro should officiate as priest and preside at the sacred feast unless his own God was being approached. If, however, it were his God, it would be clear why he presided. For none but he was a properly initiated priest of this God; and in the sacred feast we should then have the first incorporation of the Israelite leaders into the worship of Yahweh.[2] Certainly there is nothing in the story to suggest that Jethro was being initiated into the worship of Yahweh, as Meek supposes, since it is unusual for the novice to preside at his own initiation.

Further, Jethro gives to Moses instruction and advice as to the administration of justice,[3] which was regarded as a religious rather than a civil function. All of this suggests that Jethro was acting not merely as the father-in-law of Moses, but as the priest. For Moses is not represented as a youth, needing riper experience to guide him. The man who had stood before Pharaoh and who had led Israel out of Egypt was not lacking in personality or natural wisdom. On that side there was little that he needed from Jethro. But of technical knowledge pertaining to the priest's office Jethro could speak.

Yahweh was the God of Jethro and his tribe, the Kenites, and that Jethro himself was Yahweh's priest'; also Gressmann, *Mose und seine Zeit*, 1913, p. 163: 'Wie kann Jethro, der ausdrücklich als Priester der Midianiter bezeichnet wird, Jahve als den Höchsten aller Götter feiern? Das ist nur dann verständlich, wenn Jahve auch der Gott der Midianiter ist.' Cf., too, H. P. Smith, *The Religion of Israel*, 1914, pp. 50 f.

[1] Cf. *Moses*, 1947, p. 95. If Buber's supposition that Jethro was now identifying his god with Yahweh were correct, it is hard to see what significance could be attached to this. The E document, though it uses the divine name Yahweh after the call of Moses, still has a preference for Elohim, and the use of Elohim here is doubtless due to that preference. That Yahweh is the God to whom sacrifice is offered is certain. This is recognized by Meek (*Hebrew Origins*, p. 88), who also stresses the fact that Elohim and not Yahweh is the term used here. But either the choice of term is significant or it is not; and if the sacrifice was really offered to Yahweh there can be little significance in the choice of the word Elohim.

[2] Cf. Gray, *Sacrifice in the Old Testament*, 1925, p. 208: 'If the surmise is correct, then Moses was not represented in the earliest tradition merely as the son-in-law of the priest of Midian, but also as his pupil *in the priestly method* or craft, and thus the Hebrew priesthood is affiliated to the Midianite.'

[3] Ex. xviii. 13 ff. Cf. Gray, loc. cit.: 'In that case the entire narrative would present Jethro the Midianite priest as the teacher of Moses the first Hebrew priest in two chief priestly functions—the sacrificial and the oracular.'

We may further note that Jethro is said to have taken his departure from Israel after this incident.[1] Meek holds that this story, which comes from the northern document E, carried the memory of the incorporation of some Kenites in the tribe of Judah, as well as their initiation into the faith of Yahwism.[2] It is hard to see how the simple statement that Jethro departed home can be held to establish this view. It is, indeed, strange that the northern document should alone preserve the story of this visit of Jethro if the northern tribes were not amongst those Moses led, as Meek supposes. Nevertheless, it is certain that both the J and the E corpora of traditions were collections of traditions of all the tribes, and this cannot be pressed. In the J document we read that the brother-in-law[3] of Moses, Hobab, here called the son of Reuel, did join Israel,[4] but that story is divorced from this incident. Both Jethro and Hobab are called Midianites,[5] but elsewhere they are said to be Kenites,[6] and it is probable that they were members of a Midianite clan, known as Kenites.[7] We have already noted the Biblical evidence that there was a Kenite element associated with the tribe of Judah, and it is therefore

[1] Ex. xviii. 27.
[2] Cf. *A.J.S.L.* xxxvii, 1920–1, p. 104.
[3] The precise relationship of Hobab to Moses is hard to determine. In Num. x. 29, in the expression 'Hobab, the son of Reuel, the Midianite, the חתן of Moses', it is not certain whether חתן goes with Hobab or with Reuel. In Jg. iv. 11 the same term is used unequivocally of Hobab. If חתן is given its usual meaning of father-in-law, then Hobab is to be equated with Jethro. But elsewhere the father-in-law of Moses is called Reuel (Ex. ii. 18).
[4] Num. x. 29–32. The final answer of Hobab is not given in this passage, but Jg. i. 16 makes it probable that he accompanied Israel.
[5] Ex. iii. 1, xviii. 1; Num. x. 29.
[6] Jg. iv. 11.
[7] Morgenstern (*H.U.C.A.* xv, 1940, pp. 127 ff. = *Amos Studies*, i, 1941, pp. 251 ff.) says: 'Of the Kenites themselves we know very little. They were a semi-nomadic tribe, or, perhaps more exactly, clan or group of clans, whose normal abode and district of pastoral wanderings centred in the extreme south of Judah and in the border sections of Edom. Whether, in addition to following a pastoral life, they also were a clan or tribe of smiths, as their name seems to indicate and as their tribal tradition corroborates . . . can not be determined with certainty, but it is by no means improbable. They seem to have been the original worshippers of the particular Yahweh of the mountain in the desert, and from them . . . the worship of this Deity was communicated to . . . the clan or clans just emerging from Egypt.' Morgenstern holds that the oldest document used in the compilation of the Pentateuch was a Kenite document. Cf. *H.U.C.A.* iv, 1927, pp. 1–138. On the connexions of the Kenites and the Edomites cf. Glueck, *P.E.Q.* 1940, pp. 22 f., and Nyberg, *Z.D.M.G.* xcii, 1938, pp. 337 f. Lewy (*R.E.S.*, 1938, pp. 71 f.) thinks the Kenites or Midianites were Hurrians. He also holds that the name Moses is Hurrian (ibid., p. 68).

probable that this element was of the same stock as the father-in-law of Moses.

That the Kenites were Yahweh worshippers is suggested by other passages. Cain is the eponymous ancestor of the Kenites,[1] and he is said to have borne the mark of Yahweh upon him.[2] Moreover, in the days of Jehu's revolution, Jonadab, the son of Rechab is a devotee of Yahweh,[3] and we learn from the book of Chronicles,[4] itself confessedly late, that the Rechabites were of Kenite stock. The same passage associates the Calibbites and the Kenites.[5]

It has recently been claimed that there is one item of extra-Biblical evidence supporting the Kenite hypothesis.[6] This is in the form of an Egyptian text in which the place-name Yhw is found referring to a spot quite certainly in the neighbourhood of Kenite settlements, and dating from the time of Rameses II. Amongst the other places mentioned in the context are Seir, Laban,[7] and Sham'ath,[8] all of which have Edomite or Midianite connexions. It is of particular interest to note that this text is dated *circa* 1300 B.C., in the reign of the Pharaoh of the Oppression on the view I take, and therefore in the age when Moses' flight to Jethro would fall, and Grdseloff observes that it renders the Kenite origin of Yahwism more probable.

If we accept this clue, the whole complex of traditions takes on a clear pattern. If Yahweh-worshipping Kenites were associated with the southern tribes, and one of their chief leaders were Caleb, who was also Yahweh-worshipping, we could understand how by gradual penetration the worship of Yahweh could

---

[1] The Kenites are called Cain, just as the Israelites are called Israel. Cf. Jg. iv. 11.

[2] Gen. iv. 15. Cf. Stade, *Z.A.W.* xiv, 1894, pp. 250–318; Eisler, *Le Monde oriental*, xxiii, 1929, pp. 48 ff.; Vischer, *Jahwe, der Gott Kains*, 1929, pp. 40 ff.

[3] 2 Kgs. x. 15 ff. Cf. Jer. xxxv.

[4] 1 Chr. ii. 55. This verse stands at the end of a genealogy of the descendants of Caleb. On the Kenites in the Chronicler's lists cf. Eisler, *Le Monde oriental*, xxiii, 1929, pp. 99 ff.

[5] Further, Jg. v. 4, Dt. xxxiii. 2, Hab. iii. 3, 7, Zech. ix. 14 all seem to locate the sacred mountain in the Midianite country, and the Midianites and the Kenites are connected. Cf. Schmökel, *J.B.L.* lii, 1933, pp. 213 ff. Nielsen (*The Site of the Biblical Mount Sinai*, 1928, p. 9) says: 'The relation between Midianites and Kenites is not quite clear . . . the Kenites must either be a subdivision, a clan of the Midianite tribe, or, on account of their living on the border of the Midianites, are reckoned among them by the Israelite tradition.'

[6] Cf. Grdseloff, *B.E.H.J.* i, 1946, pp. 81 f.

[7] Grdseloff would connect this with Laban, Dt. i. 1.

[8] Grdseloff suggests a connexion with the Shimeathites (1 Chr. ii. 55), where the context associates them with the Kenites.

spread through the group. Just because there was no moment of the dramatic adoption of Yahwism, these tribes had no tradition that the worship of Yahweh was mediated to them first through Moses, and had no memory of its beginning. The Kenites had worshipped Yahweh from time immemorial, and hence these tribes, taking over their Yahwism from the Kenites imperceptibly, also represented it as having existed since the very beginnings of the human race. Later, when Moses fled from Egypt, where his fellow Israelites were not Yahweh-worshipping, he found refuge in the home of a Yahweh-worshipping priest of Kenite stock. There in the experience of his call he felt himself commissioned to go in the name of this God into Egypt and to bring his kindred out. When he successfully carries this enterprise through, Jethro is filled with pride and joy in the triumph of his God and initiates the Israelite leaders into the faith and practice of Yahweh-worship, and the Israelites pledge themselves to the God who has delivered them.[1] Their Yahwism thus begins in an experience of consecration, resting on the memorable experience of the deliverance from Egypt. Accordingly in their traditions they represent the worship of Yahweh as having begun in the time of Moses. In both bodies of tradition, therefore, there is substance of truth. The J document does not represent Yahwism as beginning with Moses, because for the southern tribes it did not; the E document does represent it as beginning with Moses because for the Joseph tribes it did. Since Kenites did not accompany the Joseph tribes, they rightly record in their traditions that after initiating the Israelite leaders, Jethro returned to his home; while the southern tribes, who were conscious of their Kenite element, record that Kenites came with them. Since both the northern and the southern tribes integrated traditions of all the tribes in a single account, both related their entry to Moses, and represented him as the leader of the united tribes. But if the entry was in two waves separated by a long period, as so many scholars hold, in whatever order they place the two movements, Moses cannot have been the leader of both. To accept him as the leader of the Joseph tribes seems to explain

[1] It will be seen that I do not share the extreme scepticism of Waterman, who holds that it was the entry into Egypt which was the deliverance and not the Exodus (*A.J.S.L.* lv, 1935, p. 40). No evidence, Biblical or extra-Biblical, can be produced in support of this radical rewriting of the story, and in its subjectively rewritten form it completely fails to account for the enduring impression which Israel retained of the Exodus, which is thus reduced to negligibility. A Biblical tradition cannot be maintained against clear evidence, but still less can a modern fiction, which has not even verisimilitude.

better than the contrary theory why he should be credited with introducing the divine name Yahweh in the traditions of those tribes, and also why he should not be credited with this work in the southern traditions.

Moreover, this view recognizes the supreme importance of the work of Moses.[1] Yahweh had first chosen Israel in her weakness and oppression and had sent Moses in His name to rescue her from her bondage, though she did not hitherto worship Him. Then Israel in her gratitude pledged herself to this God in undeviating loyalty. That her pledge was not always kept is clear from the record of the Old Testament itself, but the taking of the pledge was a new and highly significant thing in the history of religion. Meek here objects[2] that there was nothing new in this, since many a people has adopted another religion. It is perfectly true that there have been many cases of the adoption of a foreign religion. Sometimes it has been imposed on a subject people, or even readily adopted because of the prestige of a powerful people; sometimes, as in the case of the Kenite religion amongst the southern tribes, it has spread by gradual penetration amongst peoples closely associated with one another, and perhaps intermarrying with one another; sometimes by infiltration from a neighbouring people, as frequently in the story of Israel. But here is nothing of such a character. Here Israel's adoption of Yahweh was the response to His adoption of Israel, and the sequel to His achieved deliverance of her.

It is quite incredible that this was the pure invention of the collector, or collectors, of the northern corpus of traditions. For without it the whole story loses its vitalizing factor. If Moses really led the southern tribes out of Egypt and did not introduce them to a new name under which to worship God, but instead they had long worshipped Yahweh before his time, then the

---

[1] Powis Smith (*A.J.S.L.* xxxv, 1918–19, pp. 1–19) finds it possible to trace the origins of Israelite religion wholly to southern influences, and to leave Moses entirely out of account in the story. This is emphatically not to account for the Old Testament traditions. For he holds that Yahwism came to the northern tribes in the time of David and was due to the Judahite hegemony in that reign. It seems far more satisfactory to accept all the southern influence upon Judah to which Powis Smith calls attention, but to recognize that the Biblical traditions can only be accounted for if the Joseph tribes received their Yahwism in a wholly different way. The Song of Deborah alone is sufficient to disprove Smith's hypothesis. For it is almost certainly more ancient than the time of David and is of northern origin. Yet it clearly comes from a Yahweh-worshipping people.

[2] Cf. *Hebrew Origins*, 1936, pp. 89 f.

uniqueness of the Divine choice of Israel in the time of Moses is denied, and no ground is left on which such an idea could be based, as it was demonstrably based in the consciousness of Israel. The story is reduced to a perfectly ordinary one—of a people ascribing its deliverance to its own God. Why that should become of lasting importance in the history of religion is without explanation; and equally so why anyone—and especially in tribes that did not even share the deliverance—should convert it into something surprisingly unique.

It is often supposed that the 'Kenite theory' of the source of Mosaic Yahwism[1] reduces the work of Moses to the mere mediation to the tribes he led of the religion of his father-in-law. Nothing can be farther from the truth. If Yahwism was the worship of the Kenites from time immemorial and none knew how it had begun amongst them, then it was fundamentally different for the tribes Moses led by the mere fact of the unforgettable experience through which they were led to it.[2] It was always associated amongst them with the memory of the deliverance they had experienced. Moreover, it is not to be supposed that Moses simply transferred to Israel the Yahwism of his father-in-law without change, and that such development as took place in the religion in the course of time just happened by itself with the mere passing of the years. It is antecedently likely that under the influence of a great leader, and in the circumstances of Israel's adoption of Yahwism, some new quality would be given to their Yahwism. It is certain that a new character was given to the Passover. Whatever its significance hitherto had been, to the Israelite who had come out of Egypt it henceforth carried the memory of his deliverance, whereas to Kenites who had not shared the deliverance it could not hitherto have had such a meaning.[3]

[1] Meek (*Hebrew Origins*, p. 92) objects that the 'Kenite hypothesis' fails to solve the problem of the origin of Yahwism. It merely pushes it back from Israel to the Kenites. That is true so far as an absolute origin is concerned, and it is doubtful if any solution to that problem can be found. The 'Kenite hypothesis' does not pretend to solve it, but merely claims that Kenite Yahwism was the source of Mosaic Yahwism, until it was enriched and given a new quality through the prophetic personality of Moses. It is not necessary to suppose that the worship of Yahweh was previously confined to the Kenites, but only that Jethro was a priest of this God.

[2] Cf. Meinhold, *Einführung in das Alte Testament*, 3rd ed., 1932, p. 59: 'Wichtiger als die Frage, woher der Kult stammte, ist die, was Moses aus ihm machte.'

[3] Cf. Budde, *Religion of Israel to the Exile*, 1899, pp. 35 ff. See also Marti, *The*

It is probable that Moses gave a new Decalogue to his people. In Ex. xxxiv we have what was probably once a more primitive Decalogue[1] than that contained in Ex. xx and Dt. v. In the present text there are more than ten commands in Ex. xxxiv, but it is probable that once there were ten only. Attempts to decide which these ten were do not lead to agreed results, but the general character of the commands is inferior to that of the more familiar Decalogue, and it is commonly known as the Ritual Decalogue.[2] Yet since it contains provisions appropriate to agricultural festivals, it is generally ascribed to a period later than the Settlement in Palestine. On the other hand, it is more primitive than the Ethical Decalogue of Ex. xx, and hence this latter is assigned by many scholars to an even later date, and therefore loosed entirely from the work of Moses.[3]

Religion of the Old Testament, E.Tr., 1914, p. 62: 'Even though Jahwe was originally the name of the God of Sinai, it immediately received a higher significance under the Israelites than that which it had possessed as the God of the confederate tribes of Mount Sinai.'

[1] Cf. Messel, in *Det Gamle Testamente*, translated by Michelet, Mowinckel, and Messel, i, 1929, p. 186: 'Vi har her den eldste kjente form for en "tibudslov".'

[2] Amongst the many studies of this Decalogue mention may be made of the following: Knudson, *J.B.L.* xxviii, 1909, pp. 82 ff.; Beer, *Pesachim*, 1912, pp. 23 ff.; Cornill, in *Studien zur semitischen Philologie und Religionsgeschichte* (Wellhausen Festschrift), 1914, pp. 109 ff.; Pfeiffer, in *J.B.L.* xliii, 1924, pp. 294 ff.; Berry, ibid. xliv, 1925, pp. 39 ff.; Morgenstern, *The Oldest Document of the Hexateuch*, 1927, pp. 54 ff.; Gray, in *J.T.S.* xxxvii, 1936, pp. 245 ff. In addition to these, a further proposed selection of the original ten words of Ex. xxxiv may be found in Kennett, *The Church of Israel*, 1933, pp. 17 f.; and Köhler, *Th.R.*, N.F. i, 1929, pp. 166 f. Eerdmans (*Alttestamentliche Studien*, iii, 1910, pp. 84 ff.) denies that this ever was a Decalogue, and holds that it was of post-exilic origin. Similarly McFadyen (*Expositor*, 8th series, xi, 1916, pp. 152 ff.) argues that the emphasis on ritual was not an exclusively early characteristic. While this is true, the ritual character of this Decalogue is quite different from that of the Priestly Code, and it seems more natural to find it to be early. Morgenstern holds that it was the Kenite Code, a view with which I am in substantial agreement, as will be seen, though I should allow it greater antiquity than does Morgenstern (see following note). While he formerly held that in its original form it consisted of but eight words (cf. loc. cit., p. 91) he now believes that it was a decalogue (cf. *H.U.C.A.* xxi, 1948, p. 476).

[3] It has long been the common view of scholars that this Decalogue belongs to the period of the prophets, or even later. While there has been a steady tendency away from it during the present century, it still finds advocates. Cf. Steuernagel, *Lehrbuch der Einleitung in das Alte Testament*, 1912, pp. 259 ff.; Nowack, in *Abhandlungen zur semitischen Religionskunde und Sprachwissenschaft* (Baudissin Festschrift), 1918, pp. 381 ff.; Hölscher, *Geschichte der israelitischen und jüdischen Religion*, 1922, p. 130; Meinhold, *Der Dekalog*, 1927; Lods, *Israël*,

The Ritual Decalogue is assigned to the J document, and hence, if Moses led the southern tribes, it is hard indeed to see how he could have given them the Ethical Decalogue, if they preserved only the Ritual. Nor can it be supposed that the Ritual Decalogue would become the Ethical Decalogue by the mere passage of time. But if Moses led the Joseph tribes, and it is recognized that Israel's history lay in two streams and not in one, we have a very different situation. The southern tribes, that entered the land in the Amarna age and that gradually took over their Yahwism from their Kenite associates, would naturally take it over at the level it then had. Their Decalogue might be adapted to their new conditions in Palestine, and related to agricultural festivals, without being ethically exalted, and it might continue for long at the same level as an essentially ritual Decalogue. On the other hand, the tribes that were with Moses, and that embraced Yahwism in a historical moment of decision as the expression of their gratitude for their deliverance from Egypt, might more naturally be given a new and higher Decalogue by their great leader, Moses. Gratitude is itself ethical emotion, as fear, for instance, is not, and there is nothing surprising in a religion which is ethically based having an ethical character.[1] Hence Moses could well give the higher Decalogue

1930, pp. 365 f. (E.Tr., 1932, pp. 315 f.); Pfeiffer, *Introduction to the Old Testament*, 1941, pp. 228 ff. Mowinckel, in his important study, *Le Décalogue*, 1927, presents the view that it had its origin amongst Isaiah's disciples. Cf. too, id., *R.H.P.R.* vi, 1926, pp. 409 ff., 501 ff., *Jesaja-Disiplene*, 1926, pp. 77 ff., and *Det Gamle Testamente*, translated by Michelet, Mowinckel, and Messel, i, 1929, p. 149. Earlier, Mowinckel had subscribed to the exilic view of the origin of the Decalogue (*Psalmenstudien*, v, 1924, p. 112). Morgenstern (*Universal Jewish Encyclopedia*, iii, 1941, pp. 506 ff.) finds a series of Decalogues. The Kenite Decalogue of Ex. xxxiv he ascribes to 899 B.C.; a northern Decalogue, preserved in Ex. xx. 23–6, xxiii. 10–19, to the time of Jehu's revolution; the Decalogue of Ex. xx and Dt. v to the time of Hezekiah or Josiah; a fourth Decalogue, contained in Lev. xix. 2–18, to post-exilic times; and a fifth Decalogue, standing in Dt. xxvii. 15–26, to the fifth century B.C. On the fourth of these Decalogues, cf. Cornill, *Studien zur semitischen Philologie und Religionsgeschichte* (Wellhausen Festschrift), 1914, pp. 112 f.; Messel, in *Det Gamle Testamente*, translated by Michelet, Mowinckel, and Messel, i, 1929, p. 238; Mowinckel, *Z.A.W.*, n.f. xiv, 1937, pp. 218 ff. The first of these Decalogues Morgenstern associates with Asa's reform (cf. *The Oldest Document of the Hexateuch*, pp. 98–119; *Amos Studies*, i, 1941, pp. 236–46; *H.U.C.A.* xxi, 1948, p. 378).

[1] Cf. Budde, *Religion of Israel to the Exile*, 1899, p. 38: 'Israel's religion became ethical because it was a religion of choice and not of nature, because it rested on a voluntary decision which established an ethical relation between the people and its God for all time.' This is inadequate, as Meek points out

to the northern tribes that he led, as they declare in their traditions,[1] at a time when the southern tribes that had already adopted Yahwism at an earlier date were still at the more primitive level.[2]

It is sometimes suggested that the name of Moses' mother is the Achilles' heel of the whole Kenite theory of Yahwism. For she was called Jochebed, and this name appears to be compounded with the divine name Yahweh.[3] If, then, Moses' mother was given a theophorous name compounded with Yahweh before he was born, it cannot be supposed that he introduced the name Yahweh to the Israelites who were in Egypt. To counter this argument it is sometimes noted that our evidence for the name is found only in late sources,[4] which are without authority, or even that it is not certain that the name Jochebed is compounded

(*Hebrew Origins*, 1936, pp. 89 f.), since there is nothing inherently ethical in choice. But here it was not Israel's spontaneous choice of Yahweh, but Israel's response to His choice of her and deliverance of her.

[1] Amongst modern writers who allow that the Decalogue may go back to Moses are: Gressmann, *Mose und seine Zeit*, 1913, pp. 471 ff.; McFadyen, *Expositor*, 8th series, xi, 1916, pp. 152 ff., 222 ff., 311 ff., 384 ff., xii, 1916, pp. 37 ff., 105 ff., 210 ff.; Schmidt, in EYXAPIΣTHPION (Gunkel Festschrift), i, 1923, pp. 78 ff.; Kittel, *Geschichte des Volkes Israel*, i, 5th and 6th ed., 1923, pp. 383 ff., 445 ff.; Gampert, in *R.Th.Ph.*, N.S. xiv, 1926, pp. 184 ff.; Herrmann, in *Sellin Festschrift*, 1927, pp. 69 ff.; Volz, in *R.G.G.*, 2nd ed., i, 1927, cols. 1816 ff., *Mose und sein Werk*, 2nd ed., 1932, pp. 20 ff., and *Prophetengestalten des Alten Testaments*, 1938, pp. 51 ff.; Köhler, in *Th.R.*, N.F. i, 1929, pp. 161 ff.; Eberharter, *Der Dekalog*, 1929; Oesterley and Robinson, *Hebrew Religion*, 2nd ed., 1937, p. 168. Cf. also Hempel, *Das Schichten des Deuteronomiums*, 1914, pp. 159 f. n.; Alt, *Die Ursprünge des israelitischen Rechts*, 1934, pp. 52 ff. Spiegel (*H.T.R.* xxvii, 1934, pp. 140 ff.) argues that it goes back beyond Hosea at any rate. Not all of the writers here mentioned go so far as to claim that the Decalogue is Mosaic, but only that it may be. Beyond that, indeed, it is impossible to go. Cf. Oesterley and Robinson, op. cit., p. 168: 'We cannot say definitely that . . . they go back to Moses. . . . This much, however, we can say. Whether these commandments are the work of Moses or not, they represent very fairly the general moral standard which we may ascribe to Israel in the days preceding the Settlement.' Volz (*Old Testament Essays*, 1927, p. 30) observes that apart from the Decalogue we have no certain word from Moses.

[2] That the Decalogue has been expanded from its original form is apparent from the comparison of the two versions in Ex. xx and Dt. v. It is generally agreed that originally all the commands were probably short, like those in the second half. It is only of that original form that the Mosaic origin can be held to be possible.   [3] Cf. Meek, *Hebrew Origins*, 1936, p. 91.

[4] The name is preserved only in P: Ex. vi. 20, Num. xxvi. 59. Powis Smith (*A.J.S.L.* xxxv, 1918–19, p. 15) says it must therefore not be taken too seriously. Against this Meek (loc. cit.) rightly observes that it was hardly coined by P.

with Yahweh.[1] It is unnecessary to resort to either shift on the view which I have put forward. For if Israelite tribes with Yahweh-worshipping Kenite associates entered Palestine in the Amarna age, it would not be surprising for some intermarriage between the associated tribes to take place. Such intermarriage might easily bring a Levite family into association with a Kenite family, and hence bring a Kenite name into a Levite home. In a later age we find in the Elephantine community of Jews some Egyptian names, probably through intermarriage,[2] and it would be even more natural to find this amongst tribes associated in a common enterprise. If, as I have argued, some of the Levites who reached Shechem and were then involved in some disaster went into Egypt, a Kenite name might be found there, to be repeated in the family in another generation even though the family were not Yahweh-worshipping. On such a view the name of Moses' mother could be recognized to be a theophorous name compounded with Yahweh, but derived through some intermarriage, and bearing its witness to some Kenite blood in Moses on his mother's side.[3] Thus the name Yahweh might be known amongst the Israelites in Egypt, even though Yahweh were not the God whom they worshipped.

This view in its turn offers an explanation of Moses' flight to Jethro when he was forced to leave Egypt. If he had some Kenite blood on his mother's side, it would not be surprising for him to flee to his mother's kindred when he could not remain in Egypt. When Jacob was compelled to flee through fear of his brother's wrath, he fled to his mother's kindred.[4] For Moses to do the same would therefore be most natural. In both cases we find curiously similar incidents at the well to which they go to find their destination.

On the other hand, on my view there were still Levites who did not go down into Egypt, but who fell back on Judah. It is

[1] Gray (*Hebrew Proper Names*, 1896, p. 156) thinks the author of P did not connect the name with Yahweh, and Noth (*Die israelitischen Personennamen*, 1928, p. 111) is doubtful if it should be so connected. Bauer (*Z.A.W.*, N.F. x, 1933, pp. 92 f.) connects the name with the doubtful Yw of the Ras Shamra text.

[2] Cf. Gray, in *Studien zur semitischen Philologie und Religionsgeschichte* (Wellhausen Festschrift), 1914, pp. 174 f.

[3] Simpson (*The Early Traditions of Israel*, 1948, p. 161) conjectures that Moses' mother was an Egyptian woman, but that owing to a growing nationalism this was represented as his adoption by an Egyptian woman, and that finally his foster-mother was converted into a princess. No evidence is offered for this improbable thesis. [4] Gen. xxvii. 43.

thus that I explain the close association of Levites with Judah to which attention has been called. It is therefore likely that some relations of Moses on his father's side were to be found in Judah. It may have been through these connexions that we find the grandson of Moses in Bethlehem in the century following the Exodus.[1]

It is sometimes stated as an objection to the thirteenth-century date for the Exodus that it leaves insufficient time for the period of the Judges.[2] This argument is not valid against the view which I have presented, for it leaves the period of the Judges exactly as long as the fifteenth-century date for the Exodus makes it. On that view and on mine the Amarna age saw the entry of Israelite tribes that remained in the land continuously thereafter. In particular, I hold that the southern group, amongst which the earliest of the Judges is said to have arisen, entered in that age. The exploits of Othniel could therefore have taken place before the Exodus of the tribes that settled in the central districts. It may be noted that while this objection is not valid against my view, it is valid against that of Meek and Albright, who maintain that Judah entered the land more than a century after the Joseph tribes. For since the earliest exploits in Canaan are declared in the Biblical traditions to have been performed in this southern district, either those traditions must be declared inconvenient and therefore wrong, or the period of the Judges must be greatly compressed.

On the view that I have presented, the period from the Exodus to the founding of Solomon's Temple was rather more than 250 years. The genealogical list indicates that from Nahshon, who was of the generation of the Exodus,[3] to Solomon was covered by six generations.[4] This would require an average of somewhat more than forty years to a generation. While this might seem to be unduly high, we have evidence that supports it for some of these links. Thus Boaz appears to have been an elderly man before Obed was born. Further, since David was the seventh son of Jesse, his father may well have been over forty when he was born. Again, Solomon was born after David had transferred his capital to Jerusalem, when David must have been in the neighbourhood of forty. Solomon himself must have been in the thirties at the time of the founding of the Temple unless his birth was later in the reign of his father, when David's

---

[1] Jg. xvii. 7, 12, xviii. 19, 30.
[2] Cf. Hommel, *E.T.* x, 1898–9, p. 212.   [3] Ex. vi. 23, Num. i. 7.
[4] Nahshon, Salmon, Boaz, Obed, Jesse, David, Solomon. Cf. Ruth iv. 20–2.

M

age at his birth would need to be correspondingly increased.[1]
How long after the Exodus it was before Salmon was born we
have no means of knowing, but since we have this evidence that
an average of about forty years is required for four of the other
names, if Salmon was anywhere near forty when Boaz was born,
and Obed was anywhere near that age when Jesse was born, the
case is fully met. Where there is reasonable certainty in so many
cases, possibility can scarcely be denied in the remaining cases.
For there is no reason to suppose that this is a genealogy of
primogeniture, but on the contrary we know that in some cases
it was not.

Moreover, if we allow an average of twenty-five years each
for the eight Edomite kings who are said to have reigned before
Saul,[2] and find the one who was contemporary with Moses[3] to
be the first of them,[4] we reach a total of about 260 years for the
period from the Exodus to the founding of the Temple, and this
is in close accord with the view I have presented.

In the period of David and Solomon all the Israelite tribes
came together in a political unity that was religiously based on
their common worship of Yahweh. For by that time Yahwism
had spread through all the tribes, by whatever means it had
been introduced to them. Moreover, David sealed this unity by
bringing the long-neglected Ephraimite symbol of the Ark into
his new capital of Jerusalem. Hence, in this period there would
be some bringing together of the traditions of the various tribes
and welding of them into a unity. The actual corpora of traditions lying behind the Pentateuch are probably of later date
than this, and they bear the marks of the differing viewpoints
of centre and south. Yet underlying them both was probably the
work of collectors of traditions in the early monarchy, who
carried back the unity of the moment into a fictitious unity that
ran far back into the past.

That all the tribes were of kindred stock, and that those who
went into Egypt broke off from their kindred and about a century and a half later came and settled in their midst, is a view
which is in substantial agreement with Biblical traditions, when

---

[1] La Motte (*Interpretation*, ii, 1948, pp. 370 f.) argues that Solomon cannot
have been born until at least ten years after David entered Jerusalem, and
that he could not therefore have been much over twenty when he succeeded.

[2] Gen. xxxvi. 31 ff.   [3] Num. xx. 14.

[4] In view of the evidence above noted that Edom was not settled until
about 1200 B.C., it is improbable that the Edomite monarchy antedated the
time of Moses.

freed from the fictitious unity that has been imposed on them, and examined in the light of their contents, and against it is no serious archaeological evidence, while much can be claimed to be for it. A solid historical kernel for the work of Moses may then reasonably be accepted, and in the development that emerges we find an important clue for the understanding of the religious development of Israel. While therefore the subject of our study is primarily one of history and chronology, with a very tangled web of Biblical and archaeological evidence to make its examination appear to be remote from every important interest, it is really of fundamental importance for any study of the Old Testament, and especially for the study of Old Testament religion. When I began to be interested in this subject twenty-five years ago I did not realize this, but approached it merely as a problem which interested me by its complexity. At that time I accepted the view that Moses was a nebulous figure, of whom little more could be predicated than that he once lived,[1] and the question whether the Exodus lay in the fifteenth century or the thirteenth seemed a purely academic one that carried no significant consequences either way. It was only as the picture became clearer that its meaning became clearer. Yet I would emphasize that it is not by that meaning that my reconstruction is to be judged, but only by its fidelity to the evidence. For it is as a purely academic study that I offer it, as is fitting in the Schweich Lectures. I offer it as one who is convinced that it yields a more probable solution than its rivals, but not as one whose mind is closed against any new light that may come. Rather, with Cyprian would I say: 'Non enim vincimur quando offeruntur nobis meliora, sed instruimur.'[2]

[1] Some have denied that he was an historical person at all. Cf. Meyer, *Die Israeliten und ihre Nachbarstämme*, 1906, p. 451 n.; Hölscher, *Geschichte der israelitischen und jüdischen Religion*, 1922, pp. 64 ff.
[2] Epist. lxxi, 3 (ed. Hartel, in *Corpus Scriptorum Ecclesiasticorum Latinorum*, iii, part 2, 1871, p. 774).

APPENDIX

SUMMARY OF DATES

circa 1650 B.C. Migration of Abraham from Ḥarran.

circa 1440 B.C. Hebrew groups at Kadesh, where they sojourn thirty-eight years and become associated with Yahweh-worshipping Kenite and other groups.

circa 1400 B.C. Pressure northwards from Kadesh of Hebrew groups, together with Kenite and other elements = Ḥabiru of Amarna letters.

Simultaneous pressure from north of kindred groups, including Asher, Zebulun, Dan, and other Israelite tribes, together with other groups = SA-GAZ of Amarna letters.

Simeon and Levi reach Shechem from the south, but fail to hold it.

During following two centuries Judah and other southern tribes gradually increase their hold on the south, and northern tribes become settled in their locations.

circa 1370 B.C. Joseph taken into Egypt in reign of Ikhnaton, under whom he rises to high office.

circa 1360 B.C. Descent into Egypt of Hebrews, particularly some of those who had failed to hold Shechem.

circa 1300 B.C. Oppression under Rameses II. Hebrews set to build Pithom and Raamses.

circa 1290 B.C. Moses born.

circa 1260 B.C. Moses flees to Jethro, a Kenite kinsman of his mother.

circa 1230 B.C. Exodus from Egypt under Moses in the name of the Kenite God, Yahweh, followed by the covenant of the Exodus tribes with Yahweh, and formulation of the Ethical Decalogue.

After brief wandering for two years Joshua leads these tribes which had come from Egypt across the Jordan into central Palestine, which they occupy.

Merneptah carries out a raiding expedition into Palestine.

LIST OF WORKS CONSULTED

F. M. ABEL, *Géographie de la Palestine*, 2 vols., 1933.

J. McK. ADAMS, *Ancient Records and the Bible*, 1946.

F. E. ADCOCK, see *Cambridge Ancient History*.

W. F. ALBRIGHT, 'Historical and Mythical Elements in the Story of Joseph', in *J.B.L.* xxxvii, 1918, pp. 111–43.

—— 'A Revision of Early Assyrian and Middle Babylonian Chronology', in *R.Ass.* xviii, 1921, pp. 83–94.

—— 'A Revision of Early Hebrew Chronology', in *J.P.O.S.* i, 1921, pp. 49–79.

—— 'The Earliest Forms of Hebrew Verse', in *J.P.O.S.* ii, 1922, pp. 69–86.

—— 'Shinar-Šangar and its Monarch Amraphel', in *A.J.S.L.* xl, 1923–4, pp. 125–33.

—— 'The Archaeological Results of an Expedition to Moab and the Dead Sea', in *B.A.S.O.R.*, No. 14, Apr. 1924, pp. 2–12.

—— 'Contributions to Biblical Archaeology and Philology', in *J.B.L.* xliii, 1924, pp. 363–93.

—— 'The Topography of Simeon', in *J.P.O.S.* iv, 1924, pp. 149–61.

—— 'The Jordan Valley in the Bronze Age', in *A.A.S.O.R.* vi, 1926, pp. 13–74.

—— Review of F. M. Th. Böhl, *Genesis*, in *J.P.O.S.* vi, 1926, pp. 224–8.

—— 'The Excavations at Tell Beit Mirsim I–II', in *B.A.S.O.R.*, No. 23, Oct. 1926, pp. 2–14.

—— 'The Historical Background of Gen. xiv', in *J.S.O.R.* x, 1926, pp. 231–69.

—— 'The Second Campaign at Tell Beit Mirsim', in *B.A.S.O.R.*, No. 31, Oct. 1928, pp. 1–11.

—— 'The Egyptian Empire in Asia in the Twenty-first Century B.C.', in *J.P.O.S.* viii, 1928, 223–56.

—— Review of A. Jirku, *Die Wanderungen der Hebräer im. 3. und 2. Jahrtausend v. Chr.*, in *J.A.O.S.* xlviii, 1928, pp. 183–5.

—— 'The American Excavations at Tell Beit Mirsim', in *Z.A.W.*, N.F. vi, 1929, pp. 1–17.

—— 'New Israelite and Pre-Israelite Sites: the Spring Trip of 1929', in *B.A.S.O.R.*, No. 35, Oct. 1929, pp. 1–14.

—— 'The Third Campaign of Excavations at Tell Beit Mirsim', in *B.A.S.O.R.*, No. 38, Apr. 1930, pp. 9 f.

—— 'The Third Campaign at Tell Beit Mirsim', in *B.A.S.O.R.*, No. 39, Oct. 1930, pp. 1–10.

—— 'The Third Campaign at Tell Beit Mirsim and its Historical Results', in *J.P.O.S.* xi, 1931, pp. 105–29.

—— *The Archaeology of Palestine and the Bible*, 1932.

—— 'The Fourth Joint Campaign of Excavation at Tell Beit Mirsim', in *B.A.S.O.R.*, No. 47, Oct. 1932, pp. 3–17.

—— *The Excavations of Tell Beit Mirsim.* I. *The Pottery of the First Three Campaigns* = *A.A.S.O.R.* xii, 1932; IA. *The Bronze Age Pottery of the Fourth Campaign* = *A.A.S.O.R.* xii, 1933; II. *The Bronze Age* = *A.A.S.O.R.* xvii, 1938; III. *The Iron Age* = *A.A.S.O.R.* xxi–xxii, 1943.

—— *The Vocalization of the Egyptian Syllabic Orthography* (American Oriental Series, v), 1934.

—— 'The Kyle Memorial Excavation at Bethel', in *B.A.S.O.R.*, No. 56, Dec. 1934, pp. 2–15.

W. F. ALBRIGHT, 'A Summary of Archaeological Research during 1934 in Palestine, Transjordan, and Syria', in *A.J.A.* xxxix, 1935, pp. 137–48.

—— 'Observations on the Bethel Report', in *B.A.S.O.R.*, No. 57, Feb. 1935, pp. 27–30.

—— 'Archaeology and the Date of the Hebrew Conquest of Palestine', in *B.A.S.O.R.*, No. 58, Apr. 1935, pp. 10–18.

—— 'Palestine in the Earliest Historical Period', in *J.P.O.S.* xv, 1935, pp. 193–234.

—— 'The Song of Deborah in the Light of Archaeology', in *B.A.S.O.R.*, No. 62, Apr. 1936, pp. 26–31.

—— 'New Canaanite Historical and Mythological Data', in *B.A.S.O.R.*, No. 63, Oct. 1936, pp. 23–32.

—— 'Further Light on the History of Israel from Lachish and Megiddo', in *B.A.S.O.R.*, No. 68, Dec. 1937, pp. 22–6.

—— 'The Present State of Syro-Palestinian Archaeology', in *The Haverford Symposium on Archaeology and the Bible*, ed. by E. Grant, 1938.

—— 'A Revolution in the Chronology of Ancient Western Asia', in *B.A.S.O.R.*, No. 69, Feb. 1938, pp. 18–21.

—— 'Recent Progress in North Canaanite Research', in *B.A.S.O.R.*, No. 70, Apr. 1938, pp. 18–24.

—— 'Was the Patriarch Terah a Canaanite Moon-god?' in *B.A.S.O.R.*, No. 71, Oct. 1938, pp. 35–40.

—— 'The Israelite Conquest of Canaan in the Light of Archaeology', in *B.A.S.O.R.*, No. 74, Apr. 1939, pp. 11–23.

—— 'New Light on the History of Western Asia in the Second Millennium B.C.', in *B.A.S.O.R.*, No. 77, Feb. 1940, pp. 20–32; No. 78, Apr. 1940, pp. 23–31.

—— Review of *H.U.C.A.* xii–xiv, in *J.B.L.* lix, 1940, pp. 298–302.

—— *From the Stone Age to Christianity*, 1940; 2nd ed., 1946.

—— 'New Egyptian Data on Palestine in the Patriarchal Age', in *B.A.S.O.R.*, No. 81, Feb. 1941, pp. 16–21.

—— 'The Land of Damascus between 1850 and 1750 B.C.', in *B.A.S.O.R.*, No. 83, Oct. 1941, pp. 30–6.

—— *Archaeology and the Religion of Israel*, 1942; 2nd ed., 1946.

—— 'A Third Revision of the Early Chronology of Western Asia', in *B.A.S.O.R.*, No. 88, Dec. 1942, pp. 28–36.

—— 'Two Little Understood Amarna Letters from the Middle Jordan Valley', in *B.A.S.O.R.*, No. 89, Feb. 1943, pp. 7–17.

—— 'The Oracles of Balaam', in *J.B.L.* lxiii, 1944, pp. 207–33.

—— 'An Indirect Synchronism between Egypt and Mesopotamia, cir. 1730 B.C.', in *B.A.S.O.R.*, No. 99, Oct. 1945, pp. 9–18.

—— 'Exploring in Sinai with the University of California African Expedition', in *B.A.S.O.R.*, No. 109, Feb. 1948, pp. 5–20.

—— 'The Old Testament and Archaeology', in Alleman and Flack, *Old Testament Commentary*, 1948, pp. 134–70.

—— Review of F. M. Th. Böhl, *King Ḥammurabi of Babylon in the Setting of His Time*, in *Bi.Or.* v, 1948, pp. 125–7.

—— *The Archaeology of Palestine*, 1949.

H. C. ALLEMAN and E. E. FLACK, 'The Book of Exodus', in *Old Testament Commentary*, ed. by Alleman and Flack, 1948.

H. C. Alleman and E. E. Flack, ed. by: *Old Testament Commentary*, 1948.
—— see also F. C. Forster.

A. Alt, *Die Landnahme der Israeliten in Palästina* (Sonderabdruck aus dem Reformationsprogramm der Universität Leipzig), 1925.
—— 'Hebräer', in *R.G.G.*, 2nd ed., ed. by H. Gunkel and L. Zscharnack, ii. 1928, cols. 1668 f.
—— *Der Gott der Väter; ein Beitrag zur Vorgeschichte der israelitischen Religion* (B.W.A.N.T. 3. Folge, xii), 1929.
—— *Die Staatenbildung der Israeliten in Palästina* (Sonderabdruck aus dem Reformationsprogramm der Universität Leipzig), 1930.
—— *Die Ursprünge des israelitischen Rechts*, 1934.
—— 'Beiträge zur historischen Geographie und Topographie des Negeb', in *J.P.O.S.* xv, 1935, pp. 294–324; xvii, 1937, pp. 218–35.
—— 'Josua', in *Werden und Wesen des Alten Testaments*, ed. by J. Hempel (B.Z.A.W., No. 66), 1936, pp. 13–29.
—— Review of J. de Koning, *Studiën over de El-Amarnabrieven en het Oude-Testament inzonderheid uit historisch oogpunt*, 1940, in *A.f.O.* xiv, 1941–4, pp. 349–52.
—— 'Herren und Herrensitze Palästinas im Anfang des zweiten Jahrtausends vor Chr.', in *Z.D.P.V.* lxiv, 1941, pp. 21–39.

P. Asmussen, 'Die Einwanderung Israels in Kanaan', in *Memnon*, vii, 1915, pp. 185–207.

P. Auvray, 'Josué (Le livre de)', in *Supplément au Dictionnaire de la Bible*, ed. by L. Pirot and A. Robert, iv (fasc. xxii, 1948), cols. 1131–41.

A. M. Badawi, 'Die neue historische Stele Amenophis' II', in *Annales du Service des Antiquités de l'Égypte*, xlii, 1943, pp. 1–23.

J. Baikie, *The Amarna Age: a Study of the Crisis of the Ancient World*, 1926.
—— *A History of Egypt from the Earliest Times to the End of the Eighteenth Dynasty*, 2 vols., 1929.

W. E. Barnes, *The First Book of the Kings* (Camb. B.), 1911 edition.

G. A. Barton, 'The Habiri of the El-Amarna Tablets and the Hebrew Conquest of Palestine', in *J.B.L.* xlviii, 1929, pp. 144–7.
—— *Archaeology and the Bible*, 6th ed., 1933.
—— *Semitic and Hamitic Origins, Social and Religious*, 1934.
—— 'The Possible Mention of Joshua's Conquest in the El-Amarna Letters', in *E.T.* xlvii, 1935–6, p. 380.
—— 'Pella in the El-Amarna Tablets', in *E.T.* xlvii, 1935–6, pp. 476 f.
—— 'Danel, a Pre-Israelite Hero of Galilee', in *Mémorial Lagrange*, 1940, pp. 29–37 (= *J.B.L.* lx, 1941, pp. 213–25).

W. W. von Baudissin, *Kyrios als Gottesname im Judentum und seine Stelle in der Religionsgeschichte*, ed. by O. Eissfeldt, 4 vols., 1929.

H. Bauer, 'Die Gottheiten von Ras Schamra', in *Z.A.W.*, n.f. x, 1933, pp. 81–101.

W. Baumgartner, 'Ras Schamra und das Alte Testament', in *Th.R.*, n.f. xii, 1940, pp. 163–88; xiii, 1941, pp. 1–20, 85–102, 157–83.

N. H. Baynes, see *Cambridge Ancient History*.

A. Bea, 'Ras Šamra und das Alte Testament', in *Biblica*, xix, 1938, pp. 435–53.
—— 'Archäologisches und Religionsgeschichtliches aus Ugarit-Ras Šamra', in *Biblica*, xx, 1939, pp. 436–53.
—— 'La Palestina preisraelitica', in *Biblica*, xxiv, 1943, pp. 231–60.

G. Beer, *Pesachim* (in *Die Mischna*, ed. by G. Beer and O. Holtzmann), 1912.
—— and K. Galling, *Exodus* (H.A.T.), 1939.
S. Bendixon, *Israels Historia från äldsta tider till Herodes' tronbestigning*, i, 1948.
A. Bentzen, *Indledning til det Gamle Testamente*, 2 vols. in 3, 1941.
—— 'Nyere synspunkter vedrørende Israels invandring i Palæstina', in *D.T.T.* iv, 1941, pp. 1–26.
—— 'On the Ideas of "the old" and "the new" in Deutero-Isaiah', in *Studia Theologica*, i, 1947, pp. 183–7.
—— 'The Cultic Use of the Story of the Ark in Samuel', in *J.B.L.* lxvii, 1948, pp. 37–53.
I. Benzinger, *Die Bücher der Könige* (K.H.C.), 1899.
—— *Die Bücher der Chronik* (K.H.C.), 1901.
Bereschit Rabba mit kritischem Apparat und Kommentar, ed. by J. Theodor, 2 vols., 1912.
A. Bergman, 'The Israelite Tribe of Half-Manasseh', in *J.P.O.S.* xvi, 1936, pp. 224–54.
G. R. Berry, 'The Ritual Decalogue', in *J.B.L.* xliv, 1925, pp. 39–43.
E. Bertheau, *Das Buch der Richter und Rut*, 1845.
La Bible du Centenaire, 4 vols., 1916–48.
T. R. Birks, *The Exodus of Israel*, 1863.
W. Freiherr von Bissing, 'Das angebliche Weltreich der Hyksos', in *A.f.O.* xi, 1936–7, pp. 325–35.
J. S. Black, see *Encyclopaedia Biblica*.
F. Bleek, *Einleitung in das Alte Testament*, 4th ed., ed. by J. Wellhausen, 1878.
F. M. Th. Böhl, *Kanaanäer und Hebräer*, 1911.
—— 'Die Könige von Genesis 14', in *Z.A.W.* xxxvi, 1916, pp. 65–73.
—— 'Tud'alia I, Zeitgenosse Abrahams, um 1650 v. Chr.', in *Z.A.W.*, n.f. i, 1924, pp. 148–53.
—— *Das Zeitalter Abrahams* (Der Alte Orient, xxix, 1), 1930.
—— 'Brieven uit het archief van Mari (Tell Ḥariri)', in *Bi.Or.* i, 1944, pp. 55–8, 76–9, 101–5.
—— *King Ḥammurabi of Babylon in the Setting of his Time (about 1700 B.C.)*, 1946 (= *Mededeelingen der Koninklijke Nederlandsche Akademie van Wetenschappen*, Afd. Letterkunde, n.r. ix, No. 10, pp. 341–70).
L. Borchardt, 'Ein Onkel Amenophis' IV als Hoherpriester von Heliopolis', in *Z.Ä.S.* xliv, 1907–8, pp. 97 f.
—— 'Einige astronomisch festgelegte Punkte zweiter Ordnung im Neuen Reiche', in *Z.Ä.S.* lxx, 1934, pp. 97–103.
J. H. Breasted, *A History of Egypt*, 1906.
—— *Ancient Records of Egypt*, 5 vols., 1906–7.
—— *Development of Religion and Thought in Ancient Egypt*, 1912.
—— 'Ikhnaton, the Religious Revolutionary', in *C.A.H.* ii, 1924, pp. 109–30.
—— 'The Age of Rameses II', in *C.A.H.* ii, 1924, pp. 131–63.
—— 'The Decline and Fall of the Egyptian Empire', in *C.A.H.*, ii. 1924, pp. 164–95.
J. Bright, Review of H. H. Rowlev, *The Re-discovery of the Old Testament*, in *Interpretation*, i, 1947, pp. 83–6.
R. Brinker, *The Influence of Sanctuaries in Early Israel*, 1946.
H. Brown, 'The Exodus recorded on the Stele of Menephtah', in *J.E.A.* iv, 1917, pp. 16–20.

H. Brugsch, 'Beiträge zu den Untersuchungen über Tanis', in *Z.Ä.S.* x, 1872, pp. 16–20.

M. Buber, *Moses*, 1947.

K. Budde, *Die Bücher Richter und Samuel, ihre Quellen und ihr Aufbau*, 1890.

—— *Das Buch der Richter* (K.H.C.), 1897.

—— *Religion of Israel to the Exile*, 1899.

C. F. Burney, 'A Theory of the Development of Israelite Religion in Early Times', in *J.T.S.* ix, 1907–8, pp. 321–52.

—— *Israel's Settlement in Canaan*, 1918.

—— *The Book of Judges with Introduction and Notes*, 1920.

M. Burrows, *What Mean These Stones?* 1941.

—— 'A Comment on Professor Rowley's Paper in the February Bulletin', in *B.A.S.O.R.*, No. 86, Apr. 1942, pp. 35 f.

J. B. Bury, see *Cambridge Ancient History*.

S. L. Caiger, *Bible and Spade*, 1936.

—— 'Archaeological Fact and Fancy', in *B.A.* ix, 1946, pp. 62–7.

Cambridge Ancient History, ed. by J. B. Bury, S. A. Cook, F. E. Adcock, M. P. Charlesworth, and N. H. Baynes, 12 vols., 1924–39.

J. Capart, 'Remarques sur l'article précédent' (see under R. Weill) in *Chronique d'Égypte*, No. 41, Jan. 1946, pp. 44 f.

E. Cavaignac, 'Les Listes de Khorsabad', in *R.Ass.* xl, 1945–6, pp. 17–26.

H. Cazelles, *Études sur le Code de l'Alliance*, 1946.

B. Celada, 'Descubrimiento en Tanis de varias tumbas reales intactas', in *Sefarad*, i, 1941, pp. 415–35.

J. Chaine, *Le Livre de la Genèse*, 1948.

M. P. Charlesworth, see *Cambridge Ancient History*.

T. K. Cheyne, 'Archaeology and Biblical Criticism', in *O.L.Z.* iii, 1900, cols. 150–2.

—— 'אברך ונתון; Phinehas; Putiel', in *O.L.Z.* iii, 1900, cols. 464 f.

—— 'Joseph [in O.T.]', in *E.B.* ii, 1901, cols. 2583–94.

—— see also *Encyclopaedia Biblica*.

E. Chiera, 'Ḫabiru and Hebrews', in *A.J.S.L.* xlix, 1932–3, pp. 115–24.

J. Clédat, 'Le Site d'Avaris', in *Recueil d'Études égyptologiques dédiées à la mémoire de J. F. Champollion*, 1922, pp. 185–201.

M. Collomb, see H. Lusseau.

G. Contenau, *Manuel d'Archéologie orientale*, 4 vols., 1927–47.

S. A. Cook, 'Genealogies', in *E.B.* ii, 1901, cols. 1657–66.

—— *Critical Notes on Old Testament History*, 1907.

—— 'Simeon and Levi', in *A.J.Th.* xiii, 1909, pp. 370–88.

—— 'Levites', in *E. Brit.*, 11th ed., xvi, 1911, pp. 512–15.

—— 'Chronology. I. Mesopotamia', in *C.A.H.* i, 2nd ed., 1924, pp. 145–56.

—— 'The Rise of Israel', in *C.A.H.* ii, 1924, pp. 352–406.

—— Review of *M.J.U.P.* for March 1922 and Dec. 1923, in *P.E.F.Q.S.* 1924, pp. 199–201.

—— 'Syria and Palestine in the Light of External Evidence', in *C.A.H.* ii, 1925, pp. 296–351.

—— 'Israel and the Neighbouring States', in *C.A.H.* iii, 1925, pp. 354–87.

—— ' "The Foundations of Bible History" ', in *P.E.F.Q.S.* lxiv, 1932, pp. 88–95.

—— *The Old Testament: a Reinterpretation*, 1936.

—— See also *Cambridge Ancient History*.

G. A. COOKE, *A Text-book of North Semitic Inscriptions*, 1903.
—— *The Book of Joshua* (Camb. B.), 1918.
—— *The Book of Judges* (Camb. B.), 1918.
F. CORNELIUS, 'Berossos und die altorientalische Chronologie', in *Klio*, xxxv, 1942, pp. 1–16.
—— 'Die Chronologie des älteren Orients', in *F.u.F.* xx, 1944, pp. 75 f.
C. H. CORNILL, 'Zum Segen Jakobs und zum jahwistischen Dekalog', in *Studien zur semitischen Philologie und Religionsgeschichte* (Wellhausen Festschrift), ed. by K. Marti (B.Z.A.W. xxvii), 1914, pp. 101–13.
V. COUCKE, 'Chronologie Biblique', in *Supplément au Dictionnaire de la Bible*, ed. by L. Pirot and A. Robert, i, 1928, cols. 1245–79.
B. COUROYER, 'Les Nouveaux Textes égyptiens de proscription', in *Vivre et Penser*, i (= *R.B.* l), 1941, pp. 261–4.
—— 'La Résidence ramesside du Delta et le Ramsès biblique', in *R.B.* liii, 1946, pp. 75–98.
E. L. CURTIS, 'Chronology of the Old Testament', in Hastings's *D.B.* i, 1898, pp. 397–403.
N. A. DAHL, 'Anamnesis: Mémoire et Commémoration dans le christianisme primitif', in *Studia Theologica*, i, 1947, pp. 69–95.
G. A. DANELL, *Studies in the Name Israel in the Old Testament*, 1946.
DANIEL-ROPS, *Histoire Sainte: le peuple de la Bible*, 1943.
J. D. DAVIS and H. S. GEHMAN, *The Westminster Dictionary of the Bible*, 1944.
A. DEIMEL, 'Amraphel, rex Sennaar; . . . Thadal, rex gentium', in *Biblica*, viii, 1927, pp. 350–7.
F. DELITZSCH, see C. F. Keil.
L. DENNEFELD, *Histoire d'Israël*, 1935.
L. DESNOYERS, *Histoire du Peuple hébreu des Juges à la Captivité*, i, 1922.
P. (E.) DHORME, 'Hammourabi–Amraphel', in *R.B.*, N.S. v, 1908, pp. 205–26.
—— 'Les Pays bibliques au temps d'El Amarna', in *R.B.*, N.S. v, 1908, pp. 500–19; vi, 1909, pp. 50–73, 368–85.
—— 'Les Ḫabiru et les Hébreux', in *J.P.O.S.* iv, 1924, pp. 162–8.
—— 'Les Nouvelles Tablettes d'el-Amarna', in *R.B.* xxxiii, 1924, pp. 5–32.
—— 'Amarna (Lettres d'El-Amarna)', in *Supplément au Dictionnaire de la Bible*, ed. L. Pirot and A. Robert, i, 1928, cols. 207–25.
—— 'Abraham dans le cadre de l'histoire', in *R.B.* xxxvii, 1928, pp. 367–85, 481–511; xl, 1931, pp. 364–74, 503–18.
—— 'Les Amorrhéens', in *R.B.* xxxvii, 1928, pp. 63–79, 160–80; xxxix, 1930, pp. 160–78; xl, 1931, pp. 161–84.
E. DHORME, Review of J. Garstang's articles on 'Jericho: City and Necropolis' (in *A.A.A.* xix, 1932, pp. 3–22, 35–54), in *R.H.R.* cviii, 1933, pp. 85–8.
—— 'La Question des Ḫabiri', in *R.H.R.* cxviii, 1938, pp. 170–87.
—— 'La Question des Ḫabiri', in *Actes du XXᵉ Congrès international des Orientalistes*, 1940, pp. 123 f.
G. DOSSIN, 'Benjaminites dans les textes de Mari', in *Mélanges Syriens offerts à M. René Dussaud*, ii. 1939, pp. 981–96.
J. J. DOUGHERTY, 'The World of the Hebrew Patriarchs', in *Scripture*, iii, 1948, pp. 98–102.
E. DRIOTON and J. VANDIER, *Les Peuples de l'Orient méditerranéen. II. L'Égypte*, 1946.
S. R. DRIVER, *The Book of Genesis* (W. C.), 1904.
—— *The Book of Exodus* (Camb. B.), 1911.

S. R. Driver, *Notes on the Hebrew Text and the Topography of the Books of Samuel*, 2nd ed., 1913.

G. Duncan, *Digging up Biblical History*, 2 vols., 1931.

—— *New Light on Hebrew Origins*, 1936.

R. Dussaud, Review of L. Desnoyers, *Histoire du Peuple hébreu des Juges à la Captivité*, in *Syria*, iv, 1923, pp. 76 f.

—— 'Nouveaux renseignements sur la Palestine et la Syrie vers 2000 avant notre ère', in *Syria*, viii, 1927, pp. 216–31.

—— 'La Chronologie de Jéricho et les nouvelles fouilles de M. J. Garstang', in *Syria*, xi, 1930, pp. 390–2.

—— 'Le Sanctuaire et les dieux phéniciens de Ras Shamra', in *R.H.R.* cv, 1932, pp. 245–302.

—— 'Quelques précisions touchant les Hyksos', in *R.H.R.* cix, 1934, pp. 113–28.

—— 'Note additionnelle', in *Syria*, xvi, 1935, pp. 346–52.

—— *Les Découvertes de Ras Shamra et l'Ancien Testament*, 1937; 2nd ed., 1941.

—— 'Le Nom ancien de la ville de 'Ay en Palestine', in *R.H.R.* cxv, 1937, pp. 125–41.

—— Review of J. Simons, *Handbook for the Study of Egyptian Topographical Lists relating to Western Asia*, 1937, in *Syria*, xix, 1938, pp. 176 f.

—— 'Yahwé', in *C.R.A.I.B.L.* 1940, pp. 364–70.

—— 'Nouveaux textes égyptiens d'exécration contre les peuples syriens', in *Syria*, xxi, 1940, pp. 170–82.

—— 'La Date de Hammourabi', in *Syria*, xxi, 1940, p. 238.

—— Review of R. M. Engberg, *The Hyksos Reconsidered*, in *Syria*, xxi, 1940, pp. 343 f.

—— 'Encore la date de Hammourabi', in *Syria*, xxi, 1940, pp. 357 f.

—— *Les Origines cananéennes du sacrifice israélite*, 2nd ed., 1941.

R. M. Earle, 'The Date of the Exodus', in *The Asbury Seminarian*, i, 1946, pp. 96–104.

A. Eberharter, *Der Dekalog*, 1929.

W. F. Edgerton, 'On the Chronology of the Early Eighteenth Dynasty (Amenhotep I to Thutmose III)', in *A.J.S.L.* liii, 1936–7, pp. 188–97.

B. D. Eerdmans, *Alttestamentliche Studien*, II. *Die Vorgeschichte Israels*, 1908.

—— *Alttestamentliche Studien*, III. *Das Buch Exodus*, 1910.

—— *The Covenant at Mount Sinai viewed in the Light of Antique Thought*, 1939.

—— *The Religion of Israël*, 1947.

A. B. Ehrlich, *Randglossen zur hebräischen Bibel*, 7 vols., 1909–14.

R. Eisler, 'Das Qainszeichen und die Qeniter', in *Le Monde oriental*, xxiii, 1929, pp. 48–112.

O. Eissfeldt, *Hexateuch-Synopse: die Erzählung der fünf Bücher Mose und des Buches Josua mit dem Anfange des Richterbuches*, 1922.

—— *Die Quellen des Richterbuches*, 1925.

—— 'Die Wanderung palästinischer Götter nach Ost und West im zweiten vorchristlichen Jahrtausend', in *J.P.O.S.* xiv, 1934, pp. 294–300 (reprinted in *Ras Schamra und Sanchunjaton*, pp. 12–19).

—— *Ras Schamra und Sanchunjaton*, 1939.

—— 'Zum geographischen Horizont der Ras-Schamra Texte', in *Z.D.M.G.* xciv, 1940, pp. 59–85.

K. Elliger, 'Josua in Judäa', in *P.J.B.* xxx, 1934, pp. 47–71.

W. A. L. Elmslie, *The Book of Chronicles* (Camb. B.), 1916.

W. A. L. ELMSLIE, *How Came our Faith*, 1948.

Encyclopaedia Biblica, ed. by T. K. Cheyne and J. S. Black, 4 vols., 1899–1907.

R. M. ENGBERG, *The Hyksos Reconsidered* (Studies in Ancient Oriental Civilization, xviii), 1939.

I. ENGNELL, *Studies in Divine Kingship in the Ancient Near East*, 1943.

—— 'The text *II K* from Ras Shamra: a Preliminary Investigation', in *Horae Soederblomianae*, i, *Mélanges Johs. Pedersen*, fasc. i, 1944, pp. 1–20.

—— see also *Svenskt Bibliskt Uppslagsverk*.

A. ERMAN, *The Literature of the Ancient Egyptians*, E.Tr. by A. M. Blackman, 1927.

—— *Die Religion der Ägypter: ihr Werden und Vergehen in vier Jahrtausenden*, 1934.

H. W. FAIRMAN, 'Preliminary Report on the Excavations at 'Amārah West, Anglo-Egyptian Sudan, 1938–9', in *J.E.A.* xxv, 1939, pp. 139–44.

S. I. FEIGIN, *Missitrei Heavar: Biblical and Historical Studies* (written in Hebrew), 1943.

A. FERNÁNDEZ, 'El santuario de Dan', in *Biblica*, xv, 1934, pp. 237–64.

—— *Commentarius in librum Josue* (Cursus Scripturae Sacrae), 1938.

F. V. FILSON, see G. E. Wright.

J. FINEGAN, *Light from the Ancient Past*, 1946.

C. S. FISHER, 'Bethshean', in *M.J.U.P.* xiv, 1923, pp. 227–48.

E. E. FLACK, see H. C. Alleman, and F. C. Forster.

F. C. FORSTER, H. C. ALLEMAN, and E. E. FLACK, 'The Book of Judges', in *Old Testament Commentary*, ed. by Alleman and Flack, 1948, pp. 354–71.

J. K. FOTHERINGHAM, see S. Langdon.

A. FRIDRICHSEN, see *Svenskt Bibliskt Uppslagsverk*.

J. FRIEDRICH, *Aus dem hethitischen Schrifttum*, i (Der Alte Orient, xxiv. 3), 1925.

R. FRUIN, 'De bijbelsche Chronologie van den uittocht uit Egypte tot den bouw van den eersten Tempel', in *N.T.T.* xxiii, 1934, pp. 316–25.

C. J. GADD, 'Tablets from Chagar Bazar, 1936', in *Iraq*, iv, 1937, pp. 178–85.

—— 'Tablets from Chagar Bazar and Tall Brak, 1937–38', in *Iraq*, vii, 1940, pp. 22–66.

A. VON GALL, 'Ein neues astronomisch zu erschliessendes Datum der ältesten israelitischen Geschichte', in *Beiträge zur alttestamentlichen Wissenschaft* (Budde Festschrift = B.Z.A.W. xxxiv), 1920, pp. 52–60.

K. GALLING, *Biblisches Reallexikon* (H.A.T.), 1937.

—— 'Hyksosherrschaft und Hyksoskultur', in *Z.D.P.V.* lxii, 1939, pp. 89–115.

—— Review of H. Stock, *Studien zur Geschichte und Archäologie der 13. bis 17. Dynastie Ägyptens*, 1942, in *Deutsche Literaturzeitung*, lxvi–lxviii, Heft 1–2, Oct.–Nov. 1947, cols. 13–16.

—— see also G. Beer.

A. GAMPERT, 'Les "480 ans" de 1 Rois vi, 1', in *R.Th.Ph.*, N.S. v, 1917, pp. 241–7.

—— 'Le Décalogue', in *R.Th.Ph.*, N.S. xiv, 1926, pp. 184–209.

A. H. GARDINER, 'The Defeat of the Hyksos by Kamōse: The Carnarvon Tablet, No. 1', in *J.E.A.* iii, 1916, pp. 95–110.

—— 'The Delta Residence of the Ramessides', in *J.E.A.* v, 1918, pp. 127–38, 179–200, 242–71.

—— 'The Geography of the Exodus', in *Recueil d'Études égyptologiques dédiées à la mémoire de J. F. Champollion*, 1922.

—— 'The Geography of the Exodus: An Answer to Professor Naville and others', in *J.E.A.* x, 1924, pp. 87–96.

A. H. GARDINER, 'Tanis and Pi-Ramesse: a Retraction', in *J.E.A.* xix, 1933, pp. 122–8.

—— *Ancient Egyptian Onomastica*, 2 vols. of text and 1 vol. of plates, 1947.

—— *see also* B. Gunn.

S. GAROFALO, 'L'Epicinio di Mosè', in *Biblica*, xviii, 1937, pp. 1–22.

J. GARSTANG, 'Jericho', in *P.E.F.Q.S.* 1930, pp. 123–32.

—— *Joshua–Judges*, 1931.

—— 'The Chronology of Jericho', in *P.E.F.Q.S.* 1931, pp. 105–7.

—— 'The Walls of Jericho', in *P.E.F.Q.S.* 1931, pp. 186–96.

—— 'A Third Season at Jericho: City and Necropolis', in *P.E.F.Q.S.* 1932, pp. 149–53.

—— 'Jericho: City and Necropolis', in *A.A.A.* xix, 1932, pp. 3–22, 35–54; xx, 1933, pp. 3–42; xxi, 1934, pp. 99–136; xxii, 1935, pp. 143–68; xxiii, 1936, pp. 67–76.

—— *The Heritage of Solomon: an Historical Introduction to the Sociology of Ancient Palestine*, 1934.

—— 'The Fall of Bronze Age Jericho', in *P.E.F.Q.S.* 1935, pp. 61–8.

—— 'The Story of Jericho: Further Light on the Biblical Narrative', in *A.J.S.L.* lviii, 1941, pp. 368–72.

J. and J. B. E. GARSTANG, *The Story of Jericho*, 1940.

L. GAUTIER, *Introduction à l'Ancien Testament*, 3rd ed., 2 vols., 1939.

H. S. GEHMAN, *see* J. D. Davis.

I. J. GELB, 'Shanhar', in *A.J.S.L.* liii, 1936–7, pp. 253–5.

—— *Hurrians and Subarians* (Studies in Ancient Oriental Civilization, xxii), 1944.

M. GEMOLL, *Israeliten und Hyksos: der historische Kern der Sage vom Aufenthalte Israels in Ägypten*, 1913.

H. L. GINSBERG, *The Legend of King Keret: a Canaanite Epic of the Bronze Age* (*B.A.S.O.R.*, Supplementary Studies 2–3), 1946.

—— and B. MAISLER, 'Semitised Hurrians in Syria and Palestine', in *J.P.O.S.* xiv, 1934, pp. 243–67.

N. GLUECK, 'Explorations in Eastern Palestine and the Negeb', in *B.A.S.O.R.*, No. 55, Sept. 1934, pp. 3–21.

—— *The Other Side of Jordan*, 1940.

—— 'Kenites and Kenizzites', in *P.E.Q.* 1940, pp. 22–4.

—— 'Further Explorations in Eastern Palestine', in *B.A.S.O.R.*, No. 86, Apr. 1942, pp. 14–24.

—— 'Three Israelite Towns in the Jordan Valley: Zarethan, Succoth, Zaphon', in *B.A.S.O.R.*, No. 90, Apr. 1943, pp. 2–23.

A. GOETZE, 'The Tenses of Ugaritic', in *J.A.O.S.* lviii, 1938, pp. 266–309.

—— 'The City Khalbi and the Khapiru People', in *B.A.S.O.R.*, No. 79, Oct. 1940, pp. 32–4.

C. H. GORDON, *Ugaritic Grammar*, 1940.

—— *The Living Past*, 1941.

W. C. GRAHAM and H. G. MAY, *Culture and Conscience: an Archaeological Study of the New Religious Past in Ancient Palestine*, 1936.

G. B. GRAY, *Studies in Hebrew Proper Names*, 1896.

—— 'Children Named after Ancestors in the Aramaic Papyri', in *Studien zur semitischen Philologie und Religionsgeschichte* (Wellhausen Festschrift), ed. by K. Marti (B.Z.A.W. xxvii), 1914, pp. 163–76.

G. B. GRAY, *Sacrifice in the Old Testament: its Theory and Practice*, 1925.
—— 'Passover and Unleavened Bread; the Laws of J, E, and D', in *J.T.S.* xxxvii, 1936, pp. 245–53.
B. GRDSELOFF, 'Edom, d'après les sources égyptiennes', in *B.E.H.J.*, No. i, pp. 69–99.
H. GRESSMANN, 'Sage und Geschichte in den Patriarchenerzählungen', in *Z.A.W.* xxx, 1910, pp. 1–34.
—— *Mose und seine Zeit: ein Kommentar zu den Mose-Sagen*, 1913.
—— 'Ursprung und Entwicklung der Joseph-Sage', in ΕΥΧΑΡΙΣΤΗΡΙΟΝ (Gunkel Festschrift), i, 1923, pp. 1–55.
O. GRETHER, *Das Deboralied* (Beiträge zur Förderung christlicher Theologie, xliii. 2), 1941.
J. S. GRIFFITHS, *The Exodus in the Light of Archaeology*, 1923.
J. M. GRINTZ, 'The Immigration of the First Philistines in the Inscriptions', in *Tarbiz*, xvii, 1945–6, pp. 32–42; xix, 1947–8, p. 64.
M. J. GRUENTHANER, 'The Date of Abraham', in *C.B.Q.* iv, 1942, pp. 360–3; v, 1943, pp. 85–7.
W. J. GRUFFYDD, 'Moses in the Light of Comparative Folklore', in *Z.A.W.*, N.F. v, 1928, pp. 260–70.
A. GUILLAUME, 'The Ḫabiru, the Hebrews, and the Arabs', in *P.E.Q.* 1946, pp. 64–85.
H. GUNKEL, *Die Psalmen* (H.K.), 1926.
—— 'Mose', in *R.G.G.*, 2nd ed., ed. by H. Gunkel and L. Zscharnack, iv, 1930, cols. 230–7.
—— see also *Die Religion in Geschichte und Gegenwart*.
B. GUNN and A. H. GARDINER, 'New Renderings of Egyptian Texts. II. The Expulsion of the Hyksos', in *J.E.A.* v, 1918, pp. 36–56.
A. GUSTAVS, 'Abd-ḫiba = Put-i-Ḫepa', in *O.L.Z.* xiv, 1911, cols. 341–3.
—— 'Der Gott Ḫabiru', in *Z.A.W.* xl, 1922, pp. 313 f.
—— Review of A. Jirku, *Die Wanderungen der Hebräer im 3. und 2. Jahrtausend v. Chr.*, in *T.L.Z.* l, 1925, cols. 603–5.
—— 'Was heisst ilani Ḫabiri?' in *Z.A.W.*, N.F. iii, 1926, pp. 25–38.
—— 'Subaräische Namen in einer ägyptischen Liste syrischer Sklaven und ein subaräischer (?) Hyksos-Name', in *Z.Ä.S.* lxiv, 1929, pp. 54–8.
—— 'Der Gott Ḫabiru in Kerkuk', in *Z.A.W.*, N.F. xvii, 1940–1, pp. 158 f.
—— 'Die Aussprache von TAR-mi in subaräischen Namen', in *A.f.O.* xiv, 1941–4, pp. 201 f.
A. HALDAR, *Associations of Cult Prophets among the Ancient Semites*, 1945.
J. HALÉVY, 'Les Habiri et les inscriptions de Ta'annek', in *R.S.* xii, 1904, pp. 246–58.
H. R. HALL, 'The Middle Kingdom and the Hyksos Conquest', in *C.A.H.* i, 2nd ed., 1924, pp. 299–325.
—— *The Ancient History of the Near East*, 7th ed., 1927.
F. H. HALLOCK, 'The Habiru and the SA.GAZ in the Tell El-Amarna Tablets', in S. A. B. Mercer's *The Tell El-Amarna Tablets*, ii, 1939, pp. 838–45.
M. HAMZA, 'Excavations of the Department of Antiquities at Qantîr (Faqûs District)', in *Annales du Service des Antiquités de l'Égypte*, xxx, 1930, pp. 31–68.
G. L. HARDING, 'Recent Discoveries in Trans-Jordan', in *P.E.Q.* 1948, pp. 118–20.
—— see also O. Tuffnell.

J. Hastings, ed. by, *Dictionary of the Bible*, 5 vols., 1898–1904.

P. Haupt, 'Die Schlacht von Taanach', in *Studien zur semitischen Philologie und Religionsgeschichte* (Wellhausen Festschrift), ed. by K. Marti (B.Z.A.W. xxvii), 1914, pp. 193–223.

W. C. Hayes, *Glazed Tiles from a Palace of Ramesses II at Kantir* (Metropolitan Museum of Art, New York, Papers, No. 3), 1937.

P. Heinisch, *Das Buch Exodus*, 1934.

H. F. Helmolt, ed. by, *The World's History: a Survey of Man's Record*, 8 vols., 1901–7.

J. Hempel, *Die Schichten des Deuteronomiums: ein Beitrag zur israelitischen Literatur- und Rechtsgeschichte*, 1914.

—— *Die althebräische Literatur und ihr hellenistisch-jüdisches Nachleben*, 1930–4.

R. B. Henderson, 'Akhnaton and Moses', in *C.Q.R.* xcvii, 1923–4, pp. 109–31.

L. Hennequin, 'Fouilles et champs de fouilles en Palestine et en Phénicie', in *Supplément au Dictionnaire de la Bible*, iii, 1934–8, cols. 318–524 (appeared in 1936).

A. Herdner, Review of R. de Langhe's *Les Textes de Ras Shamra-Ugarit et leurs rapports avec le milieu biblique de l'Ancien Testament*, in *Syria*, xxv, 1946–8, pp. 131–8.

J. Herrmann, 'Das zehnte Gebot', in *Sellin Festschrift: Beiträge zur Religionsgeschichte und Archäologie Palästinas*, 1927, pp. 69–82.

H. F. Heyes, *Bibel und Ägypten*, i, 1904.

G. Hölscher, *Die Profeten: Untersuchungen zur Religionsgeschichte Israels*, 1914.

—— *Geschichte der israelitischen und jüdischen Religion*, 1922.

—— 'Levi', in Pauly-Wissowa-Kroll, *Realencyclopädie der klassischen Altertumswissenschaft*, xii, 1925, cols. 2155–208.

H. Holzinger, *Exodus* (K.H.C.), 1900.

F. Hommel, *The Ancient Hebrew Tradition as illustrated by the Monuments*, E.Tr. by E. McClure and L. Crosslé, 1897.

—— 'Babylonia', in Hastings's *D.B.* i, 1898, pp. 214–30.

—— 'The True Date of Abraham and Moses', in *E.T.* x, 1898–9, pp. 210–12.

S. H. Hooke, *In the Beginning*, 1947.

H. Höpfl, *Introductio specialis in Vetus Testamentum*, 5th ed., revised by A. Miller and A. Metzinger, 1946.

C. F. Houbigant, *Biblia Hebraica cum notis criticis et versione latina ad notas criticas facta*, 4 vols., 1753.

B. Hrozný, *Histoire de l'Asie Antérieure, de l'Inde et de la Crète (jusqu'au début du second millénaire)*, 1947.

P. Humbert, 'Une mention d'Asher dans les sources de Philon de Byblos?', in *R.E.S.-B.* 1941, pp. 61–6.

C. H. Inge, see O. Tuffnell.

J. W. Jack, 'The Israel Stele of Merneptah', in *E.T.* xxxvi, 1924–5, pp. 40–4.

—— *The Date of the Exodus*, 1925.

—— *The Ras Shamra Tablets: their Bearing on the Old Testament*, 1935.

—— 'Recent Biblical Archaeology', in *E.T.* xlviii, 1936–7, pp. 549–51.

—— 'Biblical Archaeology', in *A Companion to the Bible*, ed. by T. W. Manson, 1939, pp. 172–203.

—— 'New Light on the Habiru–Hebrew Question', in *P.E.Q.* 1940, pp. 95–115.

F. James, *Personalities of the Old Testament*, 1939.

C. F. JEAN, ' "Ḥammurapi" d'après les lettres inédites de Mari', in *R.Ass.* xxxv, 1938, pp. 107–14.

—— 'Chronologie de l'Ancien Testament', in *Initiation Biblique*, ed. by A. Robert and A. Tricot, 1939, pp. 426–36.

—— 'Ḥammurapi, d'après les textes inédits de Mari', in *Actes du XXᵉ Congrès international des Orientalistes*, 1940, pp. 116 f.

—— Review of F. M. Th. Böhl, *King Ḥammurabi of Babylon in the Setting of His Time*, in *Bi.Or.* v, 1948, pp. 127 f.

A. JIRKU, 'ⁱˡᵘḤa-bi-ru = der Stammesgott der Ḥabiru-Hebräer?' in *O.L.Z.* xxiv, 1921, cols. 246 f.

—— 'Neues keilinschriftliches Material zum Alten Testament', in *Z.A.W.* xxxix, 1921, pp. 144–60.

—— 'Zum historischen Stil von Gen. 14', in *Z.A.W.* xxxix, 1921, pp. 313 f.

—— *Die Wanderungen der Hebräer im 3. und 2. Jahrtausend v. Chr.* (Der Alte Orient, xxiv. 2), 1924.

—— 'ᴳᵒ̈ᵗᵗᵉʳHabiru oder Götter der Ḥabiru', in *Z.A.W.*, N.F. iii, 1926, pp. 237–42.

—— *Geschichte des Volkes Israel*, 1931.

—— 'Aufsteig und Niedergang der Hyksos', in *J.P.O.S.* xii, 1932, pp. 51–61.

—— *Die ägyptischen Listen palästinensischer und syrischer Ortsnamen* (*Klio*, Beiheft xxxviii, N.F. Heft 25), 1937.

—— *see also* E. König.

FLAVIUS JOSEPHUS, *Opera*, ed. B. Niese, 7 vols., 1885–95; Text and E.Tr. by H. St. J. Thackeray and R. Marcus (Loeb edition), 7 volumes (incomplete), 1926–43; E.Tr. by W. Whiston, 1825 edition, 2 vols.

H. JUNKER, 'Pḥrnfr', in *Z.Ä.S.* lxxv, 1939, pp. 63–84.

E. KALT, *Biblisches Reallexikon*, 2 vols., 2nd ed., 1938–9.

E. KAUTZSCH, 'Das Buch Josua', in *H.S.A.T.*, 3rd ed., i, 1909, pp. 305–39.

—— 'Das Buch Josua', in *H.S.A.T.*, 4th ed., i, 1922, pp. 328–66 (chapters xii–xxiv revised by H. Holzinger).

—— ed. by, *Die Heilige Schrift des Alten Testaments*, 3rd ed., 2 vols., 1909–10; 4th ed., ed. by A. Bertholet, 2 vols., 1922–3.

C. F. KEIL and F. DELITZSCH, *Biblical Commentary on the Books of Samuel*, E.Tr. by J. Martin, 1866.

R. H. KENNETT, *Old Testament Essays*, 1928.

—— *The Church of Israel*, 1933.

F. G. KENYON, *The Bible and Archaeology*, 1940.

C. KERN, 'Primum monumenta, deinde chronologia', in *J.E.O.L.* x, 1945–8, pp. 481–90.

L. W. KING, *A History of Babylon from the Foundation of the Monarchy to the Persian Conquest*, 1919.

M. E. KIRK, 'An Outline of the Ancient Cultural History of Transjordan', in *P.E.Q.* 1944, pp. 180–98.

G. KITTEL, ed. by, *Theologisches Wörterbuch zum Neuen Testament*, in progress, 1933– .

R. KITTEL, *Die Bücher der Könige* (H.K.), 1900.

—— *Geschichte des Volkes Israel*, i, 5th and 6th ed., 1923; ii, 5th ed., 1922.

H. KJAER, 'The Excavation of Shiloh 1929', in *J.P.O.S.* x, 1930, pp. 87–174.

A. M. KLEBER, 'The Chronology of 3 and 4 Kings and 2 Paralipomenon', in *Biblica*, ii, 1921, pp. 3–29, 170–205.

A. C. KNUDSON, 'The so-called J Decalogue', in *J.B.L.* xxviii, 1909, pp. 82–99.

J. A. KNUDTZON, *Die El-Amarna Tafeln*, 2 vols., 1908–15.

L. KÖHLER, 'Der Dekalog', in *Th.R.*, N.F. i, 1929, pp. 161–184.

E. KÖNIG, *Geschichte der alttestamentlichen Religion*, 1912.

—— and A. JIRKU, 'Zur Chabiru-Frage', in *Z.A.W.*, N.F. v, 1928, pp. 199–211.

J. DE KONING, *Studiën over de El-Amarnabrieven en het Oude-Testament inzonderheid uit historisch oogpunt*, 1940.

E. G. H. KRAELING, *Aram and Israel, or The Aramaeans in Syria and Mesopotamia*, 1918.

—— 'Light from Ugarit on the Khabiru', in *B.A.S.O.R.*, No. 77, Feb. 1940, pp. 32 f.

—— 'The Origin of the Name "Hebrews" ', in *A.J.S.L.* lviii, 1941, pp. 237–53.

S. N. KRAMER, 'New Light on the Early History of the Ancient Near East', in *A.J.A.* lii, 1948, pp. 156–64.

J. H. KROEZE, *Genesis Veertien: een exegetisch-historische Studie*, 1937.

M. J. LAGRANGE, *Le livre des Juges* (E.B.), 1903.

L. C. LaMOTTE, Review of L. Waterman, *The Song of Songs*, in *Interpretation*, ii, 1948, pp. 368–71.

B. LANDSBERGER, 'Ḫabiru und Lulaḫḫu', in *Kleinasiatische Forschungen*, i, 1927–30, pp. 321–34.

S. H. LANGDON, 'The Ḫabiru and the Hebrews', in *E.T.* xxxi, 1919–20, pp. 324–9.

—— and J. K. FOTHERINGHAM, *The Venus Tablets of Ammizaduga: a solution of Babylonian Chronology by means of the Venus Observations of the First Dynasty*, 1928.

R. DE LANGHE, *Les Textes de Ras Shamra-Ugarit et leurs apports à l'histoire des origines israélites* (Bulletin d'histoire et d'exégèse de l'Ancien Testament, vii), 1939.

—— *Un dieu Yahweh à Ras Shamra?* (Bulletin d'histoire et d'exégèse de l'Ancien Testament, xiv), 1942.

—— *Les Textes de Ras Shamra-Ugarit et leurs rapports avec le milieu biblique de l'Ancien Testament*, 2 vols., 1945.

—— 'Het Ugarietisch Keret-gedicht Legende, Mythus of Mysteriespel?', in *Miscellanea Historica Alberti de Meyer*, 1946, pp. 92–108.

C. LAVERGNE, *Chronologie Biblique*, 1937.

L. G. LEEUWENBURG, *Echnaton*, 1946.

C. R. LEPSIUS, *Königsbuch der alten Ägypter*, 1858.

J. P. LETTINGA, 'Ugaritica', in *J.E.O.L.* ix, 1944, pp. 116–24.

J. LEWY, *Die Chronologie der Könige von Israel und Juda*, 1927.

—— 'Ḫabiru und Hebräer', in *O.L.Z.* xxx, 1927, cols. 738–46, 825–33.

—— 'Influences ḫurrites sur Israël', in *R.E.S.* 1938, pp. 49–75.

—— 'Ḫābirū and Hebrews', in *H.U.C.A.* xiv, 1939, pp. 587–623.

—— 'A New Parallel between Ḫābirū and Hebrews', in *H.U.C.A.* xv, 1940, pp. 47–58.

M. LIDZBARSKI, *Ephemeris für semitische Epigraphik*, 3 vols., 1902–15.

E. LITTMANN, Review of D. Diringer, *Le iscrizioni antico-ebraiche palestinesi*, 1934, in *A.f.O.* xi, 1936–7, pp. 161–5.

A. LODS, *Israël des origines au milieu du viiie siècle*, 1930; E.Tr. by S. H. Hooke, *Israel from its Beginnings to the Middle of the Eighth Century*, 1932.

—— 'Archéologie et Ancien Testament', in *R.E.S.* 1936, pp. xlviii–lxxi.

A. Lods, 'Quelques remarques sur les poèmes mythologiques de Ras Chamra et leurs rapports avec l'Ancien Testament', in *R.H.P.R.* xvi, 1936, pp. 101–30.

—— 'Les Fouilles d'Aï et l'époque de l'entrée des Israélites en Palestine', in *Mélanges Franz Cumont*, ii, 1936, pp. 847–57.

A. Lucas, *The Route of the Exodus*, 1938.

—— 'The Date of the Exodus', in *P.E.Q.* 1941, pp. 110–21.

—— 'The Number of Israelites at the Exodus', in *P.E.Q.* 1943–4, pp. 164–8.

D. D. Luckenbill, 'On Israel's Origins', in *A.J.Th.* xxii, 1918, pp. 24–53.

—— 'The "Wandering Aramaean" ', in *A.J.S.L.* xxxvi, 1919–20, pp. 244 f.

H. Lusseau and M. Collomb, *Manuel d'Études bibliques*: ii. *Histoire du peuple d'Israël*, 6th ed., 1945.

W. H. McClellan, 'Jericho and the Date of the Exodus', in *Ecclesiastical Review*, lxxxviii, 1933, pp. 80–93.

J. E. McFadyen, 'The Mosaic Origin of the Decalogue', in *Expositor*, 8th series, xi, 1916, pp. 152–60, 222–31, 311–20, 384–400; xii, 1916, pp. 37–59, 105–17, 210–21.

—— 'Telescoped History', in *E.T.* xxxvi, 1924–5, pp. 103–9.

C. Mackay, 'Salem', in *P.E.Q.* 1948, pp. 121–30.

A. H. McNeile, *The Book of Exodus* (W.C.), 2nd ed., 1917.

E. Mahler, 'The Exodus', in *J.R.A.S.* 1901, pp. 33–67.

—— *Handbuch der jüdischen Chronologie*, 1916.

B. Maisler, 'Shamgar ben 'Anat', in *P.E.F.Q.S.* 1934, pp. 192–4.

—— 'Palestine at the Time of the Middle Kingdom in Egypt', in *B.E.H.J.*, No. i, 1946, pp. 33–68.

—— see also H. L. Ginsberg.

A. Mallon, *Les Hébreux en Égypte*, 1921.

—— 'Les Hyksos et les Hébreux', in *J.P.O.S.* v, 1925, pp. 85–91.

—— 'Chronique palestinienne', in *Biblica*, vii, 1926, pp. 106–18.

—— 'Les Fouilles danoises de Silo', in *Biblica*, x, 1929, pp. 369–75.

—— 'Exode', in *Supplément au Dictionnaire de la Bible*, ed. L. Pirot and A. Robert, ii, 1934, cols. 1333–42.

M. E. L. Mallowan, 'The Excavations at Tall Chagar Bazar and an Archaeological Survey of the Habur Region', in *Iraq*, iv, 1937, pp. 91–154.

—— 'Excavations at Brak and Chagar Bazar', in *Iraq*, ix, 1947, pp. 1–257.

E. Mangenot, 'Israël (Peuple et royaume d')', in *Dictionnaire de la Bible*, ed. by F. Vigouroux, iii, 1903, cols. 995–1005.

A. Mariette, *Les Listes géographiques des pylônes de Karnak*, 1875.

J. Marquart, 'Chronologische Untersuchungen', in *Philologus*, Supplementband vii, 1899, pp. 635–720.

J. Marquet-Krause, 'La Deuxième Campagne de fouilles à Ay (1934)', in *Syria*, xvi, 1935, pp. 325–45.

Sir Charles Marston, *The Bible is True*, 1934.

—— *The Bible comes Alive*, 1937.

K. Marti, *The Religion of the Old Testament*, E.Tr. by G. A. Bienemann, 1914.

G. Maspero, 'Sur les noms de la liste de Thoutmos III qu'on peut rapporter à la Judée', in *J.T.V.I.* xxii, 1888–9, pp. 53–75 (E.Tr. by H. G. Tomkins, *J.T.V.I.* xxii, 1888–9, pp. 76–112).

—— *The Struggle of the Nations*, E.Tr. by M. L. McClure, 1925 ed.

H. G. MAY, 'The Patriarchal Idea of God', in *J.B.L.* lx, 1941, pp. 113–28.
—— see also W. C. Graham.
T. J. MEEK, 'A Proposed Reconstruction of Hebrew History', in *A.J.Th.* xxiv, 1920, pp. 209–16.
—— 'Some Religious Origins of the Hebrews', in *A.J.S.L.* xxxvii, 1920–1, pp. 101–31.
—— *Hebrew Origins*, 1936.
—— 'The Israelite Conquest of Ephraim', in *B.A.S.O.R.*, No. 61, Feb. 1936, pp. 17–19.
—— 'Moses and the Levites', in *A.J.S.L.* lvi, 1939, pp. 113–20.
P. VAN DER MEER, 'Chronologie der assyrisch-babylonische Koningen', in *J.E.O.L.* ix, 1944, pp. 137–45.
—— *The Ancient Chronology of Western Asia and Egypt* (Documenta et Monumenta Orientis Antiqui, ii), 1947.
—— 'At What Time has the Reign of Menes to be Placed?' in *Orientalia Neerlandica* (Netherlands' Oriental Society Anniversary Volume), 1948, pp. 23–49.
Megiddo I, *Seasons of 1925–34, Strata i–v*, by R. S. Lamon and G. M. Shipton, 1939; II, *Seasons of 1935–39*, by G. Loud (in two parts), 1948. (University of Chicago Oriental Institute Publications, xlii and lxii.)
J. MEINHOLD, *1 Mose 14* (B.Z.A.W. xxii), 1911.
—— *Der Dekalog*, 1927.
—— *Einführung in das Alte Testament*, 3rd ed., 1932.
Mekilta of Rabbi Simeon ben Jochai, edited by D. Hoffmann, 1905.
Mekilta of Rabbi Ishmael, 1925 (Berlin reprint of Vienna edition of 1545); Text and E.Tr. by J. Z. Lauterbach (Schiff Library of Jewish Classics), 3 vols., 1933–5.
G. E. MENDENHALL, 'Mari', in *B.A.* xi, 1948, pp. 2–19.
S. A. B. MERCER, 'Merneptah's Stele and the Exodus', in *A.Th.R.* v, 1922–3, pp. 96–107.
—— 'The Religion of Ikhnaton', in *J.S.O.R.* x, 1926, pp. 14–33.
—— *The Tell El-Amarna Tablets*, 2 vols., 1939.
N. MESSEL, see S. Michelet.
A. METZINGER, see H. Höpfl.
E. MEYER, 'Der Stamm Jakob und die Entstehung der israelitischen Stämme', in *Z.A.W.* vi, 1886, pp. 1–16.
—— *Die Israeliten und ihre Nachbarstämme*, 1906.
S. MICHELET, S. MOWINCKEL, and N. MESSEL, *Det Gamle Testamente*, 3 vols. (incomplete), 1929–44.
Midrasch Tanchuma, ein agadischer Commentar zum Pentateuch von Rabbi Abba, ed. by S. Buber, 2 vols., 1885.
Midrash Tanḥuma, Choreb edition, 1927.
K. MIKETTA, *Der Pharao des Auszuges*, 1903.
A. MILLER, see H. Höpfl.
K. MÖHLENBRINK, 'Die Landnahmesagen des Buches Josua', in *Z.A.W.*, n.f. xv, 1938, pp. 238–68.
—— 'Josua im Pentateuch', in *Z.A.W.*, n.f. xviii, 1942–3, pp. 14–58.
E. MONTET, 'Les Israélites en Égypte et leur Exode du pays de la servitude', in *Mélanges Hartwig Derenbourg*, 1909, pp. 49–59.
P. MONTET, 'Tanis, Avaris et Pi-Ramsès', in *R.B.* xxxix, 1930, pp. 1–28.
—— 'Avaris, Pi-Ramsès, Tanis', in *Syria*, xvii, 1936, pp. 200–2.

P. Montet, *Le Drame d'Avaris*, 1940.
—— *Tanis: douze années de fouilles dans une capitale oubliée du Delta égyptien*, 1942.
G. F. Moore, *A Critical and Exegetical Commentary on Judges* (I.C.C.), 2nd ed., 1898.
A. Moret, *Rois et dieux d'Égypte*, 1923 ed.
J. Morgenstern, *The Oldest Document of the Hexateuch*, 1927 (reprinted from *H.U.C.A.* iv, 1927, pp. 1–138).
—— *Amos Studies*, i, 1941 (reprinted from *H.U.C.A.* xi, 1936, pp. 19–140; xii–xiii, 1937–8, pp. 1–53; xv, 1940, pp. 59–304).
—— 'Decalogue', in *Universal Jewish Encyclopedia*, iii, 1941, cols. 506–13.
—— 'The Chanukkah Festival and the Calendar of Israel', in *H.U.C.A.* xx, 1947, pp. 1–136, xxi, 1948, pp. 365–496 (unfinished).
E. W. K. Mould, *Essentials of Bible History*, 1939.
S. Mowinckel, *Psalmenstudien*, V: *Segen und Fluch in Israels Kult und Psalmdichtung*, 1924.
—— *Jesaja-Disiplene*, 1926.
—— 'L'Origine du Décalogue', in *R.H.P.R.* vi, 1926, pp. 409–33, 501–25.
—— *Le Décalogue*, 1927.
—— *Die Chronologie der israelitischen und jüdischen Könige*, 1932.
—— 'Zur Geschichte der Dekaloge', in *Z.A.W.*, n.f. xiv, 1937, pp. 218–35.
—— 'Immanuelprofetien Jes. 7: Streiflys fra Ugarit I', in *Norsk Teologisk Tidsskrift*, xlii, 1941, pp. 129–57.
—— 'Kadesj, Sinai, og Jahve', in *Norsk Geografisk Tidsskrift*, ix, 1942, pp. 1–32.
—— 'Til uttrykket "Jahvæs tjener": Streiflys fra Ugarit II', in *Norsk Teologisk Tidsskrift*, xliii, 1942, pp. 24–6.
—— *Zur Frage nach dokumentarischen Quellen in Josua 13–19*, 1946.
—— see also S. Michelet.
W. M. Müller, *Asien und Europa nach altägyptischen Denkmälern*, 1893.
—— 'Zu den altkanaanäischen Stadtnamen Jakob-el und Joseph-el', *O.L.Z.* ii, 1899, cols. 396–9.
—— 'Ägyptologisch-Biblisches', in *O.L.Z.* iii, 1900, cols. 325–8.
E. Naville, *The Store City of Pithom and the Route of the Exodus*, 1885.
—— 'Did Merneptah invade Syria?', in *J.E.A.* ii, 1915, pp. 195–201.
—— 'The Geography of the Exodus', in *J.E.A.* x, 1924, pp. 18–39.
O. Neugebauer, 'Zur Frage der astronomischen Fixierung der babylonischen Chronologie', in *O.L.Z.* xxxii, 1929, cols. 913–21.
—— 'Chronologie und babylonischer Kalender', in *O.L.Z.* xlii, 1939, cols. 403–14.
—— 'The Chronology of the Hammurabi Age', in *J.A.O.S.* lxi, 1941, pp. 58–61.
C. Niebuhr, 'Egypt', in H. F. Helmolt's *The World's History*, E.Tr. iii, 1903, pp. 587–721.
D. Nielsen, *The Site of the Biblical Mount Sinai: a Claim for Petra*, 1928.
Th. Nöldeke, 'Die Chronologie der Richterzeit', in *Untersuchungen zur Kritik des Alten Testaments*, 1869, pp. 173–98.
M. Noth, *Das System der zwölf Stämme Israels*, 1930.
—— 'Erwägungen zur Hebräerfrage', in *Festschrift Otto Procksch zum 60. Geburtstag überreicht*, 1934, pp. 99–112.
—— 'Die Ansiedlung des Stammes Juda auf dem Boden Palästinas', in *P.J.B.* xxx, 1934, pp. 31–47.

M. Noth, 'Zur historischen Geographie Südjudäas', in *J.P.O.S.* xv, 1935, pp. 35–50.

—— 'Bethel und Ai', in *P.J.B.* xxxi, 1935, pp. 7–29.

—— 'Die fünf Könige in der Höhle von Makkeda', in *P.J.B.* xxxiii, 1937, pp. 22–36.

—— *Das Buch Josua*, 1938.

—— 'Grundsätzliches zur geschichtlichen Deutung archäologischer Befunde auf dem Boden Palästinas', in *P.J.B.* xxxiv, 1938, pp. 7–22.

—— *Die Welt des Alten Testaments*, 1940.

—— *Die Gesetze im Pentateuch: ihre Voraussetzungen und ihr Sinn* (Schriften der Königsberger Gelehrten Gesellschaft, Geisteswissenschaftliche Klasse, xvii, 2), 1940.

—— 'Die syrisch-palästinische Bevölkerung des zweiten Jahrtausends v. Chr. im Lichte neuer Quellen', in *Z.D.P.V.* lxv, 1942, pp. 9–67.

—— 'Israelitische Stämme zwischen Ammon und Moab', in *Z.A.W.* n.f. xix, 1944, pp. 11–57.

—— 'Von der Knechtsgestalt des Alten Testaments', in *Evangelische Theologie*, Nov.–Dec. 1946, pp. 302–10.

W. Nowack, 'Der erste Dekalog', in *Abhandlungen zur semitischen Religionskunde und Sprachwissenschaft* (Baudissin Festschrift), ed. by W. Frankenberg and F. Küchler (B.Z.A.W. xxxiii), 1918, pp. 381–97.

H. S. Nyberg, 'Studien zum Religionskampf im Alten Testament', in *A.R.W.* xxxv, 1938, pp. 329–87.

—— 'Deuteronomion 33, 2–3', in *Z.D.M.G.* xcii, 1938, pp. 320–44.

—— 'Dan', in *S.B.U.* i, 1948, p. 342.

R. T. O'Callaghan, *Aram Naharaim: a Contribution to the History of Upper Mesopotamia in the Second Millennium B.C.*, 1948.

W. O. E. Oesterley and T. H. Robinson, *Hebrew Religion: its Origin and Development*, 2nd ed., 1937.

A. T. Olmstead, *History of Syria and Palestine*, 1931.

D. Opitz, 'Zur Ḫabiru-Frage', in *Z.A.*, n.f. iii, 1927, pp. 99–103.

J. Orr, 'Israel in Egypt and the Exodus', in *Expositor*, 5th series, v, 1897, pp. 161–77.

—— *The Problem of the Old Testament*, 7th imp., 1909.

A. Parrot, 'Notice chronologique', in *Syria*, xix, 1938, pp. 182–4.

—— *Archéologie mésopotamienne: les étapes*, 1946.

H. Parzen, 'The Problem of the Ibrim ("Hebrews") in the Bible', in *A.J.S.L.* xlix, 1932–3, pp. 254–61.

L. B. Paton, *The Early History of Syria and Palestine*, 1902.

—— 'Israel's Conquest of Canaan', in *J.B.L.* xxxii, 1913, pp. 1–53.

—— 'Archaeology and the Book of Genesis', in *B.W.* xlv, 1915, pp. 10–17, 135–45, 202–10, 288–98, 353–61; xlvi, 1915, pp. 25–32, 82–9, 173–80.

J. Pedersen, *Israel: its Life and Culture*, I–II, 1926; III–IV, 1940.

—— 'Passahfest und Passahlegende', in *Z.A.W.*, n.f. xi, 1934, pp. 161–75.

—— 'Die Krt Legende', in *Berytus*, vi, 1941, pp. 63–105.

T. E. Peet, 'The Problem of Akhenaton', in *M.E.O.J.* ix, 1921, pp. 39–48.

—— *Egypt and the Old Testament*, 1922.

Pesikta Rabbati, Midrash für den Fest-Cyclus und die ausgezeichneten Sabbathe, ed. by M. Friedmann, 1880.

W. M. Flinders Petrie, *A History of Egypt*, ii, 1896: iii, *From the XIXth to the XXXth Dynasties*, 1905.

W. M. FLINDERS PETRIE, *Hyksos and Israelite Cities*, 1906.
—— *Egypt and Israel*, 1911.
—— *Palestine and Israel*, 1934.
R. H. PFEIFFER, 'The Oldest Decalogue', in *J.B.L.* xliii, 1924, pp. 294–310.
—— *Introduction to the Old Testament*, 1941.
W. J. PHYTHIAN-ADAMS, 'Israel in the Arabah', in *P.E.F.Q.S.* 1933, pp. 137–46, 1934, pp. 181–8.
—— *The Call of Israel: an Introduction to the Study of Divine Election*, 1934.
—— 'Jericho, Ai and the Occupation of Mount Ephraim', in *P.E.F.Q.S.* 1936, pp. 141–9.
G. PIDOUX, 'Les Fouilles de Jéricho et la Bible', in *R.Th.Ph.*, N.S. xxvii, 1939, pp. 48–61.
L. PIROT, 'Abraham', in *Supplément au Dictionnaire de la Bible*, ed. by L. Pirot and A. Robert, i, 1928, cols. 8–28.
—— and A. ROBERT, ed. by, *Supplément au Dictionnaire de la Bible*, i–iv (in progress), 1928–49.
A. POEBEL, 'The Assyrian King List from Khorsabad', in *J.N.E.S.* i, 1942, pp. 247–306, 460–92; ii, 1943, pp. 56–90.
H. A. POELS, *Examen critique de l'Histoire du Sanctuaire de l'Arche*, i, 1897.
G. POSENER, 'Une liste de noms propres étrangers sur deux ostraca hiératiques du nouvel empire', in *Syria*, xviii, 1937, pp. 183–97.
—— 'Nouvelles listes de proscription (Ächtungstexte) datant du Moyen Empire', in *Chronique d'Égypte*, No. 27, Jan. 1939, pp. 39–46.
—— 'Nouveaux textes hiératiques de proscription', in *Mélanges Syriens* (Dussaud Festschrift), i, 1939, pp. 312–17.
—— *Princes et pays d'Asie et de Nubie*, 1940.
E. POWER, Review of H. J. Grimmelsman, *The Book of Exodus*, 1927, in *Biblica*, x, 1930 , pp. 101–5.
J. V. PRÁŠEK, 'On the Question of the Exodus', in *E.T.* xi, 1899–1900, pp. 205–8, 251–4, 319–22, 400–3, 503–7.
O. PROCKSCH, *Die Genesis* (K.A.T.), 2nd and 3rd ed., 1924.
G. VON RAD, 'Ισραηλ κ.τ.λ.' A, in *Th.W.B.* iii, 1938, pp. 357–9.
I. RAPAPORT, 'The Origins of Hebrew Law', in *P.E.Q.* 1941, pp. 158–67.
B. REICKE, 'Analogier mellan Josefberättelsen i Genesis och Ras Shamra-texterna', in *S.E.Å.* x, 1945, pp. 5–30.
G. A. REISNER, 'The Ḫabiri in the El-Amarna Tablets', in *J.B.L.* xvi, 1897, pp. 143–5.
Die Religion in Geschichte und Gegenwart, 5 vols., 1st ed., 1909–13, ed. by F. M. Schiele and L. Zscharnack; 2nd ed., 1927–31, ed. by H. Gunkel and L. Zscharnack.
G. RICCIOTTI, *Storia d'Israele*, i, 2nd ed., 1934; French Tr. by P. Auvray, *Histoire d'Israël*, i, 1939.
G. H. RICHARDSON, 'A Plea for Unprejudiced Historical Biblical Study', in *B.W.* xlv, 1915, pp. 160–5.
H. RIESENFELD, *The Resurrection in Ezekiel xxxvii and in the Dura-Europos Paintings* (Uppsala Universitets Årsskrift 1948, xi), 1948.
A. ROBERT, see L. Pirot.
E. ROBERTSON, 'The Period of the Judges: a Mystery Period in the History of Israel', in *B.J.R.L.* xxx, 1946–7, pp. 91–114.
H. WHEELER ROBINSON, *The History of Israel: its Facts and Factors*, 1938.
T. H. ROBINSON, *History of Israel*, i, 1932.

T. H. ROBINSON, 'The Exodus and the Conquest of Palestine', in *Theology*, xxv, 1932, pp. 267-74.

—— Review of A. Jirku, *Geschichte des Volkes Israel*, 1931, in *T.L.Z.* lvii, 1932, cols. 76-8.

—— 'The Origin of the Tribe of Judah', in *Amicitiae Corolla* (Rendel Harris Festschrift), 1933, pp. 265-73.

—— 'The Date of the Exodus', in *E.T.* xlvii, 1935-6, pp. 53-5.

—— 'The Possible Mention of Joshua's Conquest in the El-Amarna Letters', in *E.T.* xlvii, 1935-6, p. 380.

—— 'Pella in the El-Amarna Tablets', in *E.T.* xlvii, 1935-6, p. 477.

—— 'The History of Israel', in *A Companion to the Bible*, ed. by T. W. Manson, 1939, pp. 204-67.

—— *see also* W. O. E. Oesterley.

G. ROEDER, 'Pharao Achnaton von Amarna', in *Preussische Jahrbücher*, clxxxii, 1920, pp. 61-73.

S. RONZEVALLE, 'Fragments d'inscriptions araméennes des environs d'Alep', in *Mélanges de l'Université St. Joseph*, xv, 1931, pp. 237-60.

A. ROWE, 'The Two Royal Stelae of Beth-Shan', in *M.J.U.P.* xx, 1929, pp. 88-98.

—— *The Topography and History of Beth-shan*, 1930.

—— *The Four Canaanite Temples of Beth-shan*, i, 1940.

H. H. ROWLEY, *Israel's Sojourn in Egypt*, 1938 (reprinted from *B.J.R.L.* xxii, 1938, pp. 243-90).

—— 'The Eisodus and the Exodus', in *E.T.* l, 1938-9, pp. 503-8.

—— 'Zadok and Nehushtan', in *J.B.L.* lviii, 1939, pp. 113-41.

—— 'The Danite Migration to Laish', in *E.T.* li, 1939-40, pp. 466-71.

—— 'Israel's Sojourn in Egypt', in *Actes du XXᵉ Congrès international des Orientalistes*, 1940, pp. 91-3.

—— 'Ras Shamra and the Ḥabiru Question', in *P.E.Q.* 1940, pp. 90-4.

—— 'The Date of the Exodus', in *P.E.Q.* 1941, pp. 152-7.

—— 'The Exodus and the Settlement in Canaan', in *B.A.S.O.R.*, No. 85, Feb. 1942, pp. 27-31.

—— 'Two Observations', in *B.A.S.O.R.*, No. 87, Oct. 1942, p. 40.

—— 'Ḥabiru and Hebrews', in *P.E.Q.* 1942, pp. 41-53.

—— 'Early Levite History and the Question of the Exodus', in *J.N.E.S.* liii, 1944, pp. 73-8.

M. B. ROWTON, 'Mesopotamian Chronology and the "Era of Menophres" ', in *Iraq*, viii, 1946, pp. 94-110.

E. RUFFINI, *Chronologia Veteris et Novi Testamenti in aeram nostram collata*, 1924.

H. E. RYLE, *The Book of Genesis* (Camb. B.), 1921.

M. R. SAVIGNAC, 'La Région de 'Ain Qedeis', in *R.B.* xxxi, 1922, pp. 55-81.

A. H. SAYCE, 'Babylonian Tablets from Tel El-Amarna, Upper Egypt', in *P.S.B.A.* x, 1887-8, pp. 488-525.

—— 'The Cuneiform Tablets of Tel El-Amarna now preserved in the Boulaq Museum', in *P.S.B.A.* xi, 1888-9, pp. 326-413.

—— *The Early History of the Hebrews*, 1897.

—— 'On the Khabiri Question', in *E.T.* xi, 1899-1900, p. 377.

—— 'The Khabiri', in *E.T.* xxxiii, 1921-2, pp. 43 f.

C. F. A. SCHAEFFER, *The Cuneiform Texts of Ras Shamra-Ugarit*, 1939.

—— *Ugaritica*, 1939.

C. F. A. SCHAEFFER, *Stratigraphie Comparée et Chronologie de l'Asie Occidentale* (*III*e et *II*e *millénaires*), 1948.

—— 'Note sur la Chronologie de la période de transition du bronze moyen au bronze récent (1700–1500 av. notre ère)', in *Syria*, xxv, 1946–8, pp. 185–98.

H. SCHÄFER, 'Altes und Neues zur Kunst und Religion von Tell el-Amarna', in *Z.Ä.S.* lv, 1918, pp. 1–43.

V. SCHEIL, 'Notules', in *R.Ass.* xii, 1915, pp. 114–16.

—— 'Le Cylindre d'Išre-il', in *R.Ass.* xiii, 1916, pp. 5–8.

F. M. SCHIELE, see *Die Religion in Geschichte und Gegenwart*.

H. SCHMIDT, 'Mose und der Dekalog', in EYXAPIΣTHPION (Gunkel Festschrift), i, 1923, pp. 78–119.

H. SCHMIDTKE, *Die Einwanderung Israels in Kanaan*, 1933.

H. SCHMÖKEL, 'Jahwe und die Keniter', in *J.B.L.* lii, 1933, pp. 212–29.

J. N. SCHOFIELD, *The Historical Background of the Bible*, 1938.

E. SCHRADER, *Die Keilinschriften und das Alte Testament*, 3rd ed. revised by H. Zimmern and H. Winckler, 1903.

O. SCHROEDER, *Keilschrifttexte aus Assur verschiedenen Inhalts*, 1920.

A. SCHULZ, *Das Buch Josue* (H.S.A.Tes.), 1924.

Seder 'Ōlām Rabba, Warsaw ed., 1817.

K. C. SEELE, *The Coregency of Ramses II with Seti I and the Date of the Great Hypostyle Hall at Karnak* (Studies in Ancient Oriental Civilization, xix), 1940.

—— see also G. Steindorff.

M. H. SEGAL, 'The Settlement of Manasseh East of the Jordan', in *P.E.F.Q.S.* 1918, pp. 124–31.

E. SELLIN, *Wie wurde Sichem eine israelitische Stadt?* 1923.

—— 'Seit welcher Zeit verehrten die nordisraelitischen Stämme Jahve?', in *Oriental Studies* (Haupt Festschrift), ed. by C. Adler and A. Ember, 1926, pp. 124–34.

—— *Geschichte des israelitisch-jüdischen Volkes*, i, 1935.

A. VAN SELMS, 'De Archaeologie in Syrië en Palaestina (tot 587 voor Chr.)', in *J.E.O.L.* iv, 1936, pp. 207–11.

K. SETHE, 'Die Ächtungstexte feindlicher Fürsten, Völker, und Dinge auf altägyptischen Tongefässscherben des mittleren Reiches', in *A.P.A.W.* 1926, No. 5.

—— 'Der Denkstein mit dem Datum des Jahres 400 der Ära von Tanis', in *Z.Ä.S.* lxv, 1930, pp. 85–9.

A. G. SHORTT, 'The Venus Tablet', in *The Journal of the British Astronomical Association*, lvii, 1947, pp. 208–10.

D. SIDERSKY, 'Étude sur la chronologie de la première dynastie babylonienne', in *Dissertationes in honorem Dr. Eduardi Mahler*, ed. by A. Wertheimer, J. de Somogyi, and S. Löwinger, 1937, pp. 253–62.

—— 'Nouvelle étude sur la chronologie de la dynastie Ḥammurapienne', in *R.Ass.* xxxvii, 1940, pp. 45–54.

J. SIMONS, 'Palestijnsche Archaeologie', in *J.E.O.L.* vi, 1939, pp. 153–63.

—— 'Caesurae in the History of Megiddo,' in *O.T.S.* i, 1941–2, pp. 17–54.

—— 'Een opmerking over het 'Aj-probleem', in *J.E.O.L.* ix, 1944, pp. 157–62.

—— 'The Structure and Interpretation of Josh. xvi–xvii', in *Orientalia Neerlandica* (Netherlands' Oriental Society Anniversary Volume), 1948, pp. 190–215.

C. A. SIMPSON, *Revelation and Response in the Old Testament*, 1947.

C. A. SIMPSON, *The Early Traditions of Israel*, 1948.

J. SKINNER, *A Critical and Exegetical Commentary on Genesis* (I.C.C.), 1912.

G. H. SKIPWITH, 'Tribal Names and Traditions of Israel', in *J.Q.R.* xi, 1898–9, pp. 239–65.

C. R. SMITH, 'The Stories of Shechem, Three Questions', in *J.T.S.* xlvii, 1946, pp. 33–8.

G. A. SMITH, *Historical Geography of the Holy Land*, 22nd ed., n.d.

H. P. SMITH, *Old Testament History*, 1911.

—— *The Religion of Israel: an Historical Study*, 1914.

J. M. POWIS SMITH, 'Some Problems in the Early History of Hebrew Religion', in *A.J.S.L.* xxxii, 1916, pp. 81–97.

—— 'Southern Influences upon Hebrew Prophecy', in *A.J.S.L.* xxxv, 1918, pp. 1–19.

S. SMITH, *Early History of Assyria to 1000 B.C.*, 1928.

—— 'A Preliminary Account of the Tablets from Atchana', in *The Antiquaries Journal*, xix, 1939, pp. 38–48.

—— *Alalakh and Chronology*, 1940.

—— *Isaiah, chapters xl–lv: Literary Criticism and History*, 1944.

—— 'Middle Minoan I–II and Babylonian Chronology', in *A.J.A.* xlix, 1945, pp. 1–24.

E. A. SPEISER, 'Ethnic Movements in the Near East in the Second Millennium B.C.', in *A.A.S.O.R.* xiii, 1933, pp. 13–54 (and separately).

L. SPELEERS, 'Égypte', in *Supplément au Dictionnaire de la Bible*, ed. by L. Pirot and A. Robert, ii, 1934, cols. 756–919.

S. SPIEGEL, 'A Prophetic Attestation of the Decalogue: Hosea 6: 5, with some observations on Psalms 15 and 24', in *H.T.R.* xxvii, 1934, pp. 105–44.

B. STADE, 'Der Text des Berichtes über Salomos Bauten, 1 Kö. 5–7', in *Z.A.W.* iii, 1883, pp. 129–77.

—— *Geschichte des Volkes Israel* (in *Allgemeine Geschichte*, ed. by W. Oncken), 2 vols., 1887–8.

—— 'Das Kainszeichen', in *Z.A.W.* xiv, 1894, pp. 250–318.

—— *Biblische Theologie des Alten Testaments*, i, 1905 (vol. ii, 1911, by A. Bertholet).

J. L. STARKEY, 'Excavations at Tell el Duweir, 1933–4', in *P.E.F.Q.S.* 1934, pp. 164–75.

—— 'Excavations at Tell ed Duweir', in *P.E.Q.* 1937, pp. 228–41.

G. STEINDORFF and K. C. SEELE, *When Egypt ruled the East*, 1942.

C. STEUERNAGEL, *Die Einwanderung der israelitischen Stämme in Kanaan*, 1901.

—— *Lehrbuch der Einleitung in das Alte Testament*, 1912.

—— 'Jahwe und die Vätergötter', in *Festschrift Georg Beer zum 70. Geburtstage*, 1935, pp. 62–71.

H. STOCK, *Studien zur Geschichte und Archäologie der 13. bis 17. Dynastie Ägyptens unter besonderer Berücksichtigung der Skarabäen dieser Zwischenzeit* (Ägyptologische Forschungen, xii), 1942.

Supplément au Dictionnaire de la Bible, see L. Pirot.

Svenskt Bibliskt Uppslagsverk, ed. by I. Engnell and A. Fridrichsen, i, 1948.

Talmud Babli, 1862–8 (Berlin edition); Text and German Tr. by L. Goldschmidt, 9 vols., 1897–1935.

Talmud Yerushalmi, 1866 (Krotoschin edition).

E. R. THIELE, 'The Chronology of the Kings of Judah and Israel', in *J.N.E.S.* iii, 1944, pp. 137–86.

P. Thomsen, 'Ai', in *A.f.O.* xi, 1936-7, pp. 94 f.

F. Thureau-Dangin, 'Nouvelles lettres d'El-Amarna', in *R.Ass.* xix, 1922, pp. 91-108.

—— 'La Chronologie des trois premières dynasties babyloniennes', in *R.Ass.* xxiv, 1927, pp. 183-98.

—— 'Iasmaḫ-Adad', in *R.Ass.* xxxiv, 1937, pp. 135-9.

—— 'Tablettes ḫurrites provenant de Mâri', in *R.Ass.* xxxvi, 1939, pp. 1-28.

—— 'Sur les étiquettes de paniers à tablettes provenant de Mari', in *Symbolae ad jura orientis antiqui pertinentes Paulo Koschaker dedicatae*, 1939, pp. 119 f.

—— 'Le Nom du prince de Jérusalem au temps d'el-Amarna', in *Mémorial Lagrange*, 1940, pp. 27 f.

—— 'La Chronologie de la première dynastie babylonienne', in *Mémoires de l'Académie des Inscriptions et Belles Lettres*, xliii, 2ᵉ partie, 1942, pp. 229-58.

O. A. Toffteen, *The Historic Exodus*, 1909.

R. Tonneau, 'Excursion biblique au Négeb', in *R.B.* xxxv, 1926, pp. 583-604.

O. Tuffnell, C. H. Inge, and L. Harding, *Lachish II: The Fosse Temple*, 1940.

A. Ungnad, *Die Venustafeln und das neunte Jahr Samsuilunas (1741 v. Chr.)* (*M.A.O.G.* xiii. 3), 1940.

—— 'Eine neue Grundlage für die altorientalische Chronologie', in *A.f.O.* xiii, 1940, pp. 145 f.

—— 'Zur Geschichte und Chronologie des zweiten Reiches von Isin', in *Orientalia*, xiii, 1944, pp. 73-101.

J. Vandier, see E. Drioton.

R. de Vaux, 'Le Cadre géographique du poème de Krt', in *R.B.* xlvi, 1937, pp. 362-72.

—— 'Les Textes de Ras Shamra et l'Ancien Testament', in *R.B.* xlvi, 1937, pp. 526-55.

—— Review of Virolleaud's *La Légende phénicienne de Danel*, and *La Légende de Keret roi des Sidoniens*, in *R.B.* xlvi, 1937, pp. 440-7.

—— 'Nouvelles recherches dans la région de Cadès', in *R.B.* xlvii, 1938, pp. 89-97.

—— 'La Palestine et la Transjordanie au IIᵉ millénaire et les origines israélites', in *Z.A.W.*, n.f. xv, 1938, pp. 225-38.

—— 'Notes d'histoire et de topographie transjordaniennes', in *Vivre et Penser*, i (= *R.B.* l), 1941, pp. 16-47.

—— 'Les Patriarches hébreux et les découvertes modernes', in *R.B.* liii, 1946, pp. 321-48; lv, 1948, pp. 321-47; lvi, 1949, pp. 5-36.

—— 'Israël (Peuple d')', in *Supplément au Dictionnaire de la Bible*, ed. by L. Pirot and A. Robert, iv, 1947-8, cols. 729-77.

J. Vernet, 'La cronologia de la primera dinastia babilonica', in *Sefarad*, viii, 1948, pp. 428-34.

F. Vigouroux, ed. by, *Dictionnaire de la Bible*, 5 vols., 1895-1912.

A. Vincent, *La Religion des Judéo-Araméens d'Éléphantine*, 1937.

L. H. Vincent, 'L'Année archéologique 1923 en Palestine', in *R.B.* xxxii, 1924, pp. 420-37.

—— 'La Chronologie des ruines de Jéricho', in *R.B.* xxxix, 1930, pp. 403-33.

—— 'The Chronology of Jericho', in *P.E.F.Q.S.* 1931, pp. 104 f.

—— 'Céramique et Chronologie', in *R.B.* xli, 1932, pp. 264-84.

—— 'Jéricho et sa chronologie', in *R.B.* xliv, 1935, pp. 583-605.

L. H. VINCENT, 'Les Fouilles d'Et-Tell', in *R.B.* xlvi, 1937, pp. 231–66.

—— 'Les Fouilles de Tell ed-Duweir = Lachis', in *R.B.* xlviii, 1939, pp. 406–33, 563–82.

—— 'Les Pays bibliques et l'Égypte à la fin de la XIIᵉ dynastie égyptienne', in *Vivre et Penser*, ii (= *R.B.* li), 1942, pp. 187–212.

—— 'L'Archéologie et la Bible', in *Mélanges E. Podechard*, 1945, pp. 265–82.

CH. VIROLLEAUD, 'L'Épopée de Keret, roi des Sidoniens d'après une tablette de Ras-Shamra', in *R.E.S.* 1934, No. i, pp. vi–xiv.

—— 'La Mort de Baal', in *Syria*, xv, 1934, pp. 305–36.

—— *La Légende de Keret, roi des Sidoniens, publiée d'après une tablette de Ras-Shamra*, 1936.

—— *La Légende phénicienne de Danel*, 1936.

—— *La Déesse 'Anat*, 1938.

—— under heading 'Séance du 30 juin', in *C.R.A.I.B.L.* 1939, pp. 329 f.

—— 'La Légende du roi Kérèt, d'après de nouveaux documents', in *Mélanges Syriens* (Dussaud Festschrift), ii, 1939, pp. 755–62.

—— 'Sur les nouveaux textes de Ras-Shamra', in *R.E.S.-B.* 1940, pp. 68–76.

—— 'Les Villes et les corporations du royaume d'Ugarit', in *Syria*, xxi, 1940, pp. 123–51.

W. VISCHER, *Jahwe der Gott Kains*, 1929.

P. VOLZ, 'Der Gott des Mose', in *Old Testament Essays* (Papers read before the Society for Old Testament Study), 1927, pp. 29–36.

—— 'Dekalog', in *R.G.G.*, 2nd ed., 1927, cols. 1816–19.

—— *Mose und sein Werk*, 2nd ed., 1932.

—— *Prophetengestalten des Alten Testaments*, 1938.

B. L. VAN DEN WAERDEN, 'The Venus Tablets of Ammiṣaduqa', in *J.E.O.L.* x, 1945–8, pp. 414–24.

G. A. WAINWRIGHT, 'Bibliography: Pharaonic Egypt (1937), i, Archaeology', in *J.E.A.* xxiv, 1938, pp. 213–19.

W. L. WARDLE, 'The Origins of Hebrew Monotheism', in *Z.A.W.*, N.F. ii, 1925, pp. 193–209.

—— *The History and Religion of Israel*, 1936.

L. WATERMAN, 'Some Determining Factors in the Northward Progress of Levi', in *J.A.O.S.* lvii, 1937, pp. 375–80.

—— 'Jacob the forgotten Supplanter', in *A.J.S.L.* lv, 1938, pp. 25–43.

C. WATZINGER, 'Zur Chronologie der Schichten von Jericho', in *Z.D.M.G.* lxxx, 1926, pp. 131–6.

E. F. WEIDNER, 'Die Königsliste aus Chorsābād', in *A.f.O.* xiv, 1941–4, pp. 362–9.

A. WEIGALL, *The Life and Times of Akhnaton, Pharaoh of Egypt*, revised ed., 1923.

R. WEILL, 'Les Hyksos et la restauration nationale dans la tradition égyptienne et dans l'histoire', in *J.As.*, 10th series, xvi, 1910, pp. 247–339, 507–79; xvii, 1911, pp. 5–53.

—— *La fin du moyen empire égyptien*, 1918.

—— 'L'Installation des israélites en Palestine et la légende des patriarches', in *R.H.R.* lxxxvii, 1923, pp. 69–120; lxxxviii, 1923, pp. 1–44.

—— 'The Problem of the Site of Avaris', in *J.E.A.* xxi, 1935, pp. 10–25.

—— 'Le Poème de Keret et l'histoire', in *J.As.* ccxxix, 1937, pp. 1–56.

—— 'La Légende des patriarches et l'histoire', in *R.E.S.* 1937, pp. 145–206.

—— 'Sur la situation historique et politique de Ras-Shamra', in *R.H.R.* cxv, 1937, pp. 174–187.

R. WEILL, 'Le Synchronisme égypto-babylonien du début du IIᵉ millénaire et l'évolution présente de la chronologie babylonienne', in *Chronique d'Égypte*, No. 41, Jan. 1946, pp. 34–43.

J. WELLHAUSEN, *Prolegomena to the History of Israel*, E.Tr. by J. S. Black and A. Menzies, 1885.

—— *Die Composition des Hexateuchs und der historischen Bücher des Alten Testaments* (Skizzen und Vorarbeiten, ii), 3rd ed., 1889.

A. J. WENSINCK, *Semitiesche Studiën uit de Nalatenschap van A. J. Wensinck*, 1941.

L. A. WHITE, 'Ikhnaton, the Great Man *vs.* the Culture Process', in *J.A.O.S.* lxviii, 1948, pp. 91–114.

H. M. WIENER, 'Pithom and Raamses', in *Ancient Egypt*, 1923, pp. 75–7.

J. A. WILSON, 'The 'Eperu of the Egyptian Inscriptions', in *A.J.S.L.* xlix, 1932–3, pp. 275–80.

H. WINCKLER, *Abraham als Babylonier, Joseph als Ägypter*, 1903.

—— 'Vorläufige Nachrichten über die Ausgrabungen in Boghaz-köi im Sommer 1907', in *M.D.O.G.*, No. 35, Dec. 1907.

—— *see also* E. Schrader.

H. E. WINLOCK, *The Rise and Fall of the Middle Kingdom in Thebes*, 1947.

F. V. WINNETT, 'The Founding of Hebron', in *Bulletin of the Canadian Society of Biblical Studies*, No. 3, June 1937, pp. 21–9.

W. WOLF, 'Der Stand der Hyksosfrage', in *Z.D.M.G.* lxxxiii, 1929, pp. 67–79.

W. C. WOOD, 'The Religion of Canaan', in *J.B.L.* xxxv, 1916, pp. 1–133, 163–279.

G. E. WRIGHT, 'Lachish—Frontier Fortress of Judah', in *B.A.* i, 1938, pp. 21–30.

—— 'The Chronology of Palestine Pottery in Middle Bronze I', in *B.A.S.O.R.*, No. 71, Oct. 1938, pp. 27–34.

—— 'Epic of Conquest', in *B.A.* iii, 1940, pp. 1–40.

—— 'Two Misunderstood Items in the Exodus-Conquest Cycle', in *B.A.S.O.R.*, No. 86, Apr. 1942, pp. 32–5.

—— 'The Literary and Historical Problem of Joshua 10 and Judges 1', in *J.N.E.S.* v, 1946, pp. 105–14.

—— 'The Present State of Biblical Archaeology', in *The Study of the Bible Today and Tomorrow*, ed. by J. R. Willoughby, 1947, pp. 74–97.

—— and F. V. FILSON, *The Westminster Historical Atlas to the Bible*, 1945.

A. S. YAHUDA, *The Accuracy of the Bible*, 1934.

V. ZAPLETAL, *Das Buch der Richter* (E.H.A.T.), 1923.

H. ZIMMERN, *see* E. Schrader.

O. ZÖCKLER, *The Books of Chronicles* (Lange's Bibelwerk), E.Tr. by J. G. Murphy, 1876.

I. ZOLLER, 'Syrisch-palästinensische Altertümer', in *M.G.W.J.* lxxii, 1928, pp. 225–41.

L. ZSCHARNACK, see *Die Religion in Geschichte und Gegenwart*.

INDEXES

(a) SUBJECT

O

(b) AUTHORS

(c) SCRIPTURE